The Singularities of London, 1578

DEDICATION

In memory of
IRENE SCOULOUDI
whose Foundation continues
to support the work of
this Society

The Singularities
of London, 1578

Les Singularitez de Londres, noble, fameuse Cité,
capital du Royaume d'Angleterre:
ses antiquitez et premiers fondateurs

by

L. Grenade

(Biblioteca Apostolica Vaticana, MS Reg. lat. 672)

Edited by

Derek Keene and Ian W. Archer

with the assistance of
Emma Pauncefort and Ann Saunders

LONDON TOPOGRAPHICAL SOCIETY
Publication No. 175
2014

©

LONDON TOPOGRAPHICAL SOCIETY
3 Meadway Gate
London NW11 7LA
2014

ISBN
978 0 902087 620

CONTENTS

EDITORS' PREFACE

More than twenty years ago Derek Keene became acquainted with L. Grenade's distinctive account of London from references to it in the translation by G. W. Groos of *The Diary of Baron Waldstein* (1981), which covers his travels in England in 1597-8. Both texts had entered the Vatican Library as part of Queen Christina of Sweden's collection, but had come into her possession by different routes. A photostat copy rapidly supplied by the Vatican Library demonstrated the extraordinary interest of Grenade's text and prompted an idea to publish an edition and commentary. Attempts to contact Mr Groos, in a sense the grandfather of this volume, failed and other duties intervened to prevent the project from progressing. Recently, as more time has become available, Ann Saunders has been a staunch supporter of the enterprise and its publication by the London Topographical Society, and her characteristic blend of enthusiasm and exhortation has helped to bring it to a timely conclusion. The Biblioteca Apostolica Vaticana generously gave permission for the text and translation to be published and for the reproduction of Figs 5-8. Derek Keene is especially grateful to Ian Archer for having agreed to join him as co-editor and for contributing his unique and stimulating knowledge of many relevant fields. The outcome is a joint work.

Ian Archer first heard of the manuscript through Richard Cooper, and benefited from characteristically invigorating discussions of it. Emma Pauncefort, supported by the London Topographical Society, provided a very helpful initial transcription and translation, revised by the editors, who are extremely grateful to Michael Hawcroft for his careful further checking of both transcription and translation. Ian Archer would like to thank Lotte Fikkers for her translation of Lucas de Heere's account. For advice on specific elements in the introduction and notes we are grateful to Julian Bowsher, Susan Cerasano, Alastair Duke, Guido Marnef, Michael Hawcroft, David Kathman, Peter Marshall and James Raven. In Belgium the following scholars kindly consulted their own resources for information on the Grenade (or Granado) family, but unfortunately without result: Marc Boone, Guido Marnef, Anne-Laure Van Bruaene, and Monique Weis.

Special thanks are due to the staff of the Vatican Library for their kind welcome and excellent advice. We would like to thank archivists, librarians and others at the Bodleian Library, Oxford, the British Library, the Folger Shakespeare Library, the Huntington Library, the Institute of Classical Studies, the Institute of Historical Research, the Library of the University of Ghent, the London Metropolitan Archives, the Mercers' Company, the

National Archives, Senate House Library (Historic Collections), Suffolk Records Office, and the Warburg Institute.

In this edition we have answered many questions concerning Grenade and his text, which is significant both for the information it provides on London topography and for what it tells us about the way in natives and strangers together thought about the nature and history of the city, at a time when issues concerning religion and nationality were especially fraught. In organising their thoughts they both drew on ancient traditions and used new tools and modes of discourse, then rapidly evolving in several parts of Europe. As usual in research, answers provoke further questions, among the most interesting of which are those concerning the international contexts in which Londoners and families such as Grenade's lived; and there remain questions concerning the identity and career of L. Grenade himself.

DEREK KEENE AND IAN ARCHER

HON. EDITOR'S ACKNOWLEDGEMENTS

The importance to the history of sixteenth-century London of Grenade's manuscript in the Vatican Library was first recognised by Derek Keene; to him and to Ian Archer of Keble College we owe the extensive and meticulous Introduction and Notes.

The Society's publications are always well illustrated. In this case, the aim has been to provide more or less contemporary images of landscapes, buildings, and people described by Grenade, who appears to have been a periodic visitor to London over a period of about thirty years.

In procuring the illustrations, the Society is particularly grateful to Sheila O'Connell of the British Museum for figures 9, 11, 17, 21, 28, 30, 33a, 35-40, 47, 49, and 51, and to Jeremy Smith and David Tennant of London Metropolitan Archives for figures 1, 18, 23, 41, and 54. St John's College, Cambridge have generously permitted the use of their portrait of William Bendlowes (Fig. 61), and their archivist Mrs K. J. McKee has provided helpful information. Philip Burden has been equally generous with his panorama of the north bank of the Thames (Figs 10 and 25). We have also received support from Dr Jane Bridgeman and Mrs Diana Peston. We owe the Index to Roger Cline and Derek Keene.

The Ashmolean Museum in Oxford has permitted the reproduction of details from Anthonis van den Wyngaerde's preparatory drawings for his panorama of London destined for the walls of the Prado Palace in Madrid though now destroyed (Figs 13-16, 22, 27, 31, 32, 34, 52). The Museum of London has authorised reproductions from the three existing plates of the Copperplate Map (Figs 2-4, 12, 20, 24, 26, 42, 43, 45, 46, 50, 53, and 58).

Three bodies and one individual have, generously and freely, allowed reproductions of material in their possession; they are the Dean and Chapter of Westminster Abbey (Fig. 19), the Society of Antiquaries with the Tower of London (Fig. 29), the Cheapside procession (Fig. 44), and St Paul's (Fig. 60), and the British Library (Figs 55-57). Mrs Valerie Jackson-Harris has permitted the reproduction of an unique engraving by Frans Hogenberg (Fig. 48). The University of Ghent has contributed a superb scan of the Lucas de Heere representation of ceremonial dress (Fig. 59). The Society thanks them all.

Finally, above all, we owe thanks to Graham Maney of Outset Services and Steve Hartley of Scorpion Creative. To my husband's support I owe more than I can say.

ANN SAUNDERS
Editor of the London Topographical Society

MAPS OF LONDON

Full reproductions of the first state of the map of London in
G. Braun and F. Hogenberg, *Civitates Orbis Terrarum* vol. 1
(Antwerp and Cologne, 1572) and of prints from the three
surviving plates of the larger-scale Copperplate map,
surveyed during the 1550s (perhaps shortly before 1559),
from which the Braun and Hogenberg map was derived.

Enlarged extracts from these maps are used throughout
the translation of Grenade's text to illustrate the sites
and buildings he describes.

Fig. 1. London, Westminster and Southwark in the 1550s: B & H Map (1572). The map is derived from the Copperplate Map. © *London Metropolitan Archives, City of London.*

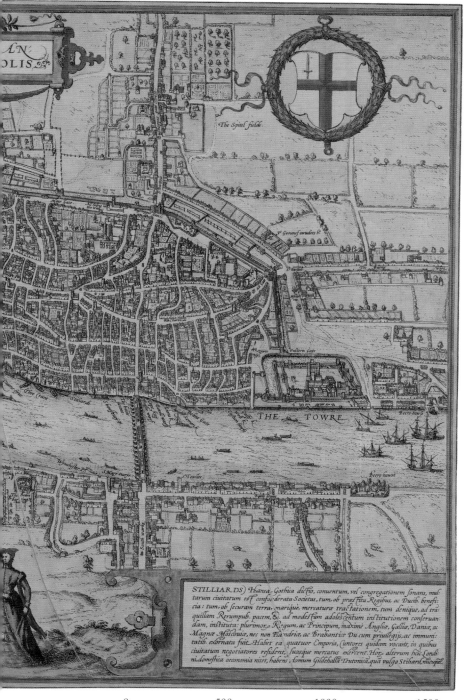

The Spitel fielde

AN-
OLIS

Maior Gate

y Gorner founders P.

Postern Gate

THE TOWRE

Beere haw

S. Mary Ouerie

Newlie

Beere hawse

STILLIAR, DS) Hansa, Gothia dicto, conuentum, vel congregationem sonans, mul-
tarum ciuitatum est confœderata Societas, tum, ob prestita Regibus, ac Ducib. benefi-
cia: tum, ob securam terra, marique, mercatura tractationem, tum denique, ad tra-
quillam Rerumpub. pacem, & ad modestam adolescentum institutionem conseruan-
dam, instituta: plurimor. Regum, ac Principum, maxime Angliæ, Galliæ, Daniæ, ac
Magna Moscouiæ, nec non Flandriæ, ac Brabantiæ Du cum priuilegijs, ac immuni-
tatib. cōrnata fuit. Habet ea quatuor Emporia, (untores quidam vocant, in quibus
ciuitatum negotiatores resident, suosque mercatus ćercent. Hor. alterum hćc Londi-
ni, domestica œconomia niti, habens domum Gildehalla Teutonica, qua vulgo Stihard, nūcupat.

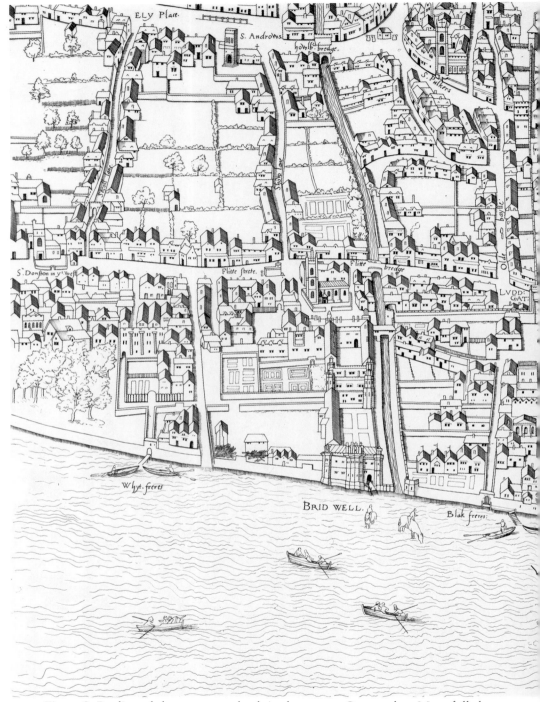

Fig. 2. St Paul's and the western suburb in the 1550s. Copperplate Map, full sheet.
© *Museum of London.*

Fig. 3. City centre and river frontage in the 1550s. Copperplate Map, full sheet.
© *Museum of London.*

CRY CHVRCH
CHE

S. helens.

Ledden hall

S. And: vnder
Chaft

Fanf Churcu

S. Denys.

Richardston

Towre ftretet

Markk

S. Mary

S. Dvnft

Prefhe waff

Fig. 4. Moor Field and the Bishopsgate suburb in the 1550s. Copperplate Map, full sheet. © *Museum of London*.

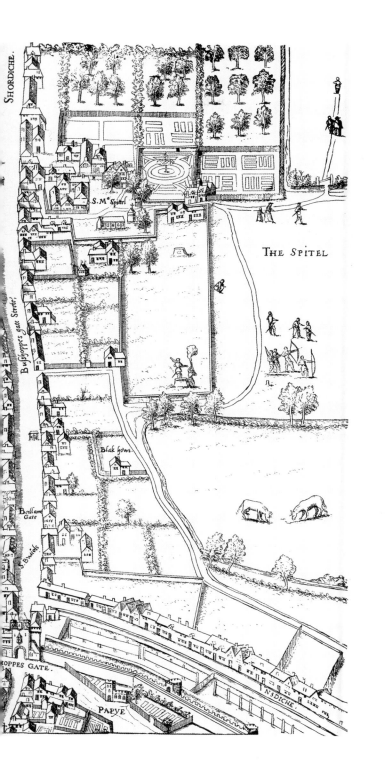

SHORDICHE.

S. Mᵃ Spitl

THE SPITEL

Buſſhoppes gatt Streete;

Blak hows

Bedlam Gate

S. Butlds

HOPPES GATE.

PAPYE

NSDICHE.

LIST OF ABBREVIATIONS

BAV   Biblioteca Apostolica Vaticana

BL   British Library

HMC   Historical Manuscripts Commission. See List of Printed Work and Theses

KW   *The History of the King's Works*. See List of Printed Works and Theses

LMA   London Metropolitan Archives

MOLA   Museum of London Archaeology [successor to MOLAS] (with number of publication)

MOLAS   Museum of London Archaeology Service (with number of publication)

PRO   Public Record Office (part of the National Archives (UK), Kew)

LRS   London Record Society, with publication number

LTS   London Topographical Society, with publication number

ODNB   *Oxford Dictionary of National Biography* (Oxford, 2004). Online edition 2008: http://o-www.oxforddnb.com.catalogue

INTRODUCTION

This lively, original and informative account of London, written in French and completed in 1578, occupies an important place among sixteenth-century descriptions of the city. Offering a distinctive view of London, it is not a traveller's record, nor a history, nor a guidebook, but an example of the long-established genre of *laudes civitatis* ('Praises of the City'), which had its origin in Antiquity. Indeed, it has some resemblance to the earliest and best-known of such *laudes* concerning London, William FitzStephen's description, written in 1173-4 as the preface to his life of the city's most famous saint, Thomas the martyr, archbishop of Canterbury. Our author, one L. Grenade (presumably a man, as perhaps indicated by a distinct interest in law, punishment and weapons), may have had some knowledge of this much earlier account, first printed in 1598, and it is possible to identify some of the more recent sources which he drew on or which shaped his plan for the work.

Grenade's text describes a selection of particular and noteworthy things (*Singularitez*) in London (Fig 5), often providing an original and informative view, and presents a good deal of historical, quasi-historical, and mythical background. Much of that background is derived from recent editions of popular summaries of English history, most notably Richard Grafton's *An Abridgement of the Chronicles of England* (1563, 1564, 1570 or 1572) and John Stow's *A Summarie of Englyshe Chronicles* (1565, 1566a, 1566b, 1567, 1570, 1573, 1575). Grenade certainly consulted one of the first four editions of Stow's work, and possibly others, but miscopied the date of the foundation of London given there and by Grafton.[1] Among the physical features he identifies four buildings of special note: St Paul's Cathedral, London Bridge, the Tower of London and the Royal Exchange. He writes in praise of and in gratitude for the city's welcoming reception of religious refugees. With a distinctively Protestant outlook, he characterises London as a city of peace, good order, good government, and charitable institutions. He has much to say about laws and regulations and takes a special interest in London's legal culture. The splendours of legal and civic ceremonial and dress excite his interest. He also provides information on entertainments, public monuments and infrastructure, markets, and food supply. There are important aspects of London in the period which he omits entirely, either because he was not interested in them or because he judged them not to be sufficiently distinctive. In an Epistle (*Epistre*) at the beginning, he addresses his text to the lord mayor and aldermen of the city (Fig. 6), and later on

---

1. See below, pp. 148-9 and notes 16, 17.

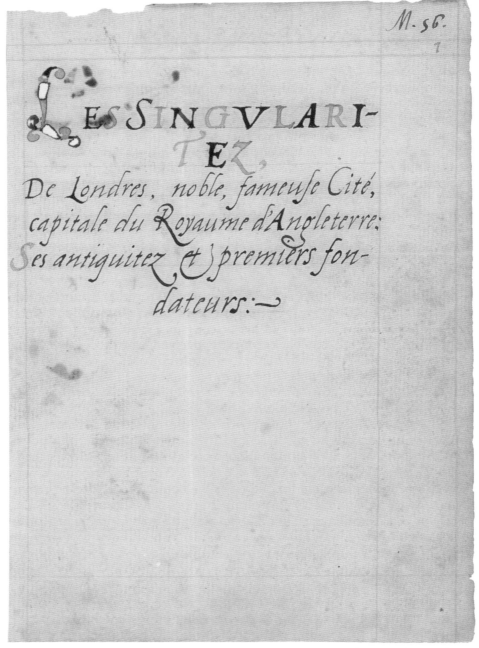

Fig. 5. Title page of Grenade's text (BAV MS Reg. Lat. 676, fol. 1ʳ). The number
M.56. at top right indicates that the MS was later in the collection of Paul Pétau,
book dealer, (1568-1614). © 2014 *Biblioteca Apostolica Vaticana*.

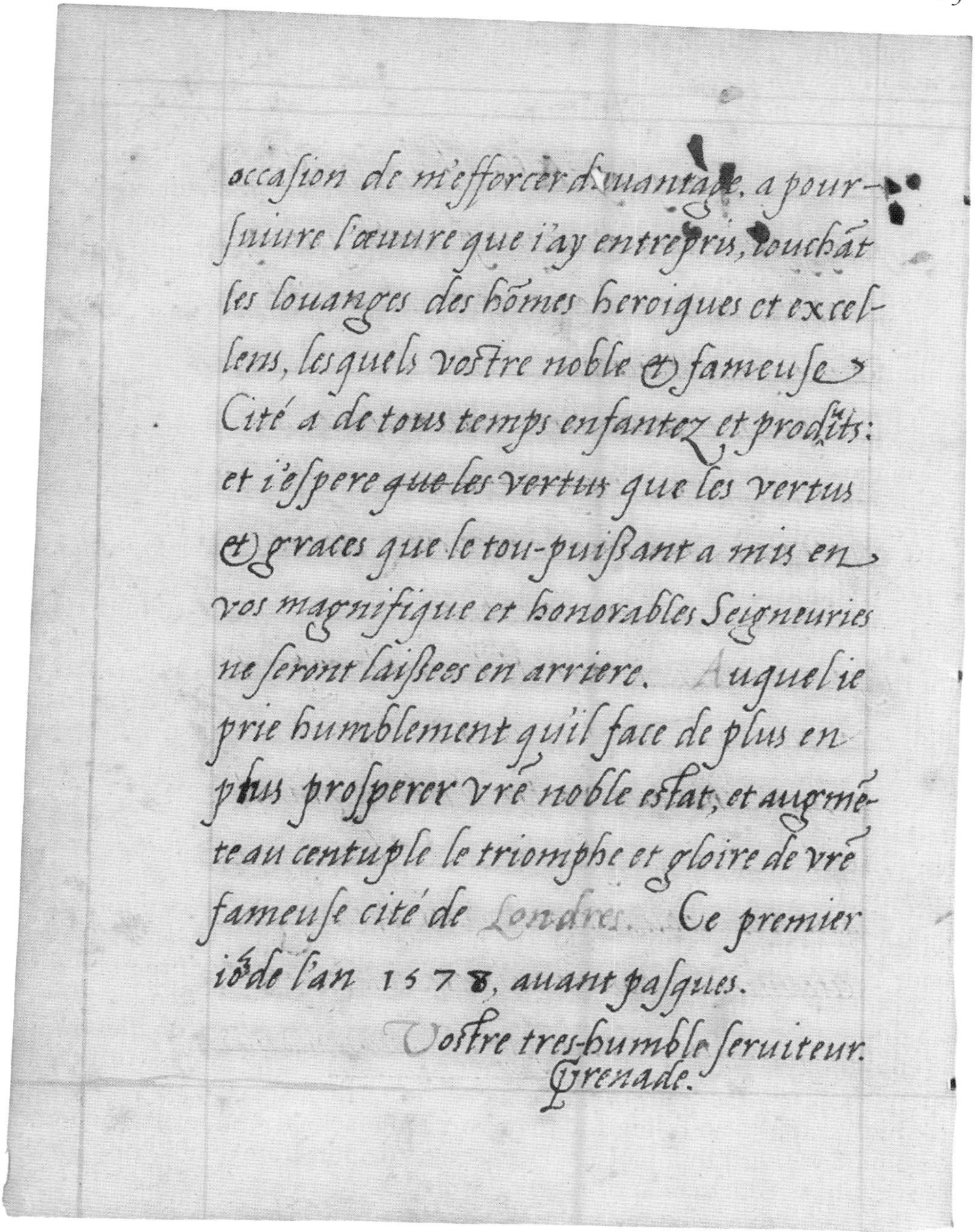

occasion de m'esforcer d'auantage, a pour-
suiure l'œuure que i'ay entrepris, touchât
les louanges des hômes heroiques et excellens, lesquels vostre noble & fameuse
Cité a de tous temps enfantez et produits:
et i'espere que les vertus que les vertus
& graces que le tou-puissant a mis en
vos magnifique et honorables Seigneuries
ne seront laissees en arriere. Auquel ie
prie humblement qu'il face de plus en
plus prosperer vré noble estat, et augmé-
te au centuple le triomphe et gloire de vré
fameuse cité de Londres. Ce premier
iô de l'an 1578, auant pasques.

Vostre tres-humble seruiteur.
Grenade.

Fig. 6. The end of Grenade's 'Epistle' addressed to the Lord Mayor and Aldermen,
with the date and his name 'L Grenade' (BAV MS Reg. Lat. 676, fol. 4ᵛ). Note the
corrections to the text, the blots from the opposite pages, and the use of red ink for the
ruled frame, *Londres* and some capital letters. © *2014 Biblioteca Apostolica. Vaticana.*

correctly identifies the 'present mayor', as Sir Thomas Ramsey, who held office in 1577-8.

One of the most distinctive and original features of Grenade's account is his sense of London's setting in the landscape, its overseas connections and its internal space. These, and especially the last, inform the arrangement of much of his material. That spatial sense seems to reflect a familiarity with maps, and in particular a map of London, making this account of a European city among the first, if not the first, to have been shaped in that way.

The author puts his name at the end of the initial Epistle (Fig. 6), but we know little about him. He seems to be related to a long-established family of Protestant refugees in London and to have been a periodic visitor to the city, his earliest known visit being in about 1550 (Chapter 5). At the time of writing, after many travails, he was seeking comfort and rest in London, presumably with his family. At other times he probably resided, or had resided, somewhere under the rule of the French monarch. His surviving text may well have been a draft of a small volume intended for presentation to the lord mayor and aldermen of London, but there is no record of such a presentation and the text is too untidy to have served in that role. This text was later in the collection of a Parisian bibliophile and then in that of Queen Christina of Sweden, after whose death in Rome it was purchased for the Biblioteca Apostolica Vaticana, where it is now MS Reg. Lat. 672.

These and other topics are further discussed in the following parts of this Introduction. The notes to the translation explain and discuss specific sites, practices and events which Grenade described.

1. THE MANUSCRIPT AND ITS PROVENANCE

Physical characteristics of the book

BAV MS Reg. Lat. 672 is a small, bound volume, the ninety-two folios of which (including fols 1 bis, 24 bis, 35 bis and 75 bis) each measure 141 mm wide by 194 mm high. Close examination of the structure of the book is not possible, on account of the tight binding. The text is written on about eight quires of paper. No watermarks are visible, other than from the wires of the paper frame. The ink, especially the red ink used for some words and letters and for other purposes, often penetrates the paper and is visible on the reverse. The lead ruling and the writing in black ink was probably done on unbound sheets, but blots on facing pages demonstrate that at least some of the larger red letters in titles were added after binding.

The leather covering the spine was renewed in 1853-4, as indicated by the arms of the Cardinal Librarian Angelo Mai (in office 1853-4) and those of Pope Pius IX (1846-78). In the 1960s new flyleaves were added to strengthen the binding and it was probably then that the foliation was rationalised by means of additions in pencil. The leather-covered boards are much earlier in date and may well belong to the original binding.[2] Both the upper and the lower covers are decorated with an identical tooled and gilded panel design (Fig. 7) enclosing the royal arms of England, within the Garter, as they were under Elizabeth I (1558-1603). Comparison with the British Library's online database of bindings suggests that this could be an English 'trade' binding of about 1580.[3] Use of the royal arms, however, does not necessarily indicate that the binding was done in England. The pages have gilded edges.

The hand and the layout of the text

The text is in a competent humanist (italic) hand of the mid or later sixteenth century, probably that of a professional scribe but hastily written and with many corrections: words struck through; insertions above the line, in spaces between words, and occasionally in the margins; and a few erasures. Certain passages are in a secretary hand (indicated in the transcription by 𝕭𝖑𝖆𝖈𝖐𝖑𝖊𝖙𝖙𝖊𝖗). These concern epitaphs and inscriptions, and a few terms associated with law and government (Fig. 8). Some epitaphs are in a smaller version of the humanist hand, perhaps because the original inscriptions used a similar script.

The text on each page is written on 15 lead-ruled lines within a panel framed by red lines at top and bottom and on each side. The red lines run the full width or height of the pages. The text is justified, but this has resulted in irregularities in the spacing between words: in some case words have been jammed together and in others excessive space has been left between them (cf. Figs 6, 8). An additional vertical red line defines a margin (to the right on a recto and to the left on a verso) in which the scribe, using a smaller version of the hand in the main text, inserted notes identifying the topics discussed and occasionally including extra information. An additional horizontal red line at the top defines a space for running headings, as follows:

fols 1 bis-4ᵛ:	*Epistre* (red, on both recto and verso)
fols 5ᵛ-8:	*Preface* (red, recto and verso)
fols 9ᵛ-13:	*Les singularitez* (on verso in red) *de Londres* (on recto in red)
fols 13ᵛ-87ᵛ:	*Les singularitez* (on verso in black) *de Londres* (on recto in black), with occasional omissions.

2. Special thanks are due to the Vatican Library conservation staff for their comments on the binding.

3. See https://www.bl.uk/catalogues/bookbindings under the shelfmark c82a13 (with references to other trade bindings).

Fig. 7. BAV MS Reg. Lat. 676, back cover of the binding, with the royal arms of England as they were under Elizabeth I. © 2014 *Biblioteca Apostolica Vaticana.*

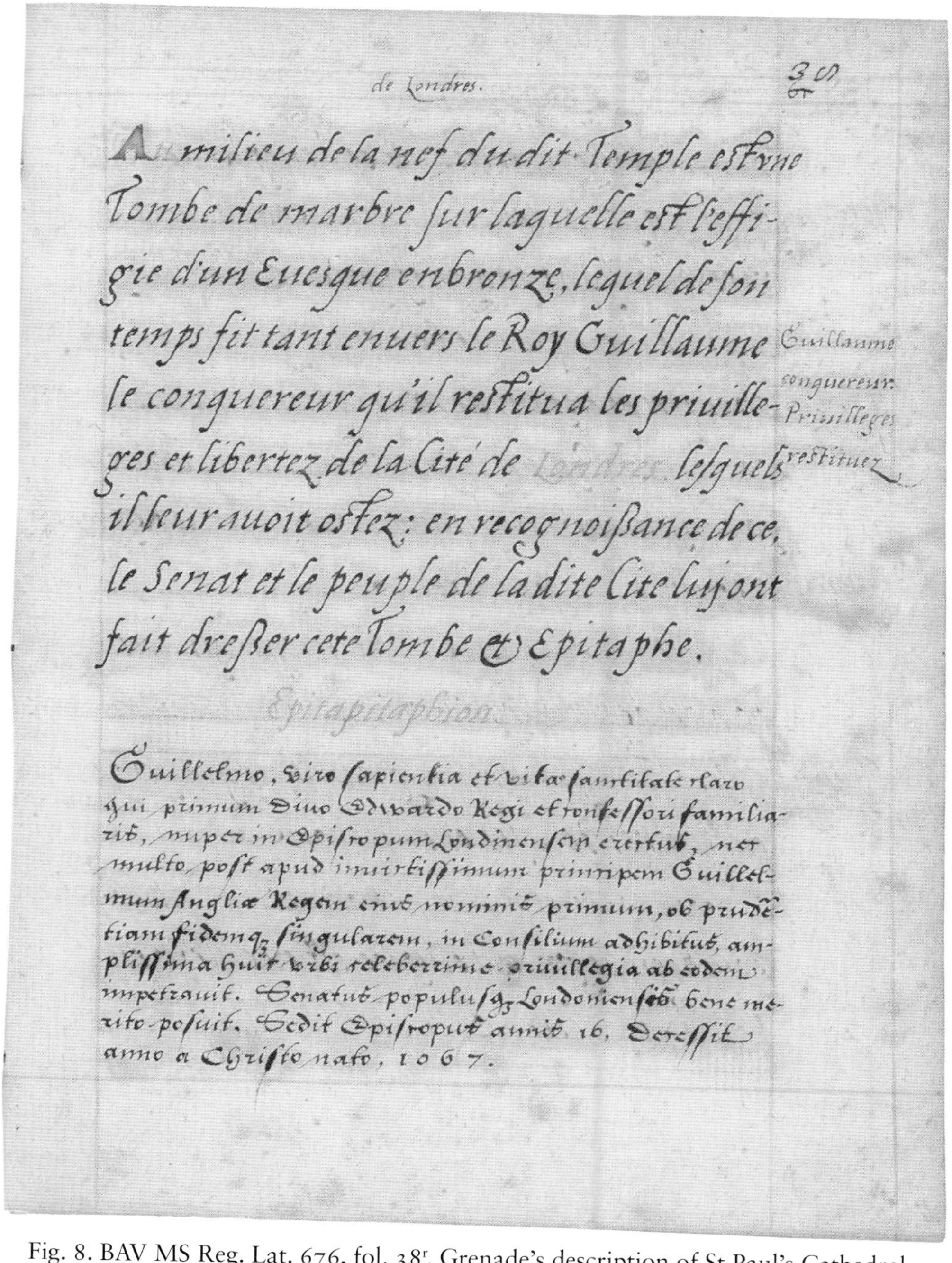

de Londres.

A milieu de la nef du dit Temple est vne
Tombe de marbre sur laquelle est l'effigie d'un Euesque en bronze, lequel de son
temps fit tant enuers le Roy Guillaume
le conquereur qu'il restitua les priuilleges et libertez de la Cité de Londres, lesquels
il leur auoit ostez: en recognoissance de ce,
le Senat et le peuple de la dite Cité luy ont
fait dresser cete Tombe et Epitaphe.

Epitaphion

Guillelmo, viro sapientia et vitæ sanctitate claro
qui primum Diuo Edwardo Regi et confessori familia-
ris, nuper in Episcopum Londinensem erectus, nec
multo post apud inuictissimum principem Guillel-
mum Angliæ Regem eius nominis primum, ob pruden-
tiam fidemq3 singularem, in Consilium adhibitus, am-
plissima huic vrbi celeberrimæ priuillegia ab eodem
impetrauit. Senatus populusq3 Londoniensis bene me-
rito posuit. Sedit Episcopus annis 16, Decessit
anno a Christo nato, 1067.

Marginal notes: Guillaume conquereur. Priuilleges restituez

Fig. 8. BAV MS Reg. Lat. 676, fol. 38ʳ. Grenade's description of St Paul's Cathedral, illustrating the use of secretary hand for the epitaph of Bishop William. Note layout of the page, marginal note, running heading, the earlier page number, and the uses of red ink. © 2014 Biblioteca Apostolica Vaticana.

The main text contains many initials and other letters in red. These mark the beginnings of chapters and sentences and are often preceded by extra space, inserted so as to justify the line, but they do not conform to any consistent scheme and so are an unreliable guide to paragraphing. Red ink is also used to pick out letters in main headings. The initial letters of chapters are large and elaborate. Some other red letters in the main text are larger or heavier than others there, but not according to any consistent scheme. It seems that the use of red ink is primarily decorative rather than to define sections of the text. The name *Londres* is almost always in red.

In the transcription the body of the text is set out according to the line lengths of the manuscript and includes words or phrases which have been struck through, but no attempt has been made to represent the manuscript's variations in the size, elaboration or colour of capital letters. The marginal notes have been positioned as closely as possible as in the manuscript, but avoiding its frequent word breaks.

Pagination and foliation

Originally, the *Epistre* ('Epistle': the initial address to the lord mayor and aldermen, but identified as *Epistre* only in the running headings), the *Preface* and *Les Singularitez* were each paginated or foliated separately using Arabic numerals, which were occasionally employed for internal cross-reference. The title folio was originally numbered 1, but the next folio, containing the beginning of the *Epistre,* was also identified as 1, with its verso numbered as 2. Subsequently, perhaps in the seventeenth century, a system of folio numbers was introduced, beginning with the first folio of the *Epistre.* Several folio numbers were duplicated. From fol. 10 onwards, the folio numbers replace an earlier (perhaps original) system of pagination, beginning with p. 3 (now fol. 10r) and continuing to p. 163 (now fol. 88r). Recent pencil additions have rationalised this system. The evolution of the numbering can be summarised as follows:

Section	Numbering		
	*c.*1578	17th century	1960s, as corrected in pencil
title page	fol. 1	fol. 1	fol. 1
Epistre	pp. 1-2, fols 2-4^v	fols 1-4^v	fols 1 bis^r-4^v
Preface	none	fols 5-8	fols 5-8
Les Singularitez	pp. 1-163 [pp. 1 and 2 not bearing numbers]	fols 9-88 [fols 10-88 originally numbered pp. 3-163]	fols 9-88 [including fols 24 bis^{r-v}, 35 bis^{r-v}, 75 bis^{r-v}]

Punctuation and suspension marks

The scribe used commas, semi-colons (rarely), colons, stops and brackets, but with some inconsistency. So far as possible the transcription follows the original. More modern practice has been followed in the translation. Suspension marks indicating the omission of n or m are used extensively in the text.

The status and provenance of the text

Written on relatively poor quality paper and containing many scribal corrections, the text cannot have been intended as a version for presentation to the lord mayor of London. It may, however, have been intended as the draft for a presentation copy or as the basis for an English version with the same purpose. There is no record of such a presentation ever having been made, and so it is possible that the author abandoned or was prevented from completing the project at this stage and that he or another person then had the text bound and put it aside.

The next known owner of the manuscript, indicated by the distinctive catalogue or shelf mark M.56. on folio 1, was Paul Pétau (1568-1614), scholar, bibliophile, numismatist and magistrate, who was based in Paris, where he was active professionally from at least as early as 1588.[4] He may have acquired the book from Grenade himself or in the Paris book market. Given Grenade's interest in legal matters and Pétau's study of jurisprudence and his role a *conseiller* in the Paris *parlement*, it is possible that the two men were acquainted. On Paul's death his collection passed to his son Alexandre Pétau, who greatly enlarged it. Scholars who used the collection included Isaac Vossius in 1641. In his later role as librarian to Queen Christina of Sweden, Vossius heard that Alexandre wished to sell a large part of the collection, and so in 1650 he visited Paris and made a hurried selection of books and manuscripts to be acquired for the queen's library, a total of about 2,000 items for a price of 40,000 *livres* according to a contemporary report, but perhaps numbering about 1,300. This collection, presumably including Grenade's manuscript, was shipped from Paris to Stockholm, where it arrived in June 1651. Following Christina's decision to convert to Catholicism and her abdication in 1654, the Pétau collection was among the sixty chests of books that she took to Antwerp in the summer of that year. Vossius joined her shortly afterwards, laid out the collection in the upper gallery of the Antwerp Bourse, put it in order, and compiled a catalogue, which he signed in October 1655. By that time Christina had formally converted and with the boxes of books set out for Rome, where she was to be based for much of the rest of her life. In 1656 the catalogue

---

4. *Biographie Universelle*, xxxii. 32; see note to fol. 1, on p. 146 (n. 1) below.

was revised by the addition of identifiers for those items which had not been part of the Pétau collection.

Towards the end of her life Queen Christina nominated her friend Cardinal Azzolino as her sole heir so as to pay her debts. Soon after her death in Rome in April 1689, Azzolino himself died and her collections passed to his heir, from whom Pope Alexander VIII (1689-91) purchased her library for the Vatican. Bernard de Montfaucon's summary catalogue of the manuscripts formerly belonging to Queen Christina, presumably made during his visit to Rome in 1698, but not published until 1739, notes Grenade's text under the heading *Libri Historici* as no. 760, entitled *Les singularités de Londres et antiquités d'Angleterre*. About that time it was renumbered as Reg. Lat. 672.[5]

2. THE GRANADOS: THE IDENTITY OF THE AUTHOR AND HIS FAMILY

At the end of his Epistle to the lord mayor and aldermen, the author identifies himself as L. Grenade (Fig. 6). Apart from the Spanish Dominican friar, the Venerable Luis de Granada (*alias* Louis de Grenade), whose collected works were published in Venice in 1578 and whose devotional writings were being translated into French and published in Paris by 1572,[6] no other person of that name at that time has been identified. It is possible that our author adopted the name as a nom-de-plume, but that seems unlikely given the relative prominence of his family in London and the purpose of his work.

L. Grenade's text reveals several elements of his identity. French was his language of choice and he compares true French with the corrupt form used by English lawyers (Chapters 2, 12). He had seen Strasbourg cathedral (Chapter 8) and his knowledge of Larchant in the Gâtinais (Chapter 4) suggests that he was familiar with, or at least aware of, the shrine there, destroyed by Huguenots in 1567. His strong interest in the laws and regulations of London, in English judges and senior lawyers and their training and ceremonies suggest that he had studied jurisprudence and the possibility

5. This summary of the migration of Grenade's manuscript is based on Wilmart 1937-45: i. vii-xii; Blok 2000: 103, 274, 281, 325-9, 331-2, 353-7, 462-70, 475, 483-4. For the catalogues, see Bignami Odier 1962; Monfaucon 1739: ii. 14-61, 96-7; *Les manuscrits* 1964: 44. A catalogue of Queen Christina's library in Stockholm at the end of 1649, before the acquisition of the Pétau collection but after the arrival of the many manuscripts acquired by her father Gustavus Adolphus (d. 1632) and as a result of subsequent military action during the Thirty Years War, includes nothing identifiable as Grenade's text: Callmer 1971.

6. Grenade, L. de 1572, 1578, 1579.

that he was a practising lawyer or magistrate. In the Preface, where he lists earlier writers on the history of cities, he refers to 'the capital of my own nation', of which a history had been written. Since features of his own work appear to have been modelled on Gilles Corrozet's publications on Paris, discussed below, Grenado's capital was presumably Paris. This seems more likely than Brussels, the capital of Brabant where his family had had strong connections. No such history had been written of Brussels. Grenade's strongly Protestant outlook pervades the whole work,[7] which was intended as an expression of gratitude to the City of London for the welcome it had afforded to religious refugees, and for the many kindnesses that both he and his family experienced from the city, as he explained in the Epistle. At the time of writing he was staying in London to comfort himself after enduring many journeys and travails. He may have been a regular visitor to the city and mentions having for the first time seen the pennants and vanes on the Tower of London more than 27 years previously, which would have been in about 1550 or earlier (Chapter 5). His writing suggests knowledge and possibly even direct experience of the extreme anti-Protestant violence in Paris in 1572 (the 'St Bartholomew's Day Massacre') and the Spanish sack of Antwerp in 1576 (the 'Spanish Fury'), and perhaps also family memories of earlier persecution in the Low Countries from the 1520s onwards. In Grenade's account, the Protestant King Edward VI, 'good King Edward', is cast as a heroic figure, not least on account of his support of new charitable institutions (Chapters 2, 9, 12).

Grenade's family in London was probably that which bore the name of Granado, Granade, Grenade, or Grenado. Its first recorded member in the city was James Granado, who in October 1539 married Mawdlen Kyldermans in the city church of St Denis Backchurch.[8] A year later, as Jakes Granado, he was an esquire of the king's stable, a position that he held, more or less, for the remainder of his life. When knighted by the duke of Somerset in September 1547, following the campaign in Scotland, he was described as a Brabanter.[9] His name suggests that he or his family had originated in Granada. Like many Spanish Protestants, he had probably taken refuge in Antwerp,[10] a dependency of the duchy of Brabant, of which Brussels was the capital. Although Mary of Hungary, as governor of the Netherlands (1531-55), favoured religious toleration, her brother, the Emperor Charles V, insisted on the suppression of Protestantism. It may have been under her regime that Granado, a Spaniard who presumably had special expertise concerning horses, decided to move to England.

7. See below, pp. 49-51.
8. *Reiester Booke*: 1.
9. Holinshed. 1577: ii. 1633; Holinshed, 1587: iii. 991.
10. We owe this suggestion to Alastair Duke and Guido Marnef.

Kyldermans was a common family name in the Low Countries. Magdalen may have been a member of the Keldermans family of sculptors and architects in Mechelen (Malines, close to Antwerp), one of whom designed the new residence there for Margaret of Austria, aunt and predecessor of Mary of Hungary.[11] A more likely candidate for Magdalen's father, however, is one Joies Keldermans, a merchant in the Low Countries who in 1546 was associated with the Londoner and royal agent, John Dymock, in gathering and attempting to export foodstuffs and other supplies for the garrisons of King Henry VIII.[12] At this time John Dymock was said to be James Granado's brother in law. In her will drawn up in 1585 Magdalen left to her daughter Katherine a 'flower of gold with diamonds and pearls' and diamond ring which her 'sister Dymocke' had given her. This sister was probably the Anne Dymmoke, who in January 1553, along with Lady Magdalen Granado, was granted denization for life, the only women in a long list of such grants.[13] It seems likely that Magdalen and Anne were daughters of Joies Keldermans. The two women may have been in need of some protection on account of the absence of their husbands, both of whom were often overseas. Moreover, Dymock was in dispute with the Merchant Adventurers and later in the year was committed to the Fleet Prison, while Granado may, as on other occasions, have been suspected of being in league with the French: in October 1553 he was granted a general pardon.[14]

While based in London James Granado was primarily a royal servant and soldier, but initially may also have engaged in commerce for in 1542 he was granted a licence to export 300 tuns of beer.[15] As a soldier, he was in 1543 a member of the army for Flanders. In the following year he probably participated in the English capture of Boulogne, since in June and July 1545 the French held him in captivity in Dieppe.[16] Injured during fighting outside Boulogne in April 1546, he was captured and taken to Etaples, but was soon allowed to return and gave a full report for the English Lord Lieutenant concerning French intentions and military preparations. This may have been his first experience as a diplomatic intermediary.[17] He next fought in Scotland and distinguished himself at Pinkie Cleugh (September 1547), after

11. Eichberger 2003.

12. *L&P Hen VIII*: xxi. nos 350-1, 368-9, 1062, 1238, 1328; Adams, Archer, and Bernard (ed.) 2003.

13. *CPR Edward VI*: v. 208; PRO, PROB 11/68, fol. 345.

14. Ramsey 1975: 47-9; *CPR Philip and Mary*: i. 451.

15. *L &P Hen. VIII*: xvii. no. 39.

16. *L &P Hen. VIII*: xviii. no. 832; xx. nos 926, 1195.

17. *L &P Hen. VIII*: xxi. nos 682, 779.

which he was knighted.[18] King Edward VI rewarded his services with grants to him and his wife Magdalen of annuities for life totalling £75 and leases of land in Devon, and in 1553 granted denization for life to Lady Magdalen.[19] In 1549 James Granado was taxed as a 'stranger' dwelling in the city of London, in the precinct of All Hallows parish in Tower Ward. In fact the house, which lay towards the south end of Mincing Lane, was in the parish of St Dunstan in the East.[20] This was convenient for his interests in London, close both to the Tower of London for military matters and to Billingsgate for its commercial and other connections with the Low Countries and France. Following her widowhood, remarriage and second widowhood Lady Magdalen kept up this house (along with other residences in the country) and died there in 1585.[21]

There were others with the surname Granado who seem also have been in the service of Henry VIII and may have been relatives of James. In 1543 Giles Grenado, a Frenchman and servant of 'Mr Knevet' (perhaps Henry Knyvet, a soldier and the younger son of Sir Thomas Knyvet, Master of the Horse under Henry VIII) reported that the French were assembling in Normandy a fleet and munitions to be sent to Scotland. In 1547 Thomas Granado was paid for riding in post to Stephen Vaughan, presumably before September 1546, when Vaughan, a London merchant, resigned his post as the king's chief financial agent in Antwerp.[22]

An undoubted member of the family was Bernard or Bernardine Grenado (d. 1571), probably James's younger brother. In 1540 it was reported to Henry VIII, that the Emperor Charles V, his consort having died, would not marry again, but would advance his brother's children. To bring them along in riding Charles had sent them to 'Granathois', whom the reporter noted was the brother of 'Jacques in the King's Stable'.[23] Bernardine was presumably a riding master active somewhere in Habsburg territory, probably in the Low Countries or nearby. He later moved to England and in 1564 and 1567 was dwelling in Tower Ward near Lady Magdalen, by then a widow. In the taxation record Bernadine was described as her 'brother' and both of them were entered under the heading 'Dutchmen'. According to the

18. Patten 1548.

19. *L &P Hen. VIII*: xxi. 9, 648; *CPR Edw. VI*, iii. 206; v. 208; *CPR Philip & Mary*, iv. 271-3.

20. Kirk and Kirk 1900-1908: i. 168; *CPR Elizabeth, 1560-6*, 560.

21. Kirk and Kirk 1900-1908: i. 339; *Tudor Subsidy Rolls*, no. 373; PRO, PROB 11/68, fols 345-7.

22. *L & P Hen. VIII*: xviii. no. 106; xxi. no. 775; Blanchard 2004c.

23. *L & P Hen. VIII*: xvi. 253. The two boys would have been the later Emperor Maximilian II, born in 1527, and Ferdinand II, later Archduke of Austria, born in 1529. Bernard Granado was also known as Barnard, Bernardo, and Barnardine.

assessors, Bernadine had settled in England about six years later than Lady Magdalen, and so had perhaps been based in London since about 1545.[24]

In October 1551 James Granado was put in charge of a mission to the French court, to deliver a gift of horses with their apparel to King Henri II, the Dauphin, the Princess Elizabeth and the Constable. The mission was a success and the French king rewarded James handsomely.[25] Bernardine may have had a role in this mission, for early in 1551 he had been appointed a squire of the stable and in 1552 was granted a Crown lease of lands in Somerset.[26]

As Protestants the Granados' position weakened under Queen Mary and in October 1553 a general pardon was granted to James and Bernardine.[27] When discussions over Mary's marriage were in progress, 'the Grenades', of whom the emperor Charles V's ambassador in London was suspicious, appear to have played a role as intermediaries, and had conversations with the representative of the King of the Romans (brother of the Emperor Charles V), who thought that his son (Ferdinand, archduke of Austria, a former pupil at Bernardine's riding school) stood a better chance of being accepted as Mary's consort than the emperor's son (Phillip II of Spain).[28] In February 1554, during Wyatt's rebellion, the 'elder Granado' (James) was imprisoned along with many others. After the defeat of the rebels, the imperial ambassador reported James Granado to be suing for a safe-conduct to go to Flanders, and supposed him to have supported the plot, stating that he had always spoken ill of the emperor and the Spaniards, was a partisan of Princess Elizabeth, and a thorough heretic devoted to the new religion; if he went to the Low Countries there would be a danger of him working for the French, on which account he should be watched; moreover, his brother was even worse than him. Later, James was reported to have performed good service to Queen Mary on the day of the defeat of the rebels, as a result of which the slanders against him ceased, and the emperor was pleased with him and promised to be his good lord so long as he supported Queen Mary.[29] This suggests that James Granado still had possessions in the Low Countries.

By 13 May 1554, however, James had been thrown into prison. This was occasioned by an investigation being made in Calais to discover who was conspiring with the French with a view to an attack on the town: Granado, who had been in Calais for many days while travelling to and from Brussels,

24. Kirk and Kirk 1900-1908: iii. 329, 339.
25. *CSP Foreign Edw. VI*, nos 464, 465, 487, 500, 511.
26. *CPR Edw. VI*: iii. 290; *VCH Somerset*: viii. 116.
27. *CPR Philip and Mary*: i. 451.
28. *CSP Spain*: ii. 357.
29. *CSP Spain*: xii. 85, 130-3, 157-8; *CSP Foreign, Mary*, 75-6.

fled towards the French, but was chased and caught under a bed. Moreover, he resented no longer being employed by the Queen and had quarrelled with the Earl of Arundel and the Master of the Horse. At this time three Spaniards were arrested and imprisoned at Gravelines on account of outrages against Granado, but Granado and others declared themselves satisfied and an appeal was made to Mary of Hungary as governor of the Low Countries to show mercy to the prisoners so as to maintain peace among those of different nationalities.[30] James Granado then appears to have been restored to a position in the English royal household, but on 4 May 1557, when he was riding in front of the King and Queen in her privy garden, the bridle broke and his horse dashed him against a wall so that he died.[31] To the Spaniards, this must have seemed a convenient accident.

The Granados had connections with English merchants, including at least one acting as a royal agent overseas. In 1548-9 John Dymock, a London draper who, as we have seen, was probably married to Lady Magdalen Granado's sister, Anne, was sent to Lüneburg (Lower Saxony), a principality of the empire now predominantly Lutheran and in opposition to the emperor. Dymock, who in 1546 had been an English agent to the Hanse towns, was procuring soldiers near Hamburg for service in Scotland and Boulogne and also paid the pension due to a former duke of Lüneburg. Both Hamburg and Bremen feared an attack via Denmark from imperial troops led by 'the Rhinegrave',[32] if they allowed Dymock's recruits to pass. At about the same time Dymock and other English merchants had purchased large quantities of munitions and illegally exported them via Amsterdam to England. This matter continued to rankle with Mary of Hungary in 1554, when in England a suit concerning these exports was brought against William Dansell (or Damsell). Dansell had been assistant and then successor to Stephen Vaughan in Antwerp and c.1550-2 had been governor of the Company of Merchant Adventurers there, and was now mistakenly described as the brother-in-law of James Granado. In 1550-2, during the recession in the Antwerp cloth trade, Dymock had been one of the principal complainants against the Merchant Adventurers. In May 1553 he was committed for a while to the Fleet Prison in London, but in 1561-2 was playing a key role as an intermediary between the English and the Swedish courts,

30. *CSP Spain*: xii. 253, 274-5.
31. Machyn 1848: 135-6.
32. Johann-Philipp, Wild- und Rheingraf zu Daun (1520-66), a military leader who recruited *Landsknechte* in Germany and was frequently employed by the king of France, where he was naturalised as *comte sauvage du Rhin et du Salm*. He may sometimes have been confused with his brother Phillip-Franz (1518-61), also Rheingraf and a military leader. Both were Lutherans and had lands in the Rhineland Palatinate, the Duchy of Lorraine and the Empire. Potter 1993-4.

in connection with a possible marriage between Elizabeth I and King Erik.[33]

The Granados also had high-ranking connections. A month after James's death in 1557 Christina, dowager duchess of Lorraine, wrote to Queen Mary on behalf of his widow and daughter, about whom she had recently spoken to the queen in London. At the same time she asked the earl of Pembroke to support her recommendation. Christina, a niece of the Emperor Charles, had come with Margaret of Parma to visit Mary's court, with the aim, it was said, to take Princess Elizabeth and give her in marriage to the Duke of Savoy, a plan which Mary blocked. Christina had a claim to the throne of Denmark, Norway and Sweden and as regent of Lorraine was in 1552 forced by the French invasion to flee to the Low Countries and to give up her son as a hostage in the French court. In 1558 she aspired to succeed her aunt Mary of Hungary as governor of the Netherlands, but Margaret of Parma was appointed instead. Christina had presumably benefited from some service – diplomatic, military or commercial – provided to her by James Granado or perhaps by Bernardine or some other member of the family. Queen Mary's response to her request in 1557 was immediately to grant to Lady Magdalen the reversion of the lease of lands in Devon, which she and James had held from the Crown, for the term of her life and free of rent.[34]

In 1559 Queen Elizabeth's favourite, Robert Dudley, earl of Leicester, sent Bernardine Granado, described as 'the queen's servant', to the Low Countries to buy horses for the queen.[35] About this time Bernardine was buying horses for the queen in Cologne and elsewhere, gathering them in Bruges and arranging for them and for military supplies to be shipped via Antwerp. He was unpopular in that region, being suspected of buying the horses for his own use rather than the queen's, and the regent of the Netherlands was cautious about granting an export licence. Bernardine, who perhaps had commercial and other interests in Lorraine, also acted as a diplomatic intermediary, enabling the queen's ambassador in Brussels to speak both in Flushing and in Antwerp to the Rhinegrave. At that time the Rhinegrave resided near Nancy in Lorraine and was perhaps to be sent to Scotland in the service of the French Crown, but wished to offer horses to the English queen. The aim seems to have been to detach the Rhinegrave from his allegiance to France and perhaps to reopen contacts with the

33. *CSP Foreign, Edw. VI: 1547-54*, 27, 30-3, 142-3; *CSP Spain*: xii. 195-7, 205; *CSP Foreign, Elizabeth*: i. preface n.5; *CSP Foreign, Elizabeth*: xi. nos 60, 104. See also Bindoff, ed. 1982: s.n. Damsell; Ramsay 1975: 47-9, 51, 53, 106, 106, 224-5; Adams et al. 2003:74, 110-11, and n. 255; Doran 1996: 33-5.
34. *CSP Foreign, Mary*: nos 628-9; *CPR Phil. and Mary*: iii. 283; iv. 271-2.
35. Adams 1996: 155.

dowager duchess of Lorraine, who continued to advise her son, the duke, and to act as regent in Lorraine during his absence.[36] Nothing more is known of Bernardine until his death, in the parish of St Dunstan in the East, in 1571, when he left £100 to Lady Magdalen's granddaughter.[37]

In November 1564 Lady Magdalen married Sir Robert Chester, a widower and former gentleman usher of the chamber who in 1544 had been among the twenty-five archers who formed Henry VIII's bodyguard when the king left Calais for Boulogne. Chester had estates at Royston, where the wedding was celebrated, and elsewhere in Hertfordshire. On the same day Magdalen's daughter Katherine was married to Robert's son and heir Edward, Royston being settled on the couple in tail male. A month later the wedding of Magdalen and Robert Chester was celebrated again in London at St. Dunstan's in the East. Thereafter Magdalen was known as Lady Chester. Sir Robert died in 1574 and Edward had died by October 1585, when Magdalen made her will and herself died a few days later. Edward had fathered two children, of whom Robert came into possession of Royston about 1586, when he would have attained his majority.[38] Lady Magdalen wished to be buried next to the body of her first husband, Sir James Granado, in the chapel of St Mary at the church of St Dunstan in the East. Among her many charitable legacies were sums to be distributed to the poor members of the French and the Dutch churches in London and to the poor in her parish of St Dunstan; she also left a gown each to 'my Lady Ramsey' and her two executors. 'Lady Ramsey' may have been the philanthropic Lady Mary Ramsey, wife of Sir Thomas Ramsey, the lord mayor of London to whom L. Grenade addressed his *Singularitez de Londres*. If there really was a connection between the two ladies and it had any bearing on L. Grenade's identity and on any link he may have had with Thomas Ramsey, it presumably would have been established by the time of Mary's marriage to Ramsey in 1578.[39]

L. Grenade seems likely to have belonged to this complex family of the Granados, members of which appear to have been active up to the 1570s as horsemen, merchants, soldiers, royal servants, diplomatic intermediaries, and possibly spies in England (especially London), Scotland, the Low Countries (especially Brabant), Saxony, France, and probably also Lorraine

36. *CSP Simancas*: i. no. 76; *CSP Foreign, Elizabeth*: i. nos 1116, 1254, 1353, 139; *CSP Foreign, Elizabeth*: ii. nos 223, 240, 554. Rhinegrave Johann-Phillip was in Flushing in August 1559: Potter 1993-4, pt. 2: 34.

37. *Register of St Dunstan*: 138; Bernardine's legacy is mentioned in Magdalen's will: PRO, PROB 11/68, fol. 345ᵛ.

38. *VCH Hertford*: iii. 260, which mistakenly identifies Edward Chester with the soldier in the Low Countries, who died at sea in 1577; see Trim (2004); *Register of St Dunstan*: 94.

39. Archer 2004a.

and the Rhineland. When, about 1550, L. Grenade first saw the pennants
on the Tower of London, James Granado was at the peak of his career and
possibly introduced him to the Tower. Protestant beliefs held them together,
but did not prevent them doing business or otherwise associating with
Catholic rulers in France and Lorraine and perhaps maintaining property
in Brabant. While James and his brother sought refuge in London, L.
Grenade or his parents appear to have done so in an area under French rule.
This may have been in the kingdom of France, or in those parts of Lorraine
– the three dioceses of Metz, Toul and Verdun – which came under French
control in 1552. Residence in Lorraine would put him within reach of
Strasbourg, the cathedral of which he had seen, and only a few days' journey
from Paris, which he may have known well. It may have been L. Grenade's
part of the family which had the closest links with the dowager duchess of
Lorraine, although it seems likely that Bernardine and others also visited
that region. All of the Granados were probably francophones and perhaps
only Lady Magdalen could have been regarded as 'Dutch'. When L. Grenade
visited London he would probably have stayed at her house in Mincing Lane
(Fig. 9) and she may have been able to introduce him to the lord mayor in
1577-8. Moreover, his account of the city displays a distinct interest in the
neighbourhood of her house: the Tower, Billingsgate and the Eastcheap
Shambles.

3. GENRE AND THE AUTHOR'S SENSE OF SPACE

Grenade's main purpose was not to write a straightforward guide to London
– although his text could fulfil that purpose to a limited extent – nor an
account of its history, but to select those features which he judged most
worthy of praise. He does this from the point of view a Protestant who had
knowledge and perhaps direct experience of recent persecution and whose
family, along with other religious refugees, had found a welcoming haven
in the well-governed and orderly city of London, which in light of recent
experience would have presented a strong contrast to Antwerp or Paris.

The genre is that of the *laus civitatis*, which had its origins in Classical
antiquity. Indeed, Grenade's text has a remarkable, if perhaps unconscious,
resemblance to the most famous example of that genre concerning London,
the description of the city which in 1173-4 William FitzStephen had written
as an introduction to his life of London's most famous citizen, St Thomas
of Canterbury, murdered on the order of King Henry II.[40] FitzStephen
deployed a scattering of classical gobbets and allusions in expressing his

40. The text used for this discussion is that in *Vita Sancti Thomae*, which is the published
text nearest both to the original and to the one likely to have been known in London in
Grenade's time: Robertson (1875).

essentially accurate and convincing portrayal of the twelfth-century city.[41]
Grenade was more cautious with his display of learning, which he largely
confined to the names of the ancient writers on cities cited in his Preface. In
a similar fashion, however, FitzStephen in the prologue to his description
had cited Plato on the form of the commonwealth (*respublica*) and Sallust
on the situation of Africa as precedents for his account of the site and of
the commonwealth of London. Grenade also displayed a special concern
for the site of London and several times referred to the city as a commonwealth (*republique*). Likewise both authors emphasised London's wealth
and its trading connections with distant parts of the world. For the latter,
FitzStephen quotes verses based on extracts from Virgil's *Georgics*. Both
FitzStephen and Grenade praise London's setting in a well-ordered and
fertile landscape and mention the distinctive occupations of certain districts
within the city, especially along the waterfront. Both deal with its fortresses:
three in FitzStephen's time, but only the Tower in Grenade's. Both praise
London's civic institutions, laws, good order, charity, and welcoming
of strangers (*hospites*), but only FitzStephen complained, certainly with
justification, of drunkenness and frequent fires. Both commented on markets
and the great quantities of foodstuffs available. With recent history in mind,
FitzStephen noted the great size of the citizens' army, while Grenade noted
the quantity of armaments at the Tower and the Londoners' prowess in
archery. Both emphasized London's role as a capital and as a site of learning
and disputation. Grenade, who had probably studied law, took a special
interest in the role of disputation in the training at the Inns of Court and
Chancery. The disputations noted by FitzStephen were more varied, but one
of their aims was to promote rhetorical powers of argument and persuasion,
essential in both politics and the law. Both authors dealt with sports and
pastimes, including the baiting of bulls and bears. Grenade disapprovingly
noted the new theatres, while FitzStephen with evident approval declared
that instead of theatrical spectacles and stage plays London had holier
representations of miracles and the passions of the martyrs. Both authors
had the same understanding of London's antiquity and foundation, derived
mainly from Geoffrey of Monmouth's fictitious 'History of the Kings of
Britain'. Both of them emphasised the role of Brutus, the legendary Trojan
founder of the city.

Such topics crop up in many medieval and later descriptions of cities, but
in this case the similarity of the two ensembles is remarkable. The two
authors, however, arrange their subject matter in different ways. There is
no hint in Grenade's text that he was drawing directly on twelfth-century

---

41. Scattergood (1996) mistakenly questions the essential accuracy of FitzStephen's
account on the basis of its rhetorical dressing.

sources, while it is clear that he used contemporary publications such as John Stow's *Summarie of the Chronicles* and Richard Grafton's *Abridgement of the Chronicles*, popular works on English history, neither of which focused solely on London. This similarity of topics may simply reflect the truth that the essential character of London in 1578 was already established four centuries earlier, but there is a possibility of a more direct connection. FitzStephen's description was first printed in 1598, at the end of the first edition of Stow's *A survay of London*. Grenade cannot have seen this volume, but it is possible that he knew Stow and had consulted either the thirteenth-century text of FitzStephen's description which Stow at some time had in his possession or Stow's transcription of it. It is unlikely that he would have had access to the version of FitzStephen's description which had been entered the early fourteenth-century civic collection of customs and memoranda known as the *Liber Custumarum*, although that text may have promoted awareness of FitzStephen's characterization in civic circles, with which Grenade probably had some contact.[42]

Medieval descriptions of cities seem not to have been informed by a strong unifying tradition, but they nevertheless drew on a common pool of topics, which in a number of cases, including those of FitzStephen and Grenade, were ordered in a coherent fashion. An eighth-century Lombard text, for example, recommended that a city first be praised by reference to its real or mythical founder, then in successive descriptions of its site, its natural resources and the achievements of its citizens in peace and war, recommendations which in one form or another seem to have had a wide effect over a long period. Such ideas had their roots in the travel literature of the ancient world, written for those who wished to understand what they saw, and of which the only complete surviving example is the 'Description of Greece' by Pausanias (fl. *c.* AD 150).[43] In fifteenth-century Italy there evolved a more systematic approach, derived from classical models and facilitated by Italian developments in regional cartography. About 1500, for example, the Venetian authorities laid down a four-part scheme for reports on distant territories and cities, which owed much to Biondo Flavio's *Italia Illustrata*, published in 1453 and a pioneer in new ways of describing cities and their territories.[44]

In his initial Epistle and Preface Grenade first explains his own and his family's appreciation of London. Then he elaborates the extent of the city's fame, notes that no history of London has been written, reviews ancient

---

42. Watson 1969: 2-3, 5, 56 (no. 200); cf. Brooke and Keir 1975: 88. For other indications that Grenade may have known Stow, see pp. 148 (n. 15), 166 (n. 108).
43. Hyde 1966; for ancient travel literature, see Hornblower and Spawforth 2003: 1129 (Pausanias (3)), 1534 ('tourism') and references there cited.
44. Manley 1995: 137; for Biondo Flavio, see below, pp. 40-41.

writers on cities, regrets that others have written the history of the capital
of his own nation—thereby depriving him of the opportunity of doing it
himself—and praises London's religious outlook. Thereafter the greater part
of his account is topographically arranged, but not according to the established internal divisions of the city — the wards and parishes — which were
to serve as an enduring framework for later descriptions of London, whose
boundaries would have been invisible to outsiders and were sometimes a
matter of uncertainty or dispute among established residents. Likewise, he
hardly noted the limits of the city jurisdiction, except at Temple Bar
which, since it was on the way to Westminster, was a formal ceremonial site
(Chapter 2). This approach provided little opportunity for thematic
treatment: he took things as they came, using the circuit of suburbs outside
the city walls and some of the principal streets within as his organising
framework (Fig. 9).

He begins (Chapter 1) with the name London and the city's foundation
by the Trojan Brutus, the excellence of whose choice of site he demonstrates
by means of the view from Highgate Hill, the earliest record of such a
panorama. This reveals the Thames, the ships from overseas coming up river
to the city, and traffic upstream towards Oxford. A spacious and fertile plain
surrounds London and it is possible to see the hills in the distance and the
villages in the immediate environs of the city.

There follow five chapters dealing with the suburbs, taken clockwise and
beginning at Ludgate, where (Chapter 2) he takes the street to Westminster,
describing sights and institutions in order, including a brief notice of the
lawyers' Inns. With the less extensive but very populous suburb outside
Newgate (Chapter 3) he takes a similar approach and includes the important
water conduit near the church of St Sepulchre and the entire surroundings
of Smithfield. He then (Chapter 4) deals with the suburban area on the
northern side, outside the gates of Aldersgate, Cripplegate, Moor Gate
(which did not lead into an inhabited area), Bishopsgate and Aldgate, counting the last as the sixth of the suburbs but saying nothing about it except
for the meadows and conduits beyond, which he appears not to have visited
and in any case confused with areas to the north and west of the city. The
seventh suburb, containing St Katharine's Hospital (Chapter 5), is
approached via The Tower of London, exaggerating the role of the Tower's
Iron Gate as a city gate. Here he begins with a full account of the Tower
itself, which he identifies as one of the four especially impressive structures
in London, the others being St Paul's, London Bridge, and the Royal
Exchange, each of which he describes in detail. He deals only briefly with
the suburb itself, noting its sailors and varied crafts, one of his rare mentions
of the numerous crafts and trades of London. He compares the last suburb
(Chapter 6), Southwark, to that near Westminster, but devotes most
attention to the bull- and bear-baiting there and to London Bridge.

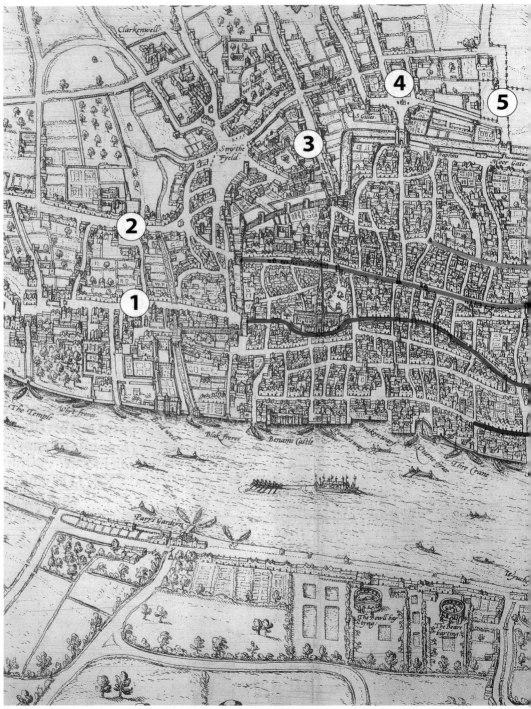

Fig. 9. Central area of B & H Map (1572) showing the order in which Grenade described the suburbs and the four 'main thoroughfares' around which he organised his account of the city within the walls. © *British Museum*.

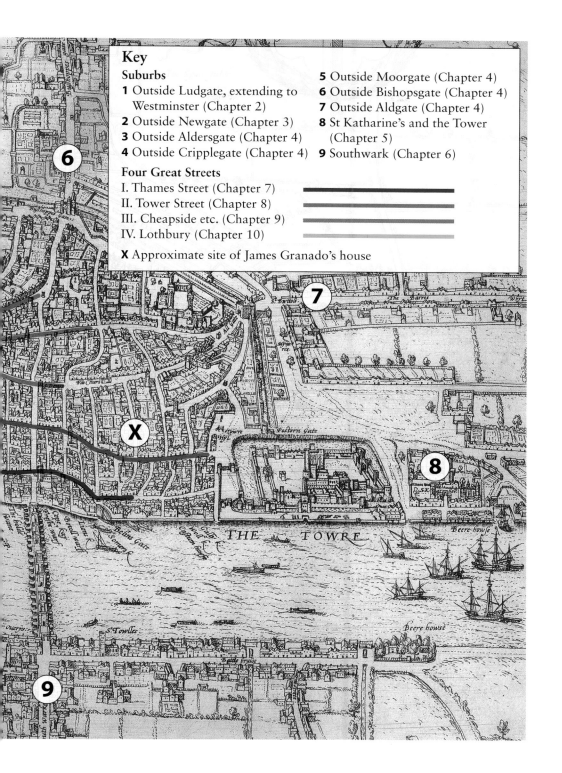

Key

Suburbs

1 Outside Ludgate, extending to Westminster (Chapter 2)
2 Outside Newgate (Chapter 3)
3 Outside Aldersgate (Chapter 4)
4 Outside Cripplegate (Chapter 4)

5 Outside Moorgate (Chapter 4)
6 Outside Bishopsgate (Chapter 4)
7 Outside Aldgate (Chapter 4)
8 St Katharine's and the Tower (Chapter 5)
9 Southwark (Chapter 6)

Four Great Streets

I. Thames Street (Chapter 7)
II. Tower Street (Chapter 8)
III. Cheapside etc. (Chapter 9)
IV. Lothbury (Chapter 10)

X Approximate site of James Granado's house

Inside the city walls he arranges his material according to what he identifies as the 'four great and principal thoroughfares' which cross the city
from east to west. This is a convenient arrangement, a form of classification
by grid on the lines of a memory theatre, but it ignores the discontinuities,
marked by changes in width and direction, along these 'streets' as he defines
them, noting that their names change along their length as they pass through
different neighbourhoods (Chapter 7). Although he notes markets and some
clusters of occupations, he does not take account of the local networks of
streets and lanes which contributed to the formation of these neighbourhoods. Moreover, he ignored the numerous singular things to be found in
the one major and many significant streets running from north to south, of
which several had distinctive roles in connecting the landing-places along
the river frontage with the city's inland markets. The first of these great
streets is Thames Street (Chapter 7), which he covers only from Billingsgate
to the Steelyard, noting its exceptionally crowded nature and the great
wealth of some of its mercantile inhabitants. The second great street
(Chapter 8), which he calls Tower Street, runs from Ludgate to The Tower,
and so he begins with an account of St Paul's. He then passes along Watling
Street, with its drapers' shops, into Candlewick Street (Cannon Street)
and past London Stone to the Eastcheap shambles, to which he devotes
considerable attention. After them he notes only the Tower.

The third street (Chapter 9) begins at Newgate where, prompted by the
remains of the former Franciscan Friary, he provides an extended account
of the three new hospitals established under King Edward VI. Cheapside
comes next, where like many visitors he was impressed above all by the
shops of the goldsmiths and those of other luxury trades. He provides
valuable descriptions of the Eleanor Cross, the Standard and two other
water conduits or fountains, but omits one at the west end of Cheapside.
At Cornhill this 'street' divides into three. He says little about Broad Street,
but managed to fit in a mention of Gracechurch Street where, well to the
south, there was a fine conduit and market. Returning to the west end of
Cornhill he describes the luxury shops in Lombard Street, after which the
street beyond Gracechurch Street led to Aldgate. Then he dealt with shops
in Cornhill and the great set piece of the Royal Exchange. For this new
building he provides great praise, as would befit a man who probably knew
Antwerp well, together with the fullest description by any author and
measurements otherwise unrecorded. Grenade then progressed past the
conduit in Cornhill to Leadenhall, after which the street was said simply to
lead to Aldgate.

The fourth street, Lothbury (Chapter 10), is hardly described, but serves
to introduce Guildhall, the seat of city administration and justice, which lay
just to the north and is described in great detail, along with an inaccurate
historical account of the development of city government and descriptions

of civic elections and ceremonial. Acquaintance with the mayor may have helped him gain access to this heart of communal privilege.

At this point, Grenade drops the topographical approach and, in a logical succession, devoted the last three chapters to aspects of city government, law and social policy. First (Chapter 11) he deals with the elections of the lord mayor, sheriffs and aldermen and the role of the city companies (which he calls *Halles*, translated here as Halls) — especially the twelve leading ones — in government, craft regulation, and charity. Then follows a long and detailed account of the new lord mayor's ceremonial entry to the city. Secondly (Chapter 12), he surveys the laws and policies of the city, including the charitable provisions made by the 'Halls' and the regulation of markets, before embarking on a detailed account of legal education at the Inns of Court and Chancery and of the ceremonies associated with the admission of Serjeants-at-Law, the highest ranking lawyers below the Crown judges. He perhaps knew a Serjeant and may even have attended the recent ceremonies in 1577. This detailed interest in regulation and the legal profession suggests that Grenade himself was a magistrate or lawyer.

Finally, in a hastily compiled conclusion (Chapter 13), Grenade reviews the liberties of the city and its royal charters, returns to the subject of archers (cf. Chapter 4), notes the citizens' commercial privileges and their hunting rights, and among all the singularities of London highlights and praises the Londoners' good customs, honesty, charity, piety, and kindness, which will stand them in good stead at the Last Judgement.

Grenade's account of London focuses on spectacular buildings and sites of wealth, authority and power. He describes two great churches, but mentions only two others, the former church of the Franciscans and that of the Knights of St John, both now converted into parish churches. Private houses attract attention only if elaborately decorated. He is interested in retail trade rather than manufacturing crafts and so the high-class shopping streets (most notably Cheapside, Lombard Street, Cornhill and London Bridge, along with the relatively new developments along Fleet Street and the Strand) emerge clearly from his account. He gives attention to striking infrastructure such as conduits or fountains and to monuments such a crosses. Even within the walls his accounts of the 'great thoroughfares' tail off as they approach the Tower and Aldgate and, to the west, beyond the Steelyard. The area covered is one with which wealthy English, Dutch, French or Italian merchants and elite English consumers of expensive imported goods would have been familiar.

Grenade's visualisation of the city seems conditioned by the use of maps, certainly the map of London published in the first volume of Braun and Hogenberg's *Civitates Orbis Terrarum* (1572; see Fig 1), which tends to exaggerate the continuity and width of the east-west streets across the city and so could have suggested to Grenade the 'four principal thoroughfares'.

He may also have modelled this idea on the twelfth-century notion of the four principal royal highways crossing England, 'very broad as well as splendid', as described by Henry of Huntingdon,[45] but accessible to Grenade in Stow's *Summarie of Englishe Chronicles* (e.g. 1567, fol. 12) where they were attributed to Molmutius Dunwallo and his son Belinus. He may also have had access to sheets of the Copperplate map (Figs 2-4), which in particular could have informed his account of archery and recreation in Moor Field. The Braun and Hogenberg map, derived from the Copperplate, would also have shaped his perception of the fields and small settlements in the immediate environs of London, while if he had access to a print of Christopher Saxton's map of Kent, Sussex, Surrey and Middlesex, the plate of which was finished in 1575, he would have gained a good idea of the wider pattern of settlement, of the hills to the south of London and of the Thames upstream from the estuary to beyond Windsor.[46] Saxton's map perhaps guided and clarified his view across London from Highgate. (Chapter 1).

This use of a map fulfilled the intentions of the publisher of *Civitates Orbis Terrarum*, who hoped that use of the new series would not be restricted to the learned and in 1571 wrote that it would commend itself to purchasers if the proper names of places, churches and gates were written in the native language. A few years later, advertising his product, he wrote of the pleasure of gazing at the volumes 'in one's home and far from all danger'.[47]

4. A POSSIBLE MODEL FOR 'LES SINGULARITEZ DE LONDRES'

While Grenade's *Singularitez* and FitzStephen's description of London have many themes in common, the organisation of the two texts is very different. In the latter respect, Grenade seems to have drawn on the account of Paris by Gilles Corrozet (1510-68), perhaps the most popular account of any European city published during the sixteenth century and almost certainly the perhaps deliberately unidentified history of the 'capital of my nation' which Grenade mentions in his Preface. First published in 1532, thirteen further editions or revised impressions of Corrozet's work were published before 1578, up to and including those of 1576 and 1577, which differed radically from their predecessors. This publication continued to be enlarged and reissued into the seventeenth century.[48] The title of the first edition, *La Fleur des antiquitez, singularitez et excellences de la plus que noble et*

45. *Historia Anglorum*, 24-5.
46. Skelton 1970: 14.
47. Skelton 1966: vii, ix.
48. Bonnardot (1880).

*triomphante ville et cité de Paris, capitalle du royaulme de France auec la
généalogie du roy Françoys premier de ce nom,* may have inspired Granade's
title, *Les Singularitez de Londres, noble, fameuse Cité, capital du Royaume
d'Angleterre: ses antiquitez et premiers fondateurs.* Corrozet himself was
probably inspired by the title of Jean Lemaire des Belges's *Les Illustrations
de Gaule et singularitez de Troye,* first published in Paris between 1511 and
1513, and to which he refers in his discussion of the foundation of Paris.[49]
Grenade, perhaps inspired by Corrozet, also cites Lemaire des Belges's work
(fol. 6), but not as a direct source of information, although it may have
inspired him to mention the Babylonian historian Berossos.[50]

Apart from the addition of the phrase *adioustees oultre la premiere
impression Plusiers singularitez estans en ladicte ville* to the title of a second
impression in 1532 and to subsequent impressions, the title of Corrozet's
account remained the same until a reordered and revised edition was published in 1550 as *Les Antiquitez, histoires et singularitez de Paris, ville capitale du Royaume de France. Auec priuilege du Roy pour vi. ans.* Corrozet
revised and republished the 1550 edition in 1561 as *Les Antiquitez,
chroniques et singularitez de Paris, ville capitale du royaume de France, avec
les fondations et bastimens des lieux: les sépulchres et épitaphes des princes,
princesses et autres personnes illustres: corrigées et augmentées pour la
seconde édition par G. Corrozet Parisien.* This was the last of the editions
produced under Corrozet's eye and there are reasons to believe that this was
the one that Grenade would have used.

Although sometimes described as a guidebook, and certainly capable of
being used in that way, especially in its later editions, Corrozet's work originated as a chronological account of the development of Paris, celebrating
its role as a capital, as expressed in its cumulative sequence of major buildings, culminating in the reign of François I, and updated in successive
impressions.[51] The royal genealogy was among its most important components. From the second impression of 1532 to that of 1543, the work also
included lists of streets and churches, details of the daily consumption of
food and drink, accounts of a walk across Paris and of another around the
Bois de Vincennes (both measured in paces), a list of the street cries of Paris,
and a few other matters, all derived from a pamphlet printed *c.*1500.[52] For
the edition of 1543, the list of streets and lanes was greatly enlarged, to a

49. fol. 5ᵛ of the 1533 edition; p. 6 of the reprint of the second impression of the 1532
edition (Paris, 1874).
50. See below, pp. 147-8, n. 11.
51. The accounts in Liaroutzos 1998: 37-121 and Skenazi 2003: 117-66 provide
valuable background; see also Hodges 2008: 41-75.
52. For the pamphlet, see *Les rues et eglises* in the list of Printed Works.

total of 413, with the addition of details concerning how the streets connected to each other and notes of the churches and other sights to be seen
along them (occupying fols 34^r-71^v). These new details, advertised on the
title page, gave the publication a special value as a guide to the city and the
intricacies of its street network.

The new editions of 1550 and 1561 dropped most of the material added
in 1532, apart from the list of streets (but shorn of much of the detail added
in 1543) and the lists of churches and colleges. These editions, as Corrozet
explained, were intended as a history of Paris from its foundation, together
with an account of its monuments, and they entirely replaced the earlier editions. They were, however, less useful as guides to finding one's way around
Paris than the edition of 1543 had been. On this basis, it has been argued
convincingly that Corrozet decided to associate his new edition with a map
and was the patron or promoter of a new version, updated to 1550, of a
large-scale map of Paris which had first been produced shortly before
1530.[53] The new map, prepared by Olivier Truschet and Germain Hoyau,
acknowledged Corrozet by quotation from his works, including an acrostic
verse containing his name. The map includes many street names, apparently
derived from Corrozet's list of 1543 and on the map itself it is stated that
Paris contained 287 streets and lanes. Since the street-names now appeared
on a map, Corrozet could omit the details of their location and intercon-
nection from the lists of streets in his editions of 1550 and 1561. There is
no indication in his text, however, that Corrozet drew upon on a map for
organising his account of the city. In this important respect Grenade's
approach differed from Corrozet, whose text does not provide a clear sense
of the landscape and setting of Paris. Moreover, such overviews of the
Parisian landscape as there are in Corrozet's work his work derive from the
pamphlet of *c*.1500 and belong to a perambulatory mode of city description,
which in the case of Paris can be traced from the thirteenth century
onwards.[54] The pamphlet, in particular, included an account of the overall
dimensions of Paris, expressed in the number of paces counted in a day's
walk between some of the principal monuments on the periphery, while on
the next day, it was said, a similar walk encompassed the Bois de Vincennes.
Both walks involved interesting social encounters. In adopting a perambulatory framework for much of his description of London, Grenade may have
been aware of that tradition, either directly or through Corrozet. Grenade
may also have been influenced by Corrozet's lists of streets, which in his

53. Dérens 1980.
54. See Géraud 1837 for the 13th-century 'Dictionarius' of Jean de Garlande (pp. 580-
612) and the 15th-century 'Les rues de Paris en vers' (pp. 578-9).

editions of 1543, 1550 and 1561 included brief references to the churches and other notable features to be encountered along many of them.[55]

The resemblances between Grenade's work and that of Corrozet are both thematic and presentational, and conservative rather than innovative. Corrozet's edition of 1561 includes an address at the beginning which recalls that the ancients praised each other by reference to the *villes excellentes* which had nourished them, citing the speeches of Thucydides and others. Grenade may have had this passage in mind when in his Preface he listed the ancient authors who had written on the history of cities and when, in the Epistle (fol. 9), he announced his intention to produce a work on the famous men of London.

Both authors began the main text of their works with interpretations of the names of their cities and accounts of their supposed founders, Trojans or Greeks in the case of Paris and Trojans in the case of London. Each of them also praises the founder for his choice of site by reference to the city's present situation. The manner in which they dated the origins and principal phases of their cities is similar: Corrozet did so by reference to by reference to the Incarnation, the Flood and the foundation of Rome, while Grenade did so according to the Incarnation and the Creation and only rarely by other means, taking his dates from Grafton's *Abridgement* and Stow's *Summarie*. Grenade's description of St Paul's Cathedral (Chapter 8), for which he provides the earliest known reasonably accurate dimensions, may have been inspired by the dimensions given in Correzet's account of the cathedral of Notre-Dame in his editions of 1550 and 1561, where they replaced a simpler set in earlier editions which had been borrowed from the pamphlet of *c.*1500. It is noteworthy that Grenade's set of dimensions follow the scheme used by Corrozet. Moreover, in his editions of 1550 and 1561 Corrozet introduced the extensive recording of monuments and epitaphs, which may have prompted Grenade to provide similar information for St Paul's. He perhaps selected the memorials of famous men associated with London whom he intended to cover in a future work and some, such as Sir Nicholas Bacon and Sir John Mason, with whom his family may have been acquainted. The prominence of St Paul's and Westminster Abbey in Grenade's account of London matches that of Notre-Dame and St-Denis in Correzet's record of the monuments of Paris. If Grenade looked at any earlier editions of Corrozet, he would have encountered the estimate of the daily consumption of meat in Paris, which may have prompted his remarks on that topic in London (Chapter 9). Another point of resemblance concerns the monumental aspects of the supply of drinking water. Grenade pays considerable attention to six of the public water conduits (which he identifies

---

55. Corrozet 1550: fols 189-97[v].

as *fontaines*) in London, acknowledging them to be impressive structures and often the work of charitable citizens. In his edition of 1550 Corrozet noted the king's impressive reconstruction in that year of the historic *fontaine des Innocents*, and for the first time included in his work a list of the sixteen such conduits in Paris.[56]

Corrozet addressed the early editions of his work to the *illustres et notables bourgeoys de Paris*, and that of 1561 to the *nobles et illustres familles de Paris*. In addition, he dedicated those of 1550 and 1561 to Claude Guiot, secretary and counsellor to the king, controller of the audience of the chancery and *prevôt des marchands de Paris*, a figure in some respects comparable to the lord mayor of London. Beneath the dedication of 1561, Corrozet's name appears as *Vostre humble G. Corrozet*, a conventional phrase, but similar to Grenade's subscription to his Epistle addressed to the lord mayor (a figure less elevated politically than Guiot) and aldermen of London. Grenade's Epistle, however, may have been inspired by 'The Epistle Dedicatory', addressed to the 'lord Mayor of the cite of London, the right worshipful Aldermen his brethren, and the commoners of the same citie' which John Stow included in the 1567 and later editions of his *Summarie*, subscribing himself as 'Your moste humble John Stowe'.

We may conclude that, in all likelihood, Grenade had read, or skimmed, at least the later editions of Corrozet's work on Paris, in particular that of 1561, aspects of which informed the presentation and to some extent the topics, of his own, very different, *laudes* of London.

New ways of visualising and writing about cities?

In the 1561 edition of his work Corrozet questioned aspects of the traditional history of Paris, especially its mythical origins. Later editions omitted such material entirely. Grenade, by contrast, was more conservative and adhered to the Galfredian version of London's Trojan origins. If he was aware that such stories had been demonstrated to lack any historical basis, he chose, diplomatically, to present the traditional and still widely believed version in his praises of London addressed to the lord mayor and aldermen. Moreover, this was at a time when those traditions were being actively developed, as demonstrated by the naming of the two effigies of giants in Guildhall (Chapter 10).[57]

Both authors were influenced by the Humanist recovery of classical texts and some of the formal aspects of the classical approach to the praise of cities, the presentation of information about them and the famous men with

---

56. Corrozet 1550: fols 180, 200.
57. See also below, pp. 48-9, 175-6 (note 159).

which they were associated. Biondo Flavio's *Italia Illustrata* was probably an important but indirect influence, not least on account of its geographical approach to the setting of cities, its combination of historical information with that concerning monuments, and its systematic accounts of famous men.[58] While this represents a recovery of earlier, more ordered approaches to the praise and description of cities, very few of the fourteenth- and fifteenth-century plan-views and sketches of cities offer coherent presentations of their street patterns, their emphasis being on town walls, watercourses, and major monuments shown in isolation. Street maps, as we now understand them, and as they were understood in antiquity, did not proliferate until well after 1500 and even then their compilers were slow to adopt precise measurement and surveying techniques in place of the pacing out of dimensions and sketches from high viewpoints.[59] In their contrasting deployment of city maps, Corrozet and Grenade mark an interesting transition in the perception and description of urban forms. Corrozet appears to have realised that his work on Paris would be more accessible if accompanied by a detailed map and adjusted his text accordingly, while others prepared a map which drew on his material. For Grenade, the surviving text of whose work suggests that it was compiled in haste, the task of praising London was facilitated by the existence of a good recently published map of London, and perhaps another of its region, which assisted his understanding of the setting of the city and suggested ways in which he might organise his thoughts about it and identify its highlights.

Corrozet's work was an important influence on ways of thinking about cities, in particular in connection with the revival of models for works which would inform the traveller about a city in preparation for a future visit. A prime mover in this development was Theodore Zwinger's *Methodus Apodemica*, which took as its starting point the notion that travel was a stimulus to learning (as Biondo Flavio had found with his research concerning Italy) and developed a hierarchical system of categories and sub-categories, summarised in synoptic tables (but not in maps), which readers would find useful when planning a journey or attempting to comprehend the features of any territory or city they might wish to visit. So far as cities were concerned, the topics and themes were much the same as those apparent in classical descriptions or *laudes,* or in *Italia Illustrata,* but the ordering and breaking down of the material fostered new thinking about urban environments as ordered sets of natural, social, religious, economic and political spaces. Elements of this approach are apparent in Grenade's thinking

---

58. Hyde 1966; Biondo Flavio 2005-10: *passim.*
59. Pinto 1976; Harvey 1980: 66-83; Harvey 1987.

about London, and he may have been aware of specific developments associated with Zwinger's approach. This logical structure owed much to the ideas of Peter Ramus (1515-72), under whom Zwinger had studied in Paris, developed in order to reform the curriculum by classifying and subdividing knowledge so that those who were short of time could learn quickly. The system was further elaborated by Bassiano Landi in Padua, where Zwinger had completed his doctorate. A notable feature of Zwinger's work was his use of four urban case studies to demonstrate the applicability of his encyclopaedic ideas. Of these, the study concerning Paris is striking and depended entirely on the 1550 or the 1561 edition of Corrozet's work, especially its ordered lists of noteworthy features, parts of which were repeated verbatim. Zwinger's ideas were taken up by later English authors, but had little impact upon the genre of English urban description in which, perhaps following Corrozet's example, separately published town maps came to have an important role. [60] Nevertheless, Zwinger's work probably contributed to sharpening perceptions of the hierarchy urban spaces. As ideas concerning the role of towns in the circulation of information and ideas came to be more systematized and diffused, so the town itself came to suggest frameworks for the organisation of knowledge, initially in *La Piazza Universale*, an encyclopaedia of professions and crafts published in 1585, and later in a comprehensive encyclopaedia of nature, where knowledge was imagined as being situated in a market place or *fondaco* and categorised according to porticos, loggias and shops.[61]

5. THE DISTINCTIVENESS OF THE TEXT

Grenade's account manifests many of the characteristic features of the accounts of foreign visitors to England.[62] They shared his sense of the highlights of the city: the Tower, the Royal Exchange, London Bridge, and St Paul's were all on the 'must-see' list. Like them he takes an interest in civic ceremonial (the elections and inaugurations of the lord mayor and sheriffs) and in the leisure activities of the citizens (Grenade makes it clear that he has been to animal baitings, but distances himself from the theatrical productions). But he includes a lot that they do not. He has a much stronger interest in the history of the city and of its frameworks of law and custom,

---

60. Zwinger 1577; Dérens 1980: 225-30; Felici 2009; Sellberg 2014; Manley 1995a: 135-40 mentions later English publications on the art of travel which drew on Zwinger. There is a hint of such ideas in Grenade's *Preface* (below, p. 59).
61. Garzoni 1585; Serpetro 1653.
62. Bentley and Walpole 1757; Sneyd 1847; Rye 1865; von Bülow 1892; von Bülow 1895; Chotzen and Draak 1937; Williams 1937; Barron, Coleman and Gobbi 1983; Folger Shakespeare Library, MS V.a.316.

although he misunderstands many of them, presumably in common with most citizens; he has much more to say about charity, and offers several exemplars of civic philanthropy. In many ways he can be compared with Stow, whose *Survey* was not to appear for another twenty years, though Grenade was able to draw upon Stow's histories for some of his material.[63] It is interesting that Grenade proposed later to undertake a survey of the heroic men who had shaped the urban fabric and the city's charities, a standard feature of *laudes civitatis*, adumbrating Stow's own list of honourable citizens incorporated into the *Survey*. Like Stow, Grenade takes us on a perambulation of the city, though his sense of its topography owes more to recently produced maps than to the administrative boundaries of wards and parishes which dominate in Stow. There is in fact astonishingly little in Grenade about the city's parish churches, although he noted their remarkable number and his references to St John Clerkenwell and Christchurch Newgate indicate that he approved of the conversion of the churches of former religious orders to parochial use. Grenade is at pains constantly to stress his selectivity: 'I do not desire to recite each one [of the city's privileges] in detail, but merely a selection' (fol. 85v); 'out of concern for brevity, I have left aside several matters pertaining to the said … Exchange' (fol. 56v). So it becomes more intriguing on which matters he chooses to allocate more space. For example, he shows considerable interest in the city's infrastructure (more proportionately, given the constraints of space, than Stow): he tells us a lot about the water supply, not simply presenting the conduits as exemplars of charity, but making claims, admittedly inaccurate, about the numbers of households served; he is fascinated by the markets, particularly the meat markets, and he notes the impressive facilities at Billingsgate.

Grenade was of course writing in a very different genre from either the foreign travellers or Stow. His tract was a panegyric to the city, piling up the superlatives both about the capital's buildings and about its virtuous magistrates. London is a 'noble and triumphant city' (fol. 78v); its policies are 'so well ordered that nothing better is possible' (fol. 78); its magistrates bear 'traces of the majesty of God' (fol. 64v). Although there are very few specific comparisons (apart from the comparison of St Pauls with the cathedral in Strasbourg), one would be forgiven for thinking that London was the premier city of Europe, though an exception should be made for the capital of his own nation (presumably Paris, at that time a greater city than London). Grenade is keen to celebrate London as a global city: the flattering remarks about London's growing fame, reflecting its participation in frameworks of international exchange, is much stronger than anything Stow himself

---

63. There is a large literature on Stow. For an introduction, see Archer 1995; Collinson 2001; and the essays in Gadd and Gillespie 2004.

claimed (though Stow does include a passage from FitzStephen which antici-
pates the later rhetoric), and the theme was much stronger in the hands of
Stow's seventeenth-century continuators. Grenade's metropolitan booster-
ism reads rather curiously for a city which in the 1560s has been described
as a 'satellite of Antwerp',[64] which by 1578, however, had become a city to
flee from rather than migrate to. A feature of the panegyric mode is a
disregard of negative characteristics. This is very evident from a comparison
with the Venetian relation of *c.*1500 which complains about thieves and
robbers, and criticises the institution of apprenticeship. Alessandro Magno
also suffered from robbers in the vicinity of the city, and picked on the poor
quality of the beer.[65] But virtually the only things Grenade criticises are the
use of law French in the courts, and possibly the state of some of the Tower
ordnance. Whereas Stow has a strong sense of the environmental degradation
brought about by the expansion of the city in his lifetime, Grenade is silent
on these themes. Stow refers to concentrations of poverty in some of the
suburbs and riverside parishes; the closest Grenade gets to this is his neutral
description of occupational groups in the precinct of St Katharine's by the
Tower, although he several times refers to the wretchedness of the poor in
the streets, but as a group for control rather than sympathy. One might also
set Grenade's account of the London hospitals in which the vision and
aspirations of the Edwardian founders appears not yet tarnished with the
disillusionment evident in the much more jaundiced account (*c.*1582) drawn
up by the former renter of the hospital, John Howes, where there is a much
stronger sense of promise unfulfilled, not to mention a whiff of corruption.[66]
Grenade's praise for matters as varied as the watch, local policing, street
lighting, and cleaning stand oddly against the fulminations of aldermanic
rhetoric, excoriating local officials for their manifold failures.[67] His praise
of the virtuous citizenry stands in stark contrast to the content of the Paul's
Cross jeremiads where London appeared as a Babylonian perversion of the
ideal.[68] These juxtapositions however alert us to the need to be as sensitive
to the conventions governing the content of mayoral precepts or a Paul's
Cross sermon as we are to the rhetoric of civic praise.

   One of the key elements in the encomium to the city is its repeated iden-
tification as the 'city of peace'. For Grenade, London is not Babylon, but its
positive antitype, the new Jersualem (which could be translated from
Hebrew as 'city of peace'). In this respect, however, Grenade also has in
mind one real way in which London was different from many of the cities

---

64. Ramsay 1975: 33.
65. Sneyd 1847; Barron, Coleman, and Gobbi 1983.
66. Tawney and Power 1924: iii. 421-43.
67. Compare Griffiths 2008: *passim.*
68. Lake 2001.

he knew. It was indeed a city of peace in the sense that it had not been scarred by religious strife. Contemporaries were all too acutely aware of the fate of Paris in the 'massacre of St Bartholomew's Day' in 1572 and Antwerp in its sack by Spanish troops in 1576. Around the time Grenade was writing the London bookstalls carried such titles as George Gascoigne's tract *The Spoil of Antwerp*, the ballad *A warning song to cities all to learn by Antwerp's fall*; and other pamphlets, *Heavy news to all Christendom from the woeful town of Antwerp come; A godly exhortation unto England to repent him of the evil and sinful ways showing the example and destruction of Jerusalem and Antwerp*.[69] Preaching at Paul's Cross on 9 December 1576 Thomas White, drawing on Matthew 12:25, warned his auditory of the perils of division: 'a Citie deuided can not long stande. He that knoweth both buildings, & their cause of ruines, hath tolde vs so. *Parris* is a pattern not of long ago, and *Antwerp* an example but of yesterday'.[70] Such sentiments would have resonated strongly among the exile community with which Grenade was so well connected.

The danger of reading a text written in the panegyric mode is to write it off as unrepresentative, inaccurate, and misleading. But quite apart from the interesting question as to why such a tract should be written at this time, to which we shall return, there are a number of areas in which Grenade's account demands our attention. While it is true that Grenade creates a sense of accuracy through what turn out to be spurious statistics – on the number of communicants in St Sepulchre's, or the volume of meat consumption in the city, or the number of spectators in Cheapside on lord mayor's day, for example – it is striking that he should have made the effort. The notion that one might infer the population of the city from the amount of meat it consumed is interesting, and not at this date part of the discourse of thinking about cities in England. A similar urge to quantify is apparent in his regular recourse to measurement, estimating the height of the Cheapside and Charing Crosses, the dimensions of St Paul's and the Guildhall, and so on. But however variable his accuracy (some of the figures seem very 'hit and miss'), Grenade's quest for specificity demonstrates his commitment to what has been called the 'culture of fact'.[71] In this he also reflected a European 'culture of numbers' which had been developing since the eleventh century, not least in response to the growth of megacities such as Milan and Paris. No European city description before the eighteenth century matched Bonvesin's contemporary account of late thirteenth-century Milan in its numerical range and precision. Paris, however, appears to have maintained a culture of urban numbers from about that time onwards, elements of

69. Gascoyne 1576; *Warning* 1577; Arber 1875-94: ii. 137b, 140, 154.
70. White 1578a: 56-7.
71. Shapiro 2000.

which are preserved in Corrozet's works, which probably influenced Grenade's view of London.[72]

As far as the buildings of the city are concerned, while many details might be replicated in other accounts, Grenade offers us among the earliest accounts of structures as important as the Royal Exchange (with especially important details on its dimensions, and the materials used in its construction) and the Shoreditch theatres (with estimates of capacity). His descriptions of the key city edifices bear comparison with those of Stow, but whereas Stow's primary concern is with fixing the buildings in time, Grenade shows much more interest in their uses by people in the present. His account of the base of the Hanseatic merchants in the Steelyard, for example, includes details of their communal life and form of government. The description of the Exchange bustles with details of the variety of activities that took place there: as an assembly point for merchants with designated zones for different nationalities, as a shopping centre; as a centre for news and the organization of postal services; and as a venue for evening concerts by the city's musicians. It is striking also that he refers to the presence of women traders not in the walks of the Exchange — a male preserve as the earlier mercantile assemblies in Lombard Street had probably been — but as shopkeepers, holding stalls in the galleries and basement. While it would be wrong to deny that Stow has any sense of the city's economic functions (like Grenade he refers to concentrations of occupations), Grenade offers a more insistent sense of London as a commercial emporium, especially in relation to its shops: he gives estimates of the numbers of drapers' shops in the Candlewick/Watling Street quarter, and of the goldsmiths' shops in Cheapside (Goldsmiths' Row) and Lombard Street. He characterizes London as the most commercial (*marchande*) town in the Christian world, otherwise using that adjective only to describe London Bridge and Lombard Street. Moreover, he bestows special praise on the port of Billingsgate and displays a knowledge of the tonnage of the ships which came up the river to London with goods from overseas. Such concerns may reflect commercial interests in his family.

On the ceremonial life of the city, Grenade provides one of the earliest narrative accounts of the procession inaugurating the new lord mayor; although it is nearly contemporary to those by the herald William Smith (1575) and (albeit less well known) the exiled Dutch artist de Heere (c. 1573-5), it offers several unique details, including the gunpowder special effects around St Paul's churchyard. He mentions the pageants (to which literary scholars too often limit their analysis), but shows more interest in the gradation of the procession, and its articulation in distinctions of dress.

---

72. See Hyde 1966; Murray 1978: 163-87, 197-8; above, pp. 37-40 and below, pp. 104-5, 166, n. 8.

Stow, as is well known, did not comment on the lord mayor's procession at all, preferring a nostalgic account of the Midsummer watch.[73]

Another unusual feature of Grenade's account when compared to those of contemporaries is the level of interest in city laws and customs. Although he might have muddled the details of city elections, there is rather more on this theme than in Stow. Foreign visitors regularly recorded the lord mayor's inaugural show, which was clearly a major attraction, but (with the noticeable exception of de Heere) said less about elections. The account of city customs might look rushed and disorganised, but it is striking that Stow does not really provide anything comparable, for all that he knew the records on which such an account might be based. Grenade is highly selective, mixing material derived from the chronicles referring to customs which were probably extinct by the time he was writing with material based on recent statutes, such as the 1572 vagrancy measures, which were not strictly matters of city custom. Other key elements of custom are ignored. Nothing is said about the city's orphanage custom (a jewel in the civic crown by the city's own lights, and something on which de Heere lavished considerable attention)[74] nor about the Thames conservancy (the regulation of the river from Staines to the Medway) which has received much less attention from historians than it deserves, but which was being keenly defended by the city as Grenade wrote.[75] It is easy to criticize Grenade's account, but it is remarkable for its time, especially given the reticence of the aldermen about publicizing the content of the city's charters.

Also marking out Grenade from other visitors is the clear evidence (set out in our notes) that he consulted the vernacular chronicle accounts of John Stow and Richard Grafton, which themselves drew on a rich vein of civic and other annalistic writing. Stow and Grafton were bitter rivals in the commercial marketplace of print, accusing each other of plagiarism and inaccuracy, but Grenade drew on both of them at different points in his account.[76] The fact that this material was circulating within the multilingual community of London merchants, travellers, and savants adds a tantalizing additional dimension to what Daniel Woolf has described as the 'social circulation' of the past in sixteenth-century England, because although we know that the chronicles enjoyed considerable popularity (there were at least five editions of Stow's *Summarie* printed between 1565 and 1590 and

---

73. Sayle 1931: 2-3; Chotzen and Draak 1937: 19-20; Stow, *Survey* i. 101-4; Manley 1995a.
74. Norton 1575-6: 10-11 (from BL, Additional MS 33271, fols 28-31); *Breefe discourse* 1584; Chotzen and Draak 1937: 24.
75. LMA, COL/CA/01/01/019, fols 109v, 113v, 390; COL/CA/01/01/020, fol. 371v; COL/CA/01/01/022, fol. 136.
76. Devereux (2000).

at least nine editions of his *Abridgement* between 1573 and 1598; Grafton's *Abridgement* appeared in five editions between 1563 and 1572), it is novel to see them circulating beyond an English audience.[77] How many more foreigners received their perceptions of London through a reading of vernacular histories? We do not know, but it is worth stressing the potential for cultural and intellectual exchange across language barriers in Elizabethan London. The Granados were part of a cosmopolitan community able to move easily between communicating, probably, in English, French, Dutch, and Italian, and in their case Spanish too. Deborah Harkness has shown how alien merchants well integrated into the local community, like Jacob Cools (or James Cole, resident in Lime Street, a regular correspondent with his uncle the cartographer Abraham Ortelius, and closely connected to the botanist Matthew L'Obel, whose daughter he married, as well as a friend of numerous London merchants, artisans, and intellectuals) could act as key cultural brokers, bridging the divides between the exiles and the host community, but also connecting to networks of international commercial and intellectual exchange.[78]

Although less well educated than Cools who was a well read Latinist, and knowledgeable about topics as varied as botany, fossils, and the history of coins, Grenade may have participated on the fringes of this kind of milieu. His own educational formation is unclear. He may have had a basic training in law, but there is little evidence of deep learning in *Les Singularitez*. He recorded the Latin inscriptions in St Paul's accurately, but his references to classical sources (which he may have known only in French) seem no more than dressing designed to impress or to elevate his subject matter. It is perhaps this which helps explain the fact that he did not question the British history myths based on Geoffrey of Monmouth (*c*.1136) which attributed the unification of Britain and the founding of London as 'Troynovaunt' to the Trojan Brutus. Polydore Vergil had subjected all this to a withering attack in 1513, which received a mixed reception from the English intellectuals, but because it served the purposes of Henry VIII's imperial kingship its eclipse was a long drawn out process.[79] At the time Grenade was writing, the chroniclers were moving towards a position where they acknowledged the unknowability of some elements of the distant past, but they would still trot out the nostrums of the British history.[80] As Holinshed put it, 'the originall in maner of all nations is doubtfull, and even the same for the more part fabulous (that always excepted which we find in the holie scriptures) I

77. Woolf 2003; Archer 2004; Wheatley 2002, 184. For more on the genre of chronicling in the later sixteenth century, see Woolf 2000.
78. Harkness 2001.
79. Kendrick 1950; Levy 1967; Ferguson 1993.
80. Woolf 2005.

wish not any man to leane to that which shall be here set down as to an infallible truth, sith I do but onlie shew other mens coniectures', but that did not stop him from including the key elements of the myth.[81] Likewise John Stow, in the *Survey of London*, cited Livy in an effort to distance himself from the improbabilities of the stories he then went on to recount: 'Antiquitie is pardonable, and hath an especial priviledge, by interlacing divine matters with humane, to make the first foundation of Cities more honourable, more sacred, and as it were of greater maiestie'.[82] Grenade does not sound any of these cautionary notes, but apparently swallows the foundation myths wholesale. But similar stories were part of the traditional history of Paris and other French and Italian cities, which proved tenacious through the sixteenth century and beyond. Corrozet, more seriously learned than Grenade, hung on to the Trojan element in Paris history up to the edition of 1561, in which he expressed a little doubt; it was only the later editions, after Corrozet's death, which cut it all out. In any event, in addressing and praising Londoners it would have been impolite to question matters in which many believed, at least in such a matter which was outside the sphere of religious belief.

6. MOTIVES: THE POSITION OF THE STRANGER IN ELIZABETHAN LONDON

Why did Grenade write his tract? Why did he intend to present it to the lord mayor and aldermen? The answer perhaps lies in the ambiguous position of the stranger population of the city and Grenade's determination that the city's rulers sustained their commitment to supporting them.

Crucial to understanding Grenade's purpose is his religious position. The text is framed by references to the support of London for the victims of religious persecution. His dedication to the lord mayor and aldermen celebrates 'this magnificent city [which] has on many occasions opened her breast to harbour close to her most noble bowels the Church of the Lord Jesus, at those times when rope, sword and fire were pursuing it on all sides' (fol. 2v). In his peroration he imagines the Day of Judgment when religious refugees who have benefited from London's support will offer up their thanks. 'At that time, they will hear the voice of the Lord, which will say unto them: I was a stranger and you took me in' (fol. 87v). Edward VI, under whose reign the evangelical project flourished and the stranger churches were founded, is referred to as 'a miracle to the world, on account of the great favours God had bestowed on him' (fol. 17v). Grenade fully endorses the Edwardian hospital project which by the time he was writing

81. Holinshed 1577: i, *History of England*, 1; Ashe 2013, 153-8.
82. Stow, *Survey*: i. 1.

was identified as an evangelical undertaking (albeit at the expense of acknowledging some of the confessional ambiguities involved). The friars are identified as 'vermin'; his remarks on Cheapside Cross reveal his suspicion of catholic imagery as 'superstitious' (fol. 44); Catholicism is tellingly identified as the religion of Antichrist. There are two providentialised invocations of Elizabeth, calling on God to see to her long preservation, while the city's peace is likewise seen as a 'blessing of God' (fol. 64). One might infer from all this a militant Calvinist position, a commitment to the 'Protestant International'. But there are other straws in the wind. His iconoclasm would not have extended to attacks on funeral monuments, the inscriptions on which he carefully records, and he would doubtless have endorsed the position adopted in the royal proclamation of September 1560 banning the 'breaking or defacing of any parcel of any monument, or tomb, or grave'.[83] He was happy with the continued practice of tolling for the dead, and he enthused about funeral sermons, matters over which the radicals marked out their differences from the establishment. Perhaps even more surprising is his respect for the musical tradition of Westminster Abbey and St Paul's; singling out organs at a time when they had fallen silent in almost all London churches was odd.[84] Among the striking omissions of the text is any mention of the stranger churches; Grenade's apparent respect for Elizabeth's hybrid settlement suggests that he may have worshipped in an English parish church, probably St Dunstan in the East, where his family was firmly embedded.

London's already sizeable alien population was boosted in the sixteenth century by refugees from the religious persecutions on the continent, beginning in the 1530s, and greatly accelerating from the 1560s. The remarkable surveys of the strangers taken by the London authorities at the behest of the government enable us to chart the development of the community, though one needs to be very sensitive with the figures to ensure that one is comparing analogous areas.[85] The best discussion, by Lien Bich Luu, shows that 4,534 aliens were listed as resident in London, Middlesex and the suburbs in 1563, increasing to 6,704 in 1568, and 7,143 in 1573. The pressure eased off thereafter with figures of 4,047 and 4,141 recorded in 1581 and 1583, though there was another wave of migration in the later 1580s. There are problems about under recording, and it is alarming to find that the stranger churches recorded 1,828 members in 1573 who do not appear in the returns, suggesting that these figures must be regarded as minima; the true population may have been nearer 10,000.[86] This population was more

83. Hughes and Larkin 1964-9: ii. 146-8.
84. Willis 2010.
85. Kirk and Kirk 1900-8.
86. Luu 2005a: 91-8.

linguistically diverse than in the fifteenth century. In 1483 82% of aliens were Dutch or German speaking, and only 2% French; by 1571 the respective figures were 61% and 20%.[87] To judge from the church membership list of 1571, most of the French speakers (68%) in fact came from the Francophone portions of the Low Countries (164 from Flanders, 107 from Hainault, and 27 from Brabant); only 27% came from France.[88]

Grenade is at pains to celebrate the welcome that had been afforded the religious refugees. The English government had in 1550 offered the Dutch and French their own churches in the Austin Friars and in the former hospital of St Anthony in Threadneedle Street. Suppressed under Mary, the churches were restored under Elizabeth and allowed to worship according to their own liturgy. Although they provided a worrying model for puritan critics, the stranger churches prospered under the benevolent eye of Edmund Grindal, bishop of London in the 1560s.[89] Grindal also recommended Hieronimus Ferlitus to the Mercers' Company in 1565, and from this date the Italians began to use the Mercers' chapel as a meeting place. It is noteworthy that there were few Italians among the congregation; at least 63 of the 161 people recorded as worshipping there in 1568 were from the Low Countries, and it is possible that Grenade attended occasional services here given that it seems to have attracted the more intellectually inclined.[90]

But not all the English were as welcoming to the strangers as Grenade suggests. Although the bonds of charity were strengthened by confessional ties to promote sympathy for religious refugees, many doubted that the newcomers were really the victims of religious persecution. Some feared that under cover of the migration, all kinds of political subversives might be entering the country, 'papists, anabaptists, libertines, drunkards, common women … murderers, thieves, conspirators' according to William Cecil's agent William Herle.[91] Such fears were readily fuelled by the surveys which revealed alarmingly that an astonishingly high number of aliens (37% in 1573) appeared to be of no church at all.[92] There was a concerted effort by the Privy Council and city authorities in 1573-4 to secure the removal of strangers who had 'crept in by colour of religion', though it does not seem to have been particularly effective.[93] The Privy Council was lobbied by the city again in September 1579 for the removal of strangers from the liberties.[94]

---

87. Luu 2005a: 99-104.
88. Littleton 1996: 32-3.
89. Pettegree 1986; Collinson 1983.
90. Boersma and Jelsma 1997: 24-7.
91. Cited by Luu 2005a: 96
92. Luu 2005a: 109-10.
93. LMA, COL/CA/01/01/020, fols 115, 166, 167v, 177v-8, 239v, 299.
94. LMA, COL/CA/01/01/021, fols 481, 485v.

Among ordinary Londoners, many saw the aliens not as refugees but as economic migrants. Although Cecil recognised the economic benefits to be derived from an infusion of alien skills, many English artisans did not see things the same way. Evil May Day of 1517 when apprentices had rioted against alien merchants and craftsmen cast a long shadow, and there were repeated murmurings against the newcomers.[95] In 1567 libels appeared on the city streets showing 'galowys and as it wer hanging of strangers'; a porter was hanged in Cheapside for spreading rumours among apprentices that 'the nyght folowynge wowlde be ye lyke stire agaynst straungers as was at Evyll May Day'. In 1573 when aliens complained that they had been abused in the streets by apprentices and servants, the aldermen required the companies to instruct their members not to mistreat aliens, while the aliens were told to stay indoors between 9 pm and 5 am.[96] Although the authorities clamped down heavily at the merest hint of anti-alien disturbance, the grievances of the artisans received a hearing among some of the more respectable sections of London society. In 1570 Richard Porder, minister of St Michael Cornhill used a sermon in St Paul's to accuse the aliens of evading trading regulations and claimed that they were not genuine religious refugees, rather they had come to take Englishmen's livings and 'eat by trade the bread out of our mouths'.[97] In 1573 the wardmote inquest of Cornhill petitioned against the 'contynuall and daily resorte of straungers of divers nacions to this cytty', which they claimed causes great scarcity of victuals, the increase of rents, and the proliferation of beggars.[98] The problems of aliens, poor migrants, and lewdness tended to be collapsed into each other in the 1570s.[99] Aliens were already subject to a raft of discriminatory legislation, but in 1574 common council passed an act limiting apprenticeships to those whose father had been born in England, which had the effect of preventing even denizens from apprenticing their sons.[100] In 1576 the city's remembrancer, Thomas Norton, was instructed to draft a bill for parliament directed against aliens who allegedly brought over their pregnant wives to be delivered in England, presumably to evade this legislation.[101] Unsurprisingly not all aliens shared Grenade's warmth towards their English hosts, reciprocating the hostility. Early in March 1574 the aldermen learned that one Mordaunt de Coolworthe, a Dutchman, had declared that 'he did

95. Thirsk 1978; Archer 1991, 4-5, 131-40. But for a more nuanced account of attitudes to aliens see Goose 2005.
96. Gairdner 1880, 140-1; LMA, COL/CA/01/01/019, fol. 372.
97. Porder 1570: fols 103[r-v].
98. LMA, CLC/W/HF/001/MS04069/001, fols 11v-12.
99. LMA, COL/CA/01/01/020, fol. 178.
100. Selwood 2010:, 41-2, 91-2; Luu 2005b.
101. LMA, COL/CA/01/01/021, fol. 38v.

hope to tarye in England when Englishe men should eate there turdes & drink there pisse'.[102]

Grenade's approach was more subtle. In praising the city for its hospitality towards religious refugees, one might see Grenade as seeking to promote their cause at the heart of city government. It was perhaps an example of the conventional renaissance device of *laudando praecipere*, offering counsel through praise. As Francis Bacon was to put it succinctly: 'Some praises come of good wishes and respects, which is a form due, in civility, to kings and great persons, laudando praecipere, when by telling men what they are, they represent to them, what they should be.'[103] We don't know whether Sir Thomas Ramsey, the lord mayor to whom Grenade proposed to present his tract, had any particular leanings towards the stranger communities — his will suggests a conformist Protestant outlook, though the probable connection between his wife and Lady Magdalen is suggestive[104] — but there were certainly other members of the London elite whose ties with the communities were strong. John Bodley, the draper father of the founder of the Bodleian Library, was an elder in the French church; Bartholomew Warner, William Winthrop and Michael Blount all served in the Italian church.[105] In 1578, the year Grenade intended to present his work to the court of aldermen, the goldsmith and Master of the Mint Richard Martin joined their ranks. Martin and his wife Dorcas were noted sympathisers with the Presbyterian movement. He had brokered some of the collections for the French refugees in 1572; in 1582 he was to be a key London contact for Jean Malliet, the agent sent from Geneva to solicit aid for the beleaguered city.[106] There can be no doubting the emotional strength of the ties developed by some of the London godly for their persecuted co-religionists. Another Presbyterian sympathiser, the mercer Richard Culverwell, bequeathed to his daughter a gold chain given to him by the queen of Navarre 'as a remembrance of the honourable zeal of that good queen, which frankly gave that chain to me, and many other her jewels of great value to others for the furtherance and defence of the gospel and such as sincerely profess the same'.[107] Grenade's tract might therefore be understood as both a token of thanks for the support already given, but also as a way of urging the London elite to still more vigilance in the common cause of the gospel.

---

102. LMA, COL/CA/01/01/020, fol. 170r-v.
103. Bacon 1996, vi pt 1, 582.
104. TNA, PRO, PROB 11/75, fols 306*v*–309; for Lady Magdalen, see above, pp. 21-7.
105. Collinson 1983: 267-8, 270, 272; Boersma and Jelsma 1997: 28-9, 216, 256, 257.
106. Challis 2004; Beilin 2004; Collinson 1983: 270; Adams and Greengrass 2003: 181, 184, 185, 189, 194, 196.
107. Collinson 1983: 271-2.

ENGLISH TRANSLATION

For the notes to the translation, see pp. 146-90

[fol. 1]

M.56.[1]

THE SINGULARITIES

Of London, noble, and famous city,
capital of the Kingdom of England:
its antiquities and first founders.

[fol. 1ᵛ blank]

[fol. 1 bis]

To the very stately Lord.
My lord the Mayor of
London.
And to the honourable Lords
Aldermen, his good brethren[2]

When first I set out to write this little treatise, through which I have undertaken to describe the rare and particular singularities of your noble and renowned City of London, most noble and honourable Lords, if I had paused [fol. 1 bisᵛ] simply to reflect, on the one hand, upon your greatness and excellence, and on the other, my insignificance and low station, comparing one and the other, I should never have contemplated nor dared to undertake this work, and even less to present it to you. However, having personally given the matter much thought I, a stranger, who by the grace of God has, while travelling, assiduously observed the singularities of the countries and commonwealths[3] through which God has caused me to pass, having finally come to this your City, in which I have stayed a while to comfort myself after

55

the many travails with which the insults of the time have burdened me, I could not help [fol. 2] but bring to the fore those things which have seemed to me most memorable and excellent in this city, for several reasons. The first is that I considered it unjust that so many attestations of the kindness, power and generosity of God, that one sees shining so brightly in an infinite number of singular distinctive things, of which your city is full, were seemingly concealed within its boundaries, and thus unknown by those who, by virtue of their ignorance of them, will take singular satisfaction from hearing an account of them. The second is a great, fervent and longstanding desire to have the opportunity to engage myself in a [fol. 2ᵛ] pursuit which might serve to adorn this noble city, in recognition of many good turns that I, and my family, have long received, and continue to receive from this city. The third is that this magnificent city has on many occasions opened her breast to harbour close to her most noble bowels the Church of the Lord Jesus, at those times when rope, sword and fire were pursuing it on all sides.[4] And not only that, but also (in a manner of speaking) nourished it with her own blood, with which she nourishes her own most tender children. The fourth is your great kindness and gentleness, on account of which I am sure that it will delight you to [fol. 3] tolerate my inordinate boldness in having undertaken this work and also my foolishness in this action. However, I hope that this effort of mine will yield profit and satisfaction to many, both my fellow countrymen and other strangers, who will become aware of it and be grateful to me on that account. On the other hand, I will have made no small gain if I manage to inspire some worthy desire in someone more adept than myself at bringing this topic to greater perfection. Finally, both supporters and detractors of your glories will seize the opportunity afforded by my work: the former, in their admiration for you, will increasingly exalt and revere you; the latter will fear [fol. 3ᵛ] you all the more.[5] In short, those are the reasons which have prompted and incited me not only to tackle this work, but also to make a modest gift of it to you which I hereby do, and with such good heart since I am certain that your humanity and gentleness will find it pleasing. But what is it that I offer you? As a gift for this New Year I present you with this City of London dressed and adorned with its most beautiful apparel and excellent jewels which I have collected together from here and there from its own cabinets. But what is it that I offer to Your Honours? I offer you London in all its excellence. But how so? She is already yours. [fol. 4] Therefore, I do so all the sooner because I appropriate the thing to itself. For it is just as if I were giving London to London, or, to express it more accurately, to give you to yourselves. What fills me with greater hope, that you might accept it in better part, is that however much in it is mine the whole is humble and small: nevertheless, as much as one discerns your honour to shine greatly there, it is great, rich and magnificent. And if I know that you noble Lords have a liking for my good will in this little present that I give to you, it will give me [fol. 4ᵛ] occasion further to strive to pursue the work that I have undertaken concerning the praise of the heroic and excellent men which your noble and renowned city has always begotten and produced.[6] And I hope that the virtues and graces with which the Almighty has endowed you, magnificent and honourable Lords will not be left behind. To Whom I humbly pray that he cause your condition to prosper more and more and increase one hundred-fold the triumph and glory of your famous city of London. This first day of the year 1578, before Easter.[7]

Your very humble servant

LGrenade

[fol. 5]

PREFACE

I have undertaken a work which, I am quite sure, will lead to many an individual accusing me of recklessness, on the grounds that it is far beyond all my abilities. However, as soon as they observe my zeal and good will, in a calm spirit divorced from all ill feeling, then it will be impossible to blame my incapacity, which rather will receive the honour of being praised just as if it were really worthy of it. And so, the hope of this has filled me with sufficient audacity to undertake this work, without which I would never have unfurled my sails to the wind — so to speak — to navigate the danger of so many hazards. [fol. 5ᵛ] But the main stimulus which instilled this desire in my heart and put a pen in my hand is that infinite number of singularities and rare things, which are seemingly unique to this country separated from the rest of the world, and which I realised have remained hitherto undivulged and therefore unknown to other nations, who are in the meantime deprived of this benefit.[8] It is true that rumour of the greatness, prosperity, singularities and splendours of London fly and run to the ends of the whole world, such that London has seen Muscovy as Muscovy has seen London. London has been carried on the back of the icy sea and its greatness, yet unsatisfied, [fol. 6] now wishes to border Cathay. And soon the honour of being frequented by this city will be bestowed on the extremities of the Levant. I am even in no doubt that soon afterwards the most distant regions will strive at length to come and visit it, bearing the rarest and most precious things they have, as in an act of homage.[9] However, all the remote countries (having heard tell of and enjoyed everything they could obtain from London) have seen, heard and enjoyed, only a shadow of a thousandth part of the excellent things that are there. For what reason should its virtues remain buried and hidden in the bosom of an eternal oblivion [fol. 6ᵛ] or within the closed mouth of Nemesis? I therefore maintain that despite the countless shortcomings of this my description — which I readily acknowledge — since I see that no-one more able than myself has come forward to publish in his writings the excellent things which are as if sown far and wide in this noble city — and above all so many such good laws and customs — my conscience would have weighed heavily upon me if I had done as others, that is, be it noted, to remain silent while possessing such good material and such a good opportunity to speak. For if the singularities, splendours and noble provisions of Nineveh have been so scrupulously extolled [fol. 7] by Herodotus, Diodorus and others; those of Babylon by Berossos and Herodotus; those of Troy by Homer, Ovid, and, in our time, Jean Lemaire de Belges;[10] those of Rome by Livy and Plutarch; those of Jerusalem by all the prophets; and those of Thebes, Numantia, Tyre, Sidon, Corinth and other such cities by many other great and excellent personages.[11] Furthermore, these cities certainly deserve that all peoples know how much the great and eternal God has each one at heart, embellishing and adorning it with so many of his favours. It is true that I would rather have taken up the task of praising the capital city of my nation, [fol. 7ᵛ] but I abstained as other clever individuals came before me.[12]

And so, with regard to my present enterprise, I will be most happy and satisfied if I might just manage to provoke someone else to do better. Moreover, I have carefully divided up the different subjects into separate chapters so that this might serve as a useful aid for readers, allowing them to best retain the information in their memory, and by this means be able to recount them to those who have not yet heard talk of them. And finally, one should not be surprised if the Lord God has desired to adorn London with so many of his graces seeing that [fol. 8] she has demonstrated great kindness and generosity, and on multiple occasions, towards the unfortunate community of Lord Jesus. For if the godless of former times have been blessed in many a way for having received and housed the children of God, acting as did Abimelech[13] for the sake of Isaac, Laban[14] for the sake of Jacob and many others, how much more would this noble city be blessed, which not only desires to be the host of the Church of God, but moreover, on shunning the Antichrist and its many idolatries, has welcomed the true religion and declares it. May the Lord God bless her, maintain her and make her grow from strength to strength until the coming of our Lord Jesus. Amen. [fol. 8ᵛ blank]

[fol. 9]

THE SINGULARITIES
Of London. Capital City of the Kingdom of England.
With its Antiquity: and who its founders were.

Chapter 1
On the foundation of London, its names, its site and the River Thames

There is a certain fool (but entirely ignorant of history) who has written that England was formerly called Britain, since its language [fol. 9ᵛ] was brief and concise.[15] This stupid etymology, however, is most worthy of such a dullard. In fact, it endows him with ears longer than those of an ass, for this name comes from an excellent Trojan named Brutus, the son of Sylvius Posthumius, who bestowed on England the name of Britain from his own name, since formerly it was called Albion.[16]

Brutus.

Britain.
Albion.

This Brutus of whom I speak, having long wandered hither and thither on the seas following the total ruin of Troy, finally reached the island called at that time Albion. And, since the country seemed a suitable place to end his voyage and his travails, having chosen a location on the River Thames, he began to build a city. [fol. 10] This was in the year of the world 2855, and 1188 years before the coming of Jesus Christ. This clearly demonstrates the antiquity of the city, for it far surpasses that of Rome and of any other city, which proudly vaunts its age. It is this city that we now call London. This happened around the time when the Levite spoken of in Chapter 19 of the Book of Judges cut up the woman into pieces on Mount Ephraim, and sent them through all the tribes of Israel.[17]

Brutus arrived in the Island of Albion.

The foundation of London.

London more ancient than Rome.

London called
New Troy.

King Lud.

So, having begun to build his city, Brutus, in honour of the city of his birth, named it New Troy. And this name remained until the coming of [fol. 10ᵛ] King Lud who in the year 68 before the coming of Jesus Christ, called it Ludunum after his own name. But since then, over time, a change has been made and it has been called Londinum, that is to say in our language *Londres*.[18]

Situation of London.

Surrounding places.

Now, Brutus could not have selected a place (I speak not only of England but even of the whole of Europe) more fitting nor more rich in everything required for the location of a place more perfect in all respects. And to prove this, I will first relate something of the neighbouring places so as to add greater lustre to all the rest.

Romulus.

Brutus.
Highgate.

Let us therefore consider (but with wonder) the environs of this noble city. For, stories of old [fol. 11] testify that in ancient times those who desired to build cities of renown were attracted by the beauty of the surrounding countryside. We read this expressly about Romulus when he wishes to found Rome, and similarly about many others. So Brutus took great heed of this, for if we stand in that elevated place called Highgate,[19] we have from there a full view of the city which with its buildings is wondrously pleasing on the eye, and in its shape and

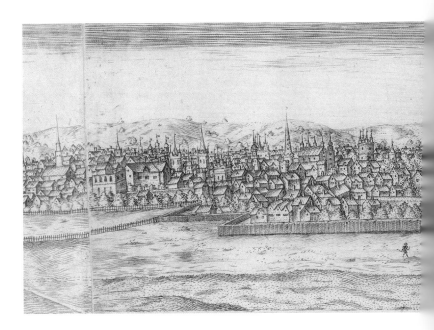

London in the
shape of a bow.

The east side.

The south side.
The country of
Kent.

The West and
the North.

The flow
of the Thames
into the sea.

The plan of the City.

Length
of the River Thames.

Oxford, the
theological town.

situation alongside the river, describes an arc of very beautiful form. Then, if we cast our gaze from there towards the east, we follow [fol. 11ᵛ] the Thames flowing gently into the arms of its father the Ocean. And turning towards the south (Figs 10 and 25), we see that lovely and rich country of Kent with its delightful view of mountains and hills, great and small, and variegated in all those qualities which pertain to a country as full of delight as it is of fertility. Finally, let us look west and north towards the descent of the Thames to the sea, O what joy to see the level plain extending as far as the eye can see, very fertile in all things. There one can see the meadows and pastures full of dairy cattle, interspersed with magnificent houses and substantial castles. [fol. 12] Now let us come to the site itself of this excellent city, which lies beside a great river called the Thames, which brings great profit and convenience to the said city. The length of this river is 30 French leagues (which is at least 60 English miles to the sea).[20] This river conveys large vessels of between two and 300 tons burden[21] to the aforementioned city: and upstream, for 18 or 20 leagues, you can take large boats on it up and down as far as Oxford,[22] the theological town of England, by

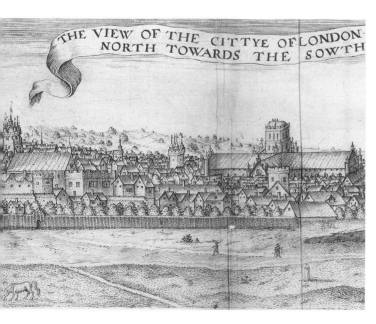

THE VIEW OF THE CITTYE OF LONDON·
NORTH TOWARDS THE SOWTH

Fig. 10. The city seen across the fields from the north west. Extract from a late sixteenth-century (1577/1598) panorama. St Paul's lacks the spire destroyed by fire in 1561. Further left are the tower of St Mary le Bow, with its distinctive arches, and the spire of St Lawrence Pountney. See Fig. 25.
© *Burden Collection.*

which means all manner of goods from all countries abound there.[23] The great ships which approach it, are accustomed on entering – and when they are opposite the magnificent royal Tower [fol. 12ᵛ] (to be discussed below) — to salute the city with great cannon shots, as if rendering thanks to God for bringing them safely to harbour.[24]

Site of London.

London is situated in the midst of a beautiful and spacious plain, which ensures that the city is well aired. She is encompassed on all sides by beautiful meadows and grassy enclosures, gardens and cultivable lands which, on account of their fertility, yield much produce every year.

the villages.

The villages (of which there is a great number in the environs) are most suitable for those who from time to time are responsible for guarding the city, for, on leaving it you can walk to them very easily since they are only about two harquebus shots [fol. 13] distant from the city.[25] Therefore, people go there in great numbers on holidays when the weather is good.

Chapter 2

On the suburbs of London: and
starting with that adjacent to
the gate called Ludgate.

8 suburbs
surrounding
London.

That on the
Ludgate side.

There are eight great suburbs around London, each of which resembles a good town as much for their size as for their singular features.

To start with that suburb by the gate called Ludgate, which extends as far as Westminster. We will put it first [fol. 13ᵛ] since it has a greater number of singularities than the others, and for this reason, we must spend longer on it.

Westminster.

This suburb is wonderfully large if we include Westminster, as indeed one should (Fig. 11 and cf. Fig. 1). And this consequently makes the main thoroughfare a good half of a French league in length. With regard to the singularities of this place, we will touch only upon the most remarkable. For, to consider all of them would be too great a number for us. Firstly, the city gate next

Ludgate very ancient.

to this suburb is of great antiquity, for it was built in the 3,800th year of the world, and 65 years before the Incarnation of Christ by a [fol. 14] Saxon King called Lud after whom it is also named the Gate of Lud.[26] Going further along the length of the main street of this suburb, by the riverside is the magnificent house of

Bridewell.

Bridewell which was built in the time of King Henry VIII, of which more will be related below.[27] Further

The great conduit
of Fleet Street.

William Eastfield.

along the length of Fleet Street, one reaches a very beautiful fountain, gushing forth water plentifully through many outlets. It was built by the late William Eastfield who was in his lifetime Mayor of London in the year 1437.[28]

4 fine Colleges.

Gray's Inn.
the two Temples.
Templars.
Lincoln's Inn.

Further along, one comes to the locality of 4 magnificent colleges of the laws of the country, very rich and opulent. The first is Gray's Inn. The [fol. 14ᵛ] second and third are the two Temples, so-called since the Templars formerly occupied the site (Fig. 12); the 4th is Lincoln's Inn (Fig. 13). Now, although these 4 colleges are mainly

inhabited by gentlemen, the children of great lords nevertheless take up residence in Gray's Inn on account of its
more airy situation.[29] It is true that there are several
other colleges, but these are the main ones. The laws
studied by the pupils are written in French, but a very
corrupt form of French, such that the French themselves
do not understand it. [30] Along the length of this street,
and particularly along the riverside, are many beautiful
and [fol. 15] magnificent palaces and houses of princes
and great lords extending up to the palace of Her
Majesty. These embellish and marvellously adorn the
whole of this quarter, and particularly the riverside.[31]
The jurisdiction of the Lord Mayor of London is divided
at Temple Bar from that of Westminster and Middlesex.

Now, we must note that this street is lined on both
sides with shops filled with all manner of merchandise
as if it were one of the fine streets of the City.[32] Moving
further along, one finds a Pyramid (Fig. 14) which

the Laws in French.

Palace and
houses of Princes
and Lords.

Jurisdiction of the
Lord Mayor
is separate.

Charing Cross.

Fig. 11. The western suburb extending from Ludgate to the Savoy, from B & H (1572). Note, from east to west, the former Bridewell Palace, the Temple, Arundel Place, and Somerset Place. © *British Museum.*

appears to be of great antiquity and from which, on account of age, several ashlar stones hang into mid-air, attached only by a little iron. However, it still stands 25 or 30 fathoms high [fol. 15ᵛ] and still has several images of Kings and others around it. Some say that it is the work of Romans from the time when Julius Caesar occupied England. Others conjecture that it was Queen Eleanor, the wife of King Edward, the first of this name, who had it erected in the year 1274.[33]

Julius Caesar.

Queen Eleanor.

St James.
Henry VIII.

Not far away is a most lovely country seat called St James (Fig. 15), which King Henry VIII had built, and to which he attached several fine parks.[34] A little further on, there is the royal Palace called Whitehall, which is so resplendent that I prefer to allow the reader to imagine its excellence than to undertake a description of it and not be able to fulfil [fol. 16] my duty.[35]

Quite near there, one enters a great and spacious court (Fig. 16) which belongs to the Palace where the

Fig. 12. The Temple area, from Copperplate Map. The parish church of St Dunstan in the West is named. Towards the river the circular Temple church can be identified from its crenellation. © *Museum of London*.

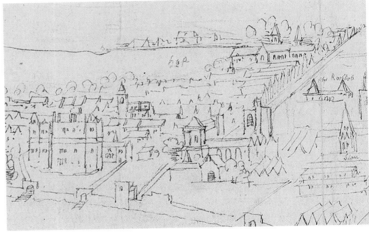

Fig. 13. Area of the Inns of Court *c.*1544, from Wyngaerde. Chancery Lane (including Lincoln's Inn) runs northwards; the large structure to the left is the house of the Bishop of Bath and Wells, later Arundel House. © *Ashmolean Museum, Univ. of Oxford*.

Fig. 14. Charing Cross, *c.*1544 from Wyngaerde. The large house towards the river is the residence of the Bishop of Durham, used by the Crown from 1536. The hamlet around the church of St Giles in the Fields lies to the north, with the Middlesex hills in the distance. © *Ashmolean Museum, Univ. of Oxford*.

Fig. 15. Whitehall Palace *c.*1544 from the east, with its private landing stage leading towards the hall built by Cardinal Wolsey, with the privy garden to the left, the gateway across King Street, the Tennis Court with four turrets, and the octagonal Cockpit. St James's park and palace lie in the distance. Sketch by Wyngaerde to accompany his panorama. © *Ashmolean Museum, Univ. of Oxford.*

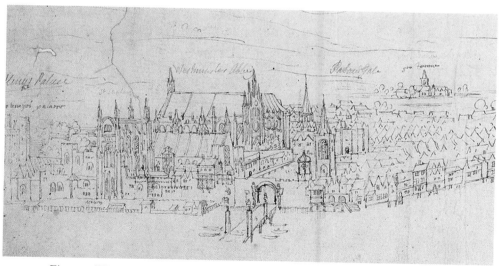

Fig. 16. Westminster Palace, Hall, and Abbey *c.*1544, from Wyngaerde. The landing stage leads into New Palace Yard, with the Hall on the left and St Stephen's Chapel at its south end.
© *Ashmolean Museum, Univ. of Oxford.*

Estates of the Realm are held, commonly called
Parliament. In this place are the most beautiful rooms
one might possibly encounter. It is also the same place
(Fig. 17) where the general pleas are held four times a
year, otherwise known as the Term. These pleas normally take place over six weeks, and great multitudes of
the people from every corner of the kingdom have
recourse to them, and this brings incredible profit to the
City of London, for then people of all ranks make
money from their work and their merchandise.[36] There
is one particularly noteworthy feature in one of [fol. 16ᵛ]

the rooms of this palace, which is that its vault is
covered and ceiled all over in a type of wood which has
the peculiarity of not gathering any dust, dirt or anything venomous. For this reason, one can never detect a
spider or its web. And although it is very old, it is still
just as beautiful as if new, and, one would say on seeing
it that great care has been taken to scour it.[37]

Let us now come to the church of the abbey of
Westminster (Fig. 16) and its singularities. This church
is outstanding for its height, which is wondrous; for its
roof, which is entirely of lead, raised high in the shape
of an ass's back so well done that it is [fol. 17] a very fine
resemblance.[38] The music of this church is outstanding,
for these are indeed the most beautiful voices (both low
and high) that it is possible to hear.[39]

At the high end of this church is a most lavish and
magnificent chapel, its exterior no less magnificently
worked in stone than the internal joiner's work in wood.
Inside is a once magnificent tomb of bronze, made in
the shape of a chapel, enriched with pillars and images
of angels and others all around in the same material. In
addition, this tomb bears a most lifelike representation
of King Henry VII, and the Queen his wife who are
buried there (Fig. 18).[40] Below, at the head of this tomb

is that [fol. 17ᵛ] of good King Edward VI who in his lifetime was a miracle to the world, on account of great
favours God had bestowed on him.[41]

There is another tomb within the choir of the said
church which is also outstandingly rich and beautiful.
The king who is buried beneath is called St Edward the
Confessor (Fig. 19). He reigned in the year 1043 and
died in the year 1066, some time before the coming of

Fig. 17. Westminster Hall south end, *c.*1620, with the courts
of King's Bench (left) and Chancery (right). ©*British Museum*.

Fig. 18. Westminster Abbey: brass tomb and effigies of King Henry VII
and his Queen Elizabeth of York. From Dart (1723).
© *London Metropolitan Archives, City of London.*

Fig. 19. Westminster Abbey: shrine of St Edward the Confessor (1279-80), inlaid with Cosmati work on Purbeck marble; the tomb of Henry III, with porphyry panels and Cosmati work (c.1280) is in the background. © *Dean and Chapter of Westminster Abbey*.

William the Conqueror. Much more will be said about him in due course. This tomb is surrounded by an iron lattice, and I have so far been able to see it only from a distance, so I could only view it from afar and accordingly I could not discern with ease either the craftsmanship or any detail. However, it appears to be most magnificent.[42] [fol. 18]

Henry III.

There are several other tombs of kings in the heart of the church. Amongst these is that of Henry III (Fig. 19) which is made of and almost covered with precious square stones richly laid out next to one another, and so gives the strong impression of a royal tomb. King Henry was the first who laid the first stone of the foundation of this Westminster church in the year of our Lord 1220.[43] He reigned for the duration of 56 years.

note.

Now, although all the tombs of the Kings and Queens which lie in this church deserve to be carefully observed and praised equally in their own right for their lavishness and beauty as much as for their antiquity, I have nevertheless contented myself with mentioning the three presently discussed, for they [fol. 18ᵛ] struck me as the most remarkable and because (as I have continually professed) I wish to be concise.

The second singularity boasted by this church is the height of its vault, exceeding as it does all those of other churches in London: and its roof covering which is lead, as mentioned.[44]

Chapter 3

On the suburb adjacent to the gate called
Newgate: and its singularities

The second suburb is that from which one enters the city by the gate called Newgate,[45] which means 'the new gate' (Fig. 20). This suburb is very large, [fol. 19] for it comprises Holborn, Smithfield and St John Street. And so, although I insisted above that the suburb of Westminster is the biggest of all the suburbs, if this present suburb were, however, to be the benchmark, I am unsure as to which suburb would be considered greater. With regard to what is notable in this suburb, there is the gate of the city called Newgate, which means 'the new gate', by which one goes from the town into the suburb. This gate is very fine in appearance, more so than any other of the City. Above it is built a wonderfully strong structure, flanked on each side by a great and strong tower. And this is not without cause, for there are guarded [fol. 19ᵛ] the prisoners who have committed crimes, and those who are sentenced to death at the sessions which are held every month. This gate was first erected by an excellent and honest man called Richard Whittington, mercer, who held the post of Mayor of London three times. He also bestowed several

Holborn Smithfield.

Newgate.

Richard Whittington.

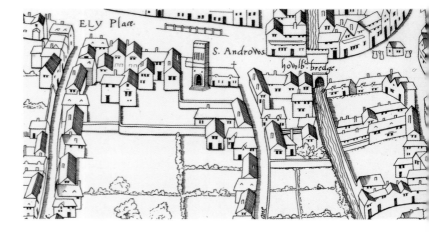

other great favours on the said city; a fact which makes his memory forever blessed before God and men.

Secondly, in this suburb is the parish called St Sepulchre which is so densely populated that there is a final count of 23,000 communicants for the holy sacraments.[46] Now, if this great number of people is found in a single parish, what number [fol. 20] might be found in the 122 parishes[47] which are in the city and its suburbs? It is true that the said Sepulchre is the biggest and most populated of all. This, however, can be acknowledged as a matter greatly to be admired.

Thirdly, and not far from St. Sepulchre, is a most beautiful fountain which gives forth jets of water from several pipes and which, someone has confirmed to me, was built at the sole expense of a gentleman called Master Lamb (which means Monsieur Agneau). At least, his arms are carved upon it, and several lambs around it. It is located at the crossroads which separate the [fol. 20ᵛ] quarter of Holborn from that of Smithfield. This fountain is so useful in this location, and so plentiful in the water that it provides water to more than 2,000 houses.[48]

Moreover, in Holborn, there are several colleges for the laws of the country, plentifully furnished with honourable pupils. All of the colleges have limited franchises; we will speak about this later.[49]

In the other part of this suburb (Figs 21 and 22) is the hospital of St Bartholomew where a great number of poor sick people and others in need are fed and kept so

St Sepulchre.
23,000 communicants.

122 parishes in London.

an admirable thing.

Lamb's conduit.

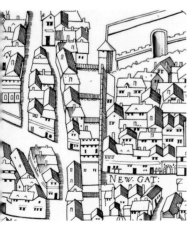

Fig. 20. Suburb outside Newgate, 1550s, from the Copperplate Map. From east to west: the church of St Sepulchre, Lamb's Conduit, Holborn Bridge (crossing the Fleet); the church of St Andrew; Ely Place, the residence of the bishop of Ely lay to the north of Holborn. © *Museum of London.*

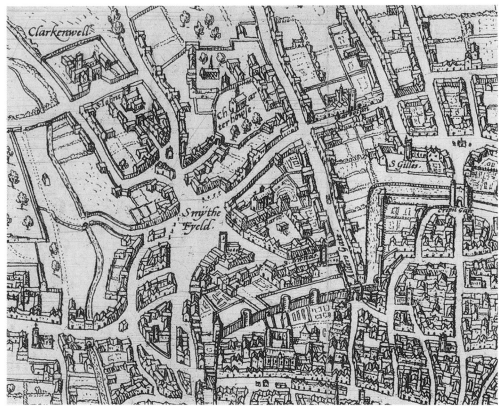

Fig. 21. Suburbs outside Newgate, Aldersgate and Cripplegate, 1550s. From B & H Map (1572), showing Smithfield and surroundings, including St Bartholomew's Hospital and the former priories of St Bartholomew, St John Clerkenwell, and St Mary Clerkenwell, and the former Charterhouse. © *British Museum.*

a musician founded the Hospital of Saint Bartholomew.

Smithfield.

clean that, although there is a common and public path open along the length of the said hospital in question, and one can see the bedrooms and beds of the invalids within, nevertheless, no bad smell can be discerned anymore than in the cleanest street of the city. [fol. 21] The building of this hospital and its chapel was begun at the sole expense and cost of one of the musicians of King Henry I, called Reyer.[50] In front of this hospital is a large and spacious square called Smithfield, which means the field of smiths,[51] which is so vast that if needed, 18 or 20,000 foot soldiers could be lined up in battle order. The former custom was to use this square as a place to throw the filth of the city. However, it is now useful for

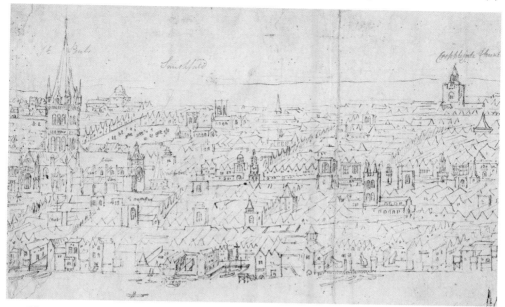

Fig. 22. View across the city from the south *c*.1544, showing Queenhithe on the river frontage, St Paul's, the Cheapside Cross and many parish churches, with Smithfield, containing people and animals, in the background. From Wyngaerde.
© *Ashmolean Museum, Univ. of Oxford.*

horse market.

Bartholomew Fair.

several necessities. Firstly, every Friday of the year there is a very fine market for horses and other beasts. Secondly, it is used for the [fol. 21ᵛ] execution of criminals who have committed some abhorrent crime; they are either burnt or put to death by other means. Thirdly, one of the finest fairs in the whole country of England, commonly called Bartholomew Fair, is held there, lasting five or six days. During this fair, the square of Smithfield and all the streets far around it, especially the square itself, is filled with so many tents with a great abundance of all sorts of merchandise that one would think one was in the heart of the most mercantile city in Christendom. And during this time, one can see the beautiful wares of London, for everything is on display then. [fol. 22] And moreover, this fair stretches across the whole of the town.

On this side too is the church of St John which used to be a rich commandery of the Knights of Rhodes, but is now a very fine parish church.⁵²

Chapter 4

On the suburbs beside the gates called
Aldersgate, Cripplegate, Moor Gate, Bishopesgate
and Aldgate called Whitechapel

I have placed four suburbs in the same chapter because it seemed to me that they do not have as many features worthy of note as the others have. Nevertheless, they are not without their own singularities, which [fol. 22ᵛ] we will not pass over in silence when the time comes. Now, what each of them has in common is a main street that runs in a straight line and is 25 or 30 paces wide at least.[53]

Length and width of streets.

Aldersgate.

The first of these four suburbs is the one by which one enters the City by the gate called Aldersgate (Fig. 21), that is to say 'the old gate', or the 'gate of the elders', for it is also said that an Alderman had it built.[54] Now, although this suburb is the smallest of all the suburbs, it still contains more than 1,000 houses.

The second is the one by which one enters [fol. 23] the City through two gates: the first is called Cripplegate (Fig. 23), which means the gate of the lame; the second is Moor Gate, the gate of the Moor (Fig. 24).[55] As one leaves the city through the gate of Moor Gate, one comes into a fine and pleasant meadow, which on feast days is full of people of every age and gender. Some practise archery there (for above all men in the world the English take the prize for archery) and indeed, they take great pleasure in it. Others, among the rest of the people there, stroll so as to enjoy the beauty and the good air of the place.[56] At one end of this meadow are two very fine theatres, [fol. 23ᵛ] one of which is magnificent in comparison with the other and has an imposing appearance on the outside (Fig. 25).[57] This theatre can hold from 4 to 5,000 people and it is said that a great Lord had it erected. Now, both of these were erected and dedicated for the performance of some plays and other spectacles, most of which comprise actions made up for pleasure rather than ones which have actually taken

Cripplegate.

Moorgate.

a fine meadow.

The Englishman, the best archer in the world.

Theatres.

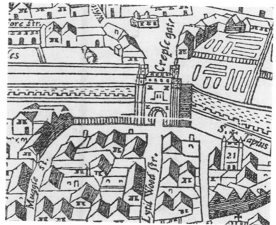

Fig. 23. Cripplegate from inside the city in the 1550s; the gate had been rebuilt in 1491, following a bequest from the Lord Mayor. The name 'S. Tapius' within the gate denotes the church of St Alphage, which adjoined the city wall. From the Woodcut Map, commonly known as 'Agas'. © *London Metropolitan Archives, City of London.*

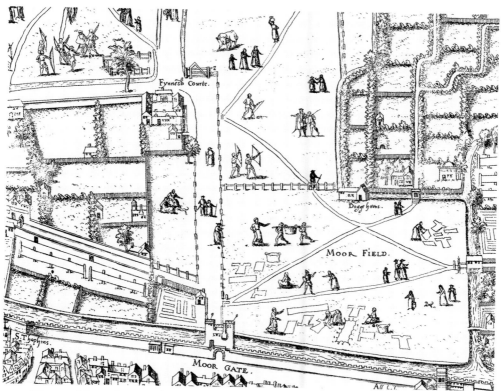

Fig. 24. Moor Gate and Moor Field in the 1550s, from the Copperplate Map. Note the diverse activities: strolling, archery, cloth-finishing, laundry, the house where the dogs for the city's common hunt were kept, and several 'garden houses' used for recreation. © *Museum of London.*

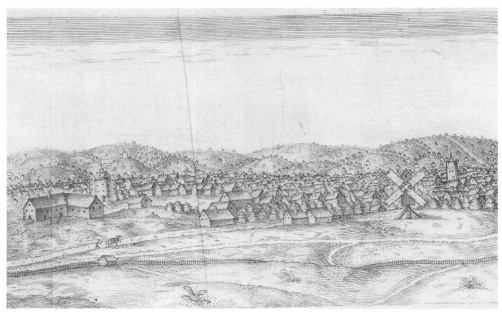

Fig. 25. View just south of east across the northern suburbs, from a late sixteenth-century panorama (see Fig. 10). The polygonal building on the left, behind the L-shaped structure, may be one of two theatres in the area: The Theatre or The Curtain. The hills beyond are on the Surrey side of the Thames. © *Burden Collection*.

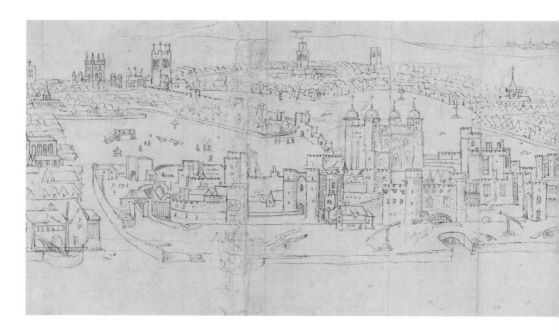

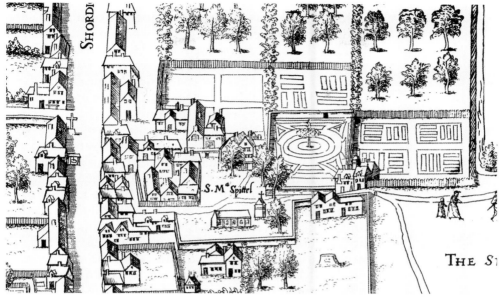

Fig. 26. The site of St Mary Spital, suppressed in 1538. This extract from the Copperplate Map clearly shows the pulpit cross, from which the sermons were preached after Easter, and the house built nearby in 1488, from which the Lord Mayor, Aldermen, and other dignitaries listened to them.
© *Museum of London.*

Fig. 27. The Tower and the eastern part of the city *c.*1544, from Wyngaerde. The six churches extending from south to north to the east of the Tower are those of St Katharine's Hospital, St Mary Graces (a former Cistercian house), Whitechapel parish, the Minoresses (former Franciscan nunnery), St Botolph without Aldgate parish, and Holy Trinity Priory (within Aldgate). © *Ashmolean Museum, Univ. of Oxford.*

place.[58] Even their agreeable appearance pleases men and any onlookers. Indeed, the wisdom of the magistrate of London recognised this. Hence the reason for placing the theatres outside the city.[59]

The Hospital of
Saint Mary.

In this suburb there is a very fine hospital called the Hospital of Saint Mary (Fig. 26). It was founded and built by a citizen [fol. 24] of London and his wife (he being named Walter Brime and she Rose) in the year 1235.[60] There is a custom of preaching a sermon at this hospital on the second day of Easter; this is delivered by one of the most excellent doctors that one can choose. It lasts three hours and is attended by the Lord Mayor, accompanied by his fellow aldermen in all their honour and magnificence. Furthermore, the bishop of London and several other great lords, and a great number of people also attend.[61] Also in this suburb is another hospital called Bethlehem, where one places the insane and those deprived of their wits.[62] Here, one attempts to restore them to good sense. [fol. 24ᵛ]. I do not know which medicines are used, only that it is said that they use the same remedies as were formerly employed to cure the mad at St Mathurin de Larchant in France, that is to say strong lashes of the whip.[63]

The sixth suburb in this sequence, which has a much straighter and wider street than all the others, is commonly called Whitechapel (Fig. 27). At the end of it are beautiful meadows, where by means of great ingenuity the water conduits for the fountains go to the city[64]. One enters the city from this suburb by a gate commonly called Aldgate, which means 'the gate of all',[65] for the inhabitants of the city were responsible for building it.

Margin notes:

Walter Brime.
Sermon on the day after Easter, lasting three hours.

Bedlam.

remedy for curing the insane.

Straight and wide street.
Whitechapel.
Fine meadows.
Water conduits.

Aldgate.

[fol. 24 bis]

Chapter 5

On the suburb called Sainte Katharine.
On its singularities. On the royal Tower,
called the Tower of London

St Katharine.
Three ways for
entering the City on
this side.

One enters the suburb of St Katharine from the direction of the city in three places: by water, through a great gate which pertains to the royal Tower, and on the other side, through a small postern outside the precinct of the said tower (Figs 27 and 28).[66] And so it does not strike me as unfitting to discuss at this point the said tower, given that in discussion of the other suburbs I have firstly spoken about the gate which affords entry into each of them. Now, amongst other things, [fol. 24 bisᵛ] I have observed in London four buildings of a wondrous structure and lavishness: therefore I shall need to dwell on them at greater length. The first is the church of St Paul. The second is the Bridge. The third is the royal Tower. The fourth structure is the Royal Exchange. But for the present we are dealing with the royal Tower and its singularities, leaving discussion of the others to their place.

4 marvellous
buildings in London.

1 St Paul's.
2 the Bridge.
3 the Tower.
4 the Exchange.

The Tower.
very ancient.
Julius Caesar.

W. Rufus.
W. the Conqueror.

Description of the
fortress of the Tower.

The Tower boasts great antiquity because Julius Cesar had its principal keep built (Fig. 29). Those who succeeded him had the rest of the fortress erected, notably William Rufus, the son of William the Conqueror, who made it as we see it today.[67] [fol. 25] It has three high walls around it, with several strong towers and deep ditches full of water which enclose them. Also visible are many platforms, well furnished with many pieces of artillery on wheels. Moreover, there is no battlement nor loophole, either in the walls or in the towers, which lacks its piece of cast artillery with its carriage. The artillery is in such abundance that some has to be placed in front of the said Tower, whether it is of bronze or of cast iron. There are so many double cannons, cannons and field pieces that they number more than 200. And there are even several pieces of iron ordnance which rust

note.

Y³ Goounefowuders h:

St Brutols

St Brutt

Byshoppes Gate

S: Denys

Fo. Churi

All Gate

Myrian rce,

Postern Gate

Towre hyll

THE   TO

Belins Gate

Lions C

Somers C

Borol warff

Cops wasf

Gresh warf

Galy
wasf
cgstum
houfe

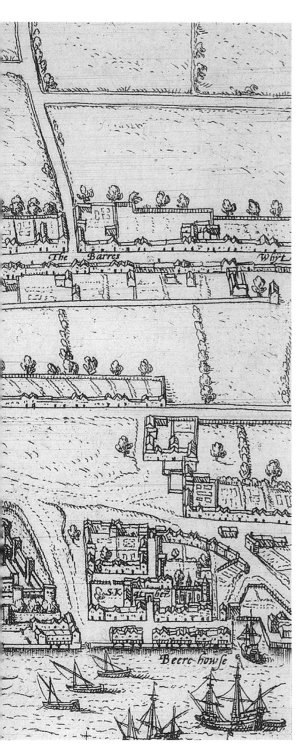

Fig. 28. The Tower of London, St Katharine's Hospital and dock and the suburb outside Aldgate in the 1550s. Although the area was noted for its industries, including gun-founding (noted on the map), it still contained many gardens. From B & H Map (1572). © British Museum.

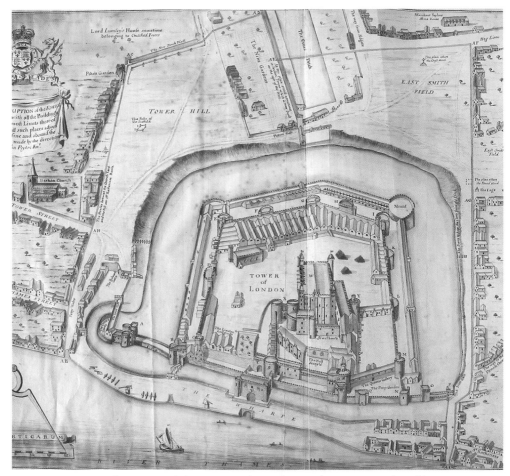

Fig. 29. Plan view of the Tower of London and its surrounding liberty,
surveyed in 1597 by William Haiwarde and John Gascoyne.
© *Society of Antiquaries of London.*

in the ground. In short, it is a matter strange to believe
for one who has not seen it.[68]

[fol. 25ᵛ]

Soldiers in ordinary
pay of the Tower.

Good common
policy.

This tower has its own permanent garrison and common guards who wear the same livery as the archers of
Her Majesty's guard. Everyday soon after 11 o'clock in
the morning, the custom is to raise the bridges and so
close the entrances to the said Tower, the guards retiring
within at the sound of a bell which is rung for that

purpose. Everything remains closed until 1 o'clock in the afternoon, when all have dined and the guards are set. And the same again at 5 o'clock in the evening. Then, at around 8 o'clock, it is opened again, both to let in those who have dined in the city, and to let out those who do not belong to the said Tower. It then remains closed until sunrise the following day, when it opens as before. [fol. 26] In short, it is so well and honourably governed in every way that no alternative could possibly better it. It is so carefully guarded for several reasons: firstly, because it is the principal fortress in England; secondly, because the royal treasures are kept there; and thirdly, since it contains an arsenal sufficient to arm more than 50,000 men with pikes, harquebuses or corselets. Finally, the tower is guarded because it acts as a prison for any great Lord or other man of rank who commits a heinous crime (above all, those accused of high treason). The offender is locked away in the Tower and cannot leave without capital punishment [fol. 26ᵛ] or complete absolution.

Good policy in guarding the Tower.

Why it is so carefully guarded.

An admirable thing.

Now, besides those things which we have mentioned, the Tower boasts a multitude of singular and exquisite things which are seen only by a few strangers, such as ambassadors and other great Lords that it pleases the king to delight by showing them these antiquities, and at the end of their tour they are saluted by a volley of cannon.[69] All who witness these things are without doubt completely awestruck, declaring it impossible to behold anywhere in Europe such a host of remarkable things.

many exceptional and exquisite things rarely shown to strangers.

When the monarch makes his entry both to the dignity of royalty and to the City of London [fol. 27] as the capital city of the kingdom, he first takes possession of the said Tower, and resides there until the day of his coronation.[70] There are four pennants with their weather vanes, 7 or 8 feet high, one on top of each of the turrets which surround the great keep.[71] The masts along with pennants and weather vanes together form a great and beautiful closed crown above the keep. Many affirm that they are all made of solid gold, which, apart from the magnificence, would be a marvellously splendid sight for, given their size and height, they could not weigh less than 200 pounds each. I know [fol. 27ᵛ]

The Tower is the first dwelling of Kings and Queens acceding to the crown.

This is in doubt.

well that it is more than 27 years since I first saw them, but neither their colour nor their lustre have changed.

In a great and broad tower which stands at the entrance of the first enclosure of the said Tower, reside the African beasts owned by her majesty which include six or seven lions and lionesses, young and old, a leopard excellently spotted, a porcupine, and a wolf. This is a most rare thing to behold since you cannot see it anywhere in the whole country unless they are specially reared.[72] So much for the Tower.

the Lions and other wild beasts of her majesty.

There are no wild wolves in England.

As for the suburb called St. Katharine, it is one of largest and most populated of them [fol. 28] all.[73] It is inhabited by a large number of sailors and of craftsmen of varying trades such as hatters, makers of harquebuses, shoemakers, brewers and many others like these. This suburb is also the destination point for a vast quantity of wood, which is brought there by boat to supply the city.[74] And although it is very expensive, it is managed in such good order that there is never a shortage.

St Katharine.

Chapter 6

On the suburb called Southwark and on the magnificence of the Bridge of London.

[fol 28ᵛ]

On the other side of the River Thames is the final suburb to be discussed. This cedes hardly to that beside Westminster in size, beauty and trade.[75] It is commonly called Southwark, that is to say 'on the southern side'.[76] Amongst those things worthy of remark is a particular spot alongside the river called Paris Garden (Fig. 30),[77] since one can see there fights between large mastiffs and a bear, a bull, a frost-nailed horse and an ape. These are held after dinner on feast-days and sometimes during the week when there are fairs. I have sometimes seen 14 mastiffs at once set loose against a [fol. 29] bear which, seizing six of them at a time, clenched them so hard between his arms that he suffocated two of them, the others being overjoyed to flee, with some difficulty, and not to return. The pleasure of a bull fight comes from when the bull is able to seize a mastiff (the mastiffs used in these fights are particularly big) using its horns; it throws the mastiff high up into the air and the mastiff, falling to the ground, either dies or breaks a limb, and so is no longer of any worth. In this suburb is the hospital of St Thomas which I will discuss later after considering Christ's Hospital on page 75.[78]

From this suburb, one enters the city by means of a [fol. 29ᵛ] great and powerful bridge, the most magnificent that exists in the whole of Europe (Fig. 31). It is built entirely of ashlar and is completely covered with houses which are all like big castles. And the shops are great storehouses, full of all sorts of very opulent merchandise. And there is nowhere in London which is more commercial[79] than this bridge. The River Thames flows beneath through 19 large arches and there is considerable ebb and flow according to the time of the tide. If a traitor has been decapitated, his head is placed at the end of a pike and displayed on this bridge for all to

Southwark.

Paris Garden.
Fighting of mastiffs, and of bears of a bull of a horse and of an ape.

Dogs crushed.

The Hospital of St Thomas.

London Bridge.

wealth of London Bridge.

the River Thames.

ebb and flow.

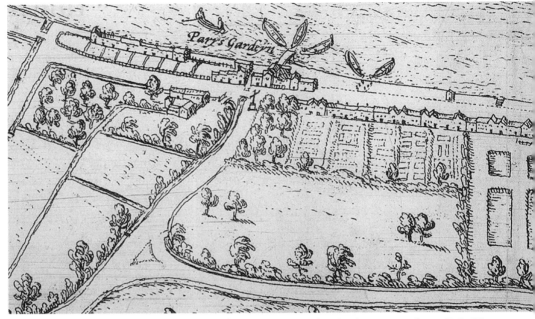

Fig. 30. Southwark from London Bridge to Paris Garden in the 1550s; from B & H (1572). The Bear-baiting and the Bull-baiting rings are clearly visible. Between them and the bridge was the London house of the bishop of Winchester. © *British Museum.*

Covered bridge.
Very ingenious
drawbridge.

The Bridge made of
wood by a priest and
afterwards in stone
by the citizens of
London.

see. I reiterate that there is no bridge in the whole of Europe which is on a great river like [fol. 30] the Thames and as formidable, as spectacular and as bustling with trade as this bridge in London. And this bridge is the second of the 4 marvellous things I noted in London for its impressive construction, as noted above. Another singular feature of this bridge is that it is covered along its whole length. There is a drawbridge in the middle of the said bridge which is made with wonderful skill. For when there is need, by means of a certain mechanism, or ingenious peg that one removes, it lifts and rises up by itself so that the bridge becomes a great fortress for this side of the city, since by this means, a whole arch of the bridge is removed. [fol. 30ᵛ] The bridge was first constructed with wood at the expense of a priest in the year 1163. And since then, in the year 1209, the magnificent citizens of London built it in stone.[80]

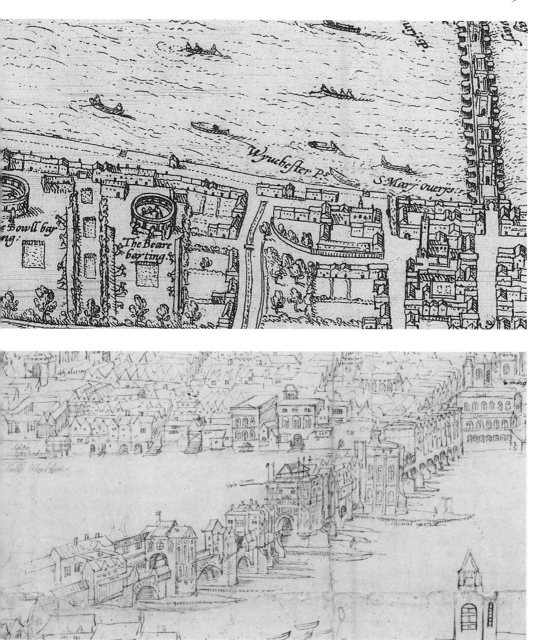

Fig. 31. London Bridge from the south-east *c.*1544, from Wyngaerde. The houses, Chapel, and Drawbridge Gate (with heads displayed on poles) made an impressive frontispiece for those approaching London upstream. The chapel ceased to be used about 1548.
© Ashmolean Museum, Univ. of Oxford.

Chapter 7

Concerning the body of the City of London:
and first of all the street called Thames Street,
the street of the Thames, and the singular
things which are in it.

Now, let us enter the City by this magnificent bridge and begin with the nearest street of the city which is commonly called Thames Street. Now, one must note that several names [fol. 31] the streets of London do not have one name for for one street. the whole of their length, but change it according to the places through which they pass. This street is one of the Four principal four great and principal thoroughfares of London since streets. it traverses the length of the city, making it very long. It Thames Street. is called Thames Street because it runs parallel to the The street of the river Thames. All along this street, there are several fine Thames. ports where boats and merchant ships drop anchor, Billingsgate. including Billingsgate (Fig. 32), which is the most famous and renowned since it is here that all sorts of [fol. 31ᵛ] foodstuffs arrive both from foreign countries Billingsgate, and elsewhere. Moreover, this port is better equipped a fine port. and more suitable than any other in the same street for receiving all kinds of ships.[81] Normally, twice every twenty-four hours, there depart from Billingsgate two great boats and many other covered vessels called tilt The Gravesend Barge boats which are filled with people, and which go the Tilt boats. between London and Gravesend (Fig. 33). Billingsgate Belinus named took its name from King Belinus who had it erected in Billingsgate from his the year of Our Lord 400 and who wished that it bear own name. his name.[82] This street is extremely narrow, even too narrow. For, owing to [fol. 32] the vast quantity of goods In the narrow street which land there, it is necessary to use many large and large waggons heavy carts to carry them. As a result, the street is often are not suitable. so blocked that sometimes passers-by are brought to a standstill for a long time. Now, this street does not boast wealth of the same grand appearance of the others, but it is nev-Thames Street. ertheless one of London's richest. And in fact, several note. Lord Mayors have been elected from its residents which worthily attests to its richness and nobility, since only

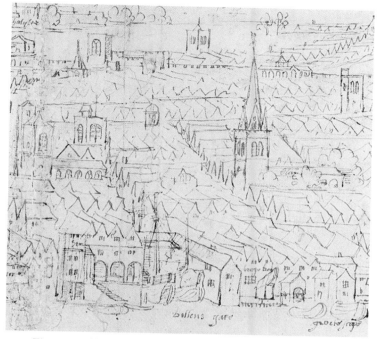

Fig. 32. Billingsgate c.1544, from Wyngaerde. The inlet
and galleried warehouses distinguished it from most other
landing places along the waterfront. The church nearby with
the prominent tower and spire was that of St Dunstan in the
East, attended by members of Grenade's family.
© *Ashmolean Museum, Univ. of Oxford.*

Fig. 33. Tilt boats with two or more sails carrying passengers to and from Gravesend:
left, in the 1550s, from B & H Map (1572), © *British Museum*; right, in the
mid-eighteenth century, from an engraving (1753) by P. Canot,
reproduced in Cruden 1843: 417.

Fig. 34. The Steelyard *c.*1544, from Wyngaerde. The twelfth-
century hall of the merchants of Cologne was where the artist
has written *Staelhof*; due south on the river frontage was the
house of the Hanse Master; in the fifteenth century the German
Hanse acquired possession of the properties to the east. Note
the crane on the open quay and the long ranges of buildings,
used as warehousing and domestic accommodation. The large
church tower is that of All Hallows the Great, adjoining the
Steelyard and where the German merchants worshipped.
© *Ashmolean Museum, Univ. of Oxford.*

note.

The house of the
Easterlings.

note.

extremely rich and virtuous people are elevated to this
dignity. [fol. 32ᵛ]

In the same street is the house of the Easterlings
(Fig. 34).[83] These people are German merchants and
make common provision for eating and drinking. They
are so regulated that their order and manner of doing
things are most honourable to behold. As long as they
are members of this household, they are not allowed to
marry. It is not, however, possible to enforce celibacy on
them. Simply, if they marry, they are no longer to belong
to the said house. They live and take meals together and

20 masters.

Inferiors.

a very honourable thing.

their table.
the Alderman.

the Alderman highly esteemed.

the Steelyard.

Privileges.
of the Steelyard.

consist of roughly between eighteen and twenty masters, and as many [fol. 33] others who are below them and their inferiors. This second rank eat at a separate table but still in the same room and, nevertheless, keep their heads uncovered, whether serving their masters at the table or eating their own meal. If an honourable person comes to this house (as often happens), with the least recourse to people and goods, he is received with great honour and well treated but only in accordance with their commons, which are as magnificent as that of any great Lord. They have a governor or superintendent who presides [fol. 33ᵛ] over them and whom they call Alderman. This is a name of an office and in that place denotes only him who presides over all those of this house. He is most respected and honoured within this body, for he is also their sole magistrate. And so, if there arises some difference between some of them over some matter, it is the Alderman who acts as judge of last resort.

The common name of this house is the Steelyard,[84] and it is most magnificent, noble and rich. It has great and excellent privileges which were conferred on it [fol. 34] by deceased kings of England, and were confirmed and upheld by Her Majesty the Queen who rules today. May God always desire to keep her under his protection and safekeeping. Amen. That is all I can think of to say about those most notable aspects of this street, leaving what remains for those who will be more discerning than myself.[85]

Chapter 8

On the street commonly called
Tower Street, 'the street of the Tower',
and its singularities

Tower Street.
several
other streets.

four principal
streets.

the street of the
Tower.

St Paul's.

Foundation of the
church of St Paul.

Very ancient church.

entire length of
St Paul's is 270 paces

the width is
120 paces.

The next street after that of the Thames, of which I have spoken, is that commonly called [fol. 34ᵛ] Tower Street. Now, it must be noted that although London has many streets traversing the city, without a great number of other lesser streets, there are, nevertheless, four great and principal ones which run from one end of the city to the other across its entire length. The street just discussed is one of these, and this one is the second. It is called Tower Street because it runs directly from the gate called Ludgate up to the great and magnificent royal Tower.[86] There are several remarkable features in [fol. 35] this street worthy of great praise. However, I will only touch upon those things which are the most rare and exquisite.

Firstly, after the gate called Ludgate where the street starts, stands the great and magnificent church of St. Paul; marvellous in several regards which will be discussed below. The histories report that Brutus built a church in New Troy which he dedicated to Apollo. On this point, many have affirmed to me that this church is that which is today called St Paul. However, some say that it was built in the year 600 of our salvation by King Æthelberht, King of Kent.[87] [fol. 35ᵛ] The reader will be at liberty to believe what he wishes. Nevertheless, whether it is one or the other, the whole displays a great antiquity. This is the third of the marvellous things which I have noted within London, and in fact those who examine it with care are astonished to see such a large building (Fig. 35). Its length inside, from the door beside the house of the bishop of London, is 150 paces or strides as far as the choir door, and from the choir door to the end more than 120 paces. Its width, from one door to the other across the church, is 120 paces.[88] Now, we should note that [fol. 35 bis] the said church is

Fig. 35. Interior of St Paul's Cathedral, looking east down
the nave. Etching by Hollar in Dugdale (1658). Hollar
simplified and tidied up the appearance of the interior,
which was notable for its length. © *British Museum.*

Church in the form
of a cross.

several magnificent
tombs.

John of Gaunt.
Edward III.

in the form of a cross and so not be astonished that its
width is so great.

In this church there are several excellent and rich
tombs of great lords, both those bearing arms and
others, of which I shall mention only the 7 which seem
to me the most remarkable. The first is that of a duke
of Lancaster called John of Gaunt, since he was born at
Ghent in Flanders. He was the son of Edward III, king
of England. He died in 1398. His tomb, on the left hand
side of the choir, is magnificently wrought of a fine
white marble. [fol. 35 bis^v] He is buried there alongside
his wife. Both of their effigies are of white marble and

Tomb of Milord
Keeper, made before
his death.

are raised on the tomb, skilfully and naturally carved and showing them holding hands.[89]

The second tomb is newly erected, and the individual who had it built is still alive (Fig. 36).[90] It is the Lord Keeper of the Seal who had it built and there are effigies of him, his two wives and his children. This tomb is the most magnificent I saw in London, for it is made of a very beautiful and fine white marble raised high, provided with a roof of the same material, and richly carved on both sides. The part above is made in the form of an ass's back. [fol. 36] The arms of the said lord are on both sides and are richly covered and dressed with their colours. This roof is supported by several columns of black, grey and white marble whose lustre is so fine that it can be admired from all perspectives. The tomb is located on the right-hand side of the choir.

Tombs of two
very ancient
Saxon Kings.

In the aisle on the other side of the choir, there are two tombs of grey marble, both fashioned in the form of ancient chests (Fig. 37). They are almost completely set within two small recesses, so that the lids cannot be opened without extracting the tombs from the recess.

Fig. 36. St Paul's: tomb of Sir Nicholas Bacon, lord keeper of the seal, erected before his death (1579) in the arcade on the south side of the choir, near the high altar. From Dugdale (1658).
© *British Museum.*

Fig. 37. St Paul's: twelfth-century sarcophagi within the
north wall of the choir containing the remains of King Sebbi
of the East Saxons (d. 694) and King Æthelred II (d. 1016),
both of whom died in London. From Dugdale (1658).
© *British Museum.*

They appear to be of [fol. 36ᵛ] very great age.[91] On one
of them this epitaph is written on a small tablet:

Sebbi, Saxon King

Here lies Sebbi, king of the East Saxons who
was converted to the faith by St. Erkenwald:
of whom the Venerable Bede in the fourth book of his
'Ecclesiastical History of the English People' made
mention: who reigned about the year of Our Lord 690.[92]

About nine or ten paces in front of this sepulchre and
on the wall of this side of the church is an excellent
tomb fashioned in fine white marble after the modern
style (Fig. 38), and finely incised with this epitaph:[93]

If any one was ever prudent and a star, Senator,
If anyone was the chorus of his country and its lover.
If anyone a suitable ambassador to foreign shores,
If anyone had a concern for justice and the good:

Mason

It was John Mason, let the whole of Britain be witness.
Let the love of princes and favour of the people be witness
In his time he saw five rulers in succession.
He was among the counsellors of four of them.
He lived three and sixty years and no more.
Here is his body covered: his spirit upholds the heavens.

Fig. 38. St Paul's: tomb of Sir John Mason (d. 1566), diplomat and perhaps an acquaintance of Grenade and his family, against the north wall of the choir. From Dugdale (1658). © *British Museum.*

John Colet.

A true likeness.

[fol. 37] On the other side, on the right-hand side of the choir against the wall, is raised, in a framework of black and white marble, the tomb of the most excellent doctor of theology, called John Colet (Fig. 39). Below is a representation of a human cadaver, while higher up is his effigy, wondrously lifelike and accompanied by this epitaph:

> Here lies Dr John Colet, Dean of this Church, eminent theologian, who following the example of St. Paul always undertook the free proclamation of evangelical doctrine, and always responded with everlasting integrity to the pure teaching of life. Alone and at his own expense he founded St Paul's School and endowed it with annual rent. He adorned a highly distinguished family with the gifts of Christ, especially a wonderful temperance and modesty. Now he delights in the pearl of the gospel, for the love of which he disregarded everything. He lived 53 years, held office for 16, and died in the year 1519.[94]

[fol. 37ᵛ] Near the door on the north side of the church, raised high on the wall to the left, is the tomb of Thomas Linacre, a man in his day very learned in

Fig. 39. St Paul's: tomb of John Colet
(d. 1519), humanist and dean of
St Paul's, in the south choir arcade towards
the west end. From Dugdale (1658).
© *British Museum.*

medicine. This tomb is entirely of white marble, and well
carved with six scrolls [or books] around its base. His
epitaph is engraved on copper and is:

> Thomas Linacre, physician of King Henry VIII, a man
> for long very learned in Greek, Latin and medicine: he
> restored to life many wearied by their age who had just
> become despondent. With wonderful and singular elo-
> quence he translated many works of Galen into Latin.
> A little before his death, at the request of friends, he pro-
> duced an excellent work 'Concerning the correct struc-
> ture of Latin speech'.[95]. He established in perpetuity two
> public lectures in medicine for the learned men of
> Oxford and one for those of Cambridge. In this city, by
> his industry he saw to the foundation of the College of
> Physicians, of which he was also elected as first presi-
> dent. Uncommonly weary of fraud and trickery, faithful
> to friends of all ranks alike *iuxta charus*, and made a
> priest a few years before he died, he left this life full of
> years and much missed, in the year of Our Lord 1524
> on the 8th day of October.[96]

[fol. 38] In the middle of the nave of the said church
stands a marble tomb on which is a bronze effigy of a

William the
Conqueror.

Privileges restored.

bishop, who in his time did so much for King William the Conqueror that the king restored those privileges and freedoms of the city of London which he had previously withdrawn. In recognition of this, the Senate and the people of this city had made for him this tomb and epitaph:

Epitaph

To William, a man renowned for wisdom and holiness of life; who first a member of the household of St Edward, king and confessor, then elevated as bishop of London, and not long after on account of his prudence and outstanding loyalty recruited to counsel that invincible prince, William king of England, the first of that name, obtained from King William the fullest privileges for this most famous city. The Senate and people of London set down [this tomb] according to his just desert. He ruled as bishop for 16 years. He died in the year 1067 from the birth of Christ.[97]

the Organs.

the music.

Henry VIII.

Church on a
Church.

[fol. 38ᵛ] The organs are not the least of the singularities of this church, for in truth, they are magnificent and produce a sound marvellous to hear when the chanters and children of the choir sing with it. Furthermore, this happens twice a day, namely in the morning and the evening. King Henry VIII had them made.[98]

It is a marvellous feature of this church that it is founded, from the choir to the end, on another fine and large church (Fig. 40) which serves as the parish church for its environs.[99]

Fig. 40. St Paul's: the thirteenth-century crypt, which accommodated the parish church of St Faith, presumably displaced by the construction of the 'new work' of St Paul's. From Dugdale (1658). © *British Museum.*

The prospect of the Parochiall Church of S.t Faith from West to East under S.t Paules.

Let us now go outside and consider how much the exterior of this great building is as excellent as its interior. [fol. 39] Its roof is singular in that it employs more than five hundred thousandweight of lead.[100] This is a most wonderful sight to behold. For, the roof is in the shape of a cross with four arms, marvellously large and long, raised high to a ridge.[101] It is said that in the year 1560, fire seized it by means of a lightning bolt and entirely consumed it.[102] Molten lead flowed through the streets right down to the river bank. Fire first took hold of the spire of the great and very tall bell-tower which sits at the roof crossing. This spire was so tall that even now one cannot see a bell-tower of such height in the whole of [fol. 39ᵛ] Europe. Great store is set by the bell-tower of Strasbourg, which is indeed very high, but, having seen both of them, I vote in favour of that of St Paul, I mean before the spire fell: for it was so high that one could see it from 25 miles away.[103]

In St Paul's churchyard, on the side of the rising sun is a very beautiful and excellent grammar school established with the personal wealth and at the charge of this Doctor John Colet of whom we have spoken above. He was the good man who first taught the people to say the Lord's Prayer, the Articles of Faith and the Ten Commandments, in English.[104]

[fol. 40] Now, let us go further on and continue along our street to 'the Drapery', that is to say at the exit from the precinct of St Paul's, where the sellers of woollen cloths begin. In this street alone are two hundred drapers' shops so full of all sorts of cloths of all prices that they appear to be more like warehouses than anything else.[105] About the middle of this street is a rock or square stone embedded deep into the ground, and above ground it is about three feet high (Fig. 41). It has a breadth of around two feet and a thickness of one foot. It is an incontestable fact, that King Lud, (of whom we have spoken twice above, and whose nation was Saxon) [fol. 40ᵛ] caused this stone to be planted for several reasons. Firstly, it was a means of perpetuating the memory of his name and the name of his nation, for first he called it the stone of Lud, that is Ludstone in the language of this country; but later, the city having taken the name 'London', the stone has likewise been called

the roof.

St Paul's burned.

height of the steeple.

the steeple of Strasbourg.

The Grammar School at St Paul's.

the street of drapers. 200 drapers' shops in one street.

London Stone.

Lud, a Saxon King.

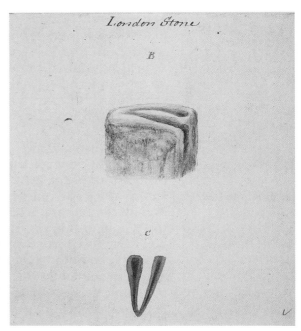

Fig. 41. London Stone,
Cannon Street, without casing.
Date of execution *c.* 1800.
© *LMA, City of London.*

London Stone. Secondly, given that the said Lud was Saxon by birth, and since this word greatly resembles the Latin word Saxum, this was a means of imprinting in memory the name of his country of birth. And thirdly, he had a stone placed there as a signpost and marker, for several have written that he extended the city from

Increase of London. [fol. 41] this stone up to the gate called Ludgate, as has been said above. This happened in the year of the world 3894, and 69 years before the coming of Christ. The stone in question is, therefore of great antiquity, especially if one considers its decayed state.[106]

The Shambles. Passing further on we come to the shambles, 200 paces from there. This shambles is amongst the most famous in London.[107] There are two points to be made

Two things to consider. in relation to this one and the others. First, is the excellence and beauty of the meat exposed for sale. The second concerns the number of beasts slaughtered there each week. As for the number, I can relate what I have

a curiosity. seen on several occasions, for I was so curious that several times on a Friday morning, on walking [fol.41ᵛ] the length of the said shambles, I would count the freshly flayed heads of beeves (not counting those which

150 heads of beeves in a shambles all at once.

were not on display) and usually came across 130, and sometimes up to 150, not counting those which were killed during the week. Now, there are in addition three other large shambles which each kill as many beasts. Apart from these, there are also six or seven others in the city and suburbs. And this is not to mention the vast quantity of meat sold in Leadenhall, to be described below. With regard to those points made above, one can ponder how extensive and good the pasture land [fol. 42] is in the whole country of England to be able to rear so many oxen for, according to the butchers' report, within London and in the suburbs 750 beeves are usually slaughtered each week, amounting to 9,000 a year.[108] Now, it is by considering the suburbs of London that one can easily judge with ease how high the number of cattle slaughtered must be in the whole of the rest of England. The calves, sheep and lambs that are slaughtered by all London butchers amount to so many that they cannot be taken into account. [fol. 42ᵛ] As for the beauty and excellence of the meat exposed for sale in the aforementioned shambles, it is not only overflowing with agreeable qualities and at the same time tender and of a delicate taste, but clean and also extremely well dressed. And so, the sight and beauty of the meat encourage people to buy it. Now, whoever studies closely what has been said with regard to this shambles and the others which are within the precincts of London will acknowledge that at no point have I spoken without reason. And so by the meat which is consumed one can guess what a large number of people inhabit it, and by the same means [fol. 43] appreciate its grandeur and magnificence. For how much meat might we think is used in the houses of the Lord Mayor and the two sheriffs throughout their tenure of office? And that does not take into account the amount consumed in the residences of Aldermen who certainly glorify their rank as much as possible, as much in that as in other matters. This astonishes those who contemplate it.

good pastures in England.

750 beeves in a week. 9000 in a year.

veals, sheep and lambs without number.

the quality and beauty of the meat.

great number of people in London.

the house of the Mayor and of the Sheriffs.

those of the Aldermen.

the finest street in London.

But we will depart from this street and let it continue straight ahead to the Royal Tower and we will come to the third, which is the most beautiful and magnificent in London, many parts of it at least, as we shall see in discussing it.

[fol 43ᵛ]

Chapter 9

On the road which begins at the gate called Newgate, On Cheapside, On the Royal Exchange and other singularities

The third and principal street of London is that which starts at the gate called Newgate (Fig. 42). This takes on several names which derive from the places it passes through, just like the other streets of London. It is the most beautiful, rich and the broadest of all those in this city. For this reason, we will not pass by its singularities without illustrating the most remarkable of them as best we can.

[fol. 44] Quite close to this gate called Newgate and running the length of the street is the place where a type of monks called Franciscans used to reside.[109] That ver-

Fig. 42. Within Newgate in the 1550s, from Copperplate Map, showing the former Grey Friars convent, subsequently occupied by Christ's Hospital, the west end of Cheapside, the butchers' shambles, and the installations of Newgate Market.
© Museum of London.

The Grey Friars
converted into
a parish church by
King Henry VIII,
then into a Hospital
by King Edward VI.

Richard Dobbes,
Mayor.

min having been driven away, this place was reduced by King Henry VIII to a parish church and was given the name Christchurch. And later, in the time of good King Edward VI, in the year 1551, it was converted into the very fine and commendable hospital that one sees today. [110] This was by the good and wise advice of the Lord Mayor of that year, called Sir Richard Dobbes,[111] and the honourable Aldermen his brethren, and other virtuous and wise citizens who were, for this end, summoned in Council as follows.

The good king Edward VI, [fol. 44ᵛ] observing the great flow of beggars who, from all regions resorted to the city of London and the wretchedness among them, wrote to the said Lord Mayor that with the assistance of his brother Aldermen, and others he deemed to be good, he thought of making some good command for the indigence of these poor people. In response, the Lord Mayor called and assembled a common council, for which 24 of the most careful and wise citizens known to him were chosen and elected, and who were to consider finding some good way of dealing with this matter. Having [fol. 45] accepted and begun this task, the council made a distinction between poor and poor, and divided them into 3 classes: the first was the sick and helpless; the second, orphans and the elderly; the third, vagabonds and idlers. For these three categories, it was decided that there be ordained three places which in fact would be hospitals, and this is what happened. For the first category, Saint Thomas of Southwark was chosen and it was ruled it would receive the sick and elderly.[112] With regard to orphans and other poor abandoned children, the aforementioned home of the so-called Franciscans was selected.[113] And for [fol. 45ᵛ] vagabonds and idlers, the lavish and magnificent residence of Bridewell (Fig. 43) was chosen.[114]

Excellent ranking
for the poor.

St Thomas.

Grey Friars.
Bridewell for
vagabonds and
the idle.

poor soldier.

the Savoy.

Now, it was agreed upon and immediately implemented that the impoverished sick, elderly and helpless and, particularly, impoverished soldiers who had fought in wars for the monarch had consequently lost a limb, would be taken in and looked after by the aforementioned hospital in Southwark. To provide for these, the good King Edward donated part of his estate and pieces of land which had formerly belonged to the Savoy.[115]

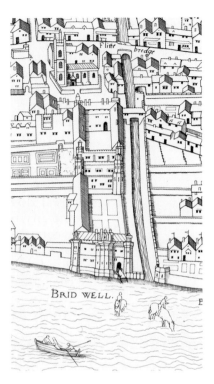

Fig. 43. Bridewell in the 1550s, from Copperplate Map. The palace occupied the west bank of the Fleet, from St Bride's church to the Thames. The covered bridge at its north end was constructed in 1522 to connect the Black Friars' precinct, where the Emperor Charles V was lodged, with the palace, where his entourage stayed. © *Museum of London.*

Christ's Hospital.

Richard Castellar, a very compassionate man.

The Cock of Westminster.

Note.

The City of London also contributed some land. And consequently, everything was built as can be seen today.

[fol. 46] With regard to Christ's Hospital, where were placed orphans and other abandoned children, it was from the outset maintained by regular alms given each week by the citizens of London and other particular charities from elsewhere.[116] However, some time afterwards God unfolded his blessing on the said hospital, by means of a man of substance, a shoemaker resident in Westminster called Richard Castel or Casteller who was a man so assiduous in the labour of his craft that, whatever the weather, he was always up and at work from 4 o'clock in the morning.[117] [fol. 46ᵛ] This earned him the designation of 'the cock of Westminster'. Nonetheless, God so greatly blessed his work (a most noteworthy fact) that from his earnings he purchased in the environs of Westminster lands, tenements, possessions and other things which brought in an income of 44 pounds sterling every year. Now, being denied any children, and with the consent of his wife who was also very honourable and virtuous, he gave all his lands and income to the said Christ's Hospital for the upkeep of the said poor children.

As for Bridewell, it was ordained that there would be confined and placed therein, either out of choice or by [fol. 47] force, all idlers, vagabonds, whoremongers, harlots and such similar lazy scoundrels so that they might be taught to earn their bread by the sweat of their brows.

There were many good outcomes from this godly ordinance. Firstly, children were removed from the hands of a large number of doxies who would roam all through the streets bringing great dishonour to the city. These children were instructed and continue to be instructed today in several skills and disciplines to give them the means to earn a living when they are grown up. Secondly, an end was put to [fol. 47ᵛ] a number of cases of soliciting, bawdiness, ribaldries and other such obscenity and lewdness. And in addition, the regulations prevented many who desired to live without doing anything from taking up thieving and robbery. Thirdly, the impoverished sick and elderly were looked after. Finally, in addition, by this means the city was freed from the noise and common outcry with which these poor people used to fill the streets. But, I will speak at greater length about this in the chapter on the good governance of the city.[118] And so, let us move on. And yet, I wish that my reader to reflect on how [fol. 48] I have drawn out this topic in order to show how the city of London is well administered by the wisdom of its governors. I hope, however, with the help of God, to extol their rare virtues in the form of a treatise on the heroic men whom throughout time this noble and renowned city has produced.[119]

And so, I resume my wanderings along this great street which is full of all manner of rich and precious wares, particularly at the place called Cheapside, for there one sees a sea of all worldly riches (Fig. 44). The goldsmiths and changers on one [fol. 48ᵛ] side of the street number about 70 shops all in a row, full of all sorts of works and vessels in gold and silver alike, gilded or to be gilded. On the other side of the street are the great and magnificent shops, or rather warehouses, of

Marginal notes:

May God wish to raise up many such people for these poor children.
Bridewell.

this was a good broom to sweep up such filth.

Great providence.

the author's excuse.

book of heroic men springing from London.

Cheapside.

70 goldsmiths' shops, apart from those elsewhere.

Fig. 44. King Edward VI's procession from the Tower, through Cheapside to Westminster on the eve of his coronation in 1547. Prominent features in Cheapside include the Cross, the Standard, the tower of St Mary le Bow, and the great stone house in front of it. As on other such occasions, citizens lined the street, houses were decorated with rich hangings, and goldsmiths mounted prominent displays in their shops. From a copy made in 1785 of a contemporary painting at Cowdray House, destroyed in 1793. © *The Society of Antiquaries of London.*

This street is more wealthy than one would know how to express.

all sorts of silken cloths (Fig. 46).[120] After these are the mercers, haberdashers, ironmongers, grocers, apothecaries etc. [121] Finally, there appear so many and such diverse varieties of wares on whatever side one turns to that it is a wonderful thing to behold, for it seems that not only Europe (signs of which are seen on all sides in this place) [fol. 49] but also all parts of the world have attempted to try to make themselves known in London by sending to it the greatest rarities which are produced in their regions.

Cheapside Cross.

Now the most eminent spot in this place called Cheapside, right in the middle of the street, is a great pyramid about 30 *brasses* high. It is completely covered in gold leaf and commonly called the cross of Cheapside because at the top of it there is a cross with the image of the crucifix and the form of a dove[122] above it, and it is daubed all over with various representations of the saints, [fol. 49ᵛ] which testify how superstitious was the

Idols are signs of superstition.

Thomas Fisher.

person who had it erected. A certain Thomas Poissonnier, gave the sum of 600 marks for it to be built.

Some have it said that he was French by nation and that at the same time, he also built that fine house which is just beside it. Now, I think that whoever affirms this has learnt this from hearsay, just as I have done. One can, however, see that the front of the house in question is strewn and covered with fleurs-de-lys. Even so, both were built in the year 1485.[123]

3 fountains.
A fair and good fountain.

There are also in the same place called Cheapside, three beautiful fountains. The biggest [fol. 50] is 20 paces in length and eight in width. It gives forth water through eleven conduits or pipes. And it is no less profitable than it is beautiful, for it furnishes two or three thousand houses with water. It was first erected in the year 1284

the Citizens.

at the expense of the citizens of London.[124] The second fountain, apart from the convenience it affords in providing water, also serves to adorn the street in question for it stands right in the middle and is built in the shape of a triumphal turret. It is commonly called The

The Standard.
John Welles.

Standard. A most honourable man called Sir John Welles who while holding the post of Mayor [fol. 50^v] of London, had it built in the year 1431.[125] This street has the particular singularity that it maintains its width of 25 to 30 paces along its whole length, apart from where the shambles are.[126]

When one begins to enter the neighbourhood of Cornhill, this street divides into three (Fig. 45);[127] the left fork is called Broad Street and extends up to the

Broad Street.

street which runs from the gate called Bishopsgate as far as London Bridge, passing by Gracechurch Street, in

Gracechurch Street.
The most beautiful fountain in London.

which there is a magnificent fountain built in the year 1490 at the personal cost and expense of an honourable knight called Sir [fol. 51] Thomas Hill. This neighbour-

a fountain abounding with water.

hood is particularly clean, for the fountain provides water to at least three thousand houses. Three times a week, a very fine market is held in the same place, selling all foodstuffs which come from the villages. [128]

But let us return to the place where we left our street [Cornhill], and we will speak of the arm which goes to the right in the street called Lombard Street. This street

Lombard Street.

is as commercial, for what it contains, as any street in London. There are more than 20 goldsmiths' shops touching and next to each other.[129] There are also hosiers, drapers, mercers, booksellers,[130] apothecaries,

the House of the
Lord Mayor.

the virtues of
My Lord Ramsey,
Lord Mayor for
this present year.

the 4 corners.

[fol. 51] haberdashers etc. Also in this street stands the house of the Lord Mayor for this year whose name is My Lord Thomas Ramsey,[131] a man most worthy of this most honourable role since he is a most good-natured, wise and a highly prudent lord. This street crosses Gracechurch Street at the place of the 'Four Corners', where the market of which we spoke a little while ago takes place.[132] The street then extends straight ahead to the gate called Aldgate.

Now, let us resume our principal street that we left at the entry to Cornhill. Here, one can see the wealthy dealers in tapestry, grocers, [fol. 52] dealers in copper ware,[133] and other rich merchandise in great abundance.

An excellent building.

Here one also finds oneself in front of one of those excellent and magnificent buildings that one could see. For this reason, it also certainly merits some time being spent to describe it.

The Royal Exchange.
Queen Elizabeth gave
it this name.

This sumptuous edifice is called the Royal Exchange, and this name was accorded to it by Her Majesty Queen Elizabeth, currently on the throne, who took the trouble to come and see this noble building in person.[134]

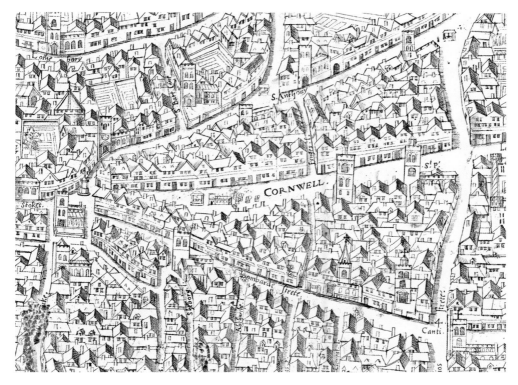

Fig. 45 *(above)*. Broad Street Street, Cornhill (Cornwell) and Lombard Street in the 1550s, from Copperplate Map. Note the Conduit and Pillory in Cornhill and the crossroads at the end of Lombard Street identified in Italian as *4 canti*. © *Museum of London.*

Fig. 46 *(left)*. Cheapside and Poultry in the 1550s, from Copperplate Map. Compare Fig. 44. The monuments include the Great Conduit, at the east end in front of the Mercers' Chapel, formerly the church of St Thomas of Acre. © *Museum of London.*

the Bourse.

Merchants assemble twice a day.

each nation to its quarter.

The Englishman.

The Frenchman.

The Fleming and Walloon.

The Italian and Spaniard.

May the eternal lord God wish to preserve Her Majesty against her enemies: Amen. The Royal Exchange, [fol. 52ᵛ] then, is what the French commonly call the Bourse, and is situated right in the heart of the city. Merchants who trade in various parts of Europe gather there twice a day, from 11 to 12 in the morning, and from five to six in the evening (Fig. 47). Each nation has its own place there, so that those who have trade to do with them can find them with ease. The English section constitutes half of the said Exchange. The French also have a particular area; the Flemings and Walloons are in another, and the Italians and Spaniards in another. However, each merchant has the freedom to go here and there throughout the said [fol. 53] Exchange according

Fig. 47. Trading at the Royal Exchange depicted by Wenceslaus Hollar, 1644. The merchants some wearing foreign dress, are grouped in 'walks' according to their specialisms, a practice already established by 1578. © *British Museum*.

post and carriers of letters.

news of several places.

the form of the Exchange.
3 walks.
the lowest.

New Venice.
the Alley in the middle.

36 Columns of dark stone.

the courtyard, 80 paces long and 60 wide.

36 columns of jasper marble.

William the Conqueror.

the entry of the Exchange.

3 columns of jasper marble.

to what his business requires. There the posts and the letter-carriers are directed, for delivery to those to whom they are addressed. There also can usually be heard reports from many countries and regions, a great convenience for those who traffic and trade as much on this side of the water as beyond.

As for the form and shape of this Exchange, it is a quadrangle surrounded by three great alleys or galleries, one on top of another. The lowest is underground, and within it, on either side there are several stalls for the sale of merchandise. [fol. 53ᵛ] Already several women dealers and merchants in linen have set up business there,[135] but I think that this place is a little too dark and out-of-the-way for it receives light only through certain iron grilles which open off the middle gallery. This underground area is called New Venice. The middle alley is where traders retire and walk when there is showery weather, for it is spacious, being six or seven paces wide and paved with squares of black and white marble intermixed, a very fine piece of craftsmanship.[136] Around this alley, there are 36 big columns of dark[137] stone, each standing to a height of 12 feet and positioned at intervals [fol. 54] of 4 paces. The inside and heart of the said Exchange is a quadrangular courtyard paved with small pebbles, 80 paces long, and 60 paces wide, and large enough to hold 4,000 merchants without using the said alley. In dry weather and during the hours already noted, traders walk conversing about their business.[138] All around the Exchange at the top of the wall on the inside, stand 36 further columns of jasper marble, placed 10 feet apart. And between two of the columns, there is a designated place within the wall to set up an image of a King or Queen of England, from among those who have reigned since [fol. 54ᵛ] William the Conqueror. These always have to be in bronze. Below[139] these columns, painted on a flat surface, are the arms and names of the kings, princes and lords of those times.

One enters the said Exchange through two large portals or entries, one on the south (Figs 48 and 49), the other on the north. These portals are flanked on each side by a great column of exquisite jasper marble, each 14 feet high, and in the middle of each portal is a similar

Fig. 48. The Royal Exchange from the south, from an engraving by
Frans Hogenberg, *c.*1569. © *Valerie Jackson-Harris.*

the Threshold.

the Arms of the
Realm.

first motto.

the second.

3rd gallery.

150 stalls.

the bell-tower of the
Bourse.

column dividing it into two parts. The threshold of these
portals is of a marble similar to that of the columns.
[fol. 55] Above the said portals, facing the Exchange,
there are raised in relief the arms and mottoes of
England, a highly exquisite piece of workmanship.[140]
The first motto reads *Honni soit qui mal y pense.* The
second reads *Dieu et mon droit.*

The third alley or gallery, which is above all the
others, is most excellent, beautiful and lavish.[141] One
climbs up to it by 25 or 30 steps which are made and
placed in flights of seven on seven. The interior of this
gallery is encircled by 150 stalls full of very valuable
wares, especially all sorts of mercer's goods.

[fol. 55ᵛ] The Exchange is roofed all round with high-
quality slate. And right above the entrance on the south
side there is a splendid turret which is particularly
prominent and well constructed. In the top and final
storey there is a small bell which has two uses: firstly,

Fig. 49. The Royal Exchange from the south-west, looking along Cornhill towards the Conduit. From *Winter*, one of a set of engravings by Wenceslaus Hollar of the Four Seasons, 1644-5. © *British Museum*.

it is sounded for the end of trade, namely at 12 o'clock in the morning, and 6 o'clock in the evening; secondly, it is used as a clock to notify traders of the time of the said Exchange.[142] Around the said tower, there are two galleries one above the other, most fittingly appointed, from which the City Waits produce wonderful sounds at 4 o'clock in the afternoon on Sundays [fol. 56] when the days are long, to the great pleasure of listeners, of whom there are very many.[143]

Now, while the said Bourse or Exchange is so magnificent and wonderful in all its parts that it amazes those who observe it carefully, how astonished should one be or how strange should one find it that one man, indeed one merchant alone, undertook and brought to completion this splendid edifice at his own costs and expense? To his honour and praise, he assumed this task and completed it, as we can see it today. This man was Sir Thomas Gresham and was for his virtues [fol. 56ᵛ]

this clock displays four faces.

the Musicians of the City.

Note.

Sir Thomas Gresham authentic promoter of the Exchange.

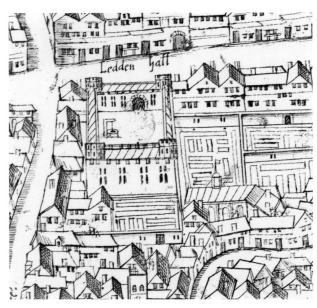

Fig. 50. Leadenhall in the 1550s, from Copperplate Map. This elegant building, completed in 1455 and intended to accommodate markets and for use as storage, presented a fine façade to Cornhill and is well represented in this sketch, although the chapel on the east side has been displaced southwards (cf. fig 51). © *Museum of London.*

and merits, elevated to the honourable rank of knight by the Majesty of Queen Elizabeth; may God wish to preserve her.[144]

Excuse.

Now, out of concern for brevity, I have left aside several matters pertaining to the said edifice, the said Exchange, such as the houses which adjoin it and are in the same enclosure, and the cellars and underground vaults.[145] I will just say that it is scarcely possible to find in the whole of Europe such a lavish edifice which serves the same purpose, and he is yet to be born who can say to the contrary. For this too Sir Thomas Gresham [fol. 57] has earned praise which will endure much more than his work.

The Conduit in Cornhill.

Now, opposite the said Exchange, on the side of Cornhill is a beautiful fountain which gushes forth water through several outlets (see Figs 46 and 48). It was built at the cost of the citizens of London in the year 1400.[146]

Leadenhall.
Sir Simon Eyre.

Walking further on, one finds a crossroads where a very fine market of all foodstuffs is held 3 times a week.[147] One also encounters there a very fine house called Leadenhall (Figs. 50 and 51), of very fine appearance.[148] An upright man called Sir Simon [fol. 57ᵛ] Eyre, a knight and Lord Mayor of London, had it built as well as a chapel nearby in the year 1445. On the door of this chapel is inscribed 'the Right Hand of the Lord raised me'. In this building called Leadenhall there is a great and spacious court, where on market days the flour of all sorts of corn is sold. This courtyard and another large porch at the back serves as a common shambles on those market days, as much for butchers from villages as for others who wish to take a stall there, with the result that sometimes there are more than 100 stalls. On account of the privileges accorded to the Freemen of London, villagers are not permitted to sell [fol. 58] any meat or other goods after midday on market day on pain of their merchandise being confiscated. And so this large street leads on to the gate called Aldgate.

100 Butchers' stalls.

Privileges of the Freemen of London.

Fig. 51. Leadenhall Chapel from the south east in 1805. The position of the chapel is correctly shown, but the artist has improved its appearance by excluding buildings which crowded up to it. From Wilkinson (1825) after a drawing by J. Whichele.
© *British Museum.*

Chapter 10

On the thoroughfare called Lothbury.
On the town hall, called Guildhall.
On the election of The Lord Mayor,
of the Sheriffs and Aldermen.

Lothbury.

Guildhall.

a little cabin was converted into a great and excellent house.

Richard Whitington a heroic man

the entry to Guildhall.

very great hall.

The fourth of the main thoroughfares of London is that which is commonly called Lothbury. It is not as long as the others, but has the honour of having near it the [fol. 58ᵛ] town hall, which is commonly called Guildhall. In the year of our Lord 1410,[149] in the very place where this building is situated stood a pitifully small and wretched shed, which has since been turned into this magnificent and glorious edifice that one sees today, at the expense of the City, and much improved thanks to the great generosity of a venerable Alderman called Richard Whittington, and of many other Aldermen who greatly desired not to spare their wealth in adorning their City with such a fine masterpiece (Figs 52 and 53).[150]

The front and entrance of this building is [fol. 59] that of a truly great and magnificent church or palace. The first part on entering the said house is a large hall, eighty

Fig. 52. Guildhall, from Wyngaerde, where identified as *Yelde halle*. Beyond the city wall to the north, the causeway from Moor Gate to Finsbury is visible. © *Ashmolean Museum, Univ. of Oxford.*

Seat of the Lord Mayor.

the Peers.

the Court of Conscience.

Note.

The Sheriffs' Court.

paces long, or thereabouts, paved with black marble tiles, perfectly laid out. [151] At one end of this hall is the judicial seat of the Lord Mayor, before whom those guilty of high treason are brought, and judged by him according to their merit. But if they are Lords, and styled with some high rank, they are brought before their peers at Westminster and judged by them.[152] [fol. 59ᵛ] On one side of this judgement hall, a court is held called the Court of Conscience.[153] Namely, when some unfortunate person is harassed by his creditor, and has nothing with which to repay his debt, the person has him called before this court, at which, having clearly proved his poverty and strong wish to repay his debt, it is settled that the debtor henceforth pays a weekly sum of 12, 8, 6, or 4 pence according to his income and means. This sum cannot, however, exceed 40 shillings. At the other end of this hall is the timber enclosure where is held the Court of the Sheriffs, who [fol. 60] judge small crimes; for example, verbal outrages or other wrongdoings concerning sums of money owed by individuals to other parties and who are in disagreement, and other similar and civil matters.

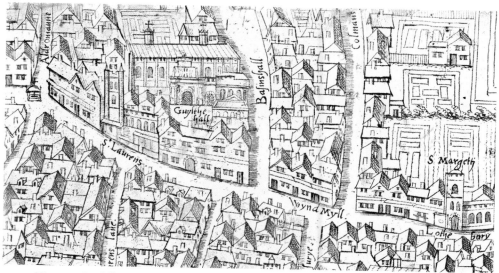

Fig. 53. Guildhall, from Copperplate Map, where labelled *Guylthe hall*. The building is accurately shown, with six windows and an elaborate projecting porch on the south side, where there was an open yard. © *Museum of London.*

Second hall.
10 or 12 steps.
two Giants, one
English, the other
Scottish.

From there, one enters another, but smaller, hall by climbing 8 or 10 stone steps. Above the entry are the effigies of two armed giants: one on the right; the other on the left, represented (as one says) almost to the life, according to the height and proportions of each one (Fig. 54). One of them was the Duke of Cornwall and the other a Scotsman, indicating the two extremities of the island. The Englishman was called [fol. 60ᵛ] Corineus

Corineus.
Goemago.

and the Scotsman Goemago. Now, they fought at close quarters for supremacy, one with a great halberd and the other with a great club fitted with 12 iron spikes. And the Scotsman was conquered and rendered subservient to Corineus; that is how the story goes.[154] In

the two Chief Justices
of England.

this hall the two Chief Justices of England hold the sessions.[155] Beside the aforementioned hall is the doorway

the chamber of the
City Council.

through which one enters the chamber which the Lord Mayor and his brothers the honourable Aldermen habitually occupy three times a week as a council for the business of the commonwealth. [fol. 61]

But since we are on the subject of the Lord Mayor, the magnificent Sheriffs and the honourable Aldermen,

Fig. 54. Giant timber statues of Gog and Magog made *c*.1707 to replace older effigies in wickerwork. They stood on columns in Guildhall on either side of and high above the steps leading up to the Mayor's Court. From a broadsheet celebrating the opening of the third Royal Exchange by Queen Victoria, 28 October 1844. © *London Metropolitan Archives, City of London.*

it will be fitting that we say something about their election and assumption of responsibility, for this greatly serves to illustrate the splendour and magnificence of London (Fig. 55). Now, since what we have to say about the Lord Mayor, his responsibility, his election and his entry into the noble city of London requires much explanation, I shall first say something about the magnificent Sheriffs and honourable Aldermen.

Richard I.

In the time of King Richard, the first of that [fol. 61ᵛ] name, the citizens of London, longing to appoint from

Fig. 55. The lord mayor, an alderman, and a liveryman: de Heere (*c.*1574b), fol. 30ʳ. © *British Library.*

Portreeves.

two Bailiffs.
King John ordained
the Mayor and the
Sheriffs.

two Sheriffs
ordinarily.

they are chosen
by the Lord Mayor.

They are annual.

ceremony.
in the election.

the office of the
Sheriffs.

dignity of the
sheriffs.

their liberality

a notable sum.

the Sheriffs have
the Shrievalty of
London and
Middlesex for
£300 a year.

those of their commonwealth a few who would take on responsibility for it and no longer to be subject to the 'Portgreves' whom King William the Conqueror had established, so successfully solicited the king that from that point onwards, the city of London was to be governed by two bailiffs. That was the year 1190, and this practice continued until the time of King John, the year 1208, when the said City obtained the authority to elect every year a mayor and two sheriffs for the government of their commonwealth and the suppression of the two bailiffs.[156] [fol. 62]

Now, as for the Lord Mayor, we will discuss him after this, so that I do not (for the reasons mentioned above) disrupt the arrangement of the work at this point.

There are normally two sheriffs and they are second in dignity to the Lord Mayor in the City of London and its appurtenances.[157] The Lord Mayor is in charge of their election and it appears likely that this is only done on the advice of his brethren, the honourable Aldermen. They are elected every year, and take up their responsibility around the end of the month of September.[158] The Lord Mayor signals who has been elected by taking up a silver cup and drinking his health during the dinner on the day of the election, designating him sheriff. Their role is (among other things) [fol. 62ᵛ] to ensure that criminal sentences are carried out against traitors, rebels, heretics, murderers, robbers and other evil-doers deserving death — no matter what their rank — or other corporal punishment. This particular function is of such significance that the sheriffs in this regard, represent not only the whole body of the City but also the whole body of the Royal Council.[159] During the period of their administration and responsibility, they maintain an open house, receiving all honourable people of stature, so that their expenditure during their administration amounts to no less than [fol. 63] seven or 8,000 écus, a considerable sum.[160] However, they can easily bear this expense thanks to the income of the shrievalty of London and Middlesex, which they have in fee farm for £300 sterling a year, and this was granted to them by King Henry III, along with other benefits that they have;[161] moreover, no-one is elected to this position who does not have the full means to bear the expense they are obliged to make.

Aldermen are assistants to the Mayor.

The Mayor has all the affairs of the City on his shoulders.

the Aldermen each have a quarter for keeping watch there.

officers of the Alderman.

London, City of peace.

Great blessing of God.

great safety.

praise of the Senate of London.

great blessing of God.

distinction between the Aldermen and the people.

the mob cap.

the long Chain of gold.

The Ephors of Sparta and the Roman Senators.

25 in the ordinary Council.

The Aldermen are the assistants of the Lord Mayor and offer him advice in his role, which is extraordinarily large, as will be discussed below. For as Lord Mayor he alone is responsible for all the matters of the city, which would be impossible [fol. 63ᵛ] for him to provide alone. The Aldermen were attached to him as his coadjutors: each of them has a quarter of the City to take care of, so as to prevent any disorder.

Each Alderman has a Deputy or lieutenant, the Deputy a Constable, and the Constable a Beadle, who are all officers of the Alderman. In short, such good order reigns that one can truly affirm that London is a City of Peace, for, an individual can, safely and at any hour, freely traverse any thoroughfare of the city for his affairs, and can carry (so people say) gold [fol. 64] in his hand without fear that someone might vex him. And this is a result of the good government which is maintained there. [162] But is it not a great blessing from God to observe such great security in such a large and well-populated City, where in many other regions one would not go three steps (in a manner of speaking) out of one's house without being robbed, plundered and often murdered? Indeed, this will be spoken about at greater length when we deal with the good laws and policies of this renowned city. Let us continue.

The Aldermen are distinguished from the rest of the people by their long robes of scarlet red or violet worn on feast-days, [fol. 64ᵛ] and, on working days, by a black velvet mob-cap 4 large fingers wide, or by a great and long gold chain which they wear around the neck, a most praiseworthy object and which solicits immense veneration from all, such that this casts doubt on whether the dignity, authority and appearance of the Ephors of Sparta or the Roman Senators of ancient times were more commendable that those of the Aldermen (Fig. 55).[163] For it is a dignity which is not at all proud but gracious, pleasant and in which one can detect certain traces of the Majesty of God who ensures that they are all the more loved and revered by worthy men, and feared and dreaded by the wicked and untamed. [fol. 65]

As for their number, they are 25 including the Lord Mayor. They were first established in the reign of King

The first institution
of the Aldermen.

Henry III in the year 1240. They numbered 35 in the beginning, and were replaced each year, but some time later they were reduced in number and their order was changed to what we see today.[164]

Fig. 56. Grenade hardly mentioned women, but depiction of all forms of dress was one of Lucas de Heere's interests. From left to right: a citizen's wife, a rich citizen's wife, a young daughter, and a country woman, the last a prominent presence in the city markets (de Heere (*c*.1574b), fol. 33ʳ). © *British Library*.

Chapter 11

On the Election of The Lord Mayor.
On the oath that he takes to her Majesty.
On his entry into the City of London,
and other triumphs and ceremonies.

Although the arrangement of this work would ideally require [fol. 65ᵛ] that one makes mention first of the Lord Mayor and those things pertaining to the taking up of his duties, it has, however, seemed to me both fitting and more appropriate (without wishing to diminish any of those things which pertain to his honour and praise) to save mention until this moment, for the reasons given above.

the election of the Lord Mayor and the Sheriffs.

Now, his election as well as that of the sheriffs takes place at the Guildhall around St Matthew's Day according to the ordinance of King John.[165] The Lord Mayor then in office and his brethren, the honourable Aldermen, conduct the election in the following manner. They chose someone who ranks just below the current post-holder, [fol. 66] but who also meets several other criteria. Firstly, he is to have the knowledge, judgment, prudence, and care, love of the country and commonwealth, sufficient wealth, as well as other such things.

Qualities of a Mayor of London.

this is the principal point.

Secondly, he is to be of a good and holy religion, for this above all is ordered and recommended by her Majesty and her council. For, if the candidate fails to satisfy one of these needs, someone else would be elected. For these reasons, whoever beholds a Lord Mayor of London can with certainty declare that he is worthy of such an honour. For, otherwise, he would not have been appointed to this role. No one is elected mayor unless he is first and foremost an Alderman. And [fol. 66ᵛ] no one is elected an Alderman unless he is a member of one of the 12 principal Halls.[166]

no Mayor without being an Alderman.

12 principal Halls.

Now, while there is a great number of Halls in London (according to the several sorts of estates and vocations) there are, however, 12 main ones, that is to say the Mercers, the Drapers, the Haberdashers, the

Fishmongers, the Grocers, the Vintners, the Spicers,[167] the Ironmongers, the Skinners, the Tailors,[168] the Salters, the Clothworkers. The Lord Mayor presides over all of these, as well as all the other companies within the jurisdiction of London. Moreover, in addition, they each have their own governors and masters who oversee the work of their particular [fol. 67] craft, so that if any one of those who are members of the said Halls does not do his duty in his craft, or if he mistreats his servants or apprentices, or if these said servants or apprentices do not fulfil their obligation to their masters, they are called before the Governor and masters of their Hall who return them to their duty correcting and chastising them according to justice.[169]

These Halls have in place an excellent system worthy of praise.[170] For if, by some disaster, someone becomes poor, the Hall to which he belongs, gives him a house and the means to live, and finally grants him a good sum of money so that he might recover. [fol. 67ᵛ] And the fact that the Companies and their members are dispersed here and there in all parts of the City, and that each of them has taken an oath to maintain its peace and unity, particularly results in the tranquillity and safety of which I spoke above. One must certainly declare the main reason to be the grace of God; but it also comes from the dignity of the Mayor who is — to speak in human terms — the source of all the good laws which, as mentioned above, exist in London.

a notable thing.

union the mother of peace and concorde.

The Senate (of which the Mayor is the premier member) is the source of good Laws.

Why the election takes place long before their entry.

The election of the mayor and the sheriffs takes place some time before they are put in full possession of their high state, [fol. 68] so that they are at leisure to make all the necessary preparations before their public entry into the City. For example, to adorn and decorate their houses (in line with their good and commendable custom) as much with paintings and joinery as other things with the purpose of receiving most honourably men of distinction and authority who will come to visit them, for a meal or otherwise. In particular, they enlarge and embellish the entries to their houses as much as is possible and, as a sign, place in front of the principal gateway on either side two great wooden pillars carved with some fine work all round and painted correspondingly. Although, [fol. 68ᵛ] as the dignity of sheriffs is inferior to that of the Lord

diverse pillars.

The entry of the Lord Mayor into the city of London on the day after St Simon and Jude.

the Halls.

Very honouable procession.

the procession towards the Thames.

the barques and boats.

great magnificence.

the beginning of conducting the Mayor by water.

Henry VI.

he take the oath of allegiance to Her Majesty.

the Princes and Lords of the Privy Council accompany him.

48 trumpets.

Drums. Fifes. Ensigns. Standards. Pennants.

Theatre.

Mayor, so the pillars of each differ accordingly.[171]

Now we come to the magnificent entry of the Lord Mayor into the City of London.[172] When this falls on the day after St Simon and Jude's day, from early morning you can see great preparations throughout the City. All the Halls, Companies and Estates assemble in a most magnificent array, each donning the hood and the livery of his hall over the long robe of fine black cloth edged with velvet and lined with fine sables, having a marvellous appearance. And once the Lord Mayor elect has been greeted, [fol. 69] and entreaties have been made to God that he might make him prosper, they form an orderly procession in front of him towards the River Thames where each of the said Companies find barges and boats all ready and magnificently pranked, on which they embark. The Lord Mayor follows, accompanied by his brethren the excellent and honourable sheriffs and aldermen, and with an incredible array and magnificence they board a rich barge, prepared to convey him to Westminster. Indeed, whoever sees the finery of the barges and boats in this convoy, their array, the number of people and the great triumph of the occasion would be astonished.

[fol. 69ᵛ] This custom of conveying the Lord Mayor by water was introduced in the time of King Henry VI in the year 1453,[173] for previously, he rode on horseback along the street of the Fleet and Temple Bar. In this fine array, therefore, the mayor is conveyed to Westminster, into the presence of Her Majesty, or those appointed in her name, to receive his oath of loyalty. Once this is done, and all the ceremonies and requirements have been accomplished, the Mayor returns by water in much greater triumph than before, for the Princes and the Lords of the Her Majesty's Privy Council accord him the honour of accompanying him along his entire return. [fol. 70] As he begins his return from Westminster, there await 48 trumpets divided up into 3 bands, namely 16 in each group,[174] with a number of tabors and fifes, banners unfurled, standards, ensigns, and many other fine spectacles.

It is customary to make a most magnificent portable theatre, completely covered with gold or silver leaf, in the shape of a mountain, which is commonly called the

Fig. 57. Pageant wagon for the Fishmongers' Pageant on
Lord Mayor's Day, 1616. See *Chrysanaleia* (1859). The 'Pageant' described by
Grenade was carried rather than drawn on wheels. © *British Library*.

the Pageant.

wild beasts.

shows of beasts.

Artillery.

train of powder.

72 *boetes* of artillery.

'Pageant' or mystery (Fig. 57).[175] On top and across the
front of it are several maidens most lavishly bedecked,
representing several virtues such as Justice, Truth,
Charity, Prudence and others similar. Also carried are
figures of several wild and strange beasts such as ele-
phants, unicorns, [fol. 70ᵛ] leopards, griffons, camels,
sirens and other such animals which are most wonderful
to behold. The artillery, however, also plays its role in a
manner that is strange and formidable to hear.
Sometimes, even, a train of gunpowder is laid out
around St Paul's cemetery (Fig 58), on top of which,
every 6 feet, is placed a large *boete*, charged and well
stopped, such that I once counted up to 72 pieces. [176]
Now, when the Lord Mayor nears this spot, these
pipes[177] are set alight by means of the train, and they

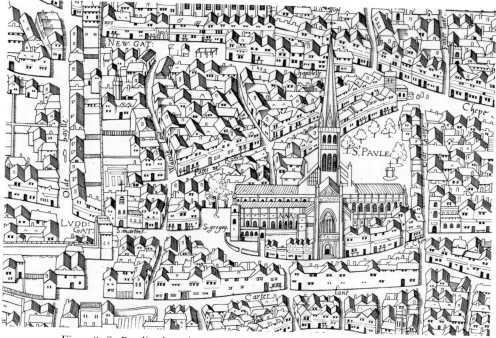

Fig. 58. St Paul's churchyard and surroundings in the 1550s, from Copperplate Map. The Lord Mayor's processional entry to the city, as described by Grenade, passed through Ludgate into the churchyard, where *boetes* were fired, and then out into Cheapside. © *Museum of London.*

Infernal Music.

a dreadful thing.

sing such a song that it seems as if the great church of St. Paul's might fall to the ground, and there is [fol. 71] not a house even in the outermost surroundings which does not shake vigorously.

On leaving the churchyard, the mayor enters the street of Cheapside, where there is such a great throng of people that, despite its width of 25 paces at least, all are so squashed that many people faint, and there would be great disorder but for the good number of men deputed to open up a space. Once all the Halls and Companies have passed by (amongst which it is good to see the procession of sergeants, for each of them, besides his great long robe, carries his silver mace in his hand),[178] the Princes and Lords of the Council follow,[179] succeeded by the Pageant and the other mysteries and triumphs: fifty or sixty [fol. 71ᵛ] honourable burgesses[180] dressed in new long robes, edged all round with a band

the street of Cheapside.

great press.

the Hall of the Sergeants (at Arms).

sixty Freemen.

Musical instruments
the Swordbearer.

of velvet two fingers wide, some having the lappets in front of velvet, others of satin and others of taffeta, as it pleases the Lord Mayor to give them, for it is his livery. After this walk the players of hauteboys, violins and other most melodious musical instruments. Then comes the sword-bearer (Fig. 59), dressed in pompous splendour both with regard to his clothes, gold chains

Fig. 59. The lord mayor riding in his processional entry into the City, accompanied by the mayor of the previous year (also on horseback) and preceded by his swordbearer on foot. Grenade's description matches this scene (de Heere (*c.*1574a), fol. 61ʳ). © *University Library, Ghent.*

and rings as well as other jewels, with his solemn mortier on his head.[181] He carries the sword upright in his hand; its scabbard is of white velvet studded with fine and rich pearls. After him comes the Lord Mayor in most [fol. 72] magnificent array with his great order and very rich collar around his neck, garbed in a great and magnificent robe of scarlet red with the Cloak of Estate trimmed with fine miniver on top, and mounted on a fine hackney in splendid harness. Briefly, it is made entirely of velvet covered all over with gilded buttons and horseshoes. The mayor of the previous year is next to him.[182] After them are the sheriffs and the Aldermen following two by two and dressed in the same apparel as the Lord Mayor, except that instead of the collar and order, they each wear a richly set gold chain, which hangs equally long, back and front. [fol. 72ᵛ]

Now, this procession and triumph lasts from eight in the morning until one in the afternoon, at which time the mayor, with all his train, enters the town hall called Guildhall, where a most excellent and most magnificent feast is ready. Even the Princes and the Lords of the Royal Council attend. Indeed, it is reckoned that the day costs the Lord Mayor at least 3,000 écus.[183] Now, in short, this is one of the most magnificent entries staged for any individual, saving always for those of emperors and kings. To be Mayor of London is, therefore, a greater honour in England than being a doge of Venice in Venice. At three o'clock in the afternoon of this day, [fol. 73] the said Lord Mayor departs from the Guildhall with the same triumph as before, save that the Princes and Lords of the royal council are not present. And thus passing along the street of Cheapside, he is led to the great church of St Paul to hear the divine service. Along this street are more than 30 or 40,000 people forming a marvellous throng, curious to admire this great magnificence. After the service, the triumph even greater than before, particularly since the light begins to fade (owing to the late hour). Along the route one can see two or 300 torches alight, and especially as night time is quieter than daytime, the melody of the musical instruments is more easily distinguished and heard. [fol 73ᵛ] To conclude, there is nothing in this day which, in a manner of speaking, should not be merry. Which is to say that after

the Lord Mayor.
the great Order of the Lord Mayor.

Pomp and great magnificence.

Order.

the town hall.

expenditure for this day.

To be Mayor in London is more than a Doge of Venice.

40,000 persons.

triumph greater than previously.

300 torches.
a peaceful night time.

Fig. 60. A representation, from a diptych painted in 1616, of the bishop of London preaching from St Paul's Cross in the churchyard to the king and queen and the lord mayor, his swordbearer, and aldermen, all accommodated in galleries against the north wall of the choir. © *Society of Antiquaries of London.*

this excellent spectacle, the people retire as joyous and happy as they could possibly be.

Now, for All Saints Day,[184] which occurs three or four days afterwards, some excellent doctor is chosen to preach in St Paul's Churchyard (Fig 60). The Lord Mayor is led there by his brethren the sheriffs and Aldermen with all the Estates and Halls of the city, garbed as on the day of his entry. It would take too long to relate in detail everything pertaining to this entry, but I will make this one final comment on the matter: that one should not be completely surprised at the use of such great magnificence for the entry of the Mayor of London, for [fol. 74] it is one of the most excellent estates which exists in the whole of the kingdom of England (within its jurisdiction) after the royal dignity. Indeed, the privileges accorded to the City convey this, that monarchs desire that its mayors, during their incumbency, have first place and yield to no man, whoever he might be, with the exception of the person of their majesties.[185] The first installation of a mayor of London was in the time of King John in the year 1209, for before that date the City was under the rule of two bailiffs, as has been said.

to be Mayor is the most honorable condition in England.

Privileges of the Mayor.

first institution of the Mayor in the time of King John.

[fol. 74ᵛ]

Chapter 12

On the laws and policies
of the City of London

Now that by the grace of God, we have described the City, adorned and embellished with its singularities and precious antiquities, along with the magnificence of the Lord Mayor and his brethren the magnificent sheriffs and honourable Aldermen as well as our ability has allowed, we must say something concerning the laws, policies, customs, privileges and liberties granted to this city by kings both ancient and modern.

We said at the beginning of this work that Brutus was the first founder [fol. 75] of London and that he called it New Troy. However, just as a cask cannot hold the wine inside it and soon leaks if not encircled by hoops, so a city can neither survive nor prosper if it has not the laws to keep in check the impudence of fools, and to uphold — and even better, to enhance the lustre of — the wisdom of the good and prudent. Furthermore, the chronicles tell us that Brutus, after having imposed his name on the City, instituted Trojan laws.[186] Now, Troy was not only the principal city in all of Phrygia, but also the most prosperous known at that time, so much so that it was envied right up the end, which was partly the cause of its destruction. Therefore, there is no doubt that it had most excellent laws which Brutus, who was Trojan, in turn transferred to his New Troy, which is today the magnificent and flourishing city of London.

These laws remained in place and in use until the time of Julius Caesar who corrupted them with the Roman laws which he introduced. And these remained in force until the time of King St Edward the Confessor, in the year 1060, who purged the laws of many corruptions which time had brought to them. And from the existing laws, he collected together those which he called the Common Laws which were more advantageous for communities, the very reason why [fol. 75 bis] he granted them this name which they still have today.[187] He was

a City without laws cannot subsist.

Brutus brought the Trojan laws to London.

the prosperity of Troy engendered a good deal of envy.

Julius Caesar brought the Roman Laws to London.

St Edward the Confessor made the Lois communes, which everywhere are called today The Common Laws.

William the
Conqueror put the
Common Laws into
French.

several benefits
would arise from
putting the laws into
good language,
purged of all
barbarity.

the intention of the
Author.

this comes from the
fear one has of
offending.

good Justice of
London.

Law against the
unruly and traitors.
Punishment.

Breakers of the peace.

succeeded by King William the Conqueror, who did not desire to make any changes, bar his wish that they be digested into the French language in which one still sees them today and which is so barbaric and corrupted that the proper Frenchman cannot understand it.[188] It would be good to hope (for the great benefit it would bring to the commonwealth) for someone to restore them to a good form of the French language. This seems to me not to be too difficult to do, but I leave the judgment of this to one more perceptive than myself, and return to my present subject.[189]

These laws, as succeeding kings have acknowledged them as beneficial, [fol. 75 bis^v] have been enriched and augmented so as to reach that state of excellence in which one sees them at present. Now, my aim is not to consider in this work the common laws which pertain to the whole of the kingdom, but only those which concern the renowned City of London and its dependencies.[190] To these laws, both the citizens and other inhabitants of this city voluntarily submit themselves and keep them sacred to such an extent that if one designates something as against the laws of the city, every person trembles and takes fright. And this demonstrates all the more the good policy and administration [fol. 76] of justice which is maintained by the city's noble senate.

Now, these laws are so numerous that were I to undertake to lay them here in detail, a much greater tome would be necessary than I aim to proffer at present. I will, however, relate a selection by which one might be able to judge the others.

1

There is a law in London against those who might speak or plot something sinister against not only the Majesty of the Prince but also the public good of the city. They are to be punished according to their desert, and likewise for those who know about but do not reveal such activities.

2

[fol. 76^v] There is a law against those who violate the peace, particularly in those places where divine service

punishment.

is held such as churches and similar places. Namely, if any person, notwithstanding their rank or condition, draws his sword in order to assault another person in these places, he is condemned to losing his hand.[191]

3

Adulterers and lechers.

punishment.

Likewise, against adulterers and lechers, to be taken to Bridewell where they are corrected and their heated bouts of madness cooled.[192]

4

vagabonds and idle persons.

Likewise, against the idle and vagrant, and this is a law which is worthy [fol. 77] of being put into practice by all nations given that laziness and vagrancy bring so many young people to a bad end. The law is this: if the guards of a certain quarter[193] come across a vagabond or idler, if he is of the city and says that he has no work, a means of procuring something for him is found. If they perceive that he does not wish to work or put himself to anything, they forcibly put him in the house called Bridewell. There he is forced to work to earn his keep, and very often his shoulders feel the rod if does not wish to do his duty. If he is 'under the peace' he is sent to his place of origin [fol. 77ᵛ] and given the money to convey himself there. Secondly, if afterwards he is found vagrant and wandering within the jurisdiction of London, his ear is pierced with a hot iron and he is banished. If he is caught there again, he is hanged and strangled.[194]

punishment.

those who are not from the town.

1, punishment

2, punishment

3, punishment

5

beggars

Likewise, against beggars and rogues. If they are of the City, the guards lead them to their quarter, where their alms are ordained, and they are ordered to stay there and no longer to go through the gates. And if they are found there again, they are taken to Bridewell.[195]

punishment.

6

Artisans.
Craftsmen.

[fol. 78] Likewise, against all artisans and people of a craft, if they do not follow the regulations concerning their workmanship, or if they offend in some matter concerning their occupations; to be punished and disciplined by the governors and masters of their Halls.[196]

punishment.

7

violent thieves.

Likewise, against those who against someone's will take or snatch something that the person owns, whether it

punishment.

be money, wares or something else; to be punished as thieves.

8

victuals.

Likewise, concerning all victuals and provisions coming from overseas; not to be sold except at the price set by the Lord Mayor, who has appointed [fol. 78ᵛ] a man especially to see to their distribution.[197]

Now, it would be sheer folly for me to wish to describe everything which pertains to the regulation of

London the noble.

London the noble. However, its policies are so well ordered that nothing better is possible. And I say this again, that London can very rightly be said to be the

Policies.

City of peace, or pacific, for during the day there are officers in each quarter, and also the Aldermen, to prevent any wrong being done to anyone and to do right to everyone. At night the Watch is stationed everywhere after nine o'clock, at which time everyone retires home at the sound of [fol. 79] a great bell which is commonly

Curfew.

called the curfew. And that originates from the ordinance of King William the Conqueror.[19] Likewise — which is worthy of great praise — there is an ordinance that from the first day of November until the first day

William the Conqueror.

of February, a hanging lantern is placed in front of each house on the street frontage, with a lighted candle which should last for three hours. And this is so closely

The Lord Mayor does well to observe this ordinance.

watched that the Lord Mayor likewise often takes pains to go through the streets at night to note and chastise defaulters. This policy is so useful that in every part [fol. 79ᵛ] of the city one can see as clearly as if it is broad daylight from six until nine o'clock in the evening, however overcast the weather might be.[199] If someone is at

good and holy ordinance.

the point of death they sound a bell in the parish of the sick person continuously for three-quarters of an hour so that all who hear it commend the poor patient to God. If he dies, it is indicated by ringing out the bell, otherwise not.[200] This good ruling was made in the time

good King Edward VI.
Sir Thomas Gresham.

of Good King Edward VI in the year 1547, when Sir Thomas Gresham was mayor. If the man who died

honorable procession.

funeral sermon.

doctrine.

charitable work.

this is very notable.

estimable work.

Haberdashers Hall.

Thomas Huntlow.

Sir John Stodey
Haberdashers Hall.

no great quarrels in
London.

belongs to a Hall, all those of the parish who are [fol. 80] of the said Hall proceed to accompany the body in order to bury it with great honour, their hoods resting on their shoulders, so as show both the black and red sides.[201] At the burial an excellent sermon is given by some learned preacher, touching on the miseries of this world, and how the cause of this is sin, and the trust that he who repents should have in the worth of the death of Jesus Christ. Finally, he concludes the sermon with the expectation of the last Resurrection, and an exhortation to lead a holy life.[202]

There are such good systems in place at these Halls that if one of its brothers becomes poor through some misfortune, his Hall gives him a house for free, and grants him a [fol. 80ᵛ] reasonable pension, and finally, provides him with a reasonable sum of money so that he might get himself back on his feet.[203] And if he dies in the same poverty, this grant is transferred to his children, which is a marvellously laudable rule. Haberdashers' Hall is obliged to provide dinner for ten impoverished members of the company or other individuals every three months, as well as to ensure each person is given a penny loaf, a small pot of ale, a piece of silver worth 4 pence in the money of England,[204] and a piece of beef worth a groat on a plate with pottage. The late Thomas [fol. 81] Huntlow, of good memory, bequeathed to the aforementioned Hall several of his inheritances for this end.[205]

Sir John Stodey who was mayor at that time, bequeathed in full to the Hall of the Vintners what we call the Quadrent, in which place the said hall now stands, and other tenements round about, including among others 13 almshouses.[206] I have mentioned these last two points at this juncture not because it would be their proper place, but because I was on the topic of Halls.

Now I return to the policies of London, then I will say something of its Privileges and Liberties.

One does not witness many quarrels in London which escalate into great scandals, [fol. 81ᵛ] for there is a particular policy amongst them that they carry staves as a ready means of defence.[207] Moreover, there are very few shops which do not have a halberd, bill, boar-spear or

quarrels.

oppressors.

'stop', 'stop'.

Arresting someone.

Thieves

25 or 30 thieves are hanged in one day. Severe laws against thieves in England.

Diligent justice.
blood letting in battery.

chimney fire.
Sermon.

4 market days each week.

filth.
London a very clean City.

false money nailed up.

watering the streets in Summer.

some other sort of cudgel with which the owners go out into the street when some fight arises, and by this means can separate the parties.

If anyone publicly does wrong towards someone else, all the bystanders take the side of the victim and try as much as they can to do justice to him.[208] If a sergeant chases and tries to arrest someone who wishes to save himself by fleeing, and cries 'stop, stop', that is to say 'arrestez', all nearby immediately come out [fol. 82] and arrest him, and so the wrongdoer cannot escape. If a sergeant is charged with imprisoning someone, he simply has to touch this person with his silver mace and the other must follow, and if he wishes to flee, the sergeant cries 'stop', etc.

Thieves are pursued to the utmost, so that if an individual who has stolen a sum of money from someone, even if of no great significance, is arrested, he will be hanged. Criminals are tried at all the Sessions, which take place once a month,[209] and there will be some occasions when they hang 25 or 30 in one day. And although the law is likewise severe against larceny, there are nevertheless many unfortunate wretches who [fol. 82ᵛ] fear neither God nor the law, even knowing its severity, but continue this malicious practice to the point at which they are apprehended by the diligence of justice. If two men fight one another and there is blood, a fine of 10 or 12 groats is levied. If a fire takes hold of the chimney of a house, there is a fine of [blank].[210]

There is public preaching every Sunday in St Paul's Churchyard, which usually the Lord Mayor, the Sheriffs and Aldermen, and a great multitude of people attend (Fig. 60).[211]

There is a market day 4 times a week, namely on Monday, Wednesday, Friday and Saturday.[212] [fol. 83] Tumbrels are arranged along all the streets of the city and three times a week they clean up and carry away the waste from the town, so that by this means it remains very clean. If someone carries a false coin, anyone is permitted to nail it to the first pillar he comes across. There is an ordinance that in summer and in hot weather every person is to throw plenty of water into the street by his house in order to avoid the putrefaction which the heat can engender; and this is all the more

water supply in
London.

from where the Judges
of England are chosen.

12 Colleges.

4 principle

8 lesser.

Inns of Court or of
Chancery.

Inner Barristers.

1 Degree.

2 Degree.

3 Degree.

4, and last Degree.

Serjeants of the Coif.

the Coife

easy since in all parts of the city there is a fountain, a pump or a well which provides abundant water.[213] [fol. 83ᵛ]

There is a particular policy regarding the election of judges which involves certain ceremonials redolent of their antiquity. I will relate what I know.

There are 12 colleges of the law in London, including 4 main ones which I have already spoken about above.[214] The 8 others are lesser, and all are Inns of Court or of Chancery. The system is as follows. When the young pupils of the 8 lesser colleges are capable of holding the common disputes which they call Moots, which comes from *motus aut motio* because they move questions, then they are called 'Disputers within the Bar' or pleaders.[215] [fol. 84] This achieved, those who have held their ground well are withdrawn from these lesser colleges and placed in one of the 4 main colleges. And they begin to work their way up the ranks of the law in the Inns of Court and nowhere else. The first degree is called 'utter barrister', namely 'Pleaders outside the Bar'. After this, they have the degree of the Readers in Chancery, namely, those who preside over the apprentices. From this position, they come to be Readers in the Inns of Court, and succeed to this rank by seniority, if they are not prevented by lack of knowledge and learning. From here, they come to a degree which they call Serjeants of the Coif (Fig. 61).[216] This last is bestowed on the individual with much ceremony and expense. For, it is from this rank that all the judges of England are chosen. [fol. 84ᵛ] Now, it happens that every 5, 7 or 8 years Her Majesty is led to understand that there is a dearth of Serjeants of the Coif from which to choose judges. At this point, Her Majesty orders that six be chosen from the Readers of the house[217] of Court. On a certain day those chosen, having invited their relations and friends, are presented to Her Majesty, who confirms them. They are then garbed with long robes, dyed half in tawny grey-violet, and half in black, and a cap of fine linen cloth is placed on their head. Then they give many gold rings first to Her Majesty, and then to many others. Then they all go to dine, where there is a sumptuous [fol. 85] feast, which the Lord Mayor, Sheriffs and the Aldermen their brethren attend. After dinner, they all

Fig. 61. William Bendlowes (1516-84), a prominent serjeant
at law from 1555, retired about 1579. This portrait, dated
1564, shows him wearing the white coif and scarlet hood
and tabard of his order. See J.H. Baker (2004).
© *St John's College, Cambridge.*

process to the great Church of St Paul to give thanks to
God, wearing their parti-coloured robes and the coif on
their head. And they must wear this dress for a whole
year. Now, when a judge is required, he is chosen from
these. And at this juncture, I will content myself with
what I have said about the policies of London.

Chapter 13

On the privileges and liberties
of the City of London.

privileges and
liberties.

their privileges are
written in the Saxon
tongue and in the
characters of the
same.

This bishop is buried
in the nave of the
Church of St Paul

on page 61 of
this book.[218]

King John confirmed
and augmented them.

King Henry III, the
same

free traffic

All Englishmen like
the game of archery.

communes around
London

3,000 archers
3,000 archers for one
prize

The privileges and liberties of the noble [fol. 85ᵛ] and triumphant city of London are so great and numerous, that I do not desire to recite each one in detail, but merely a selection which might be a means of considering the rest. These privileges were conferred upon it a long time ago by its first kings and were confirmed by their successors and greatly augmented, especially by Edward the Confessor. William the Conqueror had withdrawn their privileges, but as a result of the steadfast perseverance and entreaties of a good bishop (as mentioned above), they were restored and greatly augmented, [fol. 86] and so the city was not at all ungrateful to the bishop for this benefit. Following his death, they erected in his honour a most beautiful tomb of marble, as one sees above in the account of the church of St Paul. These liberties were confirmed by King John in 1227.[219] Furthermore, he granted the city of London a common seal that it was to hold from that point onwards, and each sheriff was granted two clerks.[220] These liberties were also confirmed by Henry III who, in a further addition, granted the city the county of Middlesex.[221] The burgesses of London enjoy the privilege of trading and dealing in any commodity throughout [fol. 86ᵛ] the kingdom of England, while others cannot trade in London without having the freedom of the city.[222]

Owing to the natural love and devotion of every Englishman, especially those of London, when it comes to archery, kings have presented the people with many empty spaces and pastures around the city in which they practise on festivals. It is true that formerly the common people of the surrounding villages caused trouble for the Londoners and have demonstrated this by their actions, but they have been punished for this.[223] This good practice has often encouraged Londoners to set up prizes, such that I have, on one occasion, counted 3,000 archers [fol. 87] all in one match for a prize. And in good weather, parishes compete against one another, and perform so well that it is a great strength for the city.

free of toll
throughout England

free warren around
London.

The citizens of London can deliver and receive their wares throughout England without paying a toll. This was granted to them by King Henry III in the year 1226.[224] He also granted them the right to hunt on a certain circuit around the city and its appurtenances.[225] Indeed, in order to uphold this possession, once a year the Lord Mayor, accompanied by his brothers, the Sheriffs and Aldermen and several other citizens go

the Mayor's Hunt.

hunting.[226] [fol 87ᵛ]

For the greatest illustration of the singularities of London, I must put first and singularly the good manners, the honesty and, above all, the charity of the noble citizens of London. And especially the piety of many, who have profited so well in the school of Jesus Christ that when he comes to judge the quick and the dead, many will come, especially a great number of those poor people banished following the quarrel concerning Jesus Christ,[227] bearing and presenting him with the benefits they received from the citizens of London at their time of dire need. At that time, they will hear the voice of the Lord, which will say unto them: I was a stranger and you took me in.[228] May you enjoy eternal life. [fol. 88]

The Author's Prayer

That is everything I have been able to discover of the beauties, kindness and perfections of this so flourishing and triumphant city of London. May the eternal and all-powerful Lord uphold this city and make it increasingly prosper. May he also maintain and fill with his favours the noble Magistracy and Senate of this city. And finally, may he desire to place under his protection the good and virtuous citizens and inhabitants of this city until the end. Amen.

End.

NOTES TO THE TRANSLATION

Title page

1. At top right in a seventeenth-century hand. This style of catalogue- or shelf-number, typically in this position on the first folio, indicates that the MS had once been part the collection of Paul Pétau (1568-1614), the French scholar, bibliophile, numismatist, and jurist, who from 1588 onwards was a counsellor to the Parlement of Paris. Many of his books were later acquired by Queen Christina of Sweden and similar catalogue numbers, sometimes in association with his name, appear in many items of the BAV, MSS Reginenses Latini and in those items from Christina's collection later acquired by the University of Leiden. See Wilmart 1937-45: *passim*; de Meyier 1947: 1-23, 25, 28, 29-31. See also above, pp. 19-20.

Epistle

2. The heading of this dedication (identified in running headings as *Epistre*) resembles that of 'The Epistle Dedicatory' which John Stow included in the 1567 and later editions of his *Summarie*, to which he put his name as 'Your most humble Iohn Stowe'; he had dedicated earlier editions to Robert Dudley, earl of Leicester. Grenade may also have been influenced by the dedication in Corrozet 1561. See above p. 40.

3. Grenade seems usually to use *republique* in the sense of *res publica* or 'common good' or 'commonwealth', not to denote the state (the kingdom of England) or the political status or structure of London, but sometimes he comes close to using it to denote the city's particular form of government with its degree of independence under the monarch. For the varying meanings of the term 'commonwealth' in early modern England, see Knights 2011; cf above, p. 29.

4. The model for this characterisation is presumably that of the Madonna holding the baby Jesus to her breast. For Londoners' response to the influx of alien migrants, see above, pp. 49-53.

5. It is not clear which detractors Grenade specifically had in mind, but it is noteworthy that Stow appended to his 1598 *Survey* the *Apologie*, drafted round about the same time Grenade was writing, *c.*1580, and possibly by the lawyer James Dalton (although all too often confused with Stow's own voice), a response to 'the opinion of some men, which thinke that the greatnes of that Cittie standeth not with the profit and securitie of this Realme'. Thomas Digges, in a characteristic intervention in the parliament of 1585, invoked the corporeal analogies to drive home the point. 'London is the belly, or if yow will, the head of England, yet I pray yow lett the legges and handes lyve by it'. Stow, *Survey*: ii. 196-217, 387n; Hartley 1981-95: ii. 112. For the changing perceptions of London in the period, see Slack 2000.

6. Grenade expresses this ambition again on fol. 48 (p. 109). So far as we are aware, Grenade did not complete this project. Praise of the noteworthy men associated with a city was a standard element in *laudes civitatis*. Several of the people Grenade mentions in this text are cast as heroes and presumably would have been included in his projected work, for example: Bishop William, Richard Castel, Simon Eyre, Thomas Gresham, and Richard Whittington. In his *Survey of London*, first published in 1598, John Stow included a long section entitled 'Honor of Citizens, and worthiness of men in the same'; those mentioned include four women (Stow, *Survey*: i. 104-17); see also above, p. 30.

7. Presumably 25 March 1578, Easter being on 30 March that year.

Preface

8. The notion of Britain as a country divided from the rest of the world originated with Virgil, *Eclogues* i.66: *Et penitus toto divisos orbe Britannos* ('And the Britons, wholly sundered from the rest of the world'). The phrase *divisus ab orbe* was used on the first of the triumphal arches celebrating the *Monarchia Britannica* at King James's entry to the city in 1604 (Smuts 2007: 235-6).

9. Grenade's celebration of London's global impact seems to anticipate Hakluyt 1903-5: vol. 5, pp. xx, xxi, xl, xliii). The Muscovy Company had received its charter in 1555; the enthusiasm about the Cathay trade probably reflected the ongoing expeditions of Martin Frobisher to seek out the north-western passage (Willan 1956; McDermott 2001). London's distant trading contacts had been celebrated by FitzStephen, in his description of London written in 1173-4, which includes a verse listing the distant lands or peoples sending expensive goods to London: Arabia, Sabaea (Yemen), the Scythians, Babylon (denoting Cairo), the Nile, China, Gaul, the Norwegians, and the Russians. The verse, otherwise unknown, was prompted by references in Virgil's *Georgics* i.57 and ii.115-17 to goods supplied to Italy from Lydia, Pontus and Cappadocia, Media, Ethiopia, India, the Sabaeans and the Seres (traders in or makers of silk in N.W. China). There is no reason to doubt the accuracy of FitzStephen's list, which Grenade may have known. Grenade would certainly have seen the text on the B & H Map (1572) which celebrated the role of the river Thames in conveying to London ships carrying 'the goods of the entire globe' (Fig. 1).

10. Author of *Les Illustrations de Gaule et singularitez de Troye*, a three-volume 'history' and reworking of the Trojan legend, published in Paris between 1511 and 1513, with subsequent reprints; his literary style was much admired; the section concerning Troy may have been the original work, not intended to be published with *Les Illustrations*, which is the less coherent of the two (Krem 1994). Grenade's use of the Dutch form of Jean Lemaire de Belges's first name, if not a scribal error, may express his antipathy to the latter's Roman Catholicism and his close association with Margaret of Austria, governor of the Netherlands from 1507 to 1530, whom he served as her librarian, and under whose rule the first Protestant martyrs were burned in 1524 and 1525. Nevertheless, Grenade may have borrowed from him the word *singularitez* for the title of his work on London, either directly or via Corrozet's book on Paris, which also cites him as an authority. See n. 11, below, and the discussion above, at pp. 36-7.

11. These ancient cities and authors became increasingly well known during the sixteenth century, not least as a result of the editions and translations of texts. Nineveh was capital of Assyria before Babylon became capital of Babylonia; the *History* of Herodotus of Halicarnassus, written before 425 BC, focuses on the Persian Wars and contains much about both cities; Diodorus Siculus, a native of Sicily, wrote a universal history to 60 BC; Berossos (fl. 290 BC), was a Babylonian scholar who wrote a Babylonian history which survives only in fragments (see Werbrugghe and Wickersham 1996). In the history of Troy and in the identity of 'Homer' as author of the Iliad, which tells the story of the Trojan War, it is difficult to distinguish reality from myth; the works of the poet Ovid (Publius Ovidius Naso, 43 BC – AD 17), especially *Metamorphoses* and *Heroides*, relate many stories concerning Troy; for the work and influence of Jean Lemaire de Belges, see above, note 10. Livy (Titus Livius, 59 BC –17 AD) wrote a substantial history of Rome (*Ab urbe condita libri*) from its origin to 9 BC; the major work of Plutarch, philosopher and biographer (d. after A.D. 120), was his 'Parallel Lives', which focuses on the lives of great men and became a major source of knowledge of the ancient world, especially after its publication in a French translation (Amyot 1558). The capture and destruction of Numantia in AD 133 marked the end of Iberian resistance to Rome; its inhabitants killed themselves rather than submit; the story became well known with the appearance of Appian's 'Spanish Wars' in 1557 and from then

on prompted much imaginative literature, especially in Spain (Dobson 2008: 12, 43-6). The Loeb Classical Library editions and translations of these works by Herodotus, Diodorus Siculus, Ovid, Livy, and Plutarch contain indexes which identify material on these cities.

    With the exception of the fragments of Berossos, French translations of all of these works would have been available to Grenade: see Amyot 1554, 1558; Bersuire 1515; Marot 1556; Salel 1545, 1570; Saliat 1556, 1570 A Latin edition of Berossos was published in Rome in 1498 and in Antwerp in 1552: see Nanni 1498 and Berossos 1552. See also de Blignières 1851 and entries in the catalogue of the Bibliothèque nationale de France. In citing Berossos, Grenade may have been influenced by Jean Lemaire des Belges, who cited Manetho, the Greek historian of Egypt, in his account of the foundation of Paris, a citation mentioned in early editions of Corrozet's account of Paris (1532-39). The spurious fragments of Manetho's supplement to Berossos were associated with the editions of Berossos published in 1498 and 1552.

12. Members of Grenade's family in London appear to have migrated from Brabant (probably Antwerp) during the 1530s, in which case he may have perceived the capital of his nation to be Brussels. On the other hand, by 1578 he appears to have identified himself as a Frenchman whose capital city was Paris, the largely historical account of which by Gilles Corrozet (d. 1568) was widely read. By 1578, when Grenade completed his text, Corrozet's work, first published in 1532, had appeared, under various titles, in at least four new editions and five reprints (some pirated) containing additional or rearranged material supplied by himself and others (Corrozet 1532, 1533, 1539, 1543,1550, 1555, 1561, 1571, and 1577). There are several indications that Grenade was influenced by Corrozet's work, in particular the editions of 1550 or 1561: for further discussion, see pp. 36-40.

13. King of Gerar: Genesis 20-1.

14. Father-in-law and uncle of Jacob: Genesis 24, 29, 31.

Chapter 1

15. The identity of this fool is uncertain. Grenade possibly alludes to Polydore Vergil, who in the dedication to King Henry VIII, dated 1533, of his *Anglica Historia* refers to 'the nature of Britain (which is now England)' (*Britanniae, quae nunc Angliae est soli natura*), but makes no reference to the brevity of its language. Polydore had thoroughly undermined the myth of the Trojan Brutus and his role in history of Britain, to which Grenade adhered. Grenade may have conflated this with a memory of the remark in Fabyan (1811: 11) that King Lud ordered New Troy to be called Lud's Town, 'which by shortness of speech we now call London', or with a memory of its almost identical rendering in Grafton, *Chronicle* 1569: 36. If Grenade came across this reference in the works of Grafton, then, if Grenade was acquainted with Stow (as seems possible: see above, pp. 29-30), the fool in question was probably Grafton.

16. Much of Grenade's version of the mythical early history and later more genuine (but frequently erroneous) history of London appears to derive from two rival publications: Grafton, *Abridgement*, of which four editions (1563, 1564, 1570 and 1572) appeared before Grenade completed his text in 1578, and Stow, *Summarie,* of which seven editions appeared before 1578 (1565, 1566a, 1566b, 1567, 1570, 1573, 1575). The account of Brutus, the foundation of London and later mythical rulers was ultimately derived from Geoffrey of Monmouth (i. 3), of which the version published in Fabyan's *Chronicles* (Fabyan 1811) was closely followed in Grafton, *Abridgement* and also in Stow, *Summarie.* Stow's version is fuller than that in Grafton (1564), but derived the dates from Grafton, who was interested in chronology and supplied a long series of dates from the origin of the world for many events before the birth of Christ, as well as the dates BC, while Stow usually supplied only dates

BC. Fabyan (1811) supplies many dates from the origin of the world, but Grafton used a system which estimated the age of the world as 1207 years less than the system employed by Fabyan, and only two years longer than in the comprehensive table published in Lucidus 1546, which he may have seen. Grenade's use of the spelling *Posthumius* indicates that he had consulted one or more of the first four or five editions of Stow, *Summarie*. This spelling was replaced by the form *Posthumus* in editions of 1570 or later (the relevant pages of the BL copy of the 1570 edition are missing). All other texts, including Grafton's, spell the name as Siluius Posthumus.

Grenade's account of London Bridge (see n. 80) indicates that he also consulted the 1570 or later editions of Stow, *Summarie* and/or Grafton, *Abridgement,* and that he could have consulted Grafton *Abridgement* 1564: see below, n. 56. His account of the Tower of London indicates that he consulted Stow, *Summarie* (1566a): see below, n. 48. More extensive comparison between Grenade's text and the successive editions of these works would probably add to this preliminary indication of Grenade's reading.

17. Grenade miscopied as 1188 the date of 1108 BC given by Grafton and Stow, who both imply that the date concerned Brutus's landing in Britain rather than the founding of London, which took place a little later. Geoffrey of Monmouth (i. 17, 18) noted that Brutus founded London about the time that the judge Eli ruled Judea and the Philistines captured the Ark of the Covenant (cf. I Samuel, iv, noting that Eli died on hearing of the theft of the Ark). Neither Grafton *Abridgement* nor Stow *Summarie* mention Eli in connection with the story of Brutus, but Grafton's much fuller *Chronicle* (1569) mentions him twice: once (p. 31) in connection with Brutus's arrival in Britain, giving a date of 2804 since the origin of the world and 1108 BC; and once (p. 36) in connection with London's foundation 456 years before Rome (putting London's foundation in the year 2755 BC according to the computation used by Grafton). The edition of John Hardyng's chronicle printed by Grafton (fol. 17) dated Brutus's landing to the year 4084 since the origin of the world, 1115 BC and the 18th year of Hely's (Eli's) rule (Hardyng 1543/4: fol. 17). Grenade presumably encountered the dating by reference to Eli in one of these works, in which case he ignored the dates they gave or perhaps he found it the Paris edition of Geoffrey of Monmouth's *History* (1508, reprinted 1517). He was probably responsible for replacing it with the story of the Levite, which may reflect his interest in punishment, combined with the fact that Eli was a Levite. Lily (1548a: fol. 57) gave the date of Brutus's arrival as 2850 years after the origin of the world. Grafton certainly consulted another part of Lily's work included in the same volume (Lily, 1548a, fol. 110; Grafton, *Chronicle* 1569: 592), as Grenade may also have done, see n. 186, below.

18. Geoffrey of Monmouth (iii.20) is the original source for the story of Lud and the evolution of the name London. Grafton (*Abridgement*:1564) dates Lud's activities to 3894 years after the origin of the world and 69 BC, and in this is followed by Stow (*Summarie*: 1565 and later editions). Grafton (*Chronicle* 1569: 36) noted that Lud's Town 'by shortness of speech became London'. Grenade himself seems to have been responsible for the form *Londinum*. For the likely origin of the name London well before Roman rule in Britain, see Coates 1998.

19. An early account of the view of London from Highgate, providing a good sense of the landscape around the city, although the more distant features mentioned would not have been visible, which suggests that Grenade supplemented the view by consulting a map. See above, pp. 35-6.

20. The actual length of the Thames is 215 English miles from its source to the sea. Grenade may be thinking here of the distance from London to the sea: to the estuary the distance is 40 miles. A text on the map which Grenade almost certainly used (Fig. 1) states that the Thames carried to London ships laden with goods from overseas over a distance of 60,000 paces. By Grenade's paces (see n. 88) this would have been 28.4 miles, and by Roman *passus* twice as long.

21. Grenade's characterization is approximately correct. In 1567-8 the ships from overseas entering the port of London included one of 200 tons, one of 400 and one of 500; the others were all in the range 7 to 130 tons, the great majority being less than 100 tons (Dietz 1972). Cargo boats on the river upstream of London would have been at the lower end of this range. The carrying capacity of the flat bottomed vessels known as shouts, which were common on the middle Thames in this period, ranged from about 12 to 40 tons, calculated by converting estimates of the volumes of wheat carried to weight (Langdon 2007).

22. This distance between London and Oxford, if 20 French leagues, was equivalent to about 40 English miles, a substantial underestimate since Oxford was 120 miles by river from London. Grenade may have been thinking of Henley-on-Thames, a major port for shipping to and from London along the river, which was 68 miles from London along the Thames. Alternatively, Grenade was thinking of the distance between London and Oxford as the crow flies (55 miles).

23. Grenade seems to mean that the goods abounded in Oxford.

24. This practice of celebrating safe arrival in the port of London, or in the shelter of the Thames, had a long history for in the early thirteenth century it was customary for the crews of ships carrying wine from Lorraine, as they passed at the Isle of Grain at the entry to the river, to sing the Kyrie, raise their standards and so progress to London Bridge (Bateson 1902: 499-500, and for the date Keene 2008b).

25. The target range of a harquebus was perhaps 200 metres, but its effective or 'battle' range may have been as little as half of that. Speed's maps of Middlesex, Kent and Surrey (1610) identify only 4 'villages' within 400m of the continuously built up area; within 1 km there were eight and within 2km eleven.

Chapter 2

26. Grafton (*Abridgement* 1564 and later editions) dates Lud's building activities in London to 3894 years from the origin of the world and 69 BC. Grenade probably copied these numbers carelessly. The name Ludgate, of English origin, probably means 'postern': Ekwall (1962), 91.

27. See Chapter 9 (pp. 107-9), note 114, and Fig. 43.

28. Mayor 1437-8; the Conduit, at the south end of Shoe Lane, was built by his executors in 1453 (Stow, *Survey*: ii. 41). Grafton (*Abridgement* 1570: fol. 109) gives a more elaborate account, stating that Eastfield built it in 1438 and providing details of water piped from Tyburn and also to the Great Conduit in Cheapside. Stow, *Summarie* does not mention this conduit

29. Given that it cost about £30 per annum to study at the inns of court, they tended to be the preserve of gentlemen to a greater extent than the universities. Wilfrid Prest's data from the slightly later period of 1590-1639 shows that 40.6% of entrants came from the upper echelons of the landed elite (peers and esquires), another 47.8% from the ranks of mere gentlemen, and just 7.8% from bourgeois-professional backgrounds. Lawrence Stone concurs with Grenade that Gray's Inn was the most aristocratic, with the names of 23 of the 74 pre-1603 peerage families in its admission register. But it was also the biggest recruiter overall. Gray's Inn was admitting 49 men per annum in the 1570s, ahead of the Middle Temple (42 per annum), Lincoln's Inn (37), and the Inner Temple (30). In the light of Grenade's remark on the importance of the quality of the air, it is interesting that almost contemporary with Grenade is the tract on civility, *Cyuile and vncyuile life,* which justifies suburban living on the grounds of the healthy air quality, and debates the merits of the city life over the countryside: 'The manner of the most gentlemen and noble men also is to house themselves (if possible they may) in the suburbes of the cittie, because most commonly the ayre there

beeinge somewhat at large the place is healthy, and through the distaunce from the bodye of the towne, the noyse not much and so consequently quiet. Also for commoditie wee finde many lodginges, both spacious and roomethy with gardaines and orchardes very delectable. So as with good government wee have as little cause to feare infection there as in the verye countrey'. Prest 1972: 27-32, 244; Stone 1965: 690-1, *Cyuile and vncyuile life* 1579: sig. L4.

30. Paolo Giovio (1548: fol. 13ᵛ) noted that in a London school interpreters of civil law taught young men the peculiar laws established by the kings which were written partly in English and partly in French, and that French was so familiar in the hall and the market place that it came to be known even by nobles and women. Both Paolo Giovio's and Grenade's accounts presumably refer to statutes, which were read aloud and discussed in law-French at the Readings held at the Inns of Court (see below, fols 83ᵛ-84 and pp. 142-3 and notes), rather than to the earlier supposed law codes written in French (see below, fol. 75 (p. 136-7), and n. 188).

31. The episcopal inns along the Strand had largely passed into lay hands in the 1530s and 1540s through a series of forced exchanges. The inns of the bishops of Chester, Llandaff, and Worcester were pulled down and incorporated into Somerset House; Durham House was in the occupation of the earl of Essex in 1572 and Sir Walter Ralegh from 1583 to 1603; the former Carlisle House was in the hands of the Russells, earls of Bedford during Elizabeth's reign; Bath House had passed to the earls of Arundel, and Exeter House to the queen's favourite, the earl of Leicester; Norwich Inn was now owned by the archbishop of York and became known as York House, but it was leased to successive lords keepers of the Seal. John Norden's 1593 map of Westminster delineates clearly the aristocratic nature of the Thames waterfront, marking from west to east, York House, Durham House, Russell House, Somerset House, Arundel House, and Leicester House. Norden also provided an account of the houses in his *Speculum Britanniae*. See Figs 11, 14; Kingsford 1916, 1917, 1920; Goldring et al. 2014: v. 132-5.

32. An early observation of fine shops along Fleet Street and the Strand.

33. Charing Cross, which stood in the middle of the road at the junction between the streets now known as Whitehall, Cockspur Street and The Strand, was the largest and most elaborate of the twelve crosses erected by King Edward I, between 1291 and 1294, to mark the places at which the embalmed body of his queen, Eleanor (d.1290), rested on its journey to Westminster for burial. The cross was a polygonal structure of considerable size containing much Purbeck marble and with a cross on top (*KW*: i. 479-85). If Grenade was estimating by means of a fathom (*toise*) of six feet, the structure would have been between 150 and 180 feet high. Cotgrave (1673) identifies a carpenter's toise of 5.5 feet, which would suggest a height of between 137.5 and 165 feet. These estimates seem very high, but may not exaggerate excessively since Wyngaerde's panorama of *c.*1544 (Fig. 14) shows the cross to have risen well above nearby buildings, including Durham House, and possibly to have been about as high as the nave roof of Westminster (101 feet to the keystones of the nave vault and about 118 feet to the ridge of the nave roof). Charing Cross, therefore, may have been more than 100 feet (30.5 m) high. For comparison, Nelson's column, which stands 50 yards north of the site of Charing Cross, is 169 feet 3 inches high. Charing Cross seems certainly to have risen higher than the Cheapside Cross (see pp. 110-111 and note 123). None of the Eleanor Crosses outside London appear to have risen much above 40 feet. John Norden described Charing Cross as an 'olde and auncient wetherbeaton monument' (Goldring et al. 2014: v. 138).

34. Henry VIII acquired the leper hospital of St James and meadows round about in 1531, and made there a 'fayre mansion and a parke' and other houses, work largely completed by 1541; the mansion, now St James's Palace, survives today: *KW*: iv 241-4.

35. Many other visitors got to see the inside of Whitehall Palace, but Grenade's description of the palaces is confined to Westminster Hall, perhaps on account of his special interest in the law courts there.

36. The number of cases heard at the royal courts in Westminster Hall was increasing rapidly in Grenade's time (Blatcher 1978: 20-2; Brooks 1986: 75-107), accentuating the economic impact of the law terms. In 1573-4 the Lord Mayor reported that the weekly consumption of corn for bread in the city was 1,571 quarters during the law term and 1,400 quarters out of term, an increase of 12 per cent (BL, MS Cotton Faustina C.II, fols 174-5; LMA, COL/CA/01/01/020, fols 182v-6.). Parliament met not in the hall, as Grenade seems to imply, but in St Stephen's Chapel.

37. In discussing Westminster Hall, John Norden explained that 'the timber wherewith it is covered came all out of Ireland for that it is observed that noe spiders webb is seene in any part of the same'. Jill Husselby, in a new edition of the extracts of Norden's *Speculum Britanniae* used by the antiquarian John Nichols, explains that it was believed that the roof of the Hall was made of sweet chestnut which 'does not attract beetles, and with less to feed on, few spiders'. But the roof was in fact of oak. If the timbers came from Ireland (which they did not), then the absence of spiders was a result of the legend of that St Patrick had banished vermin from Ireland (Goldring et al. 2014: v. 131). Grenade seems confused here and perhaps based his remarks on hearsay rather than observation, for the roof of Westminster Hall was neither ceiled nor panelled, as would be implied by his term *lambrisee*.

38. The keystones of the nave vault are 103 feet above the floor, significantly less than the vaults at Amiens and Beauvais (*KW*: i. 152-4). The ridge of the roof was about 37 feet higher, making 140 feet in all, about 15 feet higher than the ridge of the nave roof at St Paul's (see note 123).

39. Under Gabriel Goodman, dean from 1561 to 1601, the abbey became a by-word for liturgical conservatism; its organ was maintained and its choir flourished. Elizabeth's charter for the abbey provided for a musical foundation of six petty canons, ten choristers, and twelve lay vicars. Merritt 2001; MacCulloch 1999: 210-13; Carpenter 1966: 416-24; Saunders, J. 1997.

40. The brass enclosure containing the tomb of Henry VII and his queen was just to the east of the altar of the new Lady Chapel the king had built. Construction work began in 1503 and lasted ten years, costing approximately £14,000. Pietro Torrigiano accepted the commission for the tomb in 1512 and it was completed in 1518. For a comprehensive survey of the chapel, see the essays in Tatton-Brown and Mortimer 2003; also *KW*: iii. 210-22; and for the tomb, Sherlock 2005.

41. Edward VI was buried under 'the High Altar of brass' at the head of Henry VII's tomb (Sandford 1677: 497-8, which illustrates the Renaissance structure of the altar as it had been before the Interregnum). Edward might have expected to have been buried with his father Henry VIII at Windsor, but Mary chose to bury him close to his grandfather.

42. Edward the Confessor, canonised in 1161, had been buried before the high altar of the church he had built. In 1163 his remains were moved to an elevated position behind the high altar, an arrangement which was replicated when Henry III rebuilt the abbey, unfinished at the time of his death in 1272; St Edward's relics were translated to their new site in 1269; this elaborate shrine, decorated with Cosmati inlaid panels and with Cosmati pavements nearby, expressed the abbey's direct affiliation to Rome and was completed ten or more years later (Fig. 19). The shrine was severely damaged at the dissolution of the abbey (the golden feretory with its associated images of kings and saints was irretrievably lost, having been melted down), and was subject to a hasty and limited restoration by Abbot Feckenham during the Marian reaction in 1557; there was another bout of iconoclasm in 1561, but Feckenham's work has largely survived. *KW*: i. 130-59; Binski 1995: 94-101.

43. As a teenager in 1220, on the day before his second coronation (his first had been in 1216 at Gloucester, on account of the civil war) Henry III laid the foundation stone of the Lady Chapel added to Edward the Confessor's church. His own rebuilding of the church began in 1245. The date 1220 is not mentioned by Stow or Grafton and so Grenade probably learned of it during his visit to the abbey. Henry III's body lay first in the former grave of St Edward, but about 1280 his son, King Edward I, commissioned a new tomb of severely Roman design, in a position of honour close to the shrine of St Edward, with Cosmateque work and prominent porphyry panels which alluded more widely to imperial models of rule; Henry's body was translated to this tomb in 1290 and the cast metal effigy was added 20 years later. Grenade is impressed by the Cosmatesque decoration. See Fig. 19; *KW*: i. 130-2, 147-50; Binski 1995: 95, 101-2.

44. The ridge of the nave roof was significantly was higher than that at St Paul's, see notes 38, 123.

Chapter 3

45. There was a gate on this site in Roman times, and almost certainly in the ninth century; it was presumably rebuilt, probably not for the first time, during the twelfth century and was known as Newgate by 1188; it was rebuilt (probably partially) by the executors of Richard Whittington in 1423-32, and was repaired in 1555-6. By the 1590s there is evidence of some disrepair, but there was no major overhaul until 1628-30. The prison occupied a plot adjoining the gate, and dates back to at least 1187-9; it was rebuilt by Whittington's executors with a hall and chapel between 1423 and 1432. The prison's capacity is unclear, but conditions were undoubtedly overcrowded. Recorder Fleetwood records a 'great sessions' of 200 at Newgate in October 1578; an informant from 1588 claims that between 80 and 140 prisoners were brought to Newgate for every sessions, but these figures would have excluded longer term residents, including some of the seminary priests, of whom there were up to 55 at any one time. Its internal structure is unclear at this date, and the London prisons are crying out for proper scholarly investigation, but there were supposedly separate chambers for freemen and freewomen (presumably the wives and widows of citizens) respectively to the north and south of the hall; foreigners (not free of the city) were to be lodged in the 'mean chambers', while felons were housed in the two lower chambers and supposedly held in irons; the notorious 'Limbo' was the fate of those put on a bread and water diet. The semi-privatized prison administration was a by-word for corruption. The keepers needed to recoup the investment they had made in securing the office (one man spent £496 on securing the position in 1615) and were incentivized to exploit the complex structure of prison fees (laid down by act of common council in 1488, and revised by the court of aldermen in orders for the prison in 1574) to their advantage, and efforts at reform were undermined by patronage relationships. William Crowther, dismissed by the aldermen for his irregularities in 1580 was nevertheless able to draw on the support of Lord Chancellor Hatton to secure a favourable pension from the aldermen. His successor, William Dyos, was accused of corruption on a staggering scale in a report to Burghley in 1588, but he remained in office until his death in 1593. Stow, *Survey*: i. 35-7, ii. 361-2; Pugh 1970 :103-9, 188-9, 332-3, 340-2, 350, 356-63; Harben 1918: 432; Dobb 1964: 87-100; McConville 1981: 1-21; McGrath and Rowe 1991: 416, 420; HMC Hatfield: ii. 222; LMA, COL/CC/01/01/009, fols 140v-3; COL/CA/01/01/019, fols 204, 347v; COL/CA/01/01/020, fols 180v, 207v-209v, 307; COL/CA/01/01/022, fols 96, 102, 103, 104v, 154, 243v, 299r-v; COL/CA/01/01/024, fols 126v, 131, 132, 215v; COL/CA/01/01/025 fols 31r-v, 104v, 351; COL/CA/01/01/050, fols 451v-8; COL/RMD/PA/01/001, nos. 24, 116, 117, 185, 187, 188; PRO, SP12/165/5; BL, Lansdowne MS 56/5-7, fols 15-26.

46. St Sepulchre's parish, partly within and partly without the jurisdiction of the city, was indeed

the most populous parish in London, but the figure for communicants is surely wrong as only 3,400 were recorded in 1548, and 7,500 in the mid 1630s. Although the population was growing, it was at nothing like the rate Grenade's figure would imply. Kitching (1980), no. 13; Lambeth Palace Library, MS CM VIII/4, fols 4-5.

47. In 1578 there were 110 parish churches within the area on the north side of the Thames subject to the jurisdiction of the City of London, of which the parishes of five extended beyond the city jurisdiction. Further out, but within or just beyond the continuously built-up area there were five parish churches to the west, two to the north, four to the east (including the Tower), and five across the river in Southwark (from 1550, formally incorporated within the City as its twenty-sixth ward) making 126 in all. Grenade's total could have covered a slightly different selection from the outlying churches and possibly ignored some churches which served former religious precincts. It is likely that most, if not all, of the parish churches in the city, and most of those just outside, had been established by c.1100. In the 1170s FitzStephen noted that London and its suburb contained 13 conventual churches and 126 lesser parochial ones. FitzStephen's total probably applied to the city and extra-mural settlements on the north bank of the Thames, within the diocese of London; the figures may have been supplied by the archdeacon of London, whose responsibility extended beyond the city walls and a little beyond the formal limit of the city suburbs as defined by about 1220. Southwark was in the diocese of Winchester and so churches there may not have been included in FitzStephen's totals. These figures were probably recycled and adjusted from that time onwards. Commonplace books from the fifteenth century onwards often included lists of the London parishes, but the number depended in part on the area to which one referred. Richard Arnold in his so-called chronicle of 1503 (which owes a lot to the commonplace book tradition) listed 118 churches in London and the suburbs; Stow came up with the figure of 123, of which 114 were in the 26 wards of London and Southwark, 9 in the suburbs adjacent, 2 in the Duchy of Lancaster estate in the western suburbs, and 2 in Westminster. The herald William Smith (he was also a member of the Haberdashers' Company) listed 110 parish churches 'within the liberties' and 10 in the parishes adjacent to the city in 1588, as well as 12 churches 'which are not parish churches', though in an earlier version of his manuscript, commenced in 1575 but with later additions, the list is corrected by the deletion of St Sythe's in Bucklersbury (an alternative name for the church of St Benet Sherehog) to produce a revised total of 109 within the liberties. By the reign of Elizabeth, the bills of mortality were beginning to influence ways of thinking about the metropolitan space. So, the 1582 bills listed deaths within the 96 parishes within the walls, and the 11 without the walls and within the liberties; in 1603 the 8 out parishes adjacent to the city were added to the enumerations. Riley ed. 1860: i. 3, 228-38; Douce 1811: 75-7; Stow, *Survey*: ii. 137-43, 219; BL, Harleian MS 6363, fols 3ᵛ-4ᵛ; LMA, CLC/262/MS02463, fols. 2ᵛ-3v; *Number* 1582/3; Wilson 1930: 194, 200; Robertson 1996.

48. The conduit, first erected in 1498, stood next to Holborn Cross at the junction of Snow Lane, Cow Lane and Cock Lane. William Lamb, gentleman of the Chapel Royal, re-established it in 1577, supplying it with water carried more than 2,000 yards from springs in Lamb's Conduit Fields (now Coram's Fields) in a lead pipe which crossed Holborn Bridge. Stow, *Survey*: ii, 34; Archer 2004a.

49. For this, see below, pp. 65-6, 142-3 and notes 214-17.

50. The hospital and the adjoining priory initially associated with it were founded in 1123 by Rahere, a canon of St Paul's who became well-known to the king and his courtiers through his prominence at court revels; Stow later characterised him as the king's minstrel. In 1538, in the midst of the general dissolution, the city began an extensive lobbying campaign to save St Bartholomew's Hospital and a few other religious houses. In 1544 Henry VIII refounded St Bartholomew's and in 1546, in response to further pressure from the citizens

he reconstituted it as 'the House of the Poore in West Smithfield' with provision for 100 poor men and poor women. Moore 1918: ii.149-61; Barron and Davies 2007: 90-5, 149-55; Stow, *Survey*: ii. 25.

51. The name probably means 'smooth field'. For the market, see Archer, Barron, Harding (1988): 71, 93-4. FitzStephen describes the weekly horse-market in Smithfield and horse-races which accompanied it. The fair, perhaps established before 1100, was in the reign of Henry II (1154-89) in the possession of St Bartholomew's Priory. By the mid sixteenth century it had become famous for its great trade in woollen cloth. A number of the earlier executions said by sixteenth-century authors to have taken place at Smithfield, in fact had taken place at Tyburn, the historic site of capital punishment for London and Middlesex. In the sixteenth century, however, it was still used for the executions of heretics by burning and for the boiling alive of those guilty of petty treason (wives killing their husbands). Dillon 2008; Minson 2013: 106.

52. The church of the former priory of St John of Jerusalem, the headquarters of the Hospital of St John in England, founded *c*.1140 and dissolved in 1540; the headquarters of the order itself were removed to Rhodes in 1310 and in 1530 to Malta. Much of the church was destroyed in 1546, the material being used for Somerset House (Barron and Davies 2007: 294-309). The church is probably shown on Fig. 22, in the distance just west of the tower of St Paul's.

53. Grenade appears to have used a pace of 2.5 feet (see note 88). The width stated here, between 62.5 and 75 feet, is the same as that stated for Cheapside (p. 111). In a number of places the principal extra-mural streets were 80 or more feet wide.

54. The name means 'the gate of Eadred'. Ekwall 1965: 90.

55. The 'Moor' was a marshy area to the north of the city. In 1415 orders were issued to lay it out as gardens and a little postern in the city wall there was to be removed and replaced by a larger one further west; further improvements to the drainage of the Moor were made in 1512. Lobel 1989: 81.

56. Alessandro Magno, in 1562, noted the archers here and in surrounding villages (Barron, Coleman, and Gobbi 1983: 144). Grenade seems to focus on two groups: the archers, who were entirely by themselves, and those strolling to take the air, who did so among people pursuing other activities. His account may be influenced by the depiction of Moor Field on the Copperplate Map (Figs. 4, 24), which shows the archers in two separate groups and strollers among the laundresses and others at work in different parts of the meadow. B & H Map (Fig. 1) does not show these activities, although some of them are shown in a simplified form on the Woodcut Map. On archery, see Stow, *Survey*: ii. 77; Soar 1988; Gunn 2010.

57. The theatres known as 'The Theatre' and 'The Curtain', and both erected in or shortly before 1577: the former on the east side of Finsbury Fields within the former precinct of Holywell (or Halliwell) Priory and the latter about 200 yards to the south in Moorfields, both sites lying just outside the city jurisdiction. One of them appears to be represented in a panorama engraved early in the seventeenth century from a drawing made before 1598 (Fig. 25; Saunders and Schofield 2001: 41-5). In April 1576 James Burbage, an actor with Leicester's men, in association with his brother in law, the grocer and theatre entrepreneur, John Brayne, began constructing The Theatre on property leased from the dissolved priory of Holywell in Shoreditch. Costing 1,000 marks (£666. 13s. 4d.), it was a polygonal timber framed structure with three galleries; opened in the autumn of 1576, it was dismantled in 1598 and some of its timbers were used in the construction of a new playhouse that was called The Globe. The Curtain is first mentioned in 1577 and was located to the south of the priory precinct. The Curtain was said to be an 'easor' to the Theatre, and the two playhouses seem to have been shared by various playing companies, although the artistic relationship between the two

houses is unclear. The new structures in Shoreditch impressed contemporaries. Already in 1577 Thomas White had preached at Paul's Cross against 'these sumptuous theatre houses'. The sites of both theatres have been identified by Museum of London archaeologists, and excavations took place at The Theatre in 2010; these revealed it to have had fourteen sides and an external diameter of 72 feet. The site of The Curtain was discovered in October 2011, in the course of excavations south of Hewett Street and east of Curtain Road, and sections of its brick inner wall have been uncovered. See Baines 1917; Chambers 1924: ii. 383-404; Berry 1979; Ingram 1992: 182-218; Wickham, Berry, and Ingram 2000; Berry 2000; Mateer 2006; Egan 2009; White 1578b: 46; Bowsher 2012: 55-67, Hilts 2012. A collaboration between Museum of London Archaeology and Cloak and Dagger Studios has resulted in an animated reconstruction of the Theatre which can be viewed at http://www.explorethetheatre.co.uk. We are grateful to Julian Bowsher, Susan Cerasano, and David Kathman for their advice on this note.

58. Grenade alludes to two aspects of the debate over the value of spectacle, both of which can be found in Tertullian's (A.D. c.160-c.240) De Spectaculis. First, drama deals with verisimilar rather than true actions (as Aristotle points out in the Poetics), but this meant that religious moralists could easily attack it on the grounds that it portrayed lies and used actors who themselves were lying. Second, drama, like many other things, is a distraction from contemplation of divine truth and is attacked on those grounds alone by the most severe moralists; others argued that relaxation was necessary and drama could be a legitimate one. We are very grateful to Dr Michael Hawcroft for this note. Tertullian was believed to have been a lawyer as well as an interpreter of Christian doctrine, which may account for Grenade's apparent familiarity with these ideas.

59. It is curious that Grenade assumed that the lord mayor and aldermen had the power to determine the location of the theatres in areas beyond their jurisdiction. For a survey of the complexities of theatre regulation in this period, see Archer 2009, and for the city's relationship with the suburbs, see Archer 2001b.

60. This hospital on the east side of Bishopsgate, commonly known as St Mary Spital, was founded c.1200 by a group of London citizens, headed by Walter Brun (brunus, 'brown'; sheriff in 1202-3), his wife Rose, and Walter FitzAilred, alderman. They endowed it with the site, other land nearby, and rents in the city. The building appears to have been dedicated 1199×1221 (Thomas, Sloane and Phillpotts 1997; Barron and Davis 2007: 160). Walter Brun's confirmation charter of 1235 appears to refer to lands and rents acquired since the foundation, but Grenade, following Stow, Summarie (1570): fols 7-8 or Grafton, Abridgement (1570): fol. 60 or later editions of either, took the date to be that of the original foundation. The event is not noted in earlier editions of these works.

61. A passion sermon at Paul's Cross preached on Good Friday was followed by three sermons at St Mary Spital on the Monday, Tuesday and Wednesday after Easter Sunday, with a review or rehearsal sermon at Paul's Cross on Low Sunday. The Spital sermons dated back to at least Richard II's reign, but they became more elaborate in the sixteenth century, and occasions for the celebration of civic charity, in the presence of the hospital children, who were recorded as being there as early as 1553. The preaching place was in the cemetery to the south-east of the former priory site, which by the later 1570s had become an enclave for fashionable society. The preachers were chosen by the court of aldermen, in whose minutes nominations are regularly recorded, though it is not always clear who actually served. The nominees in 1577 were John Aylmer, bishop of London, Alexander Nowell, dean of St Paul's, Adam Squire, archdeacon of Middlesex, Thomas Cooper, bishop of Lincoln, and Laurence Chaderton, the distinguished puritan. In 1578 the nominees included Aylmer again, Toby Matthew, dean of Christ Church and later archbishop of York, John Still, master of Trinity College, Cambridge, Roger Goad, provost of King's College, Cambridge; William James,

Oxford academic and archdeacon of Coventry, Dr Lewes and Dr Wickham, also nominated that year, have not yet been identified. Stow, *Survey*, i. 166-8; Machyn 1848: 133 (3 April 1553); BL, Harleian MS 6363, fol. 49; Morrissey 2011: 21-2, 73-4; *Survey of London*: xxvii. 43-4, 47-50; LMA, COL/CA/01/01/021, fols 175v, 177, 294, 299v.

62. A priory of the order of St Mary of Bethlehem founded in 1247; by the fifteenth century it served principally as an asylum for poor insane and other sick persons; the city took the house under its protection in the fourteenth century and became its formal patron in 1546; from the fourteenth century onwards occasionally known as Bedlam. Barron and Davies 2007: 113-15; Andrews et al. 1997: 11-141. For treatment there, see note 63.

63. St Mathurin was believed to have had the gift of casting out evil spirits and was commonly invoked for the cure of the insane. His relics enshrined at his birthplace, Larchant (Seine-et-Marne), attracted many pilgrims seeking his intercession. French kings periodically visited the shrine, the last being Henri III in 1587. The region of Larchant experienced much fighting during the Wars of Religion and in 1567 Huguenot troops attacked and destroyed the church, removing the shrine and dispersing the relics. Grenade's opinion of 'treatment' at Larchant may have been informed by a sympathy for the Huguenots rather than by real information on treatment there, although his opinion could have been influenced by a knowledge of the shackles for restraining the insane, which pilgrimage badges indicate were suspended from the shrine, possibly as *ex voto* donations. Grenade's suspicion of the treatment of the six pauper inmates at Bethlem during the fifteenth and sixteenth centuries was well-founded: restraint, beating and correction were applied when deemed necessary, with little if any of the attention from a physician which better-off people who had lost their wits appear sometimes to have received; the house was equipped with chains, locks, manacles, fetters and two pairs of stocks. Toison 1886: 246-8, 259-60, 272-5; 1887: 327-31; 1888a: 78-9; Andrews et al. 1997: 99-106, 113-15.

64. Grenade's sense of the origin of the water was hazy and he had probably not visited the neighbourhood. He says nothing about the busy industrial and inn-keeping suburb outside Aldgate, where there was also an important concentration of butchers. Whitechapel, the area just beyond the city boundary, was traversed by numerous intermittent streams, but these were not tapped for the city's water supply. Water was first piped from Finsbury Fields, north of the city, to the conduits at Lothbury, Coleman Street , and Moor Gate in September 1546 during the mayoralty of Sir Martin Bowes. BL, Harleian MS 6363, fols 23v, 48; Stow, *Survey*: i. 17-18.

65. The name means 'old gate'.

Chapter 5

66. The 'great gate' was presumably the Iron Gate, a relatively small gate or postern with a barbican at the south-east corner of the Tower enclosure, probably of late medieval origin and in existence by 1534: *KW*: ii, 724n, iii pt 1, 269; Parnell 1993: 48-9. It is clearly identified in the plan view of 1597 (Fig. 29). The Woodcut Map names the street parallel to the river and in front of the hospital as 'Tames str.', suggesting a conceptual continuity with Thames Street to the west of the Tower.

67. The information about Julius Caesar as builder of the Tower and the work of William Rufus is probably from Stow, *Summarie* (1566a) rather than Grafton. Fabyan (1811) had made no mention of Caesar in connection with the Tower. Stow, *Summarie* (1565), fol. 14ᵛ had followed Grafton, *Abridgement* (1564) in citing Leland's view that Belinus had built the Tower (see below) but on fol. 19ᵛ also stated that Caesar built the Tower, citing as source Lydgate's *Serpent of Division*; both statements appear in subsequent editions; Stow's statement that William built the Tower, though Caesar had 'made the dongeon thereof', citing

a St Albans Abbey chronicle as authority, appears only in Stow, *Summarie* (1566a), fol. 59ᵛ. Grafton, *Abridgement* (1564), fol. 4ᵛ attributed the building of the Tower of London to Belinus, citing Leland (presumably Leland (1543), in the *Syllabus* at the end: *Bellini castrum nunc turris Londoniensis*), but in the 1570 edition dropped this in favour of the story from Lydgate, adopted from Stow. For a more detailed, but incomplete, account of the mythical history of the Tower and its impact in Grenade's time, see Wheatley 2008.

68. Grenade's views on the state of the Tower ordnance and armour are ambiguous. He seems impressed by the stores, but notes pieces on the wharf rusting into the ground. Other visitors, while noting the armour of Henry VIII, which is not mentioned by Grenade, were less impressed by the Tower's armour and ordnance. Jacob Rathgeb, secretary to the duke of Wurttemburg, visiting in 1592 remarked that the cannon 'are full of dust, and stand about in the greatest disorder'; Philip Julius duke of Stettin-Pomerania claimed in 1602 that the armour was 'not properly arranged nor kept clean', but he seemed impressed by the 200 cast pieces standing in front of the Tower, presumably on the wharf. The Ordnance office, rebuilt in 1545-7 at the enormous cost of £2,894 covered the full width of the inner bailey, and was the largest structure in the Tower complex. They were intended to be 'one house wherein all the kings majesty's store and provision of artillery, ordnance, and other munitions may be kept, guarded and bestowed', and there were also racks for the storage of armour. As the Tower became less important as a royal lodging, other areas were appropriated for storage: in the late 1560s 'two new armouries' were set up in the White Tower. The presence of the Tower stores had a significant impact on the local economy, as munitions workers, including armourers and gunsmiths, clustered in the surrounding parishes. Among the gunfounders were the Owen dynasty, operating in Elizabeth's reign from the sign of the Golden Gun in Houndsditch. The Woodcut Map and B &H Map (Figs 1, 28), both derived from the Copperplate Map, identify this gun foundry by showing a cannon in a yard, which B & H labels as 'ye goone founders h[ou]s[e]'. Rye 1865: 19; von Bülow 1892: 12-17; Williams 1937: 159-63; Bentley and Walpole 1757: 37-8; Keay 2001: 39-40, 41, 53; *KW*: iii. 269-71; Blackmore 1976: 6-9; Ffoulkes 1916: i. 67. The surviving inventories of the Tower ordnance in the Elizabethan period are helpfully printed by Blackmore 1976: 262-80.

69. It was already common, though not universal, for arriving foreign ambassadors to alight at the Tower wharf to be greeted by dignitaries and escorted through the city to their lodgings. The Spanish ambassadors, arriving on 2 January 1554, for example, were met on Tower wharf by Sir Anthony Browne, saluted with 'great shooting of guns', and then escorted through the city by Edward Courtenay earl of Devon, and Lord Garret to their lodgings at Durham Place. Machyn 1848: 50, 197; Nichols 1850: 33-4. Cf. Goldring et al. 2014: iii. 255; iv. 162-3.The Tower was a standard element of the distinguished foreign visitor's London 'package', though Thomas Platter in 1599 had to pay fees at eight separate points. Ffoulkes 1916: i. 65-8; Williams (1937): 159-63.

70. The ceremony of the creation of the Knights of the Bath usually took place on the eve of the royal entry through London which preceded the coronation. Elizabeth, however, was the last monarch to reside in the Tower on the eve of the entry (Ashbee 2008: 154-6; Harriss and Keay 2008: 163-5). Grenade implies that monarchs resided in the Tower from the moment of their accession to the eve of the coronation. That is not correct. Mary Tudor entered the city on 3 August 1553 and took up residence in the Tower, staying until 12 August, when she left for Richmond; and later St James'; on 27 September she returned to the Tower on the eve of her coronation entry. Elizabeth was in the Tower between 28 November and 5 December 1558, but she was at Somerset House between 5 and 22 December, and at Whitehall thereafter. She removed to the Tower by water accompanied by the livery company barges on 12 January 1559, presided over the knights of the bath ceremony on 13 January, performed the royal entry through the city of London on 14 January, and was crowned on

15 January in Westminster Abbey. Hamilton 1875-77: ii. 93-5, 97, 103; Machyn 1848: 180, 186; Goldring et al. 2014: i. 101-2.

71. The ogee cupolas and gilded weather vanes, gilded by the royal painter Ellys Carmyan had been added to the turrets in 1532-3, in preparation for the king's marriage to Anne Boleyn (Figs 121, 123; Keay and Harris 2008: 162-5). Grenade presumably first saw them about 1550.

72. Exotic animals had been kept at the Tower since at least as early as the thirteenth century. The Emperor Frederick II had donated three leopards in 1235 and Louis IX of France an elephant in 1255, both diplomatic gifts to King Henry III. A gift with a similar purpose was a polar bear from Norway in 1252. Magno recorded four lions (named after kings and queens) and a leopard in 1562; Platter saw six lions, a tiger, a porcupine and a wolf in 1598. By the sixteenth century the lions and the other beasts were being kept in the barbican, known as the Lions' Tower, in front of the substantial Middle Tower gateway; on this occasion Grenade uses the term *dongeon* (donjon) to denote the Middle Tower, or perhaps the outer enclosure as a whole, rather than the White Tower. Luard, ed. 1872-83: iii. 324-5, v. 489; *KW*: ii.715; Parnell 1993: 54, 61, 94; Bentley and Walpole 1757: 39; Barron et al 1983: 142; Williams 1937: 159-63.

73. The Hospital of St Katharine had been founded by Queen Matilda in 1147, with an establishment comprising a master, three brothers, three sisters, ten beadswomen, and six poor clerks. It survived the Reformation, perhaps because of the continuing patronage of the monarch's consort. The twelve-acre liberty was coterminous with the hospital precinct, and the hospital remained the leading local landowner with 98 units leased in the Elizabethan period. By a charter of 1428 the hospital had been granted extensive privileges including the right to a fair and to felon's chattels, and tax exemption; its independence from the jurisdiction of the bishop of London also meant that it enjoyed its own commissary court which seems to have survived the Reformation; a court was held in the cloister. There were abortive plans for its annexation to the Tower in 1560-1, and the city sought to buy out the franchises in 1565, but eventually settled in 1567 on the suppression of the fair, claimed by the controversial master of the hospital, Thomas Wilson, the humanist diplomat and administrator, who held the position from 1561 until 1581. It has been estimated that there were 490 households in the precinct by the 1590s. The area was prominent in the brewing and the associated coopering crafts: an assessment of 1593 shows that there were at least eight brewhouses (out of a total of 79 around the city). The prominence of munitions workers is explained by the proximity of the Tower and the ordnance office in the Minories. Stow described the area as 'pestered with small tenements and homely cottages, having inhabitants English and strangers more in number than some cities in England'. The best account of the Elizabethan liberty is in House 2006: 153-82, but see also Jamison 1952; Stow, *Survey*: i. 324; Archer 1991: 221-2, 225, 234; BL, Harleian MS 5097; LMA, CLC/199/TC/024/MS09680; BL, Harleian MS 6363, fol. 24. The earliest map of the precinct is from a survey by Gregory King and E. Bostock Fuller in 1687 and 'showing the ichnography or ground plot of all ye houses and other buildings', with 854 numbered units, can be found in LMA, CLC/199/TF/002/MS09774.

74. The wharves at Queenhithe and Three Cranes are better documented as delivery points for wood than the dock at St Katharine's, to which suppliers using the lower Thames or the River Lea presumably brought their cargoes. At the time of Grenade's writing, London stood on the cusp of the transition from a wood-based to a coal-based economy. William Harrison in 1576 had noted the pressure on woodlands in the south-east, and the aldermen made strenuous efforts to maintain fuel supplies, pressurising the woodmongers into adherence to price controls and the appropriate measures, and sending out surveyors into the surrounding counties to identify potential stocks. Edelen 1968: 275-6; Galloway, Keene, and Murphy

1996; Te Brake, 1975; Cavert 2011: 124-9, 138-9. LMA, COL/CA/01/01/020, fols 60-66 for suppliers of wood in the London region in 1573.

Chapter 6

75. This may seem a strange comparison, but Southwark was certainly prosperous and known for its many specialised crafts; it had some splendid churches and the residences of two bishops, plus several aristocratic houses and a former royal palace, which only in recent decades had begun to be broken up into smaller units.

76. The earliest recorded form of the name means 'fort of the people of Surrey', but eleventh-century and later forms mean 'southern fort': Dodgson 1996: 120.

77. The original form of the name was 'Parish Garden' which in the fifteenth century became 'Paris Garden'; a bear-baiting ring was built there between 1540 and 1546. References to bear- and bull-baiting on the Bankside proliferate from around 1540. The rings actually seem to have been in the Clink Liberty, although there may have been some doubt about its precise boundaries; they were nevertheless consistently described as being in Paris Garden perhaps because that was the landing stage for the watermen bringing spectators (cf Fig. 30). The bull-baiting and bear-baiting rings are clearly shown on the B & H Map (1572) and were presumably depicted in more detail on the Copperplate Map, but there is some doubt as to the accuracy of the locations depicted. In a lawsuit of 1620 a witness was asked 'in how many severall places on the Bankside have the game of bears and bear bayting been kept', to which the answer was 'in four severall places, viz. At Mason Steares on the Bankside, near Maidlane, by the corner of the Pyke Garden, and at the Beare Garden which was parcel of the possession of William Payne, and the place where they are now kept'. Kingsford concluded that William Payne (deputy keeper of the queen's bears, and lessee from 1540 until his death around 1574 of the Barge, the Bell, and the Cock, tenements in Southwark located between Maiden Lane and the river) had erected his pit by 1573, and probably several years earlier; that the site at the corner of Pyke Garden probably dates from shortly before 1560; and that the Mason Stairs pit was the earliest located somewhat to the west of the others, and just north of where Tate Modern now stands. When the witness refers to the 'place where they are now kept' (i.e. in 1620) he was referring to the site of the Hope Theatre, a little to the south of Payne's pit. Susan Cerasano, for whose guidance we are very grateful, suggests to us that the practicalities of housing the animals meant that bull-baiting took place in the western arena, and bear-baiting in the eastern locations. Stow, *Survey*: ii. 54; Carlin 1996: 60-1, 213n; Kingsford 1920: 155-78; Braines 1924: 87-98; Chambers 1924: ii. 448-62; Cerasano 1991; Mackinder et al 2013: 10-25; Barker and Jackson 2008: 11. These animal sports were on the standard visitor itineraries (Williams 1937: 168-70; Barron, Coleman and Gobbi 1983: 143-4, von Bulow 1895: 230; Rye 1865: 45). A few years after Grenade wrote, scaffolding collapsed at a Sabbath day bear-baiting at Paris Garden on 13 January 1583, killing eight spectators and provoking an outbreak of providentialised godly moralising (Field 1583; BL, Lansdowne MS 37, fol. 8).

78. Fol. 45^r, below (p. 107).

79. Grenade uses adjective *marchand* only of London Bridge, of Lombard Street and of the city as a whole.

80. This date for the timber construction, attributed to Peter of Colechurch, first appears in Stow, *Summarie* and Grafton, *Abridgement* in their editions of 1570, fols, 57v-8 and fol. 46, respectively. Grafton (*Abridgement* 1564: fol. 50) stated that in 1208-9 it began to be built of stone by the citizens of London and others; Stow, (*Summarie* 1565: fol. 77) copied and modified this statement. In his edition of 1567 (fol. 58r-v) Stow added further unfounded elaborations. In editions from 1570 (fol. 69v-70) onwards Stow simply stated that in this

year the arches of the bridge began to be built in stone, based on his discovery of the record *fuit fundatio archae pontis* in the 'Annals of Bermondsey' (Luard 1866: 451). The 1573 and later editions of the *Summarie* add that in 1209 the building of the bridge in stone was begun by three worthy merchants, Serle Mercer, William Alman and Benedict Botewrith. Stow eventually discovered the entry for 1176 in the 'Annals of Waverly' (Luard 1865: 240) which records that in that year the stone bridge of London was begun by Peter the chaplain of Colechurch. His later account of the bridge in Stow (*Survey*: i. 22-3) records that in 1163 Peter of Colechurch repaired and made it anew in timber as before (for which the source may have been the 'table' in the bridge chapel mentioned by Stow and by his time removed to Bridge House), that in 1176 the stone bridge was begun by same Peter, who died in 1205 and was buried in the chapel 'Annals of Waverley' (Luard 1865: 256-7). Grenade seems likely to have obtained his information from the 1570 or later editions of Grafton or Stow. According to Holinshed (1587: iii.1270, 1271), the tower at the south end of the bridge was being reconstructed at the time of Grenade's writing. Demolition work began in April 1577; the lord mayor, Sir John Langley, laid the foundation stone of the new structure on 28 August 1577, and the work was completed in September 1579.

Chapter 7

81. William Smith claimed there were 2,000 wherries on the Thames, providing employment for 3,000 men in 1575, while early in the reign of James I Georg van Schwarzstat, Baron von Hopffenbach, claimed that there were 7,000 small boats on the river (BL, Harleian MS 6363, fol. 2; Folger Shakespeare Library, MS V.a.316). The variety and distribution of vessels on the river between Westminster and the Tower is well is well illustrated by the Copperplate and B & H Maps (Figs. 1-4).

82. This mythical origin of Billingsgate is probably from Stow, *Summarie* and/or Grafton, *Abridgement* and ultimately from Geoffrey of Monmouth (iii.10), where Belinus was said to have a built a gateway with a tall tower on top and a water gate below, hence Grenade's use of the verb *edifier*. Belinus, son of Mulmutius Dunwallo, king of Britain was characterised as a great ruler, among whose supposed achievements was the completion of the four great highways across the realm, which may have prompted Grenade's notion that the city of London had four main streets. Neither Geoffrey of Monmouth nor Stow nor Grafton provide a date for Belinus; Grenade presumably made up the date given, and possibly intended 400 BC rather than AD, since in the legendary history of Britain Belinus ruled long before Julius Caesar and the Roman conquest of Britain. The port and market of Billingsgate are strikingly represented in Archer, Barron, Harding 1988: 53, 83-5. For ferries and tilt boats, see Fig. 33. The ferry between London and Gravesend was managed by the authorities of Gravesend, who had been granted it by charter in 1401, most recently confirmed in 1568; but the common ferry (in which there were 27 shares in 1573) suffered competition from at least seven tilt boats which might carry up to thirty passengers; their owners were required to pay a share of their fares to the common ferry, and fares were supposedly tightly regulated (2d in the common ferry and 4d in a tilt boat with four oars and a steersman according to the privy council schedule of 1561), but there was constant conflict between the men of Gravesend and the London watermen. Humpherus 1887: i. 111-14, 125-8; Cruden 1843: 120-1, 125, 158-60, 192-3, 199-202, 205-7; LMA, COL/CA/01/01/018, fols 323v-5.

83. This is the best account by a contemporary of the London *kontor* of the Hanseatic merchants, which occupied an enclosed site between Thames Street and the river; its two gates on to the street were closed at night (Figs 3, 34). The western part had originated in the twelfth century as the hall of the Cologne merchants; German traders from the Baltic region in the thirteenth century came to occupy the block of properties to the east, which in the fifteenth century were acquired by the German Hanse and remained in its possession to the mid nineteenth.

The name Steelyard (which originated as a reference to the sealing of cloth there) strictly applied only to the eastern part, but was commonly used for the whole. In the sixteenth century, the well-appointed twelfth-century hall still survived and the enclosure also contained a master's house and garden, a quay with a crane, warehouses and other accommodation. As with the Hanseatic *kontoren* in other northern European cities (and likewise with the houses of Italian mercantile consortia), this was an establishment where young Germans from good mercantile families learned their trade, most of them eventually returning to their home cities to pursue mercantile and political careers. The privileges which the house enjoyed and the presence there of young men leading a quasi-monastic (but not entirely restrained) life were causes of continual friction between the Steelyard and the citizens of London. During the city's controversial crackdown of 1576-7, Steelyard men were identifed as regular clients of prostitutes. Henry Boyer, a painter and Melcher Pelse regularly pimped for Steelyard men. Among the merchants named were Johan Fagotes, Hans Coxe, Derrick Christopher, Matthew Hoope, Nicholas Killinghouse, and Henry Vandome (Bridewell Court Book, vol. 3, fols 28^v, 106^v-7, 109v, 111^v, 115^v-116, 118^{r-v}). The Hanse privileges had been suspended by Edward VI's government in 1552, and although restored under Mary, their position was much weakened because of the greater leverage of the Merchant Adventurers over the government. A Hanse delegation of 1560 failed to secure more than minor concessions on customs duties, and the agreement was never ratified because of the opposition of Danzig to reciprocal rights for English merchants, a long standing sticking point. At the time of Grenade's completion of his text there was another row over the renewal of the Merchant Adventurers' privileges at Hamburg, which the Hanse used as a means of leveraging concessions. By 1579 there were only four merchants resident at the Steelyard. The problems in Antwerp were one reason for the decline of Hanse business in London. See Lappenberg 1851; Dollinger 1964; Hammel-Kiesow 2000; Ramsay 1975: 61-70, 158-62; Keene 1989; Lloyd 1991: 292-362.

84. The spelling on the Copperplate Map of the 1550s and the reduced version of it published as B & H Map (Figs 1, 3) is 'Stiliards', suggesting that Grenade consulted one of these maps: the mid sixteenth-century English spelling usually lacked the final 's' (cf. Lappenberg 1851: 179-90).

85. Grenade's treatment of Thames Street is notably limited, concentrating on sites associated with overseas trade but omitting important city landmarks and trading sites such as Three Cranes Wharf and Queenhithe to the west and the Custom House and Galley Quay to the east. See above, p. 35.

Chapter 8

86. Only the easternmost section, beyond Eastcheap, was known as Tower Street. The other components of this principal street identified by Grenade were, from west to east as named on the Copperplate Map (with the names given on the later Woodcut Map in parentheses): (Poles church, i.e. the churchyard); P. Chen (for Paul's Chain); Watleng strete (Watlinge streat), Bougge Row (Budge row), Canon Strete (Canwicke str'), Excheapp (Eschepe), and Towre strete (Towre streate).

87. The temple of Apollo is noted by Geoffrey of Monmouth (ii. 11) and Stow (*Summarie* 1567: 12), but only the latter attributes it to Belinus and states that some believe it to be St Paul's. Æthelberht, king of the people of Kent, founded St Paul's in 604.

88. In Grenade's time a commonly used pace measured 2.5 feet (Cotgrave 1673, s.n. *pas*). By this measure his estimate of the total internal length of St Paul's comes to 675 feet, an exaggeration for the true length was about 540 feet. By contrast, his estimate of the width, which would have been easier to pace out, is remarkably accurate (300 feet). His account of

the Royal Exchange (see Chapter 9) seems to confirm that his pace was one of 2.5 feet, since he described the columns around the courtyard as being set at intervals of 4 paces while the pilasters above the columns were said to be 10 feet apart.

89. The elaborate tomb of Blanche, duchess of Lancaster (d. 1368) and her husband John of Gaunt (d. 1399), whose alabaster effigies lay side by side; the tomb was on the north side of the high altar (for a description and images, see Keene et al. 2004: 140; Schofield 2011: 134).

90. This was Sir Nicholas Bacon, lord keeper of the great Seal (Grenade uses the approximately equivalent French title *Garde des Sceaux*), who had reformist views on religion and died on 20 February 1579 (Tittler 2004). Later Stow noted that the tomb was on the south side of the choir (*Survey:* i. 338), where it stood between two piers (Keene et al. 2004: Fig. 67 on p. 128). For an etching of 1657 and a surviving fragment, see Schofield 2011: 188. Grenade's description accords with the etching, which shows Bacon's effigy at an upper level and those of his wives below, but does not show any effigies of children.

91. They are the twelfth-century sarcophagi in grey or black 'marble' (presumably of Purbeck or Tournai type) of the only two kings to have been buried at St Paul's, Sebbi of the East Saxons (d. c.694) and Æthelred II of the English (d. 1016), both of whom died in London. They were in recesses behind the thirteenth-century arcade against the north wall of the choir. Keene et al 2004: 6; Schofield 2011: 45.

92. According to Bede's *Ecclesiastical History* (book III, chapter 30 and book IV, chapters 6 and 11), Sebbi (ruled from c.664 until he resigned and died in London c.694) had adhered to the Christian faith and so was not 'converted' by Erkenwald, whose episcopate (675-93) commenced under Sebbi's rule; Sebbi's co-ruler Sighere had apostasized and was reconverted by the bishop of the Mercians. By 1631 this inscription or notice had been replaced by a shorter version: *Hic iacet Sebba rex orientalium Saxonum, qui conuersus fuit ad fidem per S. Erkenwaldum, Londininsem episcopum, anno Christi 677. Vir multum Deo deuotus, actibus religiosis, crebris precibus, & piis eleemosynarum fructibus* (Weever 1631: 356). The story that Sebbi had been converted by Erkenwald was probably derived from the inscription on Erkenwald's magnificent tomb, erected c.1533 (Weever 1631: 358).

93. Sir John Mason (c.1503-66), diplomat and member of parliament; a secretary to the new ambassador to the emperor from 1537, he was in the Netherlands 1539-40; later a French secretary and tipped as ambassador to the emperor and later to Madrid; he was member of the privy councils of Edward VI, Mary and Elizabeth (Carter 2004). Given the range of his diplomatic activity, he was perhaps known to Grenade or his family. For the tomb, see Schofield 2011: 191; it was still there in 1657, when the panel containing the verses (accurately recorded by Grenade) included beneath them a statement that the tomb had been erected by Mason's wife. On a separate panel below was a statement that the verses had been composed by Mason's adopted son. Weever (1631) does not mention the tomb.

94. Colet was dean probably from early in 1504 until his death on 16 Sept. 1519, just short of 16 full years. His first tomb was unassuming, but by 1548 a more elaborate one had been erected; the one described by Grenade was presumably that being rebuilt or remodelled in 1575-6, when the Mercers' Company spent a good deal of money on marble for it; that tomb was refurbished in 1618 and is presumably the one described by Weever in or before 1631 and represented by Hollar's etching of 1657. The etching shows that the epitaph, with the text as recorded by Grenade, was placed below the cadaver. Weever recorded only a different epitaph in Latin verse, which was perhaps that stated by Trapp (2004) to have been by William Lily and noted by his son George in 1548 as hung up beside the tomb; if so, it was presumably still there in the 1620s. George Lily, however, in his encomia of his father and of John Colet, published in 1548, makes no mention of these details, noting only that the tomb was adorned with a *tabulo erudito praeconio*, which could refer to the inscription transcribed

by Grenade. Lily 1548b: 45-7; Weever 1631: 368-9; Trapp 2004; Keene et al 2004: 41, 142; cf. Schofield 2011: 137.

95. This was his *De emendata Latini sermonis*, an advanced Latin grammar published in 1524.

96. The epitaph is recorded in almost identical terms in Weever 1631: 370; the meaning of *iuxta charus* (also in Weever) is difficult to determine, but possibly means something like 'as if of the same flesh and blood'. The Royal College of Physicians, founded as a result of a petition from Linacre and others in 1518, was intended to set standards for physicians in London and the surrounding area, but, since it was unable to control the many other healers who were unwilling to cooperate, was not a success. Nutton 2004.

97. William was consecrated bishop in 1051 and so an episcopate of 16 years would have ended in 1067. In fact, he died in 1075. Stow (*Summarie* 1570: fols 37ᵛ-38ᵛ) first recorded the epitaph in English as:

> O William a man famous in wisedome
> and holines of life, who first with S. Ed-
> ward the king and confessor, being fami-
> liar, of later preferred to be bishop of Lon-
> don, and not longe after for his prudencye
> and sincere fidelity, admitted to be of coun-
> saile with the most victorious Prince Wil-
> liam king of England of that name the first,
> who obtained of the same great and large
> priuiledges to this famous Cittie, The Se-
> nate and Cittizens of London to him ha-
> uinge well deserued, have made this: Hee
> continued bishoppe xx yeares, and dyed in
> the year of Christ his natiuity 1070.

Then followed four rhyming couplets in English in which the citizens dedicate 'these marble monumentes' to him as an expression of his virtues. It seems likely that Grenade's transcription of the epitaph was more accurate than Stow's English version. Grafton (*Abridgement* 1570) followed Stow, noting that the Latin epitaph was in prose on brass. Grafton in his *Chronicle* (1569: ii. 19-20) gave the epitaphs and the couplets in both English and Latin. Weever (1631: 362) copied Stow's version of both, noting that the tomb had long since been removed, but that when the lord mayor and aldermen attended St Paul's on solemn occasions they walked to his tombstone in remembrance of their privileges he had obtained for the citizens.

98. Presumably the organs traditionally attributed to William Beton, organ maker to Henry VIII by 1537 and active to *c.*1552 (Bicknell 1996: 51-2; cf. Keene et al. 2004: 313). Platter visiting the cathedral in 1598 claimed that the service with music and organ accompaniment resembled a mass (Williams 1937: 176). For ceremonialism at St Paul's, see Keene et al. 2004: 53-4

99. The thirteenth-century Choir and Lady Chapel were raised above ground level over a crypt (Fig. 40), which at its west end accommodated the parish church of St Faith. From 1459 the Jesus Guild occupied the east end; following the final dissolution of the guild in 1561, the church of St Faith was moved to the east end.

100. The thousandweight, used to weigh lead and many other commodities, consisted of ten hundredweight of, in this case, probably 112lb each. Five hundred thousandweight amounted to 560,000 lb or 250 English tons. This weight of sand-cast lead sheet, at the probably lightest weight of 6lb per square foot, would cover 93,333 square feet, considerably less than the leaded area of the main roofs of St Paul's (see next note).

101. The lead covered roofs of the nave, choir, Lady Chapel and transepts of the church had a pitch of about 60 degrees and would have risen about 85 feet above the parapet, making them a prominent feature of the cathedral. Their surface area for roofing, excluding the space occupied by the central tower, was about 146,000 square feet, which at 6lb per square foot would require 876,000 lb (782 thousandweight). For the weight of sand-cast lead sheet, see http://www.leadsheet.co.uk/sand-cast-sheet.

102. The fire that destroyed the spire and most of the roofs below was caused by a lightning strike on 4 June 1561 (Keene et al. 2004: 51).

103. An early fourteenth-century record of the dimensions of the cathedral stated that the tower rose 260 feet above the floor of the crossing and that the spire above was 274 feet high, but that the total height was no more than 500 feet (presumably because the tower rose above the base of the spire). The true height from ground level to the top of the spire appears to have been about 400 feet (Keene 2008a: 204). It would have been theoretically possible, on an exceptionally clear day, to see the spire from many places on high ground 20 to 25 miles away. The spire of Strasbourg cathedral, completed in 1439, was 466 feet high.

104. Colet reconstituted the cathedral school (later known as St. Paul's School) in 1510-11, establishing it on a new site against the east wall of the cemetery. He sometimes preached in English and was critical of many contemporary Christian practices, but did not encourage the recitation of the Lord's Prayer etc in English. His educational programme emphasised the use of Latin and Greek in learning and he wrote a Latin accidence in English for young readers and was innovative in choosing laymen, in the form of the Mercers' Company of London, as trustees for his new school, but he was no Protestant. Nevertheless, later English reformers appropriated him as a predecessor and in 1529 William Tyndale reported that he had translated the Lord's Prayer into English. Trapp 2004.

105. Grenade appears to have left the precinct by 'Paul's Chain' near the church of St Augustine and to have proceeded along Watling Street to Candlewick Street (Cannon Street), in both of which John Stow later in the century noted many wealthy drapers as recent arrivals from Lombard Street and Cornhill. Stow, *Survey*: i. 8, 199, 217-18, 346 .

106. London Stone is first recorded in the personal name *Eadwæker æt lundene stane* noted in a rental dateable to between 1098 and 1108; the byname was associated with a twelfth-century family of prominent Londoners, which included the first mayor of the city, Henry fitz Ailwyn (d.1212), who lived nearby: Keene 2004. The stone was opposite the church of St Swithun in Candlewick Street and Stow noted that it was in the south part of the street, set deep in the ground and fastened by bars of iron to preserve it from damage by carts. Its origin and purpose, about which there has been much speculation, remains unknown. Camden suggested that it was a Roman milestone, possibly a base point for measuring road distances in Britain. In 1742 it was removed into a recess in the wall of the church of St Swithun, since when it has occupied similar, increasingly obscure, positions on the same site. Grenade provides the earliest record of its dimensions. It is now smaller. Lud's alleged Saxon origin is not mentioned by any other author. The Latin *saxum* means 'big stone'. The dates of the beginning of Lud's reign are given in Grafton, *Abridgement* 1564: fol. 7r-v. Stow (*Summarie* 1567: fol. 16) gave only the date BC, but noted that Lud 'builded London from Londonstone to Ludgate'. See also Stow, *Survey*: i. 224-5, ii. 315-16.

107. This was Eastcheap shambles, which occupied the east end of Cannon Street and the west part of what is now known as Eastcheap. For an image of the market, see Archer, Barron, Harding (1988), 57, 86. Two hundred paces (probably 500 feet) from London Stone would bring one almost to the corner of St Clement's Lane, at the west end of Eastcheap. Grenade's special interest in the Eastcheap market may have a bearing on his identity, since if he was related to James Granado he would very likely have been staying at James's former house

in Tower Ward, St Dunstan's parish, occupied until 1585 by James's widow, Lady Chester. This would have been little more than 200 yards from the eastern end of Eastcheap (see Fig. 9).

108. It is difficult to see how Grenade arrived at this total since if we allow 46 weeks of meat consumption in a year (excluding Lent, although at this date some London butchers slaughtered during Lent), the annual total would be 34,500 head of oxen, not 9,000. His minimum weekly figure for the Eastcheap shambles would suggest annual totals of 5,980 there, of 23,920 at the four large shambles in the city which he mentions, and perhaps over 30,000 including the suburban shambles. William Smith (BL, Harleian MS 6363, fol. 22ᵛ) wrote that in 1570 a report was made to the lord mayor and bench that there were killed weekly '320 beeves to say kine and oxen besides pork, veal, sheep, and lamb'; this would amount to 14,720 head of cattle in a year, for a population of perhaps 80,000 to 100,000 within the city and the suburban areas under its jurisdiction and perhaps well over 120,00 for the conurbation as a whole (Harding 1990). At the end of the sixteenth century Stow reported (*Survey*: i. 187-8) that at some former time (perhaps the 1540s, when there had been great concern over the price of meat, but see also below) the 120 butchers of the city and its suburbs had slaughtered 720 oxen weekly or 3,120 in 46 weeks (the arithmetically correct total would be 33,120). Figures for other large cities help to put these for London in perspective. In the late thirteenth century, according to a contemporary report by Bonvesin da la Riva which provides much information on the city's food supply, the butchers of Milan (a city with between 100,000 and 200,000 inhabitants), would have slaughtered 19,320 oxen (*boves*) for consumption on meat days (Chiesa (ed.), cap. IV, par. XI, pp. 110-12). Soon after 1400 the 100,000 or more inhabitants of Paris were said to consume weekly totals of oxen which would amount to 11,040 head over 46 weeks, plus calves amounting to 23,000, making 34,040 head of cattle in total (figures from the description of Paris by Guillebert de Metz in Le Roux de Lincy and Tisserand 1867: 232, 490). A late fifteenth-century estimate for Paris, which perhaps then had 100,000 inhabitants, estimated that 200 beeves were slaughtered each day, which would be 55,200 over a year (see *Les rues et eglises* and Corrozet 1539, fol. 47ᵛ; for the population of Paris, see Favier 1970: 10). The figures for the three cities seem remarkably congruent and suggest that the annual consumption of oxen implied by the totals stated by Grenade and Stow are overestimates, even if the numbers concerned an area larger than the city itself. The explanation of this may be that their totals included calves as well as oxen, despite their assertions to the contrary, but given other indications that Grenade and Stow may have known each other (above p. 30 and p. 61, note 15), it is possible that they drew on a common source or that Stow's total was derived from Grenade's estimate.

Chapter 9

109. The house of the Franciscan or Grey Friars was established on this site in 1225 and dissolved in 1538 (Barron and Davies 2007: 122-7). The distinctive form of the roof of the church is apparent in both Fig. 22 (to the east of the tower of St Paul's) and Fig. 42.

110. Here Grenade's source seems to be Grafton rather than Stow. Grafton includes details such as the committee of 24 and the classification of the poor which are not in Stow. Grafton also follows the account of the hospitals' foundation with the details of Richard Castel's charity as given by Grenade. It is also probable that Grenade was using Grafton, *Abridgement* 1563: fos 149v-50 (or his later editions of 1564, 1570, and 1572) rather than the fuller Grafton *Chronicle* 1569: 1321-3, because the latter omits the reference to the grant of lands by the city (which was misleading as the city allocated tolls to support the hospitals rather than land) included by Grenade. The fuller chronicle gave a key initiating role to Nicholas Ridley, bishop of London, but this is neither in the *Abridgement* nor in

Grenade. Grafton had been heavily involved in the establishment of the hospitals and over the period 1552-61 served at different times (sometimes concurrently) as governor of Christ's, St Thomas's, and Bridewell; he was joint treasurer of Christ's and St Thomas's from 1553 to 1557; there were occasional doubts about the state of his accounts, though whether these were related to the precarious state of the hospitals' finances, or to his personal financial difficulties more clearly evident in the later 1560s is unclear. He was buried at Christchurch Newgate. Ferguson 2004; Bindoff 1982: ii. 240-1; Slack 1980, 108-13; Kingdon 1901: 71-2; Bishop 2011: 948-9; Benbow 1993; LMA/COL/CA/01/01/016, fol 467v. Bindoff 1982 and Ferguson 2004 differ over Grafton's date of birth and the offices he held at the hospitals, but Benbow 1993 is the more authoritative source on office-holding.

111. Richard Dobbes (d. 1556), lord mayor in 1551-2. Beaven 1908-13: i. 200, ii. 210; Brigden 1988: 479.

112. This was the former Hospital of St Thomas of Canterbury, dissolved in 1540 and rededicated to St Thomas the Apostle when the new institution was established. Barron and Davies 2007:169-74.

113. This became known as Christ's Hospital.

114. Bridewell, which took its name from the spring near St Bride's church, was a substantial palace on the west side of the Fleet built for Henry VIII 1515-22 to replace the royal accommodation at Westminster destroyed by fire in 1512. After 1530, when the king acquired Whitehall, Bridewell ceased to be used by the court and served as accommodation for favoured ambassadors. In April 1553 Edward VI gave the buildings to the city to serve as a workhouse. *KW*: iv. 53-8.

115. The hospital of the Savoy, for 100 poor men, had been founded by Henry VII in 1505 on the south side of the Strand, where the residence of Peter of Savoy (d. 1268) had once stood, but was largely built after the king's death in 1509. Notable for its great size and cruciform plan, it was dissolved in 1553 and its lands given to Bridewell and St Thomas's Hospital; refounded in 1556 but in decay by 1570. *KW*: iii. 196-206; Barron and Davies 2007: 182-4.

116. Christ's Hospital opened its doors to 400 children on 21 November 1552 during the mayoralty of Sir George Barne. The hospital's primary sources of income were the collections for the poor in the city's parishes which were administered by the governors of Christ's Hospital before 1598 and the hallage dues on cloth sales at Blackwell Hall. Archer 1991: 154-63.

117. The source for this fascinating benefactor is Grafton, from whom the story passed into the chronicle tradition, being incorporated into Holinshed. Richard Castel acquired something of a folkloric status, a version of his life being included in Thomas Deloney's *The Gentle Craft* (first published probably around 1597-8), which records his marriage to a Dutchwoman and the envy of Westminster maidens. Richard Castel alias Castellar alias Cassenere was born near Guines (his father was James Cassener of Peuplinge), but was living in the London area by 1524. He arranged for annuities to be paid to his brother and sister living in Guines in 1548, but they were to renounce all other claims on the estate. His will was drawn up on 12 January 1555 and proved in August 1559. He left properties in the Westminster Long Woolstaple (off New Palace Yard and on the present Bridge Street) to Christs' Hospital, who were to pay £8 per annum to the poor of St Margaret Westminster, the benefaction to come into effect after the death of his wife, Katherine, who was probably of Dutch origin. She remarried to a Westminster gentleman, Robert Morecock and did not die until 1 June 1576, her funeral being attended by the governors of Christ's Hospital. The good relations between the hospital and the widow are clear in Katherine's sponsorship of children as hospital inmates. In 1555 the properties were rented at £23. 3s. 4d per annum; by the time Christ's obtained full possession in 1576, they were yielding £47. 17s. per

annum, part of the increase being accounted for by redevelopment work financed by the hospital in Katherine's lifetime. At the time of acquisition the Woolstaple properties were a significant element in the Christ's Hospital property portfolio, accounting for 28 per cent of rental income. It is surely unusual to see a benefaction being celebrated in 1562 several years before it actually came into effect (though a small annuity of 10s per annum was being paid out of the estate prior to the full acquisition), and one wonders whether its inclusion in Grafton's account reflected a friendship between the two men, highly probable given Grafton's prominence in hospital affairs. There is a plan of the Castel estate, *c.* 1610 by Ralph Treswell in the Christ's Hospital memorandum book. PRO, PROB 11/42B, fols 295v-6; Grafton *Chronicle* 1569: 1323; Holinshed 1577, i, *History of England*, 1714;), Deloney (1639): sigs. A3-E3v; Stevenson 1984: 150-3; LMA, CLC/210/C/001/ MS12819/ 002; CLC/210/B/001/MS12806/002, fols 33v, 38, 40, 45, 46v, 47, 47v, 48v, 53, 61v, 76v, 79, 82v, 85, 86, 88, 111v, 138, 141v, 150v, 151v, 152, 152v; CLC/210/G/A/ 004/MS128050, CLC/210/G/BCA/034/MS13008, CLC/210/G/BCA/039/ MS13013, CLC/210/G/BCA/040/ MS13014; Schofield (1987), 146-7.

118. Grenade's overall impression of London welfare is rather optimistic; other foreign visitors, particularly the Italians, were more critical, claiming that the hospitals, with the partial exception of Christ's, were small and badly maintained. By the 1570s the weaknesses of the hospital-centred social vision of the mid-century reformers were becoming apparent. With so much of the poor rate allocated to the maintenance of Christ's Hospital, there was relatively little additional resource available to address the problems of the rapidly expanding out-parishes like St Giles Cripplegate and St Sepulchre. The problem of vagrancy was insistent, and the aldermen (in spite of legislation by common council in 1570) were impotent to prevent the subdivision of tenements which was thought to encourage the migration of the poor. Recurrent plague (a generally underestimated feature of the 1570s, because not on the scale of 1563 or 1593, and not mentioned by Grenade, though there was significant mortality in 1568-71 and 1577-83) focused concern on the lack of proper hospitals for plague victims, on which subject the queen berated the city in 1580. The lack of proper training for youth was one of the major criticisms of John Howes, a former hospital official and servant of Richard Grafton, writing about poor relief in the capital *c.*1582, although there were a series of half-hearted and under-financed work schemes based on Bridewell and Christ's Hospitals. At the time Grenade was writing Bridewell was mired in bitter controversy because of its campaign against prostitution which many, including Howes, felt to be misdirected. There were repeated attempts to review the operation of the welfare system, notably in 1572 in the wake of national legislation, and again in 1579, but major reform was stymied by the lack of resources. The attention of historians of London welfare has perhaps been over-concentrated on the 1550s and 1590s, and there is a need for a reassessment of the 1570s. Archer 1991: 149-203, 232-3; Slack 1985: 61, 147; Chaney 1981: 191-2; Tawney and Power 1924: iii. 415-33; Griffiths 2003; LMA, COL/CA/ 01/01/019, fols 1, 18, 36, 131v, 425v-6; COL/CA/01/01/020, fols 108v-9, 110v, 122v-3, 126v-7v, 151v, 173; COL/CA/01/01/021, fols 136, 274, 356; COL/CA/01/01/022, fo. 136; COL/CC/01/01/019, fol. 253r-v; COL/CC/01/01/021, fols 468. 486, 502v-6v; *Orders appointed* 1582.

119. Grenade had mentioned this ambition on fol. 4^v. See above note 6, and above p. 30.

120. Moneying, and presumably also the goldsmiths who were reponsible for it, were associated with the vicinity of St Paul's from the late ninth century onwards, and perhaps from an earlier date. The concentration of goldsmiths at the west end of Cheapside, especially in the parishes of St Matthew and St Vedast and on the south side of Cheapside, was apparent in the twelfth century and later extended east to just beyond the Cheapside Cross. Parts of this area were known as 'Goldsmith's Row', but other specialised trades, including saddlers,

also occupied distinctive rows of shops in the same district. Between 1180 and 1279 the London mint and exchange were located in St Vedast parish, probably in the street on the east side of St Paul's churchyard, which after 1279, when the mint was moved to the Tower, became known as 'Old Change'. The Cheapside goldsmiths nevertheless continued to be active in the bullion trade and did a great deal of business with the Mint. By *c*.1300 an area at the east end of Cheapside, where there appears for some centuries to have been a small cluster of goldsmiths and moneyers, rapidly developed as an important focus of the money market and luxury trades, principally associated with the headquarters of Italian banking and mercantile houses and the specialised business establishments of English magnates. At that time Lombard Street acquired its modern name ('the street of the Lombards') and became the focus around which the city's financial district subsequently evolved, with the concentration of goldsmiths' shops noted by Grenade (see below fol. 51 (pp. 111-12) and n. 129). The western part of Cheapside continued to be an important focus for London goldsmiths, and in the fourteenth century the Goldsmiths' built their hall and acquired other property nearby. This concentration of goldsmiths shops, and the range and quality of the goods they displayed, were among the principal honours and singularities of London, and a key element in the setting for stately processions (Fig. 44). From about 1500 onwards they especially struck foreign visitors for their silver-ware. A Venetian at that time noted 52 goldsmiths' shops there with a such a variety and quantity of silver vessels that they exceeded that all the shops in Milan, Rome, Venice and Florence together, and in addition were notable for pewter. At the end of of the fifteenth century Thomas Wood, a leading goldsmith, built an elaborately decorated row of ten timber-framed houses, four storeys high, and containing fourteen shops on the south side of the street opposite the cross and gave it to the Goldsmiths' Company. The name 'Goldsmiths' Row' was sometimes applied to this structure. The number of goldsmiths' shops in Cheapside may well have increased by the time of Grenade's description, and his total of 70 shops seems approximately accurate and may even be an underestimate. Lists made in 1558, 1566 and 1569 of the leaseholders of houses or shops in Cheapside of the Goldsmiths' Company, and held by goldsmiths who were obliged to continue the trade there, identify 63 properties (at least half of them in St Vedast parish) and goldsmiths probably occupied other properties there which did not belong to the Company. The peak, however, may have passed: there had been a commercial recession and the drift of luxury trades into the western suburb had begun. Goldsmiths' shops were still a notable feature of Cheapside in the seventeenth century, but monarchs came to see them as old-fashioned, dilapidated, and unworthy of a capital city, and attempts were made to force goldsmiths to return to Cheapside from the suburb. Keene et al. 2004: 11, 27-8; St Paul's Cathedral Archive, Liber L (now LMA, CLC/313/B/001/MS25504), fols 20, 21, 25, 33; Mason 1988: no. 381; Challis 1992: 93, 95, 113-14; Allen 2012: 53, 74; Keene 1999; Sneyd 1847: 42-3; Reddaway 1963; Stow, *Survey*: i. 296, 344-54, ii. 351-2; Ashton 1979: 166; Griffiths 2000.

121. These other trades were still largely in their traditional locations in the eastern half of Cheapside, although like the goldsmiths they were also to be found in other parts of the city and suburbs and everywhere were intermixed with other traders. Spicers, grocers and apothecaries were predominantly on the north side of Cheapside near the Standard, but also south of Cheapside in the area of Soper Lane and Bucklersbury. Mercers, who dealt in silks and linens, congregated at the east end of the street near their Hall. Ironmongers and cutlers were a little further east, at the end of Poultry and Bucklersbury. Haberdashers who dealt with a range of clothing accoutrements, some of which had once been the preserve of mercers, were widely distributed in the eastern half of Cheapside, especially towards the east end. Similar luxury shops, but not in such large numbers, were to be found in Lombard Street (fol. 51). As was the case with the goldsmiths, some of these trades had begun to

move out of the city. Keene 1985; Keene and Harding 1987; Sutton 2005: 43-5, 444-73 and Fig. 7.1; Burch, Treveil and Keene 2011: 223-44; Stow, *Survey* says little about the distribution of these trades in Cheapside, but at i. 261 does note the grocers.

122. *Pigeon* could mean 'dove', but also denoted a blockhead or simpleton and so in this case may be a Protestant's insulting term for a representation of the Holy Ghost. In view of Grenade's remarks about its superstitious imagery, it is noteworthy that a few years after he wrote, on 21 June 1581 (Midsummer night), iconoclasts attacked some of the images at the foot of the Cross including those of Christ's resurrection, the Virgin Mary, and St Edward the Confessor. Stow, *Survey*: i. 266. For the vicissitudes of the Cross after the Reformation, see Cressy 2000: 234-50

123. Cheapside Cross (for which see Figs 22, 44 and 45) was the second most expensive, after Charing Cross, of the twelve crosses erected for King Edward I in 1291-4 to mark the resting places of the bier of Queen Eleanor on its journey to Westminster. Cotgrave (1673) identified the *brasse* as a fathom of five feet, implying a height of 150 feet, which was almost certainly an exaggeration. Nevertheless, Wyngaerde's panorama of *c.*1544 indicates that while it was not so tall as Charing Cross (see pp. 66-7 and note 33), it rose well above the houses nearby, some of the tallest of which would have been between 50 and 60 feet high. Moroever, it was shown as taller than the towers of neighbouring parish churches and a little taller than the nave roof of St Paul's, and so possibly as much as 125 feet from the street to its summit (cf. Keene 2008a: esp. 204-7). The cross was demolished in 1643: two stone fragments with armorial shields are in the Museum of London. *KW*: i, 482-4. Stow records 15th-century repairs and reconstruction and its gilding for the visit of the emperor Charles V (1522), the coronation of Ann Boleyn (1533) and the arrival of King Philip (1554); together with extensive damage and defacement later in the century: Stow, *Survey*: i, 266-7. Grenade's information on Thomas Fisher/Poissonnier is from Grafton (*Abridgement* 1570) or Stow (*Summarie* 1567: fol. 30; *Summarie* 1570: fol. 145ᵛ, where he is said to have been a mercer and to have given 600 marks toward making and newly building the Cross). A Thomas Fisher was a mercer 'out of the livery' in 1485, but the mercer in question was Alderman John Fisher who d. 1485, leaving 600 marks to rebuild, gild and repaint the 'leaden cross' in Cheapside'; Stow later corrected his account of the repair, dropping the reference to Thomas Fisher (*Acts of Court* 1936: 291; Sutton 2005: 185; Stow, *Survey*: i. 266).

124. This was the Great Conduit at the east end of Cheapside, the first of the supplies of water piped from springs outside the city which were constructed at the citizens' expense. It drew its original supply from a spring at the modern Stratford Place in Oxford Street, whence pipes of timber or lead ran past the Royal Mews near Charing Cross and then behind the gardens of houses probably on the north side of the Strand and Fleet Street, where the pipe descended to cross the Fleet near the bridge and then ascended into the city through Ludgate, where it turned north towards Newgate and then east along the north side of St Paul's churchyard and so along Cheapside. A section of the lead pipe near the churchyard was excavated in 2001. Work on the project probably began in 1237 and the original Conduit house in Cheapside, has recently been revealed as a substantial, two-storey, stone structure containing a lead cistern over a vaulted lower chamber, measuring certainly about 20 feet in width and perhaps about 45 feet in length; it was probably completed about 1245. The dimensions given by Grenade indicate that, at 2.5 feet to the pace, it was 50 feet long and 20 feet wide. Fifteenth- and early sixteenth-century chroniclers mistakenly attributed its construction to various dates in the 1280s; Grenade could have taken the date 1284 from Stow, *Chronicles* (e.g. 1570: fol. 88). This original system was subject to many later alterations. According to William Smith in 1575 (BL, Harleian MS 6363, fol. 23v) it contributed to the water supply at Fleet Street conduit, crossed the Fleet on the south side of the bridge and within Ludgate served another conduit before supplying the three

Cheapside conduits. In the 1440s water from additional springs (near Paddington Station) were fed into this system, which by then or soon afterwards was extended into Cornhill, from which, in the 1490s, branches led towards to conduits at Bishopsgate and in Gracechurch Street. In 1546 springs at Finsbury was tapped in order to supply conduits in the northern part of the city (see above, p. 82 and note 64). Religious houses also drew on extra-mural springs for piped water, an early example being the Franciscans during the 1250s, when they received water from a pipe passing under the Fleet near Holborn Bridge and then through Newgate, in a system which represented a technological advance on that recently completed by the citizens and which may later have contributed to the supply at Lamb's Conduit. What Grenade saw in Cheapside was the Great Conduit as repaired and castellated about 1480 at the expense of Thomas Ilam, work attributed to 1485 by Stow (*Summarie* 1570: fol. 145), which did not alter the essential form of the building. Grenade's estimate of number of houses which took water from the conduit is an exaggeration: it supplied about 45 households in the mid fourteenth century, a number which perhaps increased to some degree in the 1440s when additional springs were added to the supply. While it may originally have been intended that the water be free to consumers, charges were levied from the early 14th century onwards. The Conduit was also an important monument, marking a stage in royal entries and other processions and serving as a site for pageants. It came to be known as the Great Conduit after 1389-40, when a second Cheapside conduit (later the Little Conduit), not mentioned by Grenade, was constructed at the west end of the street near the church of St Michael le Quern. Keene 2001; Burch, Treveil and Keene 2011: 108-11, 178-83.

125. The Standard was in the middle of Cheapside at almost exactly the mid point along its length, where the city wards of Cripplegate, Cordwainer, and Bread Street met. In origin it may have been the oldest of the monuments in Cheapside, marking a site for punishment, militia assemblies and other gatherings, but evidence for its early existence is slight. Several punishments stated by fifteenth- and sixteenth-century authors to have taken place at The Standard in former times had been recorded by contemporaries as having taken place simply 'in Cheapside'; the earliest such reference concerns a punishment which took place in 1292-3, but the earliest contemporary reference to The Standard concerns an assembly there in 1377. The Standard was presumably not there in 1331 when a tournament was held in the open space between the Cross and the Great Conduit, although at that time it may have been a removable structure of timber. John Welles was lord mayor in 1431-2 and in 1440 was involved in superintending extensive work on the Little Conduit; in 1442 he left money for renewing the Standard in Cheapside which marked the boundary of Cheap ward, of which he was alderman; in 1443 his executors were granted a royal licence to pull down the Standard, which was made of wood, weak and old and where there was a conduit; they were to set up a new conduit in stone. The conduit was presumably supplied by the pipe which fed the Great Conduit and had perhaps been established there long before 1400. The stone structure appears to have been in the form of a pillar, on the coping of which Wells was commemorated by a carving of wells embraced by angels. Stubbs 1882: 354-5; Thomas and Thornley 1938: 21; Stow *Survey*: i. 26, 258-9, 264-5; Sharpe 1889-90: i. 499-500; *Cal LBH*: 66; *Cal LBK*: 110, 243, 249, 253; *CPR 1441-1446*: 1.

126. Grenade's estimate is probably equivalent to between 62.5 and 75 feet. Cheapside was notable for its breadth and straightness, having a width of about 60 feet its widest point. It was probably laid out in the late ninth century as a broad market street.

127. The division takes place beyond the end of Poultry, a narrow and irregular street which continued the line of Cheapside east of the Great Conduit.

128. Begun 1491 by the executors of Thomas Hill, who died during his mayoralty, 1484-5, leaving money towards bringing water to that place. The conduit was in the middle of

Gracechurch Street at the south end of the market. Stow, *Summarie* 1567: fol. 131[r-v] and 1570: fol. 147, recording verses on the conduit; Stow, *Survey*: i. 110, 211; Archer, Barron, Harding 1988: 59, 87.

129. The French alludes both to the keys (*touches*) of a harpsichord and to the goldsmith's touchstone (*touche*), a pun which the author felt required explanation.

130. The centre of the London book trade was St Paul's churchyard, in his account of which Grenade mentioned neither books nor printing. The presence of booksellers in Lombard Street reflected the neighbourhood's close commercial connections with Antwerp, from which many books were imported. At least one bookseller had moved from St Paul's to Lombard Street by 1536 (Raven 2007: 56).

131 Sir Thomas Ramsey (1510/11-1590) was lord mayor in 1578-9. He was the second son of John Ramsey of Eaton Bridge, near Westerham in Kent, and became free of the Grocers between 1537 and 1539. He served as alderman of Cheap ward from 1566, and as sheriff in 1567-8. In 1566 he had purchased the house in Lombard Street with 'a very fair forefront' (Stow, *Survey*: i. 203) built by Sir Martin Bowes. The house and two adjoining tenements were sold for £1,500 in 1608. An interesting inventory of the house was printed in 1866, but its present whereabouts is unknown (Archer 2008; Fairholt 1866). For a much less favourable impression of Ramsey, see Francis Barnham's memoir (Orlin 2008: 268-9), where his courtship of Francis's grandmother, Alice Barnham was rebuffed, because of his clumsy attempts to revise her jointure arrangements. Alice apparently declared that 'your nature [is] so bent upon covetousness as would have given me but small comfort in you'. His reputation for posterity, however, was secured through the charity of the woman he did marry, another widow, Mary Avery, née Dale (Archer 2008). Ramsey was unusual in being represented on the stage in Thomas Heywood's play, *If you know not me you know nobody, part 2* (1605), on which see Archer 2007: 178-80. Grenade may have known Ramsey through Lady Magdalen Chester's (formerly Granado) probable acquaintance with his wife: see above p. 27.

132. *Quatre cantons* is perhaps a rendering of the Italian *quattro canti*, which on the Copperplate Map, dating from the 1550s were named, in Italian, as *4 canti,* and denoted the cross roads at the east end of Lombard Street (Fig. 45). A Venetian visitor in 1562 noted that Italian merchants met morning and evening in a street, presumably Lombard Street, closed off at one end with chairs so that traffic could not enter; likewise on Sundays after mass they gathered at the *quattro canti* and made their bargains (Barron et al. 1983: 147, but given only in English translation). These assemblies prefigured later practice at the Royal Exchange.

133. Traditionally associated with Dinant, hence *dinandiers*.

134. On 23 January 1571. Stow (*Summarie* 1573: at end), recorded this event in some detail and may have been Grenade's source; the same account also appears in later editions of Stow, *Chronicles* and is quoted from that of 1604 in Saunders, A. 1997: 44. Ancient cities were provided with buildings and spaces segregated from the public streets for the protection and regulation of trade, and from the twelfth century onwards western European cites again developed similar institutions. The first Bourse took its name from an important family of innkeepers in the centre of Bruges. Before 1450 international merchants came to use the space outside the inn, 'where four streets came together' (compare note 132) and which was also bordered by the Italian consular houses, for regular trading assemblies. By 1460 a similar bourse was being held in the courtyard of a house near the great market in Antwerp, and in 1515 the yard was provided with a stone arcade for protection from the weather. In 1531 this was replaced by the 'New Bourse', a magnificent structure in what was becoming the heart of the expanding city. It enclosed a spacious courtyard surrounded by four vaulted

loggias with an arcade supported by thirty six columns in 'blue stone'. Two double gateways served as entrances and there were two towers with clocks. Trading there, largely conducted in Italian, primary concerned financial and credit transations and contracts. The New Bourse was a direct model for the Royal Exchange, which elaborated on some of its features. The pattern of evolution in London was similar to that in Bruges and Antwerp. During the fifteenth and early sixteenth centuries Lombard Street was a distinctive commercial space in the city which served as a direct link to the Place de la Bourse in Bruges and subsequently to the Bourse in Antwerp. Merchants, including many Italians, established the practice of assembling twice a day in Lombard Street to do business and the east end Lombard Street was identified as *Quattro Canti*. From 1527 a chain was placed across the street during trading, but this did not overcome problems arising from the weather, the narrowness of the street, and passers by. In the 1530s the idea of setting up a bourse at Leadenhall (see pp. 118-19, n. 148) was discussed, but that was too remote from the centre of business. Then it was planned to built a bourse in Lombard Street on the site of the Pope's Head Tavern, where the Bardi had formerly resided. A plan was drawn up but it proved impossible to acquire the site, and so attention shifted to a nearby site between Cornhill and Threadneedle Street, where the Exchange was eventually built. Saunders, A. 1997; Keene 1997; Calabi and Keene 2007.

135. Each of the two French terms used denote women and could be translated as 'female linen-draper'. Grenade was perhaps drawing a distinction between retail and wholesale dealers.

136. Grenade's pace probably measured 2.5 feet (see n. 88), suggesting that the gallery was between 15 and 17.5 feet wide, that the dark stone columns were ten feet apart (as were the jasper columns above them), and that the courtyard measured 200 by 150 feet.

137. *Bize*, is presumably from the adjective *bis, bise*, which could denote a dark grey-brown colour associated with rye bread, but could also mean 'black' (*Littré* (2005) s.n.; Huguet (1925), s. n. Cotgrave 1673 noted the same sense, but also specifically defined *pierre bise* as 'a certain hard stone of sundry colours and bright as flint, which it somewhat resembles'. The columns of *pierre bize* and *marbre jaspin* were probably of the polished limestone from quarries to the N.W. and S.W. of Namur which was widely used from the sixteenth century onwards, and especially appreciated for its varied colours and decorative patterns.

138. The sites where merchants associated with particular commodities or regions met were later known as 'walks'.

139. By au *deßus* Grenade usually means 'above' but in this case au *deßous* must have been intended since there was no space for an inscription above the columns and there is some evidence that the inscriptions were in fact below, where there was a suitable flat space (Saunders, A. 1997: Fig. 36). Grenade's account is evidence that some of these images had been erected by 1578.

140. They were inside and above the portals, facing the courtyard.

141. On her visit in 1571 the queen had especially enjoyed this galley, which by 1573 was known as 'the Pawne', after the Dutch *pandt*, the name for the galleries at the new Bourse of Antwerp (completed 1531), on which the Royal Exchange was modelled. Stow, *Summarie* 1573: s.a. 1572.

142. Later this was known as 'the time of 'Change' or of 'going on 'Change'.

143. Evening concerts at Royal Exchange were provided by the six city waits on Sundays and holidays. COL/CA/01/01/019, fol. 300; Masters 1984: 17.

144. Gresham (*c.*1518-79) was a Mercer and Merchant Adventurer active in Antwerp and also founded Gresham College: Blanchard 2004a.

145. The adjoining houses in the same enclosure may have been parts of the four blocks which

surrounded the courtyard, and perhaps included the shops at ground level facing towards the street.

146. A round, stone prison known as the Tun, standing in the middle of Cornhill since the thirteenth century, was in 1400-1 made into a conduit for water supplied from springs to the west of the city, by means of extending the pipe from the Great Conduit (q.v.), into which additional supplies of spring water had been introduced; according to Stow, there had been a well of spring water next to the Tun, on which was now erected a timber prison known as the Cage, with stocks and pillory above it; the conduit was enlarged and castellated in 1474; a proposal in 1546 to enlarge the cistern was dropped in favour of reconstructing the well and placing the pillory a little further west, as shown in the Copperplate Map of the 1550s. Stow, *Survey*: i. 190-2; Figs 45, 49).

147. The market in the street outside Leadenhall. Archer, Barron and Harding 1988: 10, 61.

148. In the twelfth century this large property, on the south side of Cornhill and just east of Gracechurch Street, had been the London home of the prominent Cornhill family. The City acquired it in 1411 and between 1440 and 1455 rebuilt the northern part of it, next to the street, as four elegant, three-storey ranges, the ground floor being an open gallery around a courtyard intended to accommodate the market for traders from the countryside previously held in the street; a part of the new building was to serve as a granary, probably a response to the grain shortage of 1439, but in the longer term this was not to be a significant use of the structure. The term 'garner', which was sometimes applied to the building, could have designated its wider role as a place for the protection of traders and for the storage of a variety of goods. Simon Eyre, a merchant and civic benefactor who was mayor 1445-6, contributed substantially to the project and in the previous year gave land to enlarge the site, where in May 1444 he was said to be about to erect a garner; he also built the chapel against the east range, according to an inscription inside the chapel. Eyre died in 1459, leaving money to support a college of priests, clerks and choristers celebrating daily in the chapel and for housing to accommodate them. A fraternity of 60 priests was established there in 1466. As a civic property, parts of the new buildings and the yards to the south came to have a variety of uses, including storage, warehousing and the accommodation of several specialised markets, not least in in textiles and iron goods. Grenade's account includes what seems to be the earliest mention of a butchers' market there. Stow noted that the inscription *Dextra Domini exaltauit me* was over the porch of the chapel rather than on the door. Stow, *Chronicles* 1570: fol. 132 (spelling *Dextera*); Stow, *Survey*: i. 153-60 (spelling *Dextra*); *Cal LBK*, 294; Masters 1974: 20-31; Archer, Barron, Harding 1988: 61, 97-8; Samuel 1989; Barron 2004b; Keene 2011: 60-1.

Chapter 10

149. Grenade could have got this date from Stow, *Summarie*, s.a. 1410, e.g. on fol. 107ᵛ of the 1567 edition. The beginning of construction is now attributed to 1411: Barron 1974: 25.

150. Whittington was responsible for the paving of the great hall and the windows; there were other benefactors, but the project required financing by a doubling of the fees for freedom admissions for several years. Barron 1974; Bowsher et al 2007: i. 182-5, ii. 361, 380. The configuration of the Guildhall precinct can best be appreciated through the plans in Bowsher et al. 2007: esp. figs. 174 (i. 183), 200 (i. 207), 218 (i. 227), 351 (ii. 378-9).

151. The hall is about 150 feet long internally; eighty of Grenade's paces would have been 200 feet. The 'black marble tiles' were presumably the Purbeck 'marble' paving paid for with a bequest of £35 from Whittington's executors. The hall fulfilled an intention to impress and to express the authority and governance of the city. Entering this great space though the splendid porch, a visitor would have seen the Court of Husting at the end of the hall to the

right, and the Sheriffs' Court at the end to the left, while directly opposite were the steps leading up towards the Mayor's Court, flanked by the effigies of the two giants. A doorway in south-west corner of the Mayor's Court (the 'utter court') gave access to the council chamber, where the court of aldermen met. For the porch, hall and the mayor's court, see Bowsher et al. 2007, respectively: i. 195-8, ii. 361-4; i. 192-5; i, 212.

152. Grenade appears to be confused: he presumably refers here to the court of Husting (the oldest of the city's courts, after the by then defunct folkmoot), which met once a week at the east end of the hall, its judges being the mayor, sheriffs and aldermen. As he correctly observes below, the sheriff's court met at the other end of the hall (cf. Barron 1974: 30). Nevertheless, the Guildhall was heavily involved in the operation of the criminal law. Treason trials did sometimes occur at Guildhall under commissions of oyer et terminer, but the lord mayor did not preside. A notorious instance was the trial of Sir Nicholas Throckmorton, acquitted by a sympathetic London jury in April 1554. Pirates were regularly arraigned at Guildhall. Recorder Fleetwood records the trial of seminary priests at Guildhall. Although the gaol deliveries of the city of London were taken at the Justice Hall in the Old Bailey, they were always preceded by sessions of peace at the Guildhall; Fleetwood describes these as 'sessions of inquiry' at which, among other things, the indictments of those who were to be arraigned for felonies at the gaol delivery the following day would be read. Patterson 1998; Bowler 1934: vii-x; Machyn 1848: 218, 220, 281, 290; Wright 1838: ii. 63, 170, 186-7, 245, 291.

153. This, apparently formalised in 1568, had grown out of the court of requests established in 1518 as a temporary measure to reduce the number of small claims (less than 40s.) needing to be determined by juries in the Mayor's Court (which had developed the power to remedy disputes in 'conscience' or, later, 'equity'). It rapidly proved popular and was eventually made permanent. Pleas concerning debts of more than 40s. could be heard by the king's courts at Westminster. Foster 1977: 17; Archer 1991: 18; Tucker 2007: 113-18, 318; LMA, COL/CA/01/01/12, fol. 137; COL/AD/01/013, fols 71, 141; Stow, *Survey*: i. 171.

154. This story is based on Geoffrey of Monmouth (i.16). Corineus, a Trojan, gave his name to his share of the island of Albion, which later became known as Cornwall; before the Trojans arrived the island had been uninhabited apart from a few giants, all of whom, except for Gogmagog, were killed by the followers of Brutus; Corineus, who liked wrestling, challenged Gogmagog to a match and killed him by hurling him on to rocks in the sea. Stow, *Summarie* does not record this story, but it was widely known and is in Grafton, *Chronicles*, i. 24-5, drawing on Fabyan (1811), and in the 1577 edition of Holinshed's *Chronicles* (i, *History of England*, 9). Representations of single giants, symbolising the city's strength and authority, had played a part in royal entries and civic processions since 1415 or before, but the earliest evidence for a pair of giants in this role concerns the entry of the Emperor Charles V in 1522, when he was welcomed at the drawbridge on London Bridge by effigies identified as Hercules and Sampson. King Philip of Spain, at his entry in 1554, at the same site encountered a similar pageant of giants, now identified as Corineus and Gogmagog. Giants with those names, identified Corineus the Briton and as Gogmagog the Albion (presumably from *Albanus*, an inhabitant of Albany, the name for Scotland) addressed Elizabeth I at Temple Bar as she left the city after her coronation entry in 1559. These names, evidently an addition to the tradition derived from Geoffrey of Monmouth, may have been adopted, on royal, civic or popular initiative, in response to the war with Scotland in 1547 and the Cornish rebellion of 1549, as an expression of the strength the English monarchy and of the City, where the giants were now, in a sense, held captive and could serve in the traditional giant's role as city champions. The association between this pair of giants and the gates or entries to the city and its authority is noteworthy and is paralleled in their position within Guildhall, presumably the normal resting place of the effigies. They were

also paraded on a variety of other occasions, including the Midsummer Watch and Lord Mayors' Shows. Stow does not mention the effigies by name, but notes that in the Midsummer Watch procession the mayor was accompanied by one giant and the sheriffs by another. In 1562 a Venetian observer, describing the Guildhall interior, mentioned the 'very fine armour hung onto the wall; some say it belonged to giants', which suggests that the effigies were dressed in impressive armour.

Grenade may have heard his version of the story of the two giants during a visit to Guildhall, but the tales told about them were unstable. Paul Hentzner, visiting in 1598, was led to believe that that the giants had helped the English when the Romans waged war upon them (Bentley and Walpole 1757: 34). The giants were still known as Corineus and Gogmagog in 1660, but the significance of the names was becoming lost and by 1700 they were generally known as Gog and Magog. In 1707-8, two new effigies, skilfully carved out of wood, were erected high on the north wall of Guildhall, opposite the main entrance and above and to either side of the steps leading up to the Mayor's Court, a position of high authority where they remained until 1815. Before 1708, however, the effigies appear to have been of wickerwork and pasteboard and were presumably quite often renewed. Grenade's description suggests that in 1578 they occupied the same position in Guildhall as their timber successors, which appear to have resembled them. The effigy of Corineus had come to be identified as that of Magog, an aristocratic figure wearing Roman armour and holding a halberd and a shield, the latter emblazoned with what may have been intended as the eagle from the arms of Richard of Cornwall (d. 1272) after he had been elected King of the Romans. The Scotsman was Gog, an appropriately wild figure wielding a chain mace with a spiked ball. The new names were presumably adopted by reference to the terrifying biblical figures of Gog and Magog (Ezekiel 38-9 and Revelation 20), whom Geoffrey of Monmouth had yoked together to make his especially repulsive giant Gogmagog. See Geoffrey of Monmouth: i.16; Thomas and Thornley 1936: li, 158, 419; Stow, *Survey*: i. 103; Hone (1823), 241, 272, 275; Nichols 1831: 52-8; Price (1886), 77, 89-95; Withington 1918-20: i. 58, 60-1, 133, 137, 141, 176, 189, 191, 199-203; Barron, Coleman and Gobbi 1983: 148; Warkentin 2004: 33, 54, 93-5, 100, 109.

155. This is the Mayor's Court (also known as the Outer Chamber), occupying the upper storey of a building begun in 1424-5 and entered from the Guildhall via its north porch; the smaller chamber to the west, which Grenade mentions next, was the Inner Chamber, occupied by the court of aldermen (Barron 1974: 30-1). It is difficult to understand what Grenade, who was confused concerning the city courts, meant by his reference to 'sessions' presided over by the chief justices. The Guildhall, however, was certainly involved in the operation of the criminal law and the sessions of gaol delivery held by the Crown justices at or near the king's prison in Newgate, and from 1539 at the new Sessions House near the prison (Pugh 1968: 310), were always preceded by 'sessions of inquiry' at Guildhall (see note 152), which may have prompted him to conclude that the chief justices presided there. His misleading account may also have been influenced by a misunderstanding of ceremonial aspects of the sessions, of which the mayor had been a justice ex officio since 1327, other city officers enjoying the same right from later dates. As a result, the mayor and sheriffs came formally to preside at the sessions, some of which were 'held' or 'kept' by the mayor and others by the sheriffs; out of respect for the city's liberties, royal justices did not normally preside within the area of the city's jurisdiction (Pugh 1968: 290-4, 310).

156. Grenade's misleading account is probably derived from Grafton, *Chronicle* 1569: 83, 115, where Grafton states that he obtained the information on 'portgreves' from Fabyan (1811). Similar accounts, but lacking the reference to 'portgraves' or portreeves having been established by William the Conqueror and being replaced in 1190 by bailiffs, appear in Grafton, *Abridgement* (1564 onwards); Stow's account in *Summarie* (1565 onwards)

repeats Grafton and resembles that in Stow, *Survey*: ii, 147-50. London and the county of Middlesex had been administered, probably since before the Norman Conquest, by royal officials known portreeves ('town reeves': the Old English name continued in use well into the twelfth century), who in terms of their responsibilities were the direct predecessors of the sheriffs ('shire reeves', jointly responsible for London and Middlesex and hardly ever described as bailiffs) of the twelfth century and later. The citizens appear to have had the right to elect the sheriffs by 1129-30, but that probably lapsed under Stephen or Henry II. The office of mayor, head of the nascent (though perhaps second) commune, emerged during the reign of Richard I, who was greatly indebted to the city for its financial support and was absent from the realm for a long period. The first mayor was recorded with that title about 1191, but was later believed to have commenced his period of office in 1189, at the beginning of Richard's reign. By his charter of 11 July 1199 King John, anxious to keep the citizens on his side, granted them the right to choose the sheriffs from among themselves, and by his charter of 9 May 1215 granted the barons of the city (an elite group among the citizens, but later identified with the aldermen) the right to choose a mayor with a yearly term of office. This distinction between the election of the mayor by the barons and that of the sheriffs by the citizens was significant and was confirmed by charters of Henry III in 1227, but dropped from later royal charters of confirmation (Birch, 1887).

157. The term 'appurtenances' may have been intended to cover the suburbs within the city's jurisdiction since historically the term 'city' had denoted only the area within the walls; the appurtenances probably also included Southwark. Moreover, the two sheriffs were also jointly responsible to the Crown for the county of Middlesex, where the lord mayor had little formal authority. See also note 190.

158. On 29 September. The account is slightly misleading. The lord mayor nominated one of the sheriffs by drinking to him at a feast, shortly before the formal election at common hall, which between 1538 and 1585 took place on Lammas Day (1 August) and thereafter on 24 June; the other was elected by the liverymen in common hall but he was usually the junior alderman who had not served, with the proviso that if all the aldermen had served another commoner was chosen. According to Beaven the earliest reference to the nomination by toast comes from 1583, so Grenade's remark is noteworthy, though the custom was probably long standing: Machyn notes sheriffs chosen at dinners at the Mercers and Merchant Taylors on 25 July 1559 and 1 July 1562, respectively, and one assumes that they would have been toasted; William Smith notes that Sir John Percival was nominated sheriff by the lord mayor drinking a cup of hippocras (wine flavoured with spices) to him in 1487. Foster 1977: 26; Pearl 1961: 52; *The History of the Sheriffdom of the City of London* 1723: 23; Beaven 1908-13: ii. xxxiii-xxxiv; Wright 1838: ii. 204-5; Machyn 1848: 241, 287; BL, Harleian MS 6363, fol. 43ᵛ; Johnson 1914-22: ii. 445-9.

159. Grenade exaggerates the role of the city and the sheriffs in criminal justice. The city had no jurisdiction over capital crimes, treason and other serious matters, which came before the king's judges. The sheriffs formally 'presided' at certain gaol deliveries and had administrative responsibilities with regard to their activities: this seems to be the basis of Grenade's misinterpretation (see notes 152 and 155, above). The sheriffs' court itself dealt with personal claims and minor crimes.

160. The écu, a gold coin in the money of France, consisted of 3 *livres* or 60 *sous tournois*. In 1500 8,000 écus would have been equivalent to approximately £2,840 sterling (Spufford 1986: 179, 201). There were heavy expectations of civic hospitality from the sheriffs which were to some extent offset by the contributions of liverymen coming to dine with them and the fees of prison administration. Precise figures for the sixteenth century are hard to come by but Sir Thomas Cullum spent at least £2,394 (his gross spending was £3,348 offset by the receipts of office of £954) on the shrievalty in 1646-7. There had been inflation in the

intervening period but hospitality was to some extent curtailed during the civil war, so perhaps Grenade was not wide of the mark. Suffolk Records Office, E2/29/1.1 (account book of Sir Thomas Cullum); Simpson 1961: 135-6.

161. In 1199 King John granted the shrievalty of London and Middlesex to the citizens of London in return for a fixed payment to the Exchequer of £300 a year; it was subsequently claimed that Henry I had made a grant in similar terms and a copy of a charter was confected to back up the claim; given the citizens' conflict with King John, they later preferred to base their claim on Henry III's charter of 18 Feb. 1227, which granted the shrievalty on the same terms as in the 1199 charter (Birch 1887: 26-7). The regalian income from London and Middlesex (sokage and other rents, profits of jurisdiction, tolls, etc) presumably amounted to much more than £300, though a mid-sixteenth century account (surviving in the Mercers' Company archives) of the charge and profits of the office is more pessimistic, suggesting the uncertainties of the income streams, as well as underlining the obligations of hospitality and providing livery to the sheriffs' officers, which were significant additional burdens. This account was explicit that if the receipts did not match the fee farm (which at this point was calculated at £377), then the sheriff would have to provide the shortfall from his own pocket. The sheriffs were entitled to waifs and strays (stray animals unclaimed after three days) and fines for frays and bloodsheds, as well any recovered stolen goods in cases where the victim of the crime did not sue, but the main element of the sheriffs' income was probably from the tolls taken at the gates and bars, except those on London Bridge which went to support the bridge. The most significant element was the duty of scavage with the tolls at Billingsgate, which was estimated as yielding between £100 and £200 in the mid sixteenth century. BL, Harleian MS 6363, fols 10v-11; Mercers' Company, Register of Writings, ii, fols 128v-32. There is evidence of growing fining out from the office in the later sixteenth century, though this may have indicated the exigencies of the hard-pressed city Chamber, rather than a loss of a sense of civic obligation: in other words, people who were known not to want to serve may have been deliberately targeted as a revenue raising device: Wunderli 1990.

162. *Pollice* normally means 'policy' or 'government' rather than 'police'. This account of local policing is somewhat over schematic. Grenade rightly emphasises the importance of the alderman's deputy (though the extramural wards had more than one), but there were many more constables, 242 according to Stow, and the beadles were not subordinate to the constables but answered to the alderman and his deputy, though they may have lost some status over the course of the sixteenth century. Grenade misses the role of the wardmote inquest, a panel of householders appointed annually on St Thomas's Day to inquire into local offences, noted by de Heere. Archer 1991, 218-25; Stow, *Survey: passim*; Barron 2004a: 124; Rexroth 2007: 60-67; Chotzen and Draak 1937: 21-2.

163. Detailed regulations for the dress of aldermen were set out in *Ordre* 1568. See also Chapter 11 (fol. 72; p. 133.). For visual representations, see Fig. 55; Archer, Barron, and Harding 1988; Schlueter 2011: 55-6 and Figs 22, 23, 24.

164. The city had had aldermen, responsible for wards (administrative areas for organising defence and internal order), since the late eleventh century or before. There were probably 24 wards early in the twelfth century, if not earlier. In 1394 one of the wards (Farringdon) was divided, making a total of 25. In Grenade's time, following a royal charter of 1550, Southwark, in the county of Surrey on the south bank of the river, was counted as a city ward with its own alderman, but the city's control there was less strictly exercised than on the north bank (Johnson 1969). The date 1240 is probably from Stow, *Summarie*, e.g.(1567), fol. 65v (1570), fol. 79, or from Grafton, *Chronicle* 1569: 123-4 (previous editions of his *Abridgement* had given the date as 1242), where it is erroneously stated that aldermen were 'first chosen' in that year while previously they had ruled the wards of the

city but held office only for a year. Grenade misunderstood his source. The accounts by Stow and Grafton may ultimately have derived from a contemporary record that in 1249 the mayor legitimately took a ward into the possession of the city and that the men of the ward, being licensed by the mayor, elected a new alderman (Stapleton 1846: 15).

Chapter 11

165. John's charter allowing the election of a mayor does not specify the date of the election. By the fourteenth century mayoral elections took place on the Feast of the Translation of St Edward (13 October) and those of the sheriffs on St Matthew's day (21 September); mayors were sworn in at Guildhall on the Feast of SS Simon Jude (28 October) and sheriffs on the day before Michaelmas (29 September); mayors and sheriffs were admitted at Westminster on the day after their oath-taking in the city (Barron 2004: 146, 151-2, 159-60). By the later sixteenth century the election of the lord mayor took place on 29 September, the day after the sheriffs had been sworn in. There is a near contemporary description of the 1575 election by Recorder Fleetwood who explains that speeches were made both by the recorder and the common sergeant setting out the awesome responsibilities of the office, but the qualities of magistracy would have been underlined also in the sermon in the Guildhall Chapel which preceded the election. A slate of three to four candidates was placed before the liverymen in common hall, from which they would choose two names to go forward to the aldermen, who would make the final selection. As one of the two names was at this time invariably the senior alderman who had not served, the process had a strong ritual element, but the mobilisation of consent was important. There were probably about 2,000-2,500 liverymen in the later sixteenth century. De Heere offers a fuller account than Grenade. HMC, Hatfield: ii. 117; Crowley 1575; Archer 1991: 19-20; Chotzen and Draak 1937: 18-19.

166. Grenade does not use *halle* in its established French senses of 'covered market', 'hall' or 'great chamber', but to denote a body, which in the sixteenth century, as today, would in English commonly have been described as a 'company' or 'guild'. That he chose not to use *compagnie*, but a word which sounded like the English 'Halls' seems significant and may reflect a usage in London with which he was familiar. Just as the Guildhall was the focus of the city's political and social identity, so most companies had (or borrowed) a hall where the fellowship met for festivities and based their judicial and administrative functions, which commonly concerned a trade. In some English cities such 'halls' can be traced back to the eleventh century. In Grenade's mind the hall may have personified the society or company which met there (as was the case with Tammany Hall in later New York). The word may also have seemed appropriate because of its association with trade, as in Paris and elsewhere. Grenade sometimes seems to draw a distinction between 'halls' and 'companies', the former perhaps being the 'Great Twelve' and the latter perhaps the other city guilds. His list on of 'halls, companies and estates' (fol. 68ᵛ, p. 129) implies a hierarchy, though a few lines later he lumps them all together as 'companies'. Elsewhere (fol. 68ᵛ, p.129) he mentions 'halls and companies' as if making a distinction (fol. 71, p. 131). This translation respects his terms, while at the same time recognising that *halle* and *compagnie* could each be translated as 'guild'. The 'estates' may have been other associations with less distinct political and economic functions, perhaps such as the 'Fraternity or Guild of Artillery' established in 1537.

167. The trade in spices was associated with the Grocers' Company; Grenade should have included the Goldsmiths instead of spicers. Otherwise his list of 'The Great Twelve' is correct.

168. The Merchant Taylors' Company.

169. Grenade's use here of the word *raison* may reflect familiarity with Roman Law and the developing idea that it was the fount of the general truth of natural law: Stein 1999: 67, 95-99.

170. Grenade's stress on their contribution to social cohesion is striking. Their wardens did indeed exercise discretionary jurisdiction over masters and apprentices and resolved many disputes informally. The companies played an important role in the support of their members through their almshouses and pensions. Archer 1991: ch. 4; Archer 2002.

171. There was only a limited number of houses appropriate to the extensive hospitality required of the lord mayor. Sir Thomas Ramsey kept his mayoralty in the house in Lombard Street (see note 131, above) formerly owned and built by Sir Martin Bowes (mayor 1545-6); and also noted that the 'fair and large builded house' in Walbrook, on the north side of the church of St Stephen and formerly owned by the earls of Oxford, hosted the mayoralties of Sir Ambrose Nicholas in 1575-6 and Sir John Hart in 1589-90. The mayor and sheriffs were expected to decorate their houses, marking them out by the distinctive pillars noted by Grenade, and their livery companies made grants, usually £40 early in Elizabeth's reign, rising to £66. 13s. 4d. in the later years, for the 'trimming' of their houses. Stow, *Survey*: i. 203, 224: Sayle 1937: 61, 74.

172. The nearest contemporary description by an Englishman of the lord mayor's day (29 October) is by the herald William Smith (*c.* 1550- 1618), 'A Breef Description of the Famous Citie of London', 1575, revised in 1588 (LMA, CLC/262/MS02463; BL, Harl. MS 6363, fols 6v-8, printed by Sayle 1931: 2-3, and Archer and Price 2011: 653-4). For Smith, see Kathman 2004. Also from this period is Lucas de Heere's account which outlines the processional order and gives details of dress (Chotzen and Draak 1937: 19-20). There is also an account of the 1584 procession by Lupold von Wedel (1544-1615): von Bülow 1895: 252-5. Orazio Busino, Venetian ambassador in 1617 provides a fuller account, but by then the show had evolved with more pageantic elements (*CSP Venetian*: xv. 15, 58-63). See also Werner 1999; Jansson and Rogozhul 1994: 162-4. See Fig. 59 for de Heere's image of the lord mayor *ainsy quil marche a son entrie*. Grenade delineates the key elements of the celebrations on 29 October (though without mentioning the lord mayor's oath taking at Guildhall on the previous day): the procession from Guildhall to the riverside and by boat to Westminster; the oath taking at the Exchequer in Westminster; the procession through the streets back to Guildhall; the lord mayor's feast; the service in St Paul's; and the torchlit departure from the cathedral. Most elements of Grenade's account can be found elsewhere, but novel elements are the arrangement of the trumpeters at Westminster, the special gunpowder effects around Paul's churchyard, and the presence of privy councillors in the procession (though on this latter point he may be in error). For modern analysis see Bergeron 1971; Hill 2010; Manley 1995; Lancashire 2002, Archer 2012, though curiously few modern commentators pay much attention to the ordering of the procession, on which contemporaries were more observant.

Grenade's own account of the procession itself, however, is somewhat perfunctory. The liveries of the other companies lined the processional route, having gone ahead of the lord mayor's party on disembarkation from their barges after the trip to Westminster. It was the lord mayor's own company, ranked according to the gradient of social power, who processed through the streets. The key elements were a group of poor men in blue gowns with red sleeves and caps carrying small shields with the arms of company worthies, the bachelors (that is non-liverymen specially selected for the occasion and themselves differentiated according to whether their gowns were trimmed with budge (lamb's wool) or foins (marten fur – the so called rich bachelors), the liverymen in their gowns and goods, and the assistants. The break points in the different elements of the procession were marked by flag and ensign bearers, musicians, and by the whifflers. Once the company hierarchy had passed, the civic elite followed: the sheriffs' officers, the lord mayors' officers, the swordbearer, the lord mayor accompanied by the previous mayor (Fig. 59), the aldermen, with the two sheriffs at the rear. By way of example, the well-documented Merchant Taylors' procession at the inauguration of Sir Thomas Roe involved 80 poor men, 80 bachelors, 30 whifflers, and probably 70 liverymen (Sayle 1931: 43-58).

173. The mayor had originally been accompanied on horseback to Westminster; the permanent switch to the waterborne procession (which was opposed by the Crown) seems to have taken place in 1453 when John Norman was mayor. There may, however, have been occasional waterborne processions before then. LMA, COL/CC/01/01/005, fols 124ᵛ, 126; Lancashire 2002: 145-8, 199-200, 289-90. The river procession embarked at Three Cranes Wharf and returned to Paul's Wharf. From there the procession passed up Knightrider Street through Paul's churchyard, and into Cheapside.

174. The usual complement of trumpeters seems to have been 24, and was provided through the king's sergeant trumpeter. De Heere claimed that there were 18 trumpeters in front of the bachelors and another 6 between them and the liverymen. Machyn 1848: 96; Sayle 1931: 21, 23, 45, 52; Chotzen and Draak 1937: 19.

175. At this date just one pageant seems to have been carried, though by the early seventeenth century the pageants were much more elaborate (cf. Fig. 57), and there were usually four or five different elements. The pageant was portable (in 1568 the Merchant Taylors paid for 16 porters for carrying it), and accompanied the procession thenceforwards; according to Smith it came after the poor men and the first set of whifflers. It was usually the result of a collaboration between artificers and literary men, so in 1568 one Keble the painter was paid £10. 13s. 4d for the pageant, while the speeches were written by Richard Mulcaster, master of the Merchant Taylors' School; repeated references to children performing in the pageants indicate that boy actors drawn from the schools were regularly used. The pageant of 1568 consisted of a figure representing St John the Baptist (the company's patron saint) and a roe deer playing on the mayor's name. St John the Baptist's call for repentance was hearkened to by the roe, a creature celebrated for its speed, wit, and good sight. 'Our roe by sight in goverrmente/ Wee trust shall Rule so well/ That by his doinge, suche may learne/ As covet to excell'. The moralising was pretty heavy-handed, but it was designed to remind the lord mayor of the responsibilities of his office. The animals featured in Grenade's account referred to elements of company heraldry, and were another regular feature: the Grocers' arms had griffins as supporters and a camel on the crest, while leopards featured on the Golsdsmiths'. Sayle 1931: 48, 52, 53-55; Machyn 1848: 73, 96, 155-6, 271; Bergeron 1971: 129; Hill 2010: 192.

176. Deafening noise was provided both on water on land. In 1568 the Merchant Taylors paid £30 for 'the gonneshott upon londe and water', and an additional 20s 'for fyer woorck wthin the Cytie upon Fower wheles' (Sayle 1931: 52). More is known about the cannnonade fired from the galley foist (Carnegie 2004; Sayle 1931: 24-5, 34-5, 47; Machyn 1848: 47, 96, 270), a small ship, usually of 18-20 tons, decked with banners and streamers, moored in the Thames and carrying 16 pieces of ordnance fired off six times over the course of the day (but curiously not mentioned by Grenade), so the emphasis here on the special effects in Paul's churchyard is particularly interesting. A *boete* was small gun of iron used in celebrations, set in a vertical position, loaded with gunpowder and plugged with a wooden stopper (James 1810: ii, Appendix, s.n. *BOETES pour les réjouissances*).

177. A pun in French, where the term *flute* or *fleute* denoted both a musical instrument (so they 'sing') and a piece of small artillery.

178. It is not clear to which group Grenade is referring when he writes of the sergeants. They are possibly the officers of the lord mayor's household who were sometimes referred to as

sergeants, but they are more probably the whifflers or gentlemen ushers who wore velvet gowns, golden chains and carried white staves. They were used to punctuate the procession, with two groups, one on front of, and one behind the pageant, and separating the poor men from the bachelors. The Merchant Taylors appointed 30 whifflers in 1568 'to see that the Bachelours Company goo in order and likewise to see that the poore men that carry the targettes kepe araye and goo in order accordingly' (Sayle 1931: 56).

179. Although some councillors attended the feast, they are not usually mentioned as part of the procession. In any event their placement in the hierarchy would not make much sense at this point in the procession.

180. Presumably citizen members of the mayor's household; cf. Barron 2004a: 157-8 for the *bourgeois* who accompanied the mayor.

181. For the swordbearer, who headed the lord mayor's household, see Barron 2004a: 156-8; Archer, Barron, and Harding 1988: 82-3; and for his dress and equipment, Jewitt and Hope 1895: ii. 101-2, 105, 108-10. From 1520 onwards the city chamberlain met the costs of the swordbearer's swords and ceremonial dress, previously supplied by the mayor, and in that year was to provide a sword and scabbard and caps of grey fur for winter and of silk for summer. In 1519 he had provided a hat for St Bartholomew's Day (24 August) 'of the most goodlyest fassyon'. At least four more swords and five scabbards were purchased or given before 1578. On ceremonial occasions the swordbearer wore a coat of damask trimmed and faced with velvet, first noted in 1539, when, for Henry VIII's muster, he was to have a coat of white damask or white satin, probably trimmed with velvet; later that year, however, one in velvet appears to have been substituted, and in addition he was to have eight coats of russet trimmed with russet velvet. By c.1574, however, his coat was of a dark damask trimmed with velvet (Fig. 59), probably the one seen by Grenade and replaced in 1587. The swordbearer also had a 'cap of maintenance' as a symbol of his standing, perhaps used on less ceremonial occasions than the lord mayor's day. This was probably the 'goodly and ryche' hat for the swordbearer presented by the lord mayor in 1546 and the 'rich hat of crimson velvet called the cap of maintenance' which was mended and garnished in 1614. De Heere's depiction (Fig. 59) matches Grenade's account. The sword is presumably the 'pearl sword' (probably that aquired in 1534 or 1545), but de Heere does not show the pearls on the white velvet scabbard. He does show the rings which Grenade described the swordbearer as wearing, but not the chains and other jewels. This hat is clearly the one described by de Heere (Chotzen and Draak 1937: 18) as a 'count's hat' (*Graeuen hote*, probably meaning a 'high hat') of grey fur (and could perhaps also be decribed by Grenade's term *mortier,* which denoted a distinctive high, round cap, now worn by certain French and German magistrates and some academics. The term *mortier* might better describe the swordbearer's white headgear worn during the summer (cf Schlueter 2011: Figs 22-5) or the smaller cap, perhaps of brown fur, which he is depicted as wearing in a representations of 1598 and 1620 (Fig. 60; Archer, Barron and Harding 1988: Plate I; Fig. 60). We are most grateful to Stuart Minson for providing transcripts from the city's Repertories and Journals up to 1546, supplementing the orders printed in Jewitt and Hope 1895.

182. Grenade describes the harness of the mayor's horse more or less exactly as de Heere (Fig. 59) had depicted it. The image of the mayor's collar and order (pendant) is especially detailed and makes a contribution towards understanding their history. The collar had originated as a collar of SS bequeathed by Sir John Allen in 1545 to the mayor and his successors. In 1567 it was enlarged by the addition of four SS, and two gold knots and two jewelled roses. In 1558 Sir Martin Bowes gave the pendant which was added to it: a gold cross set with pearls and precious stones. In 1568 £23. 19s. 10d. were spent on enlarging the collar, which was repaired in 1572, when the cross and stones were 'new made'. De Heere's image shows the collar and pendant shortly after this work and indicates that the

collar probably had 14 roses (here coloured blue) and 14 knots and perhaps 16 SS. It shows the pendant hanging from a knot and therefore indicates that the gold portcullis, from which the new pendant acquired in 1607 now hangs, was not an original feature, as was once suggested, but probably an addition made in 1607 or later. In 1895 the collar still had 14 roses and 13 knots, but the number of SS had been increased to 28. Jewitt and Hope 1895: ii. 101-15. For images of the lord mayor in other processions, see Schlueter 2011: 55-66 and Figs 21-5.

183. About £1,065 sterling at the 1500 rate of exchange. Grenade's estimate of £1,000 is probably an exaggeration. According to William Smith the feast cost £400, to which the lord mayor contributed £200 and the sheriffs £100 each. This is corroborated by our knowledge of the costs of the 1556 and 1557 feasts, which were respectively £331. 12s. 6d. and £190. 8s. 5d., the difference being accounted for by the fact that in 1556 the feast was one of meats and that in 1557 a fish dinner. Real costs would in any event be difficult to calculate because of the practice of securing gifts of venison from one's friends and allies. Sayle 1931: 3; Mercers' Company, Register of Writings, ii, fol. 144. The Mercers' register also provides us with an account, unique to the sixteenth century, of how the space in the Guildhall was allocated to accommodate all the guests: ibid., fols. 142v-3.

184. 1 November. According to the *Ordre* (1568), the mayor and aldermen went to St Paul's on All Saints Day on horseback in their scarlet gowns and cloaks after evening prayer in the Guildhall. This was one of several civic occasions in the cathedral over the course of the year: there were finely graded distinctions such as the colour of gowns to be worn (scarlet, puke, or violet), whether they went on horseback, and whether they wore their chains and tippets.

185. The lord mayor enjoyed this precedence only within the city of London.

Chapter 12

186. This story is from Geoffrey of Monmouth (i.18). A thread in Geoffrey's text concerns good rulers as lawmakers, reflecting Anglo-Norman concerns c.1130; Geoffrey included Dunwallo Molmutius and Belinus, but not Lud, among such rulers. Grafton (*Abridgement* 1564: fol. 7) added this to the accomplishments of Lud, who 'amended the laws and took away all usages that were naught', a statement recalling the preface to Justinian's *Institutes*. This was evidently intended as a signal for his characterisation of Edward the Confessor, who (fol. 30v) 'established holy laws which to this day are called King Edward's laws or the common lawes of England, for the maintenance whereof, when by the Normans they were taken away the people were much grieved and by force sought to have them again'. Grafton probably borrowed the characterisation of Edward's laws as the common laws from Lily 1548a: fo. 57v, which has *leges posteri communes appellarunt*. Stow, *Summarie* 1565, fol. 50, and in subsequent editions, shortened Grafton's account, adding a statement that Edward 'purged the olde and corrupt lawes and picked out of theym a certayne, which were most profitable for the commons, and therfore were they called the common Lawes'. Grafton (*Chronicle* 1569: 179) incorporated Stow's text. Grenade, with his interest in law and the maintenance of good order, presumably gave special attention to these passages, but it is not possible to say whether he based his text on Grafton's *Chronicle* or on some combination of the shorter works by Grafton and Stow. The supposed laws of Edward the Confessor were compiled and written down in the twelfth century, long after Edward's death, and came to have a special significance for the citizens of London since William the Conqueror had formally confirmed that they were to be as law-worthy as they had been under King Edward. Copies of the citizens' own updated version of Edward's laws, compiled at the time of their conflict with King John, were registered in the city's archives. O'Brien 1999; Wormald 1999: 407-12; Keene 2008b.

187. For Edward's laws, see n. 186.

188. King William had no such policy: his letter confirming the rights of the Londoners was written in Old English. Grenade possibly had in mind the so-called *Leis Willelme*, the earliest surviving version of which is a text in French written about 1175 and probably translated from a Latin compilation made in the early decades of the twelfth century, at about the same time as two other collections of supposedly current laws, one attributed to Edward the Confessor, from which parts of the *Leis Willelme* are derived, and the other to Henry I (Wormald 1999: 407-15). By the early thirteenth century some city regulations in London were being written down in Anglo-Norman, the business language of the city and not much different from the equivalent language in Paris. Copies of many such regulations dating from the thirteenth and fourteenth century were in the fifteenth century copied into city registers such as the *Liber Albus* (Riley, ed. 1859) and would have seemed old fashioned, but no worse, to francophones of Grenade's generation. Grenade, however, had almost certainly encountered the 'law-French', used for legal pleading and disputation and for the 'Readings' of statutes at the Inns of Court, for which his assessment would have been more accurate. Nevertheless, Grenade may have confused the Anglo-Norman of William's 'laws', which was also used for some later statutes, with law-French (see below, n. 215).

189. The problem is to determine whether what follows was taken from a code or whether it was constructed by Grenade from individual cases that he knew about.

190. By *dependances* Grenade probably meant the extra-mural suburbs subject to the city's jurisdiction, but it is possible that he was thinking of those many English towns whose customs were modelled on those of London. Cf. note 157.

191. Grenade could have known of a case in 1293, when the right hands of three men, including a goldsmith, were cut off in Cheapside on the order of the king's justices, from Stow, *Chronicles* 1570: fol. 89v.

192. The legal basis of Bridewell's activities was the charter of 1553 (which gave the governors sweeping powers of search and arrest in London and Middlesex) and city custom which had sanctioned a variety of secular penalties against sexual offenders. But the basis of its actions was never properly codified and already in the later 1570s its jurisdiction was being contested. Ingram 2002; Archer 1991: 231-3, Griffiths 2003.

193. i.e. the constables of the ward.

194. Grenade's discussion of the measures against vagrancy combines elements of city practice with the provisions of the 1572 statute. The statute laid down whipping and ear boring as the penalty for conviction at sessions on the first offence, death (albeit with the possibility of benefit of clergy) on the second offence, and death without benefit of clergy on the third (*Statutes of the Realm*, iv, pt 1, 590-1; 14 Eliz. I c. 5). Grenade is perhaps a little sanguine about the scope of work provision in the parishes which seems to have been very limited.

195. Pensions were normally available only to the resident poor, and to narrowly defined categories (the aged and impotent) though others may have benefited from occasional payments, the so-called casual poor. Pensioners were sometimes allowed to beg within their parish under licence from the authorities.

196. By the statute of 1503, Company ordinances had to be approved by the law officers, and usually contained specific provisions for the regulation of craft standards and the labour supply. Although in some companies like the Mercers craft identity was already weakening, the general picture remains one of fairly vigorous regulation. Archer 1991; Ward 1997. Compare Chotzen and Draak 1937: 25.

197. The scope of regulation was indeed wide. Since at least the thirteenth century the city had been regulating the prices salt, fish and wine and setting the weight of bread according to

the price of grain, and in the fifteenth century the machinery of regulation was extended to beer (ale was already covered), meat, and poultry. The mayor's oath included the requirement that he enforce the assizes, and see weights and measures properly regulated. The city also claimed the right of metage over all articles of consumption brought coastwise to the port of London; this facilitated the king's collection of customs, but it also involved the bringing of samples before the lord mayor to determine prices. Official meters of corn, salt, fruit, and coal were appointed by the lord mayor and aldermen, and these are probably the officers referred to. Barron 1970: 239-57, 570-8; Norton 1869: 390-2; Archer, Barron, and Harding 1988: 22.

198. The hours of the watch were from 9 pm until 5 am between Michaelmas and 1 April, and from 10 pm until 5 am from 1 April to Michaelmas. According to the articles of the wardmote inquest the curfew was marked by the tolling of the bells of the churches of St Mary Bow, Allhallows Barking, St Giles Cripplegate, and St Bride. The aldermen were rather less sanguine about the effectiveness of the watch. In October 1572, for example, in a typical precept, they ordered that watchmen should not be boys or lame men, but able men harnessed with a head piece. Platter was more nuanced, commenting of the measures against prostitution, that although close watch was kept, 'great swarms of these women haunt the town in the taverns and playhouses'. English men abroad might feel that London was a safer city. A brief exposure to the criminality and violence of the streets of Paris caused James Howell to remark in 1620 upon 'the excellent Nocturnall Government of our City of London, wher one may passe and repasse securely all hours of the night, if he give good words to the Watch'. LMA, COL/CA/01/01/019, fol. 374v; Williams 1937: 174-5; Howell 1650: 26. Cf. Griffiths 2008: 349-60. The belief that curfew was ordained by William the Conqueror appears to have originated in the sixteenth century (Grafton, *Chronicle*: ii. 9; Stow, *Survey*: i. 99-100).

199. Householders were obliged to hang out lanterns with candle lights. This is generally ascribed to Henry Barton, lord mayor in 1416-17 and 1428-9, but on little authority. By the later sixteenth century the expectation was that lights would be maintained from dusk until 9 pm between 1 October and 1 March, though precinct lanterns may have burned for longer. There were recurrent complaints that householders failed to fulfil their obligations. Roskell, Clark, Rawcliffe 1996: ii. 135-8; de Beer 1941; Griffiths 2008: 342-9.

200. Post-Reformation injunctions allowed bells to be rung for the dying, with a short peal immediately after death, and two others before and after the burial, but practice was often more liberal. Given the anxieties of some of the reformed about the tolling of bells, Grenade's endorsement is notable. The association of the practice with a civic order, is however puzzling, as the tolling of bells was a matter for regulation by the ecclesiastical authorities. Marshall 2002: 161-7. We are grateful to Peter Marshall for advice on this note.

201. The mayor in 1547-8 was Sir John Gresham (Beaven 1908-13: ii. 30; Blanchard 2004b). It was customary for liverymen to participate in the funeral processions of deceased brethren, and wills often include provisions for a funeral dinner for the livery, but they would inevitably have been drawn from further afield than the deceased's parish.

202. Grenade's endorsement of the practice of funeral sermons is notable given the anxieties they sometimes evoked in reformed circles. Marshall 2002: 156-61.

203. Such generosity so impressed Grenade that he twice gives an account of it (cf. fol. 67, p. 128); or is this repetition evidence of hasty composition?

204. The silver coin known as the groat.

205. Thomas Huntlowe (d. 1544) was sheriff of London in 1539-40. According to his will dated 13 August 1544 he requested that on its repayment the £200 he had lent to the king the

previous summer should be given to the Haberdashers' Company, and the profits used to support those living in the Haberdashers' properties rent free. It is intriguing that his bequest was also singled out for mention with the same details provided, by William Smith, who was a haberdasher. PRO, PROB 11/30, fols 104v-6; BL, Harleian MS 6363, fol. 47ᵛ.

206. Grenade's marginal note here mistakenly repeats the reference to Haberdashers Hall, when Vintners' Hall would have been intended. John Stodey, vintner (d. 1375/6), was mayor in 1357-8. In the mid fourteenth century he put together a large block of properties between Thames Street and the river, straddling the boundary between the parishes of St Martin and St James, both in Vintry. This appears to have been included in the residue of his estate which by his will of 1375 he divided between his four daughters. About 1400, when the vintners may already have used a part of the property for assemblies, they appear to have delegated one of their number, John Michol (or Michel), to acquire the rights in Stodey's former property, which by then belonged to the heirs of his daughters. About 1408 the reunited property passed from Michol's executors to five feoffees, each of whom was later a master of the Vintners' Company, which probably had full use of the property from that time onwards. The surviving feoffee, by his will of 1446, left the property to the Masters and Wardens of the Vintners to the use of the commonalty, on condition that they convert a large hall and other rooms to their use, bestow 13 small houses there on 13 poor men free of rent, and maintain the obits with which the property was charged. The remainder of the property was let for rent. A succession of feoffees continued in possession, and in 1496 one of them, a vintner, left the property under precisely the same terms as it had been bequeathed in 1446. The almshouses may have been established soon after 1446, but if the will of that year simply repeated the conditions of an earlier bequest, they could have been established earlier. By the late sixteenth century, John Stodey, who had charged the property with rent to support chantries in the church of St Martin Vintry, had been attributed a larger role in the foundation of the hall and the amshouses. Sharpe 1889-90: ii. 171, 191, 596 675n: Stow, *Survey*: i. 106, 240. The account of the early history of the hall in Glover 1971: 2-3 and Crawford 1971: 35-7, is in need of clarification.

207. Grenade's account here is a reminder that 'one of the most common activities of the London mob was to assist in law enforcement rather than breaking the law' (Shoemaker 2004: 30). The rallying cry of the apprentices on the streets may have been 'prentices and clubs', and violence may have been part of the accepted code of masculinity, particularly for young men, but sometimes they acted to enforce order, as when apprentices intervened to protect the earl of Southampton assaulted by Lord Grey's followers in the Strand in January 1601: we are told that 'therle defended hymselfe till clubbes came to succour hym' (Westminster Diocesan Archive, MS A.7, p. 3, a reference we owe to the generosity of Paul Hammer). On the other hand it is worth noting that homicide cases in the metropolitan area reveal the apparent availability of swords and rapiers to groups beyond the gentry (Jeaffreson 1886-92).

208. Englishmen were obliged to arrest anyone they saw committing a felony, and to join in the hue and cry when instructed by a constable; the sergeants discussed here probably refer to the sheriffs' officers, who carried maces, though possibly the constables are meant, for from at least 1572 they were required to carry staves of one-and-a-half ells length bearing the arms of the city and the crown for appeasing frays. Wardmote inquests were required to present the names of those who refused to assist constables and beadles in the keeping of the peace. Herrup 1987: 70-2; LMA, COL, CA/01/01/019, fol. 461; COL/CA/01/01/020, fols 12, 18v.

209. Not city courts, but Sessions of the Peace, for which, from the late fourteenth century onwards, the governors of the city were commissioned to act for the Crown. On the operation of the criminal law in London in this period, see Archer 1991: ch. 5; Griffiths

2008. Sessions of gaol delivery were held between ten and twelve times a year. It is difficult to verify the figure for executions. William Smith, writing in 1575, explained that the sessions were held every four to six weeks, and that up to 60 persons might be condemned at any one sitting, 'of which parsons so condemned there is executed in one day 20 or 30, & I have knowne 36 at a tyme to suffer'. For a slightly earlier period Machyn records numbers of executions at Tyburn, though not consistently; the highest figure was 20 on 23 February 1561; the lowest was three on 12 January 1560; more usual was between nine and twelve. Platter in 1598 claimed that between 20 and 30 persons were gibbeted at each sessions. The volume of indictments (and probably the number of executions) was rising through the reign. This was indeed a bloody period in the history of the English criminal law. Jeffreason estimates that in the reign of James I about 75 people were being executed at the Middlesex sessions; that figure should probably be doubled to take account those sentenced at the sessions held separately for the city of London. BL, Harleian MS 6363, fol. 10r-v; Machyn 1848: 223, 227, 233, 251-2, 256, 280, 286, 301; Williams 1937: 174; Jeaffreson 1886-92: ii. xvii-xx.

210. Wardmote inquests were particularly concerned with the fire risks posed by chimneys, presenting fireplaces lacking reredos (brick backings). See LMA, CLC/W/HF/001/MS04069/001 (Cornhill wardmote inquest book).

211. The open air sermons at St Paul's Cross in the area to the north-east of the cathedral were indeed major civic occasions. St Paul's Cross had been erected and was serving as a site for political assembly by 1216, and was being used as a site for preaching by at least 1387; regular attendance by the lord mayor and aldermen dates back to the 1420s. The wooden pulpit with open sides shown in the Gipkyn diptych of 1616 (Fig. 60) was built by Bishop Thomas Kempe of London in 1449. A gallery had been constructed against the wall of the north choir aisle in 1483 for the lord mayor, aldermen, and their wives; this was replaced by a more substantial sermon house in 1569. The low wall creating an ambulatory around the pulpit was built between 1595 and 1608. Although contemporary estimates of congregations of 6,000 are probably exaggerated, the sermons undoubtedly attracted a large and variegated audience, and were widely reported. Morrissey 2011: 16, 19-24; MacClure 1958; Pauls and Boswell 1989; Keene et al. 2004, 31, citing Michel 1840, 197; Tudor-Craig 2004.

212. There were general markets in Cheapside, Newgate, Cornhill, Leadenhall, and Southwark. Archer, Barron, and Harding 1988: 9-10; BL, Harleian MS 6363, fo. 22.

213. Precepts were regularly issued for the cleaning of the streets, and Mark Jenner has shown that they were increasing in frequency from the 1560s. There were serious efforts to give publicity to the measures: it was ordered in 1572 that a mayoral proclamation on the subject should be printed and a certain number set upon posts. The expectation was that householders would sweep up rubbish for collection by the raker at least every other day, and from the 1580s usually daily, though de Heere implies that the rubbish was collected only on Saturdays. Wells were to be drawn with ten bucketfuls of water to be poured down the channel to sweep away filth at least three times per week, and sometimes daily. Street cleaning was financed by a rate collected by the scavengers elected for two-year terms; the rate has been estimated as yielding around £900 (about a quarter of the size of the poor rate) at the end of Elizabeth's reign, and gives a useful benchmark for the cost of street cleaning. LMA, COL/CC/01/01/019, fol. 243v; COL/CC/01/01/021, fol. 485; COL/CA/01/01/019, fol. 321; COL/CA/01/01/021, fol. 374v. Jenner, 1992: 54-86, 112-117; Rawcliffe 2013: 135-8; Chotzen and Draak 1937, 23; Archer 2001a: 601.

214. See above, Chapter 2, fol. 14r-v (pp. 65-6). Each of the Inns of Chancery was supervised by one of the four Inns of Court (Gray's Inn, Lincoln's Inn, Inner Temple and Middle Temple).

Grenade provides a relatively well-informed description of the inns and legal training, presumably based on conversations with lawyers and possibly by observation at readings or moots and attendance at the ceremonies of the serjeants at law (see below, notes 215-16). There had been nine Inns of Chancery until 1549, when the site of Strand Inn was taken for Somerset House. The Inns of Court were often referred to as 'houses', as Grenade does on one occasion. For a concise account of this system of legal education, equivalent to a university in scale, see Baker 2002, 156-65.

215. The name of these moots derives from the Old English *mot*, meaning 'assembly' or 'court', not from the Latin words for 'movement or 'motion' as Grenade claimed. Grenade does not clearly distinguish the two principal learning exercises undertaken at the Inns of Court and Chancery. At that time moots were exercises in pleading modelled on cases heard in the Court of Common Pleas and conducted in law-French. Readings were courses of lectures given by experienced lawyers, including serjeants elect, who read out statutes and raised questions concerning them by discussing imaginary cases; one of the younger 'utter barristers' then attempted to prove that the reader's points were contrary to law; after the reader had refuted the objections, any judges or serjeants present gave their opinions. 'Inner barristers' were students admitted from the Inns of Chancery to the Inns of Court, where after about seven year's training they might expect to be called to the bar as 'utter barristers'. See Thorne and Baker 1990: liv-lxxii; Baker 2001: 227-34.

216. That is, serjeants at law. During the fourteenth century the leading pleaders at the Common Bench came to be organised as an estate or order resembling a guild, known as the serjeants at law, the highest ranking lawyers below the Crown's judges. Grenade's account of them is approximately correct, although contemporary descriptions of their ceremonial admission, feast and dress differ from his in detail and suggest that his account was a summary one and perhaps based on hearsay as well as observation. Moreover, the order of the ceremonies, which often took place over several days, varied from occasion to occasion. While monarchs sometimes attended the feast, it seems that the serjeants elect were neither presented to nor confirmed by the monarch in person, those roles being performed by the lord keeper of the great seal and the lord chief justices on the monarch's behalf. The presentation of a ring for (but rarely, if ever, to) the monarch may have been a mid sixteenth-century innovation, since it appears to be mentioned only in the accounts of the ceremonies in 1577 and later. The ceremonies and processions for newly elected serjeants, many parts of which took place in public view, were major state occasions, involving members of the Privy Council, the chief justices, other legal officers, other members of the Inns, the lord mayor and civic officers, and the relatives and friends of the serjeants. Grenade may have witnessed some of the well-recorded events in 1577, on Friday 15, Monday 18, and Tuesday 19 November, with which his account has both similarities and differences.

On the Friday the sergeants appeared before the lord keeper of the great seal at the Chancery bar in Westminster Hall, where they delivered their writs, swore their oaths and collectively gave the lord keeper a ring to be transmitted to the queen and presented rings to other officers. On the Monday they again went to Westminster and performed similarly before the lord chief justice of Common Pleas. On Tuesday, the festive day, they took formal leave of their inns and went to the Temple, where in black robes they entered the recently constructed Middle Temple Hall (completed early in the 1570s), where the two chief justices, in scarlet robes with collars of SS about their necks, the other judges and many other lawyers awaited them. After an oration, the new serjeants each knelt down before a judge, who put on the serjeant's head his linen coif and laid on his shoulders his scarlet hood. The judges then went to Westminster Hall. The new serjeants then replaced their black gowns with particoloured ones, with a tabbard over, pulling out the tail of the hood behind. They then processed in single file to Westminster Hall, with many officials before them and gentlemen and servants behind. In the hall they did reverence to the chief justice of Common Pleas and waited for the other judges, from the lord treasurer downwards, to assemble. Then, before the bar, each new serjeant in turn repeated his declarations and his writs were read aloud. Serjeant Bendlowes (Fig. 61) concluded the proceedings by putting a case before the chief justice and the court rose. The sergeants then returned to the Temple in the order as before. Once there they changed their particoloured gowns for violet ones and with their scarlet hoods on their shoulders and coifs on their heads entered the hall and stood until the lords of the Privy Council, the lord mayor and the judges were seated. Then they sat and dined, ceremoniously apart from the others. After the feast each serjeant went to his chamber in the Temple and welcomed his friends who had dined there. Then all went to St Paul's, heard a sermon and returned to the Temple by torchlight. On such occasions the serjeants distributed more than 150 gold rings.

Before the construction of Middle Temple Hall, the ceremonies were based in other inns or in great houses borrowed for the occasion, such as Ely Place or Lambeth Palace. Before the Reformation, ceremonies had been more elaborate, including visits to Our Lady of Pew and to the shrine of St Edward in Westminster Abbey and to St Stephen's Chapel. Moreover, the link between the serjeants and the city had been given greater emphasis, for the serjeants had made offerings at the church of St Thomas of Acre at the east end of Cheapside, where the citizens' patron saint, St Thomas of Canterbury, had been born. They had then processed along Cheapside to St Paul's, where they entered through the north door, making offerings at the rood there and at the shrine of St Erkenwald behind the high altar, before they were assigned their places at the pillars in the north aisle of the nave. The sergeants' distinctive dress and ceremonial were designed to emphasise their characteristics as an order with a tradition of service, and to make them stand out in the crowd when doing business at St Paul's or Westminster Hall. See Baker 1984: *passim*, esp. 269-79, 303-11.

217. Lawyers at this date often referred to their inns as 'houses'.

Chapter 13

218. See fol. 38 (pp. 101-2).

219. King John confirmed them by his charter of 17 June 1199, referring to the customs as they were in the time of King Henry I. John died in 1216; his son Henry III, by his charter of 16 March 1227, the year in which he attained his majority, confirmed them as they had been in the time of Henry I and as in John's charter. There is no surviving original of Henry I's charter, unlike those of the other royal charters to the city of that period which were carefully archived in the city treasury, and it is known only from a copy in an early thirteenth-century collection of laws and customs; it was almost certainly an early thirteenth-century forgery. Henry III's other charters to the city issued earlier in 1227 refer to the customs and liberties as they were in the time of John, but no earlier. Birch 1887: nos VII, XV.

220. The citizens appear to have acquired their common seal on their own initiative about 1216-17; the earliest royal charter to the citizens to mention it is that of 1319. No royal charter mentions the sheriffs' clerks, but the sheriffs (or their equivalents) had undoubtedly had clerks by c.1143-5, when the future St Thomas of Canterbury was employed as one: Barlow 1986, 26-7. Where Grenade's text refers to clerks it seems confused and the apostrophe in *d'eux* may be erratic. The phrase could have been intended as *auoir vn chacun deux clercs*, meaning 'each of them to have two clerks', but the MS reads *auoir vn chacun d'eux clercs*, a syntactically problematic formulation which may have been intended to mean 'each one of them to have clerks'. The latter seems to be preferable as an interprepretation, since in 1356 it was ordained that each sheriff have a chief clerk and a second clerk, plus two more if necessary; by the fifteenth century each of the sheriffs had three clerks with titles, who

were to be free of the city, plus an unknown, but probably large, number of other clerks: *Cal LBK*, 72; Riley (ed.) 1859: 519; cf. Barron 2004, 168.

221. The charter by which Henry III confirmed the shrievalty of London and Middlesex is that of 18 February 1227. The sheriffs had been responsible for both areas since the twelfth century or earlier.

222. This statement accurately reflects London's dominant role in trade throughout England, but falsely draws a contrast between the rights of citizens of London and those of citizens or burgesses of many other towns, in which it is probably influenced by the author's knowledge of Londoners' right to trade free of toll (see note 224, below). Country people and merchants from other towns had restricted rights to trade in the public markets of a town, but could not set up shop there to engage in retail trade unless they became citizens or burgesses. This applied as much to London merchants as to those from other towns, but the economic and political strength of London gave the Londoners a greater informal advantage when trading elsewhere than provincial merchants had when trading in London. The significance, if any, of the use of the term 'burgesses' rather than 'citizens' at this point is not clear; charters granting rights to Londoners from at least as early as 1155 × 1161 referred to them as citizens.

223. Conflicts over archery presumably referring to the disputes occasioned by the enclosure of the fields where the Londoners used to practice. Stow, following Edward Hall, records that in 1514 the citizens pulled down hedges in the suburbs (Islington, Hoxton, Shoreditch etc). Stow, *Survey*: ii. 77-8.

224. This right was granted to the citizens by Henry II by his charter of 1155 × 1161, as being among the liberties and customs said to have been enjoyed in the time of King Henry I. The supposed charter of Henry I, of which no original survives, was probably confected early in the thirteenth century. Birch 1887: nos III, IV.

225. The charter of Henry II granted them their hunting grounds or chases (*fugationes*), wherever they had had them in the time of Henry I. The supposed charter of Henry I stated that they had them in Chiltern, Middlesex and Surrey, locations presumably derived from FitzStephen's description of the city, written 1173-4, which listed them as Middlesex, Hertfordshire, 'the whole of Chiltern', and 'Kent as far as the river Cray'. Birch 1887: nos III, IV.

226. This was the 'Lord Mayor's Hunt', which hunted with hawks as well as hounds and in 1460 claimed hunting rights in Essex. Its hounds were kept near Moor Gate, but in 1512 were moved to a new 'Dogge hous' in Moor Field (see Fig. 24) and in 1570 still further out to a site in Finsbury Fields. Masters 1969: 99-101.

227. This characterization of the disputes between reformers and the Catholic Church and their catastrophic impact on the lives of many seems to focus on Luther's criticism of the doctrine of Transubstantiation and his quarrel with Zwingli over the nature of Christ's presence in the Eucharist. Use of the term *querelle* endows these violent clashes of views with some of the features of a legal action.

228. Matthew 25:35.

FRENCH TEXT

[fol. 1]

M.56.

LES SINGVLARITEZ
De Londres, noble, fameuse Cité,
capital du Royaume d'Angleterre:
ses antiquitez et premiers fondateurs:-

[fol. 1 bis]

A Tres-magnifique Seigneur.
Monseigneur le Maire de Londres
et aux honorables Seigneurs
Aldermans ses bons freres

Quand premierement ie suis mis a
escrire ce petit Traité, par lequel i'ay entre
pris de descrire les rares et particulieres
singularitez de vostre noble et fameuse
cité de Londres (Tres-magnifique et
honorables Seigneurs), si ie me fuße arres-

[fol. 1 bis^v]

té simplement a considerer d'une part, vostre
grandeur et excellence et d'autre part ma[1]
petiteße et baße condition, faisant conferén-
ce de l'un a l'autre, ie n'euße iamais pense ne osé entreprendre cet oeuure, et encore moins de le vous presenter. Mais
apres avoir longtemps pensé en moymes-
me (quj suis estranger, et quj par la
grace de Dieu, ay en voyageant diligemment[2]
obserué les singularitez des pais et republi-
ques par lesquelles Dieu m'a fait paßer)
estant finalement venu en cete vostre Cité,
en laquelle i'ay fait quelque seiour, pour

1. *seems to read* una.
2. mm *in* diligemment *is represented by seven minims.*

me soulager apres tant de trauaux que
l'iniure du temps m'a aportez: ie n'ay peu

[fol. 2]

faire que les choses que i'y ay obseruees tres-me-
morables et excellentes n'ayent esté mises
en auant pour plusieur raisons.   La
premiere est que i'ay consideré n'estre raisona-
ble que tant de tesmoignages de la bonté,
puißance et largeße de Dieu qu'on voit
reluire viuement en vn nombre infinj
de choses singulieres, desquelles *vostre* Cité
est pleine, fußent[3] comme enseuellies deda*n*s
les limites et circuit d'icelle? sans estre
cognues de ceux quj en estans ignorans
prendront vn singulier contentement
d'en ouyr faire le recit: La seconde est
vn grand et feruent desir que i'ay de lo*n*gtemps
eu de pouuoir m'employer a faire quelque

[fol. 2ᵛ]

chose qui seruit a la decoration de cete noble Cité:
en recognoißance de beaucoup de biens que moy
et les miens auons de longtemps receu et
receuons encore dicelle.[4]   La troisieme est que
cette magnifique Cité, a par plusieurs fois
ouuert sa poitrine pour y loger
pres de ses plus nobles entrailles l'Eglise
du Seigneur Jesus, lors que la corde, l'es
pee, et le feu la poursuiuoient de
tous costez. Et non seulement cela, mais
außj (par maniere de dire) l'a nourrie
de son propre sang, et duquel elle nourrit ses plus tendres enfans.   La quatrieme, est vostre grande benignité et douc-
c*eur* par laquelle ie m'aßeure quil vous plai-

[fol 3]

ra supporter ma trop grande hardieße d'auoir
entrepris cet œuure, et außj mon imbecillité
sur ce fait.   Or toutesfois si espere ie que
ce mien labeur raportera du proffit et, contentement a plusieurs, tant de ma nation
qu'autres estrangers a la cognoißance des-

3. sußent *in MS.*
4. dicelle *inserted above line.*

quels il paruiendra, et m'en sauront bon
gré.   D'autre part ie n'auray pas peu
profité si ie puis engendrer quelque bonne
enuie a quelqu'un plus expert que moy
de mener cette mattiere a plus grande
perfection.   Finallement, tant les amis
que les ennemis de vos grandeurs, prendront
occasion de ce mien ouurage, les vns, en
vous admirant, de vous louer et reuerer

[fol. 3ᵛ]

de plus en plus: et les autres de vous creindre
d'auantage.   Voila, en somme, cequj⁵
m'a meu et prouoqué, non seulement d'entreprendre cet œuvre, mais außi de vous
en faire vn bien humble present; ce que
ie fay maintenant⁶, et d'außi⁷ bon cœur comme
ie m'aßeure que vostre humanité et dou-
ceur l'aura pour agreable.   Mais qu'est
ce que ie vous offre? Je vous donne pour
estrenes de ce nouuel an, cete Cité de
Londres vestue et ornee de ses plus beaux
habillemens, et excellens ioyaux, que
i'ay recueillis ça et la dedans ses cabinets.
Mais qu'est ce que i'offre a vos honneurs?
Je vous donne Londres auec son excel-

[fol. 4]

lence. Mais quoy? Elle est deia vostre.
Außi fai ie cela d'autant plutost, que i'ap-
proprie la chose a son propre.   Car c'est
comme si ie donnois Londres à Londres:
ou, pour mieux dire, vous mesmes à
vous mesmes. Ce qui me donne plus de
esperance, que vous le receurez de meil-
leure part, est que combien qu'en ce qu'il
ya du mien, le tout est humble et petit:
toutesfois en tant qu'on y voit grandement
reluire l'honneur vostre, il est tres grand
riche et magnifique.   Et si ie cognois
que vos nobles Seigneuries ayent a gré
cete mienne bonne volonté, en ce petit
present que ie vous fay, cela me donnera

5. *three dots under* quj *to indicate their omission.*
6. mainenant *inserted above line to replace* ~~a present~~.
7. *for* assez? *possibly indicating that written from dictation.*

[fol 4ᵛ]

occasion de m'efforcer dauantage a pour-
suiuvre l'œuure que i'ay entrepris, touchant
les louanges des hommes heroiques et excellens, lesquels vostre noble et fameuse
Cité a de tous temps enfantez et produits⁸:
et i'espere ~~que les vertus~~ que les vertus
et graces que le tou-puißant a mis en
vos magnifique et honorables Seigneuries
ne seront laißees en arriere.　Auquel ie
prie humblement qu'il face de plus en
plus prosperer vostre noble estat, et augmente au centuple le triomphe et gloire de vostre
fameuse cité de Londres. Ce premier
iour de l'an 1578, auant pasques.

Vostre tres-humble seruiteur
LGrenade⁹

[fol. 5]

PREFACE:-

J'ay entrepris vn œuure, par lequel ie ne doute
point que ie ne sois taxé de temerité par plusieurs: car außj il surpaße de beaucoup toutes
mes facultez.　Toutesfois quand on examine-
ra mon zele et bonne volonté auec vn esprit
reposé et separé de toute mauuaise paßion:
tant s'en faut que mon insuffisance soit bla-
mée que plutost elle receura cet honneur
d'estre louee comme si elle en estoit digne.
Et außj cete esperance m'a fait prendre la
hardieße de l'entreprendre: sans laquelle
ie n'euße iamais abandonné mes voilles
au vent (par maniere de dire) pour na-
uiguer au danger de tant de perils.

[fol. 5ᵛ]

Or, la cause principale qui m'a mis cete
volonté au cœur; et la plume en main, est
vn nombre infinj de singularitez et choses
rares lesquelles sont confinees (ce semble) en
ce pais, separé du reste du monde: et lesquel-

8. u in produits *inserted above line.*
9. LG *forms a ligature; see Fig. 6.*

les i'ay cognu n'estre diuulguees, ains incog-
nues aux autres nations, quj sont cependant priuees de ce bien.   Vray est que
le bruit de la grandeur, richeße, singularitez et magnificences de Londres volent
et courent iusques aux extremitez du
monde vniversel: tellement que Londres
a veu Moscouie; Moscouie außj a veu
Londres.   La mer glaciale l'a eue sur
son dos: et non contente de cela, sa gran-

[fol. 6]

deur veut maintenant voisiner le Cathay.
Et bien tost les extremes parties du leuant
receuront cet honneur de se voir visiter par
icelle.   Mesme ie ne fai-point de doute,
que cj apres les plus lointaines regions ne
prenent bien la peine de la venir visiter: luj
portans (comme par hommage) les plus
rares et precieuses choses qu'elles ayent.
Mais tous ces lointains pais (apres auoir
ouy parler, et iouy de tout ce qu'ils ont peu
obtenir de Londres)[10] n'ont veu, ouy ne iouy
que l'ombre de la millieme partie des choses excellentes quj sont en elle. Parquoy,
failloit-il que ses merites restaßent ense-
uellis et cachez au sein d'un perpetuel ou-

[fol. 6ᵛ]

bly? ou dedans la bouche close de Nemesis?
Je maintien donc, que combien qu'en cete
mienne description y ait beaucoup d'imper-
fections, et lesquelles mesme ie cognois bien;
si est ce que voyant au'aucun plus suffisant
que moy ne s'auançoit de publier par ses
escrits les choses excellentes qui sont comme
si elles estoient semees prodigalement en
cette noble cité: et sur tout, tant de si bonnes Loix et coustumes: i'euße fait grande conscience de faire comme les autres, as-
sauoir demeurer muet, ayant si bel argument et occasion de parler.   Car
si les singularitez, grandeurs et magnificences de Niniue ont esté extollees si cu-

10. *The ms does not include a closing bracket for the parenthesis
beginning at* apres, *but this seems a likely position for it.*

[fol. 7]

rieursement par Herodote, Diodore[11] cecilien
et autres.   Celles de Babylone, par Bero-
se et Herodote. Celles de Troye, par Ho-
mere, Ouide, et de nostre temps, par Jan
le Maire de Belges. Celles de Ro*m*me par
Titeliue, et[12] Plutarche. Celles de Jerusalem
presque par tous les Prophetes. Et celles
de Thebes, Numance, Tyr, Sydon, Co-
rinthe et autres telles par plusieurs autres grans et excellens personnages.
Celles cj meritent bien außj que tous peuples cognoißent combien le grand et eternel Dieu l'a a cœur, en l'embellißant et
ornant de tant de ses faueurs.
Vray est que i'euße plutost entrepris

[fol. 7ᵛ]

de louanger la cité capitale de ma nation
mais ie m'en suis abstenu pour ce que quelques bons esprits m'ont deuancé.
Or touchant cete mienne entrepriße
donc; ie me tiendray pour bien content et
satisfait, si tant seulement ie puis prouo-
quer quelque autre a faire mieux.
Au reste, i'ay si bien distingué les matieres
par chapitres qu'il seruira de bonne aide
aux lecteurs pour mieux les retenir en
la memoire, et par ce moyen les pouuoir
raconter a ceux quj n'en ont encore[13]
ouy parler.   Et pour la fin, il ne faut
pas s'emerueiller si le Seigneur Dieu a voulu
orner Londres de tant de ses graces, veu qu'-

[fol. 8]

elle s'est monstreé si benigne et liberalle, et par
plusieurs fois, envers les poures membres de
Seigneur Jesus.   Car si mesmes les infideles au
temps iadis ont esté benis en beaucoup de sortes
pour auoir receu et logé les Enfans de Dieu,
comme Abimelech, acause d'Isaac, Laban, acause
de Jacob et plus*ieurs* autres: combien plus cete

---

11. e *inserted above line.*
12. *inserted above line.*
13. *followed by an erasure, probably of* ouy.

noble Cité, laquelle non seulement veut estre
l'hosteße de l'Eglise de .D.[14] mais außj, en reiecta*nt*
l'Anthechrist et toutes ses idolatries a receu la
vraye Religion et en fait profeßion.
Le Seigneur Dieu la benie, maintienne et face prosperer de plus en plus iusqu'a la venue
de nostre Seigneur Jesus Christ. Amen.

[fol. 8ᵛ blank except for blots from heading on fol. 9]

[fol. 9]

LES SINGVLARITEZ
De Londres. Cité capitale du Royaume
d'Angleterre.

Ensemble son antiquité: et quels ont
esté ses fondateurs

Chap. i.

De la fondation de Londres, de ses

noms, de son aßiette, et de la riviere

Tames.

Il y a quelque fol (mais du tout ignorant
des histoires) quj a escrit, qu'Angleterre
estoit iadis appellee Bretaigne, a cause qu'elle
[fol. 9ᵛ]
auoit un langage brief et succinct. Mais cette
sotte etimologie est bien digne d'un tel lourdaut.
Et de fait, elle luy fait des oreilles plus longues
que celles d'un asne: Car ce nom luy vient
d'un excellent Troyen nommé Brutus fils
de Syluius Posthumius, lequel luy donna le nom
de Bretaigne de son nom, car auparavant
elle estoit appellee Albion.
Ce Brutus duquel ie parle, ayant longtemps
erré ça et la par les mers apres la totale ruine
de Troye: finalement arriua en l'Isle dite pour
lors Albion. Et pource que le pais luy sem-

Brutus.

Bretaigne.
Albion.

Brutus arrive en
l'Isle Albion.

14. *inserted above line for* Dieu.

bla propre pour donner fin a son voyage et
a ses trauaux; ayant elleu un lieu sur le fleuue Tames, il commença d'edifier une Cité.

[fol. 10]

Commencement de Londres.

Ce fut en l'an du monde 2855, et devant la
venue de Jesus Christ 1188, ans.

Londres plus antique que Rome.

Cela monstre clairement de quelle antiquité
est cete Cité: car elle precede de beaucout celle
de Romme, et de quelconque autre qui super-
bement se vante de ses antiquitez.

Or c'est celle qu'on appelle auiourd'huj Lon
dres. Cecj aduint environ le temps que le Leui-
te duquel est parlé au 19, chap. du livre des Juges,
mit la femme en pieces en la montagne d'Ephraim, et les envoya par toutes les lignees d'Irael.

Brutus, donc, ayant commencé d'edifier
sa Cité, la nomma (en honneur de celle de
sa nativité) *Troye la nouvelle.*

Londres appellee Troye nouvelle.

Et ce nom luy dura iusqu'a la venue du

[fol. 10ᵛ]

le Roy ludus.

Roy Ludus, lequel la nomma de son nom, Ludunum, en l'an 68, avant la venue de Jesus Christ:
mais depuis, par succeßion de temps, on a changé quelque chose, et l'a on nommée Londinum
qui est a dire Londres en nostre langue.

Situation de Londres.

Or ne pouuoit Brutus choisir lieu (ie
ne dy seulement en Angleterre, mais mesmes en toute l'Europe) plus propre ne plus
enrichj de tout ce quj est requis à la situation d'un lieu accomplj en toutes choses.

Et pour le prouuer ie[15] reciteray quelque chose

Lieux circonuoisins.

des lieux circumuoisins premierement, pour
donner plus grand lustre a tout le reste.

Contemplons donc (mais auec admiration)
les enuirons[16] de cete noble Cité: car außi les

[fol. 11]

histoires tesmoignent qu'anciennement ceux
quj vouloyent edifier quelques citez fameuses
estoyent attirez par la beauté des paisages cir-

Romulus.

conuoisins; ce qui est leubien expres de Romulus quand il voulut donner commen-

15. *inserted above line.*
16. i *inserted above line.*

Brutus.

Heye gate.

cement a Romme, et plusieurs autres tout
de mesme.   Ainsi Brutus obserua bien[17]
cela parfaitement: car si nous sommes en
un lieu eminent nommé Heye gate: de[18] la nous
voyons pleinement la Cité, laquelle en ses bastimens donne un contentement merueilleux a
l'oeill: et en sa forme et situation costoyant la

Londre en forme
d'Arc.

le coste vers orient.

riuiere monstre son etendue en Arc d'une
tres belle forme. Puis apres si nous iettons
nostre veüe de la vers l'Est, nous conduisons

[fol. 11ᵛ]

la Tames coulant doucement iusques entre les
bras de son pere[19] l'Ocean.   Et nous tournans du

Le costé du Sud.
Le pais de Kent.

costé du Sud, nous voyons ce beau et riche pais
de Kent, ayant un prospect delectable de mons
et de collines grandes et petites et diversifiees
de toutes les parties quj appartienent a vn
pais accomplj tant en delectation qu'en fertilité. Finalement, si nous contemplons

Le West et le Nord.
La cheute de Tames
en la mer.

le costé du West et du Nord iusques vers la
cheute de Tames en la mer, O quel plaisir!
de voir la plaine rase par[20] longue distance estre
grandement fertile en toutes choses. La on
voit les prairies et herbages pleins de bestes a
laict, avec distinction de magnifiques ~~mag-~~
~~nifi~~ maisons et chasteaux fort apparans.

[fol. 12]

Le plant de la Cité.

Venons maintenant au propre plant de
cete excellente Cité, laquelle est aßsise sur le
bord d'un grand fleuue nomme Tames, le
quel est d'un merueilleux profit et comodité

Longueur du fleuue
Tames.

a la dite Cité. L'estendue duquel en longue*ur*
est de 30, lieues francoises, (quj sont 60, mille
d'Angleterre pour le moins)[21] iusqu'a la mer.
Ce fleuue porte grans vaißeaux de deux et 300,
tonneaux de port iusqu'a la dite Cité: et au deßus,
iusques a 18, ou 20, lieues, on conduit par
icelluy de grandes barques allans et venans

---

17. *followed by erased letter, probably* n.
18. *inserted above line.*
19. re *added above line.*
20. r *inserted above line.*
21. *terminal bracket omitted in MS.*

Oxford, ville
theologale.

iusqu'a Oxfort, ville Theologale d'Angleterre
a cause de quoy toutes sortes de marchandises, et
toutes pars y affluent.   Les grans nauires qui la abordent, ont accoustumé a l'entrée
et des qu'ils sont deuant la magnifique Tour
royalle (de laquelle il sera parlé cj apres) de salu-

[fol. 12ᵛ]

er la cité a grans coups de Canon, comme s'ils
rendoient graces a Dieu, par ce moyen, de ce
qu'il les a faits arriuer a bon port.

Aßiette de Londres.

Londres est aßise sur vne belle et spacieuse
plaine de tous costez, et par ce moyen elle
est fort bien aerée. Elle est enuironnée
de part et d'autre de tres belles prairies et
parquis herbeus, iardins et terres labora-
bles: lesquelles a cause de leur fertilité ra-
portent annuellement beaucoup de fruit.

les villages.

Les villages (desquels il y a grand nombre
es environs) sont fort propres pour ceux
quj ont garde la ville quelque temps: car
en sortant hors, on²² se promene iusqu'à
iceux fort aiseement, a cause qu'ils ne

[fol. 13]

sont distans de la Cité qu'environ doux iects
de harquebouse: außj y va le peuple a grandes
troupes les festes quand il fait beau temps.

Chap. 2.

Des faubours de Londres: et premierement de
celluy du costé de la porte nommee Ludgate.

8 faubours a l'entour
de Londres.

Il y a huit grans faubourgs a l'entour de
Londres chacun desquels reßemble a une
bonne ville: tant pour leur grandeur que
pour les choses singulieres quj y sont.

Celluy du costé de
Ludgate.

Premierement celluy du costé de la porte
nommee Ludgate: lequel s'estend iuqu'a
Westminster, nous le mettrons le premier,

21. *terminal bracket omitted in MS.*
22. *followed by erasure of* ?on.

[fol. 13ᵛ]

a cause qu'en icelluy y a plus grand nombre des singularitez qu'es autres, et pour
cete cause il nous y faudra arrester d'a-
uantage.

Ce faubourg est merveilleusement grand
si nous comprenons Westminstre auec
icelluy, comme außj il le faut: et ainsi
si sa principale rue sera d'une bonne de-
mj lieue fraçoise de longueur.

Touchant les singularitez d'icelluj, nous tou-
cherons seulement les plus remarquables: car
le tout seroit vn trop grand nombre pour nous.
Premierement la porte de la Cité, du costé
de ce faubourg, est fort antique: car elle fut
bastie en l'an du monde 3800, et avant la venue
de Jesus Christ en chair 65, ans, par un Roy

[fol. 14]

Saxon nommé Lud, a cause dequoy außj elle
est appellee, la porte de Lud. Paßant plus
outre, le long de la grand rue de ce faubourg
du costé de la riuiere est la magnifique
maison de Bridwell, laquelle fut²³ edifiee
du temps du Roy Henrj, 8, de laquelle
sera parlé plus a plain cj apres. Plus
outre, et le long du fliet, on rencontre
vne fort belle fontaine, rendant grande
abondance d'eau par plusieurs conduis.
Elle fut edifiee par feu William Estfield
en son viuant Maire de Londres en
l'an 1437. Apres cela, en procedant,
on vient a l'endroit de 4, magnifiques
Colleges des loix du pais, fort riches et
opulens. Le premier est Grays In. Le

[fol. 14ᵛ]

second et tiers sont les deux Temples, ainsj appellez., car les Templiers estoient iadis ou ceux-
cj sont a present. Le 4, est Lincolnes In.
Or combien que ces 4, Colleges soient habitez
pour la plus part de gentils-hommes, les enfans des grans Seigneurs, neantmoins, sont

---

23. t *inserted above line.*

a Grais In, a cause[24] qu'il est situé en plus bel
aer. Vray est qu'il y a plusieurs autres
Colleges, mais ceux cj sont les principaux.

les Loix en francois.

Les loix ausquelles estudient les escolliers
sont escrittes en francois, mais vn françois
fort corrompu, tellement que les françois
mesmes n'y entendent comme rien.
Le long de cette rue, et singulierement du
costé de la riuiere, sont plusieurs beaux et

[fol. 15]

Palais et maisons des
Princes et Seigneurs.

magnifiques Palais et maisons de Princes et
grans Seigneurs iusques au Palais de sa maiesté
lesquels embellißent et ornent merveilleusement tout ce quartier la, et singulierement

Jurisdiction du
Sr Maire est separée.

du costé de la riviere.   La Juridiction
du Seigneur Maire de Londres se separe a
Templebarre d'auec celle de Westminstre, et midlsex.[25]
Or il nous faut notter que cette rue[26] est pleine
de costé et d'autre de boutiques fournies de
de toutes sortes de marchandise comme si ce
fut vne des bonnes rues de la Cité.

Charing croße.

Paßant plus outre, on trouve vne Piramide
fort antique ce semble, de laquelle quelques
pierres de taille pendent, par vieillesse, en
l'aer, ne tenans qu'a vn peu de fer; toutesfois si est elle encore haute de 25, ou 30, toi-

[fol. 15v]

ses; Elle a encore plusieurs ymages de Rois et
autres[27] au tour d'elle.   Quelques vns disent
que c'est de l'ouurage des Romains, du

Jules Cæsar.
la Royne Allienor.

temps que Jules Cæsar occupa l'Angleterre. Autres, que ce fut la Royne Alienor
femme du Roy Edward premier de ce
nom quj la fit faire, en l'an, 1274.
Non guieres loin de la est vne fort belle

St James.
Henry 8.e

maison de plaisance, appellee St. James,
laquelle le[28] Roy Henry 8e fit bastir: et y
adioignit plusieurs beaux parcs.
Il y a puis apres le Palais royal, dit whit

24. se *inserted above line.*
25. midlsex *added at end of line.*
26. *added above line.*
27. *inserted to left of line.*
28. *inserted above line.*

hall, lequel est si somptueux que i'ayme
mieux laißer penser au lecteur son
excellence, que d'entreprendre la description, d'icelluy, et ne pouuoir satisfaire

[fol 16]

a mon devoir.

Aßez pres de la, on entre en vne grande
et spacieuse cour, et est celle du Palais ou lon
tient les Estas du Royaume, qu'on appelle
le Parlement.   communement le Parlement. La sont les
Salles.   plus belles Salles qu'il est poßible de voir.
La mesme est le lieu ou lon tient les plaids
generaux quatres fois l'an, autrement, le
le Terme.   Terme.   Ces plaids durent ordinairement
l'espace de six semaines: auxquels resortent
grandes multitudes de peuple de toutes
pars du Royaume: telle que cela apporte
vn profit incroyable a la Cité de Londres,
a cause²⁹ que lors gens de tous estas reçoiuent
argent de leurs ouurages et marchandises.   Il y a vne chose fort notable en vne

[fol. 16ᵛ]

proprieté de bois.   des sales de ce Palais: c'est que la voulte d'i-
celle est couuerte et toute lambrißee d'un
certain bois quj a cete proprieté de ne receuoir aucune poußiere, ordure nj chose
venimeuse: a raison de quoy on n'y vit onq'
nulle araigne ou araignee. Et combien
qu'elle soit fort vieille, si paroit elle belle
comme si fut neuue, et diroit on, a la voir,
qu'on a prins grand peine a la frotter.

Temple de   Venons maintenant au temple de
westminster.   l'Abbaye de westminster, et a ses singularitez.   Ce temple est excellent en sa
sa hauteur.   hauteur, qui est merueilleuse: en sa cou-
sa couuuerture.   uerture, qui est toute de plomb, haut elle-
uee en dos d'asne si bien agencee qu'elle est

[fol. 17]

la Musique.   dune fort belle representation. La Musicque
de ce temple est excellente: car ce sont bien les
plus belles voix (tant baßes que hautes) qu'il
est poßible d'ouir.

29. se *inserted above line.*

la Cappelle du Roy
Henry 7.ᵉ

Au bout d'en haut de ce Temple, est vne chappelle fort somptueuse et magnifique, et non
moins excellement ouuragee en pierre par
dehors, qu'en menuiserie de bois par dedans.

Sepulchre
magnifique.

En icelle est vn paße magnifique sepulchre de bronze, fait en forme de chappelle,
enrichj de pilliers et d'ymages d'anges et
autres tout alentour, de mesme matiere:
et de mesme sur icelluj la representation
au vif du Roy Henrj 7ᵉ, et de la Roine
sa femme, quj la ensevellis sont.[30] A la teste du-

[fol 17ᵛ]

Le Roy Edward 6.ᵉ

dit sepulchre en bas est celluy du bon Roy Eduard
sixieme: lequel en son temps estoit vn miracle
au monde, a cause des grandes graces que Dieux
avoit mises en luy.
Il y a vn autre sepulchre dedans le cœur
dudit Temple, lequel est außi excellentement riche et beau. Le Roy qui enterré

Sᵗ Edward confeßeur.

est deßous, est appellé St. Edward le confes-
seur: lequel regnoit en l'an 1043, et mou-
rut en l'an 1066, quelque temps auant la
venue de Guillaume le conquereur; mais
il sera encore fait mention de luy cj apres.
    Ce sepulchre est entouré de trellis de fer, et
ne l'ay encore peu voir que de loin: parquoy
ie n'ay peu bien discerner la manufacture
d'icelluj, nj la matiere dequoy il est: tou-

[fol 18]

tesfois i monstre estre fort magnifique.
ll y a plusieurs autres sepulchres des Roys a
l'entour du cœur, entre lesquels, celluy de Hen-

Henrj, 3,ᵉ

ry 3, est composé, et presque couuert, de pierres fines et quarrees richement agencees
l'une contre l'autre, et sent bien son sepulchre
royal.   Ce Roy Henrj fut le premier quj
mit la premiere pierre au fondement de ce
temple de Westminster en l'an du Seigneur

nota.

1220; Il regna l'espace de 56, ans.
OR combien que tous les sepulchres des Rois
et Roines qui reposent en ce Temple, meritent
bien d'estre fort prisez, et louez: tant a cause de

---

30. sont *inserted above line.*

leur richeße et beauté, que pour l'antiquité
d'iceux: toutesfois ie me suis contenté de faire mention des trois susdits, pource qu'ils
[fol. 18ᵛ]
m'ont semblé les plus remarcables, et que (comme i'ay touiours protesté) ie veux estre brief.
LA seconde singularité qui est au dit temple est la hauteur de sa voulte, laquelle surpaße toutes celles des autres temples de
Londres: et sa couuerture, laquelle est
de plomb come dit est.

Chap. 3.

Du faubourg du costé de la porte dite

Newgate: et de ses singularitez

Le second faubourg est celluj par lequel
on entre en la cité par la porte dite Newgate
c'est a dire la porte neuue. Il est fort grand,
[fol. 19]

Holburne Smithfield. car il comprend Holburne, Smithfield et la
rue Sᵗ. Jean.   Et combien que i'aye dit ci de-
uant que le faubourg de Westminster est
le plus grand de tous: toutesfois si cetuicj
luj estoit parangonné, ie ne sçay qui l'em-
porteroit.   Touchant ce qui est remar-
quable en ce faubourg, il y a la porte de la
Cite nommee Newgate, c'est a dire Porte

Newgate. neuue, par laquelle on va de la ville
au dit faubourg.   Cette porte est d'une
fort belle apparence, et plus que nulle autre de la Cite: sur laquelle est edifié vn corps
de logis merveilleusement fort, flanqué
de chacun costé d'une große et forte tour.
Et ce n'est pas sans cause, car la sont gar-
[fol 19ᵛ]
dez les prisonniers criminels, et ceux qu'on
iuge a mort toutes les seßions qu'on tient
tous les mois.   Cete porte fu premierement
edifiee par vn excellentement homme de bien

Richard
Whitington. nommé Richard Withinton, mercier, et
quj auoit esté trois fois Maire de Londres:

lequel fit außi plusieurs autres gra*n*s biens
a la dite cité, chose quj rend sa memoire be-
nite deuant Dieu et deuant les hommes a
iamais.

Secondement en ce faubourg, est la parrois-
se appellee St Sepulchre: laquelle est si
peuplee qu'on y trouue de compte fait
23·000, communicans aux Sacremens.

Or si ce grand nombre de personnes se
trouue en cete seule parroiße, quel no*m*bre

[fol. 20]

trouueroit on en 122 parroißes, quj sont ou
en la Cité ou es faubourgs?   Vray est
que le dit Sepulchre est la plus grande
et mieux peuplee de toutes: toutesfois si
peut on recognoistre la quelque chose
de grande admiration.

 Tiercement (et non guieres loin de la)
est vne fort belle fontaine, iettant eau
par ~~par~~ plusieurs tuyaux, laquelle (comme on m'a certifié) vn Gentilho*m*me,
nommé, 𝖒𝖆𝖎𝖘𝖙𝖊𝖗 𝕷𝖆𝖒𝖇𝖊, (c'est a dire Monsr.
Aigneau) a faite edifiée a ses propre despens. Pour le moins ses armes y sont en-
grauees, et plusieurs aigneaux a l'entour.
On l'a aßise au quarrefour qui separe le

[fol. 20^v]

quartier de Holburne d'auec celluy de Smithfield.   Cete fontaine est si vtile en cet endroit, et
si abontante en eau, qu'elle fournit plus de 2000,
maisons.   Il y a außj du costé de Holburne,
plus*ieurs* Colleges des Lois du pais, bien fournis
de honestes escolliers, lesquels ont tous leurs
franchises limitées: nous en parlerons ci apres.
A l'autre membre de ce faubourg est l'Hospital de S^t. Barthelemj, au quel grand nombre de poures malades et autres personnes ne-
ceßiteuses sont nourries, et tenues si nettement que combien qu'il y ait paßage co*m*mun
et publique tout du long dudit Hospital, et
qu'on voye les chambres et lits des malades et eux
dedans; neaumoins on n'y sent aucune mauuai-

(marginal notes)

Sr Sepulchre.

23000, personnes
communicans.

122 paroißes.
a Londres.

chose admirable.

la fontaine a
l'Agneau.

[fol. 21]

se odeur , non plus qu'en la plus[31] nette rue de la Cité.
Cet Hospital fut commencé d'edifier avec son
Temple, aux propres coust et despens d'un des
Musiciens du Roy Henrj, i, nomme Reyer.

vn musiccien
fondal'Hospital de
Saint Berthelemy.

Smithfield.

Au front de cet Hospital est vne grande
et spacieuse place nommee Smithfield, c'et
a dire le champ des mareschaux: laquelle
est si ample qu'a vn besoin on y mettroit
18 ou 20000, hommes de pié en bataille.
Cete place iadis souloit estre vn lieu ou on
iettoit les immondices de la Cité, mais maintenant elle est vtile a plusieurs choses ne-
ceßaires.   Premierement, tous les vendredis de l'an il y a vn fort beau marché de che-
uaux et autres bestes. Secondement on

marché a
chevaux.

[fol 21ᵛ]

y execute les malfaicteurs quj ont commis
quelque cas execrable, soit par feu ou autrement. Tiercement on y tient vne foire des
plus belles quj soit en tout le pais d'Angleterre, qu'on appelle communement, la foire
de Berthelemj: elle dure cinq ou six
iours. Durant laquelle foire la place de
Smithfield[32] et les rues al'entour bien
loin, singulierement icelle place est
pleine de tentes, auec grande abondance de toutes sortes de marchandises,
tellement qu'on penseroit estre au milieu
de la plus marchande ville de la chres-
tienté. Et lors voit on les belles marchandises de Londres, car tout se des plo,ye

la foire de la
Berthelemj.

[fol 22]

adonc.   Et außj cete foire s'estend par toute
la ville.   De ce coste außj est le Temple de S.ᵗ
Jean quj souloit estre vne riche Comman-
derie des Cheualliers de Rhodes, mais
maintentant est vne tres belle paroiße.

31. qu'en la plus *inserted above line*.
32. d *inserted above line*.

Chap. 4.

Des faubourgs du costé des portes dites Aldersgate, Creplegate, Moregate, Bisshopesgate et Allgate, dit Whitshapell.

J'ay compris sous vn mesme chapitre quatre faubours, pource qu'il m'a semblé n'y
auoir point tant de choses dignes d'estre
remarquees qu'es autres: combien qu'ils
[fol. 22ᵛ]
ne sont pas sans singularitez, lesquelles nous
ne paßerons ~~pas~~ sous silence en leur lieu.
Or ils ont tous cela de commun ensemble,
que leur principale rue continue en

Longuer et largueur
des rues.

longueur droite, et large de 25, a 30, pas
pour le moins.   Le premier de ces
quatre faubourgs est celluy duquel on

Aldergate.

entre en la Cité par la porte dite Aldergate, c'est a dire, la porte ancienne, ou
des anciens: car außi on dit qu'un Alderman la fit edifier.
Or combien que ce faubourg soit le moindre de tous les faubourgs, si contient il
plus de 1000, maisons.
Le second, est celluy duquel on entre en
[fol. 23]
la Cité par deux portes: la premiere est celle

Crepellgate.
Moregate.

qu'on appelle Crepellgate, c'est a dire la porte
du boiteux. La seconde est Moregate, la porte
du more.   Comme on sort hors de la cité
par la porte de More gate, on vient en vne

belle prairie.

belle et plaisante prairie, laquelle es iours
de feste est pleine de peuple de tous aages
et sexes.   Les hommes s'exercent, vne partie,

L'Anglois meilleur
tireur du monde.

a tirer[33] de l'Arc (car außj sur tous les hommes
du monde l'Anglois emporte le pris de
bien tirer). Et de fait, ils s'y plaisent merueilleusement. L'autre partie, auec le reste du peuple, se promenent pour la beauté
et bon aer du lieu.   En vn bout de

33. atirer *in MS.*

Theatres.

cette prairie, sont deux fort beaux Thea-
[fol. 23ᵛ]
tres. L'un desquels est magnifique sur l'autre
et a grande apparence par dehors. Il peut
en icelluy de 4, a 5000, personnes, et dit on que
vn grand Seigneur l'a fait faire. Or tous
deux ont este faits et dediez pour iouer en
iceux quelques Comedies et autres ieux, desquels la plus part sont choses faites a plaisir,
et quj ne furent onques. Seulement cete
belle apparence amuse les hommes, et tous
~~tous~~ les regardans. Außj la sageße du
Magistrat de Londres a bien cognu cela;
a cause de quoy ils ont esté mis hor de la
Cité.

l'Hospital de
Sainte Marie.

En ce faubourg ya vn fort bel Hospital,
appellé l'Hospital de Sainte Marie
[line space blank]
Il fut fondé et fait bastir par vn Citoyen
[fol. 24]

Walter Brime.

de Londres et sa femme: luy nommé Walter
Brime, et elle Rose, en l'an 1235.

Sermon le lendemain
de Pasques, dure trois
heures.

On a accoustumé de faire vn Sermon au-
dit Hospital le second iour de Pasques, par
vn des plus excellens docteurs qu'on peut
choisir. Il dure trois heures, et y aßistent
le Seigneur Maire, accompagné de ses freres les Aldermans fort honorablement et
magnifiquement. L'Euesque de Londres
außj et plusieurs autres grans Seigneurs,
et un tres-grand nombre de peuple.
En ce faubourg außi est vn[34] autre Hospital, auquel on met les insensez et ceux quj
sont desuoyez de leur esprit, nommé

Betlem.

Betlem. On tasche de les remettre en bon
[fol. 24ᵛ]
sens: ie ne sçay pas parquels medicamens, sinon
qu'on dit qu'on vse des remedes desquels on
on vsoit iadis a Sᵗ Maturin de Larchan en

Remede pur guerir les
insensez Rue droite
et large.

france pour guarir les fols, aßavoir force
coups de fouët.   Le sixieme faubourg
est en rang, lequel a vne rue fort droite et

34. n *inserted in space.*

White chapelle.
Belles prairies.

Conduis d'eaux.

Allgate.

large sur toutes celles des autres: il est
communement nommé White chapelle:
au bout duquel sont les belles prairies, et
en icelles les conduits des eaux des fontaines
lesquelles vont a la Cité par vn tres bel artif-
ce.   On entre de ce faubourg en la
Cité par vne porte dite communement
Allgate, c'est a dire la porte de tous, car
les habitans de la Cité l'ont faite faire.

[fol. 24 bis]

Chap. 5.

Du faubourg dit sainte Katherine. De
ses singularitez. De la Tour royalle, dite
la Tour de Londres.

Ste. Katherine.
Trois entrees pour
entrer en la Cité de ce
cousté.

On entre au faubourg de Ste. Katherine du
costé de la ville par 3. endroits: par eau, par
vne grande porte quj est des appartenances de la Tour royalle: et d'un autre costé
par vne petite poterne hors le pourpris de la-
ditte Tour.   Parquoy il ne me semble pas
mal a propos en cet endroit, de faire mention de ladite Tour, veu qu'es autres faubourgs nous avons en premier lieu parlé
de la porte par laquelle on entre a iceux.
Or i'ay remarqué dedans Londres (entre

[fol. 24bisᵛ]

4 edifices merueilleux
a Londres.

1 S.ᵗ Pol.
2 le Pont.
3 la Tour.
4 L'Exchange.

autres choses) quatres edifices de merveilleuse
structure et somtuosité: parquoy il m'y faudra arrester d'auantage.   La premiere est
le Temple de St Pol.   La seconde est le Pont.
La troisieme est la Tour royalle.   La quatrieme structure est le Royal Exchange.
    Or nous traiterons pour le present de la
Tour royalle et de ses singularitez, reser-
uant les autres en leur lieu.

La Tour fort ancienne
Jules Cæsar.

Cete Tour est fort ancienne, car Julius Cæsar
fit faire le principal dongeon d'icelle: ceux
quj sont venus par apres ont fait faire le
reste de la fortereße: et singulierement

W. Rufus.
W. conquereur.

William Rufus fils de Guillaume le conquereur, la rendit comme on la voit a present.

[fol. 25]

Description de la
forterefße de la Tour.

Elle a trois hautes murailles au tour d'elle, avec
plusieurs fortes tours et profons foßez pleins d'eau
quj les environnent. La voit on außi plusieurs
Platesformes, bien fournies de plusieurs pieces
d'artillerie sur roues. Au demourant, il n'y a
creneau ne trou tant es murailles qu'ez Tours
qui au besoin n'ait sa piece de fonte auec son
equipage.   Car il y a si grand nombre d'Artillerie, qu'on est contraint d'en laißer devant ladite
Tour, qui de bronze, quj de fer de fonte: tant
doubles Canons, Canons, et pieces de campai-
gne, plus de 200. Et mesmes y a plusieurs
pieces d'artillerie de fer qui se pourrißent
en terre. Bref, c'est chose estrange a croire
a quj ne la veu.

nota.

[fol. 25ᵛ]

Mortes payes de la
Tour.

Bonne police
ordinaire.

Cette Tour a ses mortes payes et gardes ordinaires
quj portent mesme liuree que les archers de la
garde de sa Maiesté. Tostapres onze heures deuant
midj, chacun iour ordinairement, on a accoustumé de leuer les pons et entrees de la dite
Tour les gardes se retirans dedans au son d'une
cloche laquelle on sonne pour cet effait: et n'est
ouuerte derechef iuqu'a vne heure apres midj
que tous ont disné et que les gardes sont außises.
Autant en fait on a, 5, heures de soir. Puis enuiron les huit heures on oure encore, tant pour
introduire ceux quj soupent a la ville que
pour laißer sortir ceux quj ne sont de la dite
Tour: puis reste close iusqu'au lendemain
soleil leuant qu'on l'ouure comme parauant.

[fol. 26]

Belle police en la
garde de la Tour.

Pourquoy elle est si
soigneusement gardee.

Bref elle est[35] si bien policee en toutes choses et
tant honorablement qu'il n'est pas poßible
de mieux. Elle est ainsj soigneusement gardee pour plusieurs raisons. Premierement
pource que c'est la principale forterefße d'An-
greterre.[36] Secondement pource que les thre-

35. *added above line.*
36. *sic for* Angleterre.

Chose admirable.

sors royaux sont en icelle. Tiercement pource
que la dedans est le Magazin des armes, telle-
qu'il y a (soit de piques, harquebuses ou
Corselets) pour armer plus de 50000, homes
Finalement, a cause que si quelque
grand Seigneur ou autre home notable
(sur tout les accusez de crime de leze
maiesté) a forfait, il est serré la dedans
d'ou il ne peut sortir sans punition capi-

[fol. 26ᵛ]

tale, ou absolution totale.   Or y a il en la Tour
(outre ce que nous avons dit) vne infinité

**Plusieurs choses rares
et exquises quj ne se
monstrent qu'a peu
d'estrangers**

de choses singulieres et exquises, et qui ne sont
veues que de bien peu d'estrangers, comme sont
Ambaßadeurs et autres grans Seigneurs, ainsi qu'il plait a sa Maiesté de les gratifier, aus-
quels on monstre ces antiquitez et a l'ißue
ils sont saluez d'une vollee de Canons.
Il est bien certain que ceux qui ont veu ces choses sont tous rauis en admiration: afermans
qu'il n'est pas poßible de voir en toute l'Europe plus grand nombre de choses remarquables.
Quand sa Maiesté fait son entree tant à la
dignité royalle qu'en la Cité de Londres com-

[fol. 27]

me la cité capitale du Royaume, elle prend premierement poßeßion de la dite Tour: et y abit-

**La Tour premiere
habitation des Rois et
Roines venans a la
couronne.**

te iusqu'au iour de son couronnement.
Il y a quatre banderolles auec leurs girouet-
tes de 7, a 8, piez de hauteur, vne au feste
de chacune des tourelles qui sont a l'entour
du grand dongeon. Lesquelles (tant les ar-
bres que les banderolles et girouetes, en semble vne belle et grande couronne close qui est

Ceci est en doubte.

au deßus) plusieurs afferment estre d'or
maßif: qui seroit (outre la magnificence)
vne chose merveilleusement riche. Car veu
leur grandeur et hauteur, elles ne peseroyent
moins de 200, liures chacune. Cela sçay-

[fol. 27ᵛ]

ie bien qu'il y a plus de 27 ans que ie les vy premierement, mais elles n'ont changé ny leur
couleur ny leur lustre.

En vne groſſe et large tour qui est a l'entrée
du premier dongeon de la dite tour sont les
Affricanes de sa maiesté. Entre lesquelles sont
six ou sept que lions que lionnes, ieunes ou
vieils: vn liepard excellentement moucheté:
vn Porcepy, et un loup: qui est chose bien rare
car on n'en voit point en tout le pays si on
ne les nourrit expreßement: et voila *touchant*[37]
la Tour.

les Lions et autres
bestes sauuages de sa
maiesté.

Il n'y a nuls loups
sauuages en
Angleterre.

Ste. Katherine.

Quant au faubourg dit de Ste Katherine,
ilest l'un des grans et plus peuplé entre les

[fol. 28]

autres, et est habité d'un grand nombre de ma-
riniers, et d'artisans de diuerses occupations,
comme Chapelliers, harquebusiers, cordounaniers,
braßeurs de biere et plusieurs autres tels.
La außi arriue grande quantité de bois
qu'on y amene avec bateaux pour la provision
de la Cité. Et combien qu'il y soit fort cher,
si donne on si bon ordre qu'il n'y en a iamais
faute.

Chap. 6.

Du faubourg appellé[38] Southwarke et
de la magnifience du Pont de Londres.

[fol. 28ᵛ]
DE l'autre costé de la riviere Tames est le
dernier faubourg, lequel ne cede de gueres
a celluy du costé de Westminster, nj en grandeur, ny en beauté nj en marchandise: on
l'appelle communement Southwarke, c'et
a dire du costé de midj. Entre ce qui y
est digne d'estre remarké est vn certain
endroit du costé de l'eau nomme Pari-
she-gardin, pource que'on void la le combat des grans dogues contre l'Ours, le
Taureau, le Cheual ferré a glace, et le
Singe; cela se fait les festes apres disner; et

Southwarke.

Parishe gardin.

Le combat de Dogges,
et des Ours du
Taureau du Cheval
et du Singe.

37. uchant *in MS.*
38. é *inserted.*

quelque fois sur semaisne[39]. J'ay autres fois veu
lascher 14, dogues a vne fois contre vn

[fol. 29]

Chiens estoufez.

Ours, et en embraßant six a la fois, les ser-
roit si fort entre ses bras qu'il en étoufoit
deux: les autres estoyent bien aises, aueques
peine, d'eschaper et n'y retourner plus.
Le plaisir du combat du Toreau est quand
il peut puiser quelque Dogge (ce sont chiens
fort grans) avec ses cornes, il le iette en
l'aer fort haut, et cheant en terre il meurt
ou se rompt quelque membre et ne vaut
plus rien.

**L'Hospital de
St Thomas.**

En ce faubourg est l'Hospital de St Thomas,
duquel il sera parlé cj apres sur le point de
l'Hospital de Christ, page, 75.[40]
De ce faubourg on entre en la Cité par vn

[fol. 29^v]

le Pont de Londres.

grand, puißant et plus magnifique Pont qui
soit en toute l'Europe. Il est tout de pierre tail-
lee, tout couuert de maisons qui sont toutes
commes grans chasteaux, et les boutiques

**richeße du Pont
de Londres.**

sont autant de magazins pleins de
toutes sortes de marchandises tres riches:
et n'y a lieu en Londres qui soit plus marchand que ce Pont.   Le fleuue Tames pas-

le fleuue Tames.

se pardeßous en 19, grandes arches[41], et y a grand

flux et reflux.

flux et reflux selon le temps des marees.
Si quelque traistre a esté decapité, sa teste est
mise au bout d'une perche sur ce Pont en
veue de tous. Je dj cecj de rechef qu'en Europe n'y a pont sur vne grande riviere comme

[fol. 30]

est Tames, si fort, si beau et si marchant comme
est celluy de Londres: et c'est la seconde des, 4,
choses merueilleuses que i'ay remarquees a Londres estre d'une somptueuse structure comme
a este dit cj deßus. Il y a encore cecj de

**Pont couvert.
Pont leuis fort subtil.**

singulier en ce Pont, c'est qu'on est a couuert
tout le long d'icelluy. Il y a vn pont leuis

39. *inserted above line.*
40. p. 75 *is now fol. 45.*
41. *inserted above line.*

au milieu dudit Pont, lequel est fait d'un
merveilleux artifice: car en temps de neceßité,
par le moyen de quelque engin, ou cheuille
ingenieuse qu'on oste, il se dreße et leue seul,
tellement que c'est vne grande fortereße pour
ce costé de la Cité: car par ce moyen on re-
tranche vne arche entiere de ce Pont.

[fol. 30ᵛ]

le Pont, fait de bois
par vn prestre puis a
pres de pierre par les
citoyens de Londres.

Il fu fait premierement de bois aux despens
d'un prestre en l'an 1163; et depuis en l'an
1209, il fut fait de pierre par les magni-
ficques citoyens de Londres.

Chap. 7.

Du corps de la Cité de Londres: et premier-
mement de la rue nommee Tames strete, la
rue de la Tames, et des choses singulieres
quj sont en icelle.

OR entrons en la Cité par ce Pont magnifique, et commençons par la plus prochaine
rue d'icelluy appellee communment la
rue de Tames.   Or il faut notter cecj, que

[fol. 31]

plusieurs noms en
vne rue.

les rues de Londres n'ont pas vn nom qui leur
serue tout du long, mais le changent selon
les endroits par ou elles⁴² paßent.

Quatre rues
principales.

Cete rue est vne des quatre grandes et principales de Londres car elle va le long de la
cité d'un bout a l'autre, a cause de quoy
elle est fort longue.   On l'appelle la

Tames Strete.
la rue de Tames.

rue de Tames, pource qu'elle costoye touiours le fleuue Tames.   Sur lequel, et
le long de la dite rue, sont plusieurs beaux
Ports, auxquels abordent les bateaux et nauires marchandes: entre lesquels celluy qu'on

Bellines gate.

appelle Bellinesgate est le plus celebre
et fameux, a cause que la arrivent toutes sor-

[fol. 31ᵛ]

tes de victuailles. tant celles qui vienent des pais

42. s inserted.

forains que d'ailleurs. Auß ce Port est mieux
agencé et plus propre qu'aucun autre qui soit
en la dite rue pour recevoir toutes sortes de
nauires.   D'icelluy partent ordinairement deux fois en 24, heures, deux grandes
Barques et plusieurs autres bateaux couuers,
qu'on nomme communement Tillebotes tous
chargez de gens, quj vont et vienent de Lond-
dres a Graves ende:
Bellinesgate fut ainsi nommé par le Roy Bellinus lequel le fit edifier en l'an du Seigneur
400, et voulut qu'il portast son nom.
Cete rue est fort estroite, voire et trop: car pour
[fol 32]
la grand affluance des marchandises qui la
abordent, il est neceßaire de se servir de grand
nombre de charrettes pour les transporter:
lesquelles charrettes sont grandes et lour-
des a cause de quoy la rue est souuent si
empeschée que les paßants sont longuement arrestez quelque fois.   Or n'est elle pas de grande apparence comme les autres,
mais si est elle neaumoins l'une des plus
riches de Londres. Et de fait, plusieurs
Seigneurs Maires sont elleuz d'icelle, qui
est bien un tesmoignage de sa richeße et
nobleße, car on ne constitue pas en telle
dignité sinon personnes puißamment
[fol. 32ᵛ]
riches et vertueuses.
 En cete mesme rue est la maison des Aus-
terlins. Ce sont marchans allemans: et
font vne commune despense pour le man-
ger et le boire.   Ils sont tellement reglez
que c'est une chose fort honorable de voir
leur ordre et maniere de faire. Il ne leur
est permis soy marier tant qu'ils seront de
la dite maison, combien qu'on ne les peut
contraindre au celibat: seulement s'ils se
marient s'ils se marient ils ne sont plus
de la dite maison. Ils vivent et prenent
leur repas en commun, et sont enuiron

Bellines gate,
beau port.

La Barge de
Grauesend les
Tillebos.

Bellinus nomma
Bellines gate de
son nom.

A Rue estroite,
grandes charrettes,
ne conuienent.

richeße de Tames
Strette.
nota.

nota.

la Maison des
Austerlings.

nota.

20 maistres.

de dix et huit a vingt[43] maistres, et autant d'au-

[fol. 33]

Inferieurs.

tres qui sont sous eux et leurs inferieurs:
et ces seconds ont leur table a part, mais
en la mesme salle, aiant touiours (neau-

chose fort honorable.

moins) la teste descouuerte, soit qu'ils
servent les Maistres a table ou qu'eux
mesmes prenent leur repas.

Si quelque personne honorable vient en
cette maison (comme cela auient souuent) avec le moindre accez du monde, elle y est receue fort honorablement,

Leur table.

et bien traitée seulement a leur ordinaire lequel est magnifique comme
celluj de quelque grand Seigneur.

l'Alderman.

Ils ont vn Gouuerneu[44] ou Superinten-

[fol. 33ᵛ]

dant sur eux qu'ils appellent Alderman.
C'est un nom d'office, et ne convient (leans)
sinon a celluj qui a la superintendance
sur tous ceux de cette maison. Il est fort

l'Alderman
fort honoré.

respecté et honoré la dedans, car außi
il est leur seul Magistrat: tellement que
s'il se meut quelque different entre quelques vns d'entr'eux pour quelque chose
que ce soit l'Alderman en iuge dernier
reßort.

les Stillars.

Le nom commun de cete maison est les
Stillardes,[45] laquelle est tres-magnifique et
noble et riche. Elle a de grans et excel-

Privilleges.

lens privilleges qui luj ont esté conferez

[fol. 34]

des Stillars.

par les feus Rois d'Angleterre; et confirmez et maintenus par la Maiesté de la Roine quj regne auiourdhuj, laquelle Dieu
vueille touiours maintenir sous sa protection
et sauuegarde. Amen.   Voila ce qui m'a
semblé de dire touchant les choses les plus
notables de cette rue: laißant ce qui reste
pour ceux quj verront plus cler que moy.

43. a vingt *inserted above line.*
44. Gouuerneur *presumably intended.*
45. r *added above line.*

Chap. 8.

De la rue communement dite[46] Tower streete
la rue de la Tour: et de ses singularitez

LA prochaine rue apres celle de Tames dont
nous avons parlé[47], est celle qu'on nomme com-

[fol. 34ᵛ]

Tower streate.

munement Tower streate. Or faut il noter
que combien qu'il y ait dedans Londres

plusieurs autres rues.

plusieurs rues trauersantes la cité, sans
vn tres grand nombre d'autres ruettes,

**quatre rues
principales.**

neaumoins il y en a quatre grandes et
principales, qui vont d'un bout de la
Cité iusqu'a l'autre tout du long: celle
de laquelle nous avons parlé cj deuant
en est vne, et cete ci est la deuzieme.

la rue de la Tour.

On la nomme la rue de la Tour, pource
qu'elle va droit de la porte Ludgate iusqu'a la grande et magnifique Tour royalle.
Il y a plusieurs choses remarquables en

[fol. 35]

cete rue, et de tres grande louange: toutesfois
ie ne toucheray que ce qui est le plus rare et
exquis.
Premierement, il y a (apres la porte dite Lud
gate qui est le commencement de cete rue)

St Paul.

le grand et magnifique Temple de Sᵗ. Pol,
lequel est merueilleux en plusieurs choses
desquelles il sera parle cj apres.
Les histoires font[48] mention que Brutus
fit bastir vn Temple dedans sa Troye nou-

**Commencemt. du
Temple de Sᵗ Paul.**

velle, lequel il dedia a Apollo: la deſſus
plusieurs m'ont affermé que c'est celluy
qu'on dit auiourd'huy Sᵗ Pol: mais ~~pource
que~~ quelques vns disent que ce fut le Roy Eth-
elbert Roy de kent, en l'an 600, de nostre salut:

[fol. 35ᵛ]

Le Lecteur sera en liberté d'en croire ce qu'il

---

46. *inserted above line.*
47. r *omitted.*
48. t *inserted above line.*

Temple fort antique.

voudra: touteffois soit l'un soit l'autre, le
tout monstre vne grande antiquité.
C'est ici la 3ᵉ, de 4, choses merueilleuses
que i'ay remarquees dedans Londres; et
de fait ceux qui le contemplent d'un Esprit
attentif sont tous estonnee de voir vn si
grand bastiment. Sa longueur (dedans
oeuure) est depuis la porte du costé de la
maison de l'Euesque de Londres, de 150,

longeur en tiere de St.
Pol est de 270, pas.

pas, ou es iambees iuques a la porte du
cœur: et de la porte du cœur iusques au
bout d'en haut 120, pas: et de largeur
d'une porte a l'autre, trauersant le dit

la largeur est de,
120, pas.

Temple, 120, pas. Or faut il noter que

[fol. 35 bis]

Temple croisé.

le dit Temple est en une forme de croix, parquoy
ne se faut esbair sil est si large.

plusiers magnifiques
Sepulchres.

Il ya en ce Temple plusieurs excellens et
riches Sepulchres de grans Seigneurs
tant de robe court qu'autres. Entre lesquels ie feray mention de 7, seulement,
pource qu'ils mont semblé les plus remarquables.   Le premier est celluy d'un

Jean de Gand.

Duc de Lancastre nommé Jean de Gand
pource qu'il naquit a Gand en flandres:

Edward, 3.

il estoit fils de Edward 3ᵉ, Roy d'angleterre. Il trespaßa l'an 1398. Son
sepulchre est a l'entour du coeur a
main senestre, magnifiquement ela-
bouré, d'un fin marbre blanc. La il est

[fol. 35 bisᵛ]

enterré avec sa femme: les efigies de tous deux
sont en marbre blanc enleuées sur le dit
Sepulchre naiuement bien taillees se
tenans par la main.

Milorde keeper his
Sepulker, made before
his death.

Le second est neuf, et celluy qui l'a fait faire n'est pas encore trespaßé, c'est Monsʳ.
le Garde des Seaux quj l'a fait⁴⁹ faire, duquel
l'effigie et celles de ses deux femmes et
Enfans sont la. Ce sepulchre⁵⁰ est le
plus magnifique que i'aye veu en Lon-

49. *inserted above line.*
50. *The text reads* sepulpulchre.

dres: car il est d'un tres beau et fin marbre blanc haut esleué garnj d'une tres-
magnifique couuerture de mesme es-
tofe, richement entaillee a double sons,[51]
la partie de deßus faite en dos d'asne,

[fol. 36]

les armoiries du dit Seigneur sont d'un
costé et d'autre richement entaillees
et agencees de leurs couleurs. Cete
couuerture est soustenue de plusieurs
colomnes de marbre noir, gris et blanc:
d'un si beau lustre qu'on s'y peut mirer
de tous costez. Il est a main dextre a l'entour du coeur.

A l'allee de l'autre ~~costre~~ costé du cœur
y a deux Sepulcres de marbre gris, faits
en faßon de coffres a l'antique, ils sont
dedans deux petis cabinez comme
enchaßez, tellement qu'on ne peut
leuer les couuercles sans sortir les Sepulcres hors dudit cabinet. Ils monstrent

Sepulchres de deux Rois Saxons fort antiques.

[fol. 36ᵛ]

estre fort antiques. sur l'un desquels est escrit
cet Epitaphe en vn petit tableau.

Seba. Roy Saxon.

Hic iacet Seba Rex orientalium Saxonum quj
conuersus fuit ad fidem per sanctum Erkenwaldum: de quo venerabilis Beda in 4° libro eccle-
siastica historia gentis Anglorum mentionem fa-
cit: quj regnavit circa annum Domini, 690.

Enuiron neuf ou dis pas plus avant contre la
muraille de ce costé est vn tres excellent Sepulchre de fin marbre blanc fait a la mo-
derne, bravement taillé avec cet Epitaphe.

Si quis erat prudens vnquam sidusque, Senator,
    si quis erat patriæ chorus, amansque suæ.
Si quis ad externas legatus idoneus oras,
    si cuj Justiciæ cura, bonique, fuit:

Mason.

Js Masonus erat, sit tota Britania, testis.
    Testis amor procerum,[52] sit populjque, favor:
Tempore quinque suo regnantes ordine vidit.
    Horum a consilijs quatuor ille fuit.

51. *Probably* sens *was intended.*
52. *MS reads* proocerum.

Tres et sex decies vixit et non amplius annos.
   Hic tegitur corpus: spiritus astra tenet.

[fol. 37]
De l'autre costé a main dextre du cœur, contre la muraille, est esléué en bße[53] de marbre
noir et blanc, le sepulcre d'un tres excellent

Jo. Colet.

Docteur en Theologie, nommé Jean Colet, Au-
deßus est la forme d'une anatome humai-
ne: et encore plus haut l'efigie d'icelluy,

Efigie naiue.

si au vif que merueilles, auec cet Epitaphe.

Hic situs est, D. Jo. Coletus, huius Ecclesiæ decanus,
   Theologus
insignis: qui ad exemplum S. Paulj semper egit
   gratuitum Euan-
gelicæ doctrinæ præconem, ac sinceræ doctrinæ
   perpetua vitæ
sinceritate respondit. Scholam Paulinam suo
   sumptu solus et
instituit, et annuo redditu dotauit. Genus honestißimum
Christj dotibus cohonestauit, præcipua[54] sobrietate
   mira ac pudici-
tia. Nunc fruitur euangelico margarito, cuius amore neglexit
omnia, vixit an. 53, administerauit, 16. obijt an. 1519.

[fol. 37ᵛ]
Aupres de la porté du costé du nord haut
éleué dedans la muraille, a main gauche
est le Sepulcre de Thomas Linacer ho*m*me
fort docte en medecine de son temps. Ce sepulcre est tout de marbre blanc et bien ~~en-~~
entaillé, aiant six volumes rangez en sa
base. Son Epitaphe graué en cuiure, est tel.

   Thomas Linacrus Regis henrici octaui medicus vir
et grecæ et latinæ atque in re medica longe eruditissimus:
multos ætate sua languentes. et qui iam animum
   desponderant
vitæ restituit. Multa Galeni opera in latinam linguam
mira et singulari facundia vertit. Egregium opus de
emendata structura[55] latini sermonis amicororum rogatu
   paulo

---

53. *MS reads* bße (*for* baße, *meaning 'base'*) *or, possibly* oße, *with
   a suspension mark above the* o. *The latter could be a garbled
   abbreviation for* ossature, *meaning 'framework', which also
   could make sense in the context.*
54. *Probably a misreading of* præcipue.
55. *MS has* s, *followed by a blank space for about six letters.*

ante mortem edidit.   Medicinæ studiosis Oxoniæ publi-
cas lectiones duas, Cantabrigiæ unam, in perpetuam
    stabi-
liuit. In hac urbe Collegium medicorum fieri sua industria curauit:[56] Cuius et presidens primus ellectus est.
fraudes dolosque mire, perosus, fidus amicis omnibus
    ordi-
nibus iuxta charus aliquot annos antequam obiret
    præsbiter
factus plenus annis ex hac vita migrauit, multum desi-
deratus anno Domini 1524 die 8 octobris.

[fol. 38]
Au milieu de la nef du dit Temple est vne
Tombe de marbre sur laquelle est l'effigie d'un Euesque en bronze, lequel de son
temps fit tant enuers le Roy Guillaume

Guillaume Conquereur Privilieges restituez.

le conquereur qu'il restitua les privilleges et libertez de la Cité de Londres lesquels
il leur auoit ostez: en recognoißance de ce,
le Senat et le peuple de la dite Cite luj ont
fait dreßer cete Tombe et Epitaphe.

Epitapitaphion[57]

Guillelmo, viro sapientia et vitae sanctitate claro
qui primum divo Edwardo Regi et confessori familia-
ris, nuper in Episcopum Londinensem erectus, nec
multo, post apud inuictissimum principem Guillel-
mum Angliæ Regem, eius nominis primum, ob pruden-
tiam fidemque singularem, in consilium adhibitus, am-
plissima huic urbi celeberrime privillegia ab eodem
impetrauit. Senatus populusque, Londonienses bene me-
rito posuit. Sedit Episcopus annis 16. Decessit
anno a Christo nato 1067.

[fol. 38ᵛ]
Entre les singularitez de ce Temple, les Orgues ne sont des moindres, car, a la ver-
rité elles sont magnifiques, et les fait

les Orgues.

la musique.

merueilleusement bon ouir quand les
chantres et enfans de cœur chantent auec,
comme außj cela se fait chacun iour deux

56. *For ... medicorum fieri sua industria curauit,* Weever *(1631),*
    p. 370 has ... medicorum sua industria fieri curavit.
57. Epitaphion *presumably intended.*

Henri, 8,

fois, aßauoir au matin et au soir. Le Roy
Henri 8ᵉ, les fit faire.

Temple sur Temple.

Cecj est merueilleux en ce Temple, qu'il est
fondé, depuis le cœur en haut, sur vn
autre Temple beau et grand, et qui sert
de parroiße a ses ~~es~~ enuirons.
Sortons maintenant dehors et considerons
combien ce grand edifice est excellent en
son exterieur come il l'est dedans.

[fol. 39]

la couuerture.

Sa couuerture est singuliere, a laquelle a
esté employe plus⁵⁸ de cinq cens milliers de plomb,
chose merueilleuse a voir: car la dite couuerture estant en forme de croix a quatre bras
merueilleusement gros et longs, hauts
elleuez en dos d'asne. On dit qu'en l'an

Sᵗ Paul bruslée.

1560, le ~~feu~~ feu s'y print par le moyen d'une
foudre, par lequel elle fut du tout consu-
mée: le plomb fondu couloit par les rues
iusques bien bas du costé de la riuiere.
Ce feu se print premierement a l'aiguille
d'un gros et tres-haut clocher qui est aßis
au milieu du croison de cete couuerture.

hauteur de clochier.

Laquelle aiguille estoit si haute qu'on ne
voit encore telle⁵⁹ hauteur de clochier en toute

[fol. 39ᵛ]

le clochier de
Strasbourg.

l'Europe.   On fait grand cas de celluy de
Strasbourg, et de fait il est fort haut, mais
les aiant veuz tous deux ie donne m'a voix
a celluy de Sᵗ Paul, ie dy auantque l'esguil-
le tombast: car il estoit si haut qu'on le voyoit
de, 25, mille.

le College de
Grammaire a
Sᵗ Paul.

Au Cemitiere de Sᵗ. Paul du costé de Soleil
leuant, est vn tres beau et excellent College de
Grammaire fondé aux propres cousts et
despens de cet excellent Docteur Jean Colet,
duquel est parlé ci deßus. Ce fut ~~ce fut~~ cet
homme de bien qui enseigna le peuple a dire
l'oraison Dominicale, les artiqlles de la foy et
les commandemens de Dieu en langue vul-
gaire premierement.

58. *inserted above line.*
59. lle *inserted above line.*

[fol. 40]

Or paßons outre et reprenons nostre rue a
la Drapperie, c'est a dire a l'ißue du pourpris
de S^t. Paul, ou commencent les vendeurs

la rue des drapiers.

de draps. En cette seule rue sont deux

*200, boutiques de
drappiers en vne rue.*

cens boutiques de drapiers tant pleines
de toutes sortes de draps et de tous pris, que
plustost ce sont magazins qu'autre chose.
Environ le milieu de cette rue y a vn grand

la pierre de Londres.

Saxe ou Pierre quarree, plantee profonde-
ment en terre, et hors de terre enuiron
trois piez de haut. Elle est large environ
de deux piez, et espeße d'un.
C'est vn point tout arresté que le Roy

Ludus Roy Saxon.

Ludus (duquel a esté parlé deux fois
cj deßus, et qui estoit Saxon de nation).

[fol. 40ᵛ]

fit planter la cete piere et pour ~~pour~~ plusieurs
raisons. Premierement pour perpetuer par
icelle la memoire de son nom et le nom de
sa nation; car, pour le premier: il la nomma
la Pierre de Lud: et au langage du pais
elle signifie cela aßavoir 𝕷𝖚𝖉𝖘𝖙𝖔𝖓𝖊: mais
depuis la Cité aiant prins le nom de Londres, on a ausi dit la Pierre de Londres.
Secondement, pource que le dit Ludus estoit Saxon de natiuité, et que ce mot simbolise
fort auec ce mot latin 𝕾𝖆𝖝𝖚𝖒, par ce moyen
il mettoit en memoire le nom de son pais naturel: et pour le troisieme, il fit là poser cete
pierre pour enseigne et marque, car plusieurs ont escrit qu'il accreust la Cité depuis

[fol. 41]

*accroißement de
Londres.*

cete pierre iusqu'a la porte de son nom Ludgate come a este dit ci deuant. Cela auint en
l'an du monde 3894, et deuant la venue de
Jesus Christ, 69, Außi ladite Pierre est fort
antique a voir sa caducité.

la Boucherie.

Paßons outre, et venons iusqu'a la Boucherie
a 200, pas de la. Cete boucherie est des plus
fameuses de Londres. Deux choses sont a con-

*deux choses a
considerer.*

siderer en icelle et es autres außj: la premiere
est la bonté et beauté des chairs qui sont la
exposees en vente. La seconde est le nombre

des bestes qu'on y tue chacune semaine.
Quant au nombre; ie puis dire ce que

curiosité. i'ay veu plusieurs fois: car i'ay esté si curieux
par plusieurs fois les vendredis matin en pas-
[fol. 41ᵛ]
sant le long de la dite boucherie, de compter les
testes des bœufs qu'on auoit fraichement es-
corchez (sans celles qui pouuoyent estre
hors de monstre) mais ordinairement
i'en ay trouué 130, et quelques fois

150, testes de bœufs iusqu'a 150, sans ceux qu'on tue sur
en vne boucherie tout semaine. Or y a il encore trois autres
a vne fois. grandes Boucheries esquelles il s'en tue
bien autant en chacune. Il y en a aus-
si (outre celles la) encore six ou sept autres
particulieres, tant en la ville qu'ez faubourgs, sans le grand nombre de chairs
qu'on vend a Leaden halle, de laquelle sera
parlé cj apres. Par les choses susdites on peut

bons pasturages en penser combien grand et bon pasturage il
Angleterre. [fol. 42]
y a tout le päis d'Anglerre[60] pour nour-
rir tant de beufs: car selon le raport
des bouchers on tue coutumierement
dedans Londres ou es faubourgs par

750, beufs par chacune semaine 750 beufs: qui
semaine. 9000 par an. seroit par an 9000,   Or c'est seulement (notez) en la ville et faubourgs
de Londres.   Parquoy on peut aiséement iuger par cela combien grand
doit estre le nombre de ceux qu'on
tue en tout le reste d'Angleterre.

veaux, mouttons Les veaux, moutons, et aigneaux
et aigneaux sans qu'on tue en toutes les boucheries
nombre. de Londres, sont en si grand nombre
qu'on n'en peut tenir le compte.
[fol. 42ᵛ]

bonté et beauté Quant a la beauté et ~~beauté~~ bonté[61] des chairs expo-
des chairs. sées en vente esdites Boucheries, elle sont
non seulement graces superfluement, et
auec cela, tendres et delicatement sauou-

60. *for* Angleterre.
61. *Inserted above line over* ~~beauté~~.

reuses mais außi tresbien et nettement
dreßees: tellement que la veue et beauté
d'icelles incite les personnes a en achetter.
Or qui pensera de pres a ce qui a esté dit
touchant cete Boucherie et les autres qui
sont dedans les appartenances de Londres,
cognoistra que ie n'en ay poin parlé sans
cause: et par la viande qui s'employe
en icelle, on peut a peu pres coniecturer
combien le nombre est grand du peuple qui y habite: et par mesme moien

grand nombre de
peuple a Londres.

[fol. 43]

venir a la contemplation de sa grandeur et
magnificence. Car combien pensons nous
qu'il s'employe de viande es maisons du
Seigneur Maire et des deux Sheriefes durant
le temps de leur administration? Sans y aious-
ter celles des Aldermans, lesquels, sans doute,
honorent leur estat au poßible, tant en cela
qu'en autres choses.   Cela rend estounez ceux
quj le considerent. Mais nous sortirons de
de cete rue, et la laißerons aller d'un droit
fil iusqu'a la Tour royalle, et viendrons
a la troiseme qui est la plus belle et mag
nifique de Londres, au moins en plusieurs
endrois comme on verra en la discourant.

la maison du Maire
et des Sherifs.

celles des Aldermans.

la plus ble belle rue
de Londres.

[fol. 43ᵛ]

Chap. 9.

De la rue commence a la Porte dite
Newgate, Du Chepside, Du Royal
Exchange, et autres singularitez.

LA troisieme et principale rue de Londres est celle qui commence a la Porte dite
Newgate: laquelle a plusieurs noms
les endroits qu'elle paße les luy donnent,
comme außi les autres tout de mesme.
C'est la plus belle, la plus riche, et la plus
large de toutes celles qui sont en la Cité:
a cause de quoy nous ne paßerons les sin-
singularitez d'icelle sans illustrer les

plus remarquables le mieux que nous
pourrons.

[fol. 44]

Aßez pres de cete porte dite Newgate, et le
long de cete rue est le lieu ou souloit estre
vne sorte de Moines appellez Cordeliers.
Lequel lieu fut reduit par le Roy Henrj 8ᵉ,
(cete vermine chaßee) en Eglise parroiciale,
et luy fut donné le nom d'Eglise de Christ.
Et apres cela (du temps du bon Roy Edward
6ᵉ, en l'an 1551) elle fut erigee en vn tres beau
et louable Hospital comme on le voit auiour-
d'huy: et ce par le bon et sage avis du Seigneur
Maire de cete annee la nommé Sir Richard
Dobbes, et des honorables Aldermans ses
freres, et autres vertueux et sages Citoyens
qui furent pour cet effect appellez en Conseil comme s'ensuit.   Le bon Roy Edward.

[fol. 44ᵛ]

6ᵉ, voyant la grand'affluance des mendi-
ans qui de toutes pars resortoyent en la
cité de Londres, et la misere qui estoit en
tr'eux, escriuit au dit Seigneur Maire
qu'estant aßisté de ses freres les Aldermans, et d'autres tels comme il verroit
estre bon, il auisast de donner quelque
bon ordre a la neceßité de ce poure peuple.
La deßus le dit Seigneur Maire fit con-
uoquer et aßembler vn Conseil commun,
auquel furent choisis et elleuz 24, citoyens et des ~~plus~~ plus prudens et sages
qu'on peut cognoistre, afin qu'ils aui-
saßent de trouuer quelque bon expedi-
ent sur cet affaire: lesquels, ayant

[fol. 45]

prins cete negotiation en main, firent distinction entre poure et poure, en enfirent
3, ordres. Le premier estoit, des malades[62]
et impotens. Les second, des Orphelins et
vieilles gens. Le troisieme, des vacabons
et faineans. Pour lesquelles trois sortes de gens, il fut auisé qu'on ordon-

les Cordeliers
changez en Eglise
parroiciale par le Roy
Henry, 8, puis en
Hospital par le Roy
Edward, 6.

Richard Dobbes,
Maire.

Ordre excellent pour
les poures.

62. la *inserted above line.*

neroit trois places, qui seroyent a la verité Hospitaux, et fut ainsi executé.

St Thomas.

pour le premier, Saint Thomas du
Southwarke fut choisi et ordonné
pour les malades et vielles gens. Pour
les Orphelins et autres poures enfans
abandonnés, fut ordonné le dit

les Cordeliers.

lieu desdits Cordeliers. Et pour les

[fol. 45ᵛ]

Bridwell pour les
vacabons et faineans.

vacabons et faineans fut ordonné le
grand et magnifique logis de Bridwell.
Or il fut arresté et quant et quant executé, que les poures malades, vieilles-
gens et impotens: et singulierement les

poure soldat:

poures soldats qui es guerres du Roy au-
royent perdu quelque membre, seroyent receuz et entretenus au dit Hospital de Sowthwark. Pour aquoy fournir le bon Roy Edward donna certaines
terres et poßeßions, qui auparavant

la Sauoye.

appartenoyent a la Sauoye.   La Cité
de Londres au̶ß̶i̶ y donna außi quelques
terres, tellement que le tout fut reduit
au bon ordre qu'on y voit auiourd'huy.

[fol. 46]

l'Hospital de Christ.

Quant a l'Hospital de Christ, ou furent
mis les orphelins et autres enfans abandon-
nez, il estoit du commencement entretenu
par les aumosnes ordinaires que faisoient
chacune semaine les Citoyens de Londres
et autres particulieres charitez d'ailleurs:
mais quelque temps apres Dieu desploya
sa benediction sur le dit Hospital, par
le moyen d'un homme de bien, cordoa-
nier demourant a Westminster, nommé

Richard Castellar.
homme fort
pitoyable.

Richard Castel, ou Casteller, homme
fort aßidu au labeur de son mestier:
en sorte que (quelque temps que ce fut)
il estoit touiours de bout et a l'œuure
auant quatre heures du matin, telle-

[fol. 46ᵛ]

le Coq de
westminster.

ment que par cela on l'appelloit le Coq de
Westminster. Neaumoins Dieu benit

Nota.

tellement son labeur (chose bien remar-
quable) que de son gain il achetta es enuirons de Westminster, terres, tenemens, pos-
seßions et autres telles choses, iusqu'au
reuenu de 44, liures sterling, par an.
Or ne se voyant nuls enfans (auec le con-
sentement de sa femme, qui estoit außi
tres honneste et vertueuse) il donna
toutes ces terres et reuenus au dit Hospital de Christ pour l'entretenement desdits
poures enfans.

Dieu wueille susciter
plusieurs tels bons
personnages a ces
poures enfans.
Bridwell.

Quant a Bridwell, il fut ordonné pour
y enfermer et mettre par gré ou par for-
[fol. 47]

c'estoit vn bon balay
pour ballier telles
ordures.

ce tous faineans, vacabons, rufians, pu-
tains et telles canailles oisiues, pour là
leur apprendre a gaigner leur pain a
la sueur de leur visage.
De cete sainte ordonnance procedoient
plusieurs biens. Premierement on

Grande providence.

ostoit les enfans d'entre les mains d'un
grand nombre de bellistreßes qui ~~cou~~
couroyent ça et la par les rues au grand
deshonneur de la Cité, et les faisoit on
instruire (comme außi fait on encore)
en plusieurs arts et disciplines, tellement qu'ils ont le moyen de gaigner
leur vie quand ils sont grans.
Secondement, on coupoit broche a
[fol. 47ᵛ]

plusieurs maquerallages, paillardises, ru-
fienneries et autres telle vilenies et dis-
sollutions. Et outre ce, on empeschoit, que
plusieurs, voulans viure sans rien faire, ne s'addonnaßent finallement a
desrober et destroußer.
Tiercement, les poures malades et vieilles
gens furent entretenus.   finalement,
außi, la cité fut vuidee, par ce moyen,
d'un bruit et cry ordinaire que faisoient lesdits poures par les rues. Mais
ie parleray d'auantage de cecj au chapitre des bonnes pollices de la Cité: parquoy paßons outre. Cependant ie

desire qu'on ~~qu'on~~ considere que

[fol. 48]

excuse de l'auteur.

i'ay prolongé d'auantage ce propos, a fin
de monstrer combien la Cité de Londres
est bien pollicee par la sageße de ses gouuerneurs. Mais i'espere (auec l'aide
de Dieu, d'extoller leurs rares vertus

liure de homes
heroiques sortis
de Londres.

au traicté des hommes heroiques
que cete noble et fameuse cité de
tous temps produis: par quoy ie repren
mes erres le long de cete grande rue,
laquelle est pleine de toutes sortes
de riches et precieuses marchandises: singulierement a l'endroit appellé

Chepseid.

Chepside, car la on voit comme vne
mer de toutes richeßes mondaines.
Les Orfeuures et Changeurs d'un

[fol. 48ᵛ]

70 boutiques
d'orfeures sans ceux
qui sont ailleurs.

costé, en nombre de soixante et dix boutiques tout d'un rang, pleines de toutes
sortes d'ouurages et vaißeaux, tant d'or
que d'argent, dorez ou a dorer.

Cete rue est plus
riche qu'on ne sauroit
exprimer.

D'autre costé, les grandes et magnifiques boutiques (ou plutost magazins) de toutes sortes de draps de soye.
Puis les merciers, aberdashers, quin-
quailliers, großiers, apoticaires et.c.
finallement tant et de si diuerses sortes de marchandises de quelque costé qu'on se tourne, que c'est chose merueilleuse a voir: car il semble que non
seulement l'Europe (de laquelle on ap-
percoit les marques en ce lieu de tous

[fol. 49]

costez) mais außj toutes les parties du
monde ont tasché de se faire cognoistre
a Londres, en luj enuoiant les choses
les plus rares qui croißent en leurs
quartiers.
Or au lieu le plus eminent de ce lieu
de Chepside, voire au milieu de la rue

La Croix de Cheside.

est vne grande Piramide, de la hauteur de 30, braßes ou enuiron, toute
couverte de fueille d'or, communement

appellée la croix de Chepside, pource
qu'a la sime d'icelle ya vne croix auec
l'Image du crucifix et la figure d'un
pigeon au deßus, par tout a l'entour
remplie de divers Images des Saints

[fol. 49ᵛ]

les Idoles sont signes
de superstition.

Thomas Fisher.

qui tesmoignent aßez combien estoit su-
perstitieux celluy qui la fit faire.
Un certain Thomas Poißonnier, donna
pour la faire, la somme de 600, marcs.
Quelques vns veulent dire qu'il estoit
françois de nation, et qu'en vn mesme
temps il fit außi edifier cete belle maison
qui est a costé d'icelle. Or i'estime que
ceux qui l'ont dit l'ont ouy dire comme
moy: toutesfois on voit encore le deuant
de la dite maison tout semé et remplj
de fleurs de lys: neaumoins l'une et
l'autre furent edifiees en l'an 1485,
Il y a außi ence mesme endroit de
Chepside, trois belles fontaines: la plus

3, fontaines.

[fol. 50]

grande desquelles est de 20, pas de long
et huit de large. Elle rend son eau par
onze conduis ou tuyaux: et est non
moins profitable que belle: car elle for-
nit eau pour deux ou trois mille maisons. Son commencement fut en l'an
1284, et fut edifiee aux despens des
Citoyens de Londres. La seconde fontaine, outre la comodite de l'eau, sert
ausi d'ornement a la dite rue: car elle
est aßise droit au milieu; elle est faite
en forme de Tourelle triomphale.
On l'appelle communement l'Estan-
dard. Un tres-honorable homme nommé Sir Jean Welles pour lors Maire

Belle et bonne
fontaine.

les Citoyens.

l'Estandart.

Jean welles.

[fol. 50ᵛ]

de Londres, en l'an 1431, la fit faire.[63]
Cete rue a cela de singulier qu'elle continue d'un bout iusqu'a l'autre en largeur

63. la fit faire. *added in a space in small letters.*

de 25 a 30 pas, excepté a l'endroit des boucheries.
Quand on comence d'entrer a l'endroit
de Cornehill, cete rue se diuise en trois,
dont la partie qui va a senestre, est appellee broade streate, et se va rendre a la rue

Broad Streat.

qui va de la porte nommee Bisshopesgate
iusques sur le pont de Londres, pas-
sant par gracious streate en laquelle est

Graciousstreate.

vne magnifique fontaine, laquelle fut

*la plus belle fontaine
de Londres.*

edifiée l'an 1490, aux propres cousts
et despens d'un honorable Cheuallier nommé
[fol. 51]
Sir Thomas Hill. Elle est fort propre en
cet endroit, car elle fournit d'eau a trois
mille maisons pour le moins.

*fontaine foisonnant
en eau.*

En ce mesme endroit se tient vn tres-
beau marché trois fois la semaine pour
toutes victuailles venans des villages:
mais nous retournerons a l'endroit ou
nous auons laiße nostre rue, et parlerons
du bras qui va a dextre, en la rue dite

Lombardes streate.

Lombardes streate. Cete rue est autant
marchande, pour ce qu'elle contient,
que rue de Londres. Il y a plus de 20
boutiques d'orfeures touche a touche
l'un de l'autre; la sont les chaußetiers
Drapiers, merciers,[64] libraires, apoticai-
[fol. 51ᵛ]
res, aberdashers, et.c. En cete rue est

*la Maison du
Siegneur Maire.*

außj la maison du Seigneur Maire
de cete presente annee, du quel le nom
est Mons.ʳ Thomas Ramesey: homme

*les vertus de Monsʳ.
Ramsey Lord Maire
pour cete presente
année.*

vrayement digne de cette charge tres
honorable, pour estre fort debonnaire,
saige et bien auisé Seigneur.
Cette rue trauerse Gracious streate a
l'endroit des quatre cantons ou se tient

les, 4, cantons.

le marché duquel nous parlions n'a
guieres: puis elle prend sa route droit
vers la porte dite Allgate.

---

64. s *of* merciers *inserted above line.*

Or reprenons nostre principale rue que[65] nous
auions laißee a l'entree de Cornehill.
La voit on les riches tapißiers, großiers,

[fol. 52]

dinandiers, et autres riches marchandises a grande abondance. La außi on
trouue en front vn des excellens et magnifiques edifices qu'on puiße voir a
l'oeil: parquoy außi il merite bien qu'on
employe quelque peu de temps a la description d'icelluy.

Ce somtueux edifice est appellé, Le
Royall exchange. et ce nom luj fut
donné par la Maiesté de la Roine Elisabeth, apresent regnante: laquelle[66] print bien
la peine de venir voir en personne ce
noble edifice: le Seigneur Dieu eternel
vueille conseruer sa Ma.té contre tous ses
ennemis Amen. Le Royal Exchange

[fol. 52ᵛ]

(donq) que les françois appelle communement la Bourse, est aßis droit au
millieu de la Cité: au quel conuienent,
deux fois le iour, les marchans qui trafic-
quent en diuers endrois de l'Europe, et ce
de, 11, a 12, heures du matin; et de cinq
a six heures de soir.   Chacune nation
y a son quartier, afin que ceux quj ont
affaire a eux les trouuent plus aiséement.
Le quartier des Anglois est la moitié dudit Exchange: les francois sont außi en
un certain endroit: les flamens et wal-
lons en vn autre, et les Italiens et espa-
gnols en vn autre. Cependant chacun
d'eux est en liberte d'aller ça et la par le dit

[fol. 53]

Exchange selon que ses affaires le requie-
rent.   La s'adreßent les postes et porteurs de lettres pour les deliurer a qui elles
s'adreßent.   La außi on entend ordinairement nouuelles de plusieurs con-

Excellent edifice.

Le royal Exchange.
La Roine Elisabeth
luy donna ce nom.

la Bourse.

les March.
s'aßemblent deux
fois le iour.

chacune nation a son
quartier.

L'Anglois.
Le François.
Le Flamen et
wallon L'Italien
et Expagnol.

poste et porteurs de
lettres.

nouuelles de plusieurs
endrois.

65. inserted above line.
66. lle *inserted above line.*

trees et regions, qui est vne grande comodité pour ceux qui trafiquent et mar-
chandent tant de ça que dela la Mer.
Quant a la forme et façon du dit Exchange, il est en quadrangle, enuiron-
né et ceint de trois grandes allees ou
galeries l'une sur l'autre.   Celle qui
est la plus baße est soubsterraine: en laquelle, d'un costé et d'autre, sont plusieurs estaux a vendre marchandise,

la forme de l'Exchange.

3, allees.

la plus baße.

[fol. 53ᵛ]
et deia quelques lingeres et marchandes
de toilles y estallent, mais ie pense que
le lieu est vn peu bien obscur et solitaire:
car elle ne reçoit veue par certains
treillis de fer qui respondent a l'allee du
milieu.   On appelle ce lieu soubsterrain
La nouuelle Venise. L'allee du milieu
est celle ou les marchans se retirent et
pourmenent[67] quand le temps est pluui-
eux: car elle est ample de six a sept pas
de large, pauee a quarrons de marbre
blanc et noir entremeslez d'un fort bel
ouurage.   Il y a a l'entour de cet allé
36, großes Colonnes de piere bize, de
12, piez de haut d'une piece, plantees

Venise la neuue.
l'Allee du milieu.

36. Colonnes de piere bize.

[fol. 54]
de quatre pas loin l'une de l'autre.
Le dedans et cœur du dit Exchange, est
vne place en quadrangle, aßez ample pour
contenir 4000, marchans, sans la dite al-
lée: pauee de menus cailloux: longue de 80,
pas et large de 60,   La se promenent les
Marchans en temps sec et deuisent de leurs
affaires es heures sus dites.   Au haut
de la muraille, du costé du dedans, tout
au tour du dit Exchange, sont 36, autres
Colonnes de marbre iaspin en table, situees
a 10, piez l'une de l'autre; et entre deux
vne certaine place dedans la muraille
pour y poser l'ymage d'un Roy ou Roine
d'Angleterre, de ceux quj ont regné depuis

la place de 80, pas, de longe, et 60, de large.

36 Colonnes de marbre iaspin.

67. promenent *presumably intended; may indicate that the text was written from dictation.*

[fol. 54ᵛ]

William Conquer*eur.*

Guillaume le Conquereur: lesquelles doi-
uent estre de Bronze.   Au deßus de ses
Colonnes sont en platte peinture les armes
et noms des Rois, Princes et Seigneurs
qui ont esté en ce temps[68] là.

l'entree de
l'Exchange.

On entre au dit Exchange par deux grans
Portaux ou entrees, l'un du costé de midi.
et l'autre du costé d'Aquilon. Lesdits portaux sont flanquez des deux costez, d'u-

3. Colo*n*nes de
marbre Jaspin.

ne große Colonne de fin marbre Jaspin,
de la hauteur de 14, piez chacune: et
au milieu des dits Portaux, une semblable Colonne qui les mi part en deux.

le Sueil.

Le Sueil desdits Portaux est de marbre
semblable aux Colonnes.

[fol. 55]

Au deßus desdits Portaux, au front du
dit Exchange sont enleuees en boße les

les Armes du
Royaume
premiere deuise.
la seco*n*de.

armes et deuises d'Angleterre d'un ouurage fort exquis.   La premiere deuise est *Honni soit qui mal y pense*. La seconde

3ᵉ, gallerie.

est *Dieu et mon droit*.
La troisieme allee ou gallerie, et qui est
au deßus des autres, est tres excellente,
belle et riche.   On y monte par, 25,
ou, 30, degrez qui sont faits et posez
par Estages de sept en sept.   Cete gal-
erie est entouree par le dedans, de

150, Estaux.

150, estaux pleins de tres riches marchandises, sur tout de toutes sortes
de merceries.

[fol. 55ᵛ]

Le dit Exchange[69] est couuert tout au tour de
fine ardoise: et droit au deßus ~~deßus~~ de
l'entree du costé de Midj, est vne bra-
ue Tourelle fort eminente et bien faite,

le clocher de la
Bourse.

au plus haut et dernier estage est vne
campanelle laquelle sert a double vsage: premierement on la sonne qua*n*d
l'exchange est fini, aßavoir a 12, heu-

68. s *inserted above line.*
69. *the link at the foot of the recto supplies* Le dit.

cet horologe a
mo*n*stre a quatres
faces.

les Musiciens de la
Cité.

res de matin, et a 6, de soir.   Secondement elle sert d'horologe pour auertir
les Marchans du temps du dit Exchange.
Au tour de la dite Tour y a deux galleries
l'une sur l'autre, faite fort proprement,
esquelles les ioueurs d'instrumens de la
Cité font merueilles de sonner, les dimen-

[fol. 56]

ches a 4 heures apres midj aux longs iours,
au grand contentement des escoutans, desquels le nombre est fort grand.
Or combien que la dite Borse ou Exchange soit si magnifique et merueilleux en
toutes ses parties qu'il rend estonnez ceux
qui le contenplent[70] attentiuement: combien se doit on émerveiller et trouuer

Nota.

estrange, qu'un ho*m*me, voire vn Marchant seul a entrepris et parfait a ses
propres cousts et despens vn si somtueux
edifice? Il l'a entrepris et en est venu
a bout comme on le voit auiourd'huy

Sir Thomas Gresham
az autheur du
Excha*n*'

a son honneur et louange. C'est Sir
Thomas Gresham qui par ses vertus

[fol. 56ᵛ]

et[71] merites a esté elleué au degre honorable
de Cheuallier par la Ma.ᵗᵉ de la Roine
Elisabeth, laquelle Dieu vueille preseruer.

Excuse.

Or i'ay laißé plusieurs choses apparte-
nantes au dit edifice du dit[72] Exchange,
comme sont les Maisons qui sont con-
tigues a icelluy, et qui sont du mesme
pourpris: et les Celliers et Caves soubs-
terraines, a cause de breueté.   Seulement i'ose dire en vn mot, qu'il ne se
trouuera en toute l'Europe gueres de
si somptueux edifice pour ce a quoy il
est dedié: et celluy est encore a nais-
tre qui peut dire du contraire.
Parquoy außj Sir Thomas Gresham

---

70. contemplent *presumably intended.*
71. at foot of fol 56ᵛ.
72. dit *inserted above line.*

[fol. 57]

s'est acquis vne louange quj durera
encore beaucoup plus que son ouurage.

Le Conduit de
Cornehill.

Vis a vis dudit Exchange, du costé de Corne hill est vne belle fontaine qui donne son eau par plusieurs
conduis. Elle fut edifiee aux despens des Citoyens de Londres, en l'an
1400.

Marchant plus outre on trouue vn
carrefour, au quel se tient, 3, fois la
semaine vn fort beau marché de toutes victuailles. On rencontre la aus-
si vne fort belle maison nommee Leden

Leden hall.

hall, de tres belle representation. Un

Sir Simond Eyre.

homme de bien, nommé Sir Symond

[fol. 57ᵛ]

Eyre, Cheuallier et Lord Maire de Londres la fit bastir, et außj vne Chapelle
tout au pres en l'an 1445, sur la porte
de cete Chapelle est escrit, Dextera Dominj
exaltauit me. En cete maison de Le-
denhall y a vne grande et spacieuse Court
ou lon vend es iours de marché la fari-
ne de toutes sortes de blés; Cete Court
et vn autre grand porche qui est au
derriere, sert de Boucherie commune
esdits iours, tant pour les Bouchers du
village qu'autres quj y veulent estaler:

100, estaux de
Bouchers.

tellement qu'il s'y trouueront quelque
fois plus de 100, Estaulx.   Il n'est
permis aux vilageois de vendre aucu-

[fol. 58]

ne viande ne autre chose le midi du iour
de marché paßé sur peine de confiscation
des marchandises, a cause des privilleges

Privilleges des
Bourgeois de
Londres.

des frimans de Londres: et ainsi cete grande rue s'en va de la rendre a la Porte
dite Algate.

Chap 10.

De la rue dite Lothburie. De la
maison de ville, dite GuildeHall.
De l'election du Seigneur Maire,
des Sheriefz et Aldermans.

LA quatrieme des principales rues de
Londres, est celle qu'on appelle communement

Lothburie.

Lothburie. Elle n'est pas si longue que les
autres, toutesfois elle a cet honneur d'auoir
[fol. 58ᵛ]
la Maison de ville vers elle, laquelle on ap-

Guildhall.

pelle communement Guilde Hall.
En l'an du Seigneur 1410, au propre lieu
ou cete maison est aßise estoit vne fort petite

vne petite logette fut conuertie en vne grande et excellente maison.

loge et contemptible, laquelle, depuis a
esté erigée en ce magnifique et excellent edifice qu'on y voit auiourd'huy,
au despens de la Cité, et beaucoup auan-
cée par la grande liberalité d'un

Richard Whitington homme heroique.

venerable Alderman nommé Richard
Whitington, et de plusieurs autres
Aldermans, quj voulurent bien n'es-
pargner leur propre bien pour orner
leur Cité d'un si beau chef d'œuure.

l'entree de Guildhall.

Le front et entree de cete Maison est
[fol. 59]
comme celle d'un bien grand et magnifique Temple ou Palais.

sale fort grande.

Le premier membre de la dite maison, en entrant, est vne grande sale,
de quatre vingts pas de long, ou enuiron, pauée en quarrons de marbre noir
fort proprement agencez.

Siege du Sʳ. Maire.

En un des bouts d'icelle est le Siege iu-
dicial du Seigneur Maire, deuant lequel sont menez les criminels de leze
Maiesté, et par luj iugez, selon leur merite. Mais s'ils sont Seigneurs, et sont
qualifiez de quelque haut degré,

les Pers.

ils sont menez deuant leurs Pers a
Westminster, et la iugez par eux.

[fol. 59ᵛ]

la Court de
conscience.

Au costé de ce Pretoire, on tient vne
Court, laquelle on appelle, *La Court de
Conscience*. C'est a dire, quand quelque
poure personne est inquietee par son crediteur, et n'a dequoy payer: elle le[73] fait appel-
ler deuant la dite Court, a laquelle ayant
bien certifié sa poureté et le bon vouloir
qu'elle a de bien payer: on ordonne que
le debiteur payera chacune semaine au
crediteur (en rabatant sur la debte) 12,

Nota.

ou, 8, ou 6, ou, 4, deniers, selon le gain
et poßibilité du debiteur. Mais cete coust
ne peut cognoistre de plus de 40 Shelings.

La Court des
Sheriefz.

A l'autre bout de cete Sale est le Parquet
ou se tient la Court des Sheriefz, lesquels

[fol. 60]

iugent des choses casuelles, comme, parolles outra-
geuses et autres torts, des sommes d'argent
deues des vns aux autres desquelles on est en
different, et de choses semblables et ciuiles.

Sale seconde.

De la on entre ~~en une autre~~ en vne autre
Sale, moindre toutesfois, par la montee de

10. ou 12. degrez

8, ou 10, degrez de pierre. Au deßus de
l'entree de laquelle sont les effigies de deux

deux Geans l'un
Anglois, l'autre
Escoß.

Geans armez, l'un a dextre l'autre a
senestre, representees (comme on dit)
au plus pres du vif, selon la grandeur
et proportion d'iceux. L'un desquels
estoit Duc de Cornewall: l'autre estoit
Escoßois, qui sont les deux extremitez de l'Isle. L'Anglois estoit nommé

[fol. 60ᵛ]

Corineus. Goemago.

Corineus et l'Escoßais Goemago.
Or ils combatirent corps a corps pour
la superintendance; l'un avec une
grande halebarde, l'autre auec vne
grose maßue, ferree a 12 pointes de
fer, et fut l'Escoßois vaincu et rendu tri-
butaire a Corineus, voila ce qu'on en dit.

les deux Chefs
Justices d'Angleter.

En cette sale les deux Chefz Justices
d'Angleterre tiennent les Aßises.

73. le *inserted above line.*

la chambre du
Conseil de la ville.

A costé de la dite Sale, est la porte par
laquelle on entre en la chambre, ou
le Seigneur Maire et ses freres les honorables Aldermans entrent trois fois
la semaine ordinairement en Conseil
pour les affaires de la republicque.

[fol. 61]

Mais puis que nous sommes sur le propos du
Seigneur Maire, des magnifiques Sheriefs
et des honorables Aldermans: il sera bon
que nous disions quelque chose de leur ellection
et entree en leur charge: car cela sert grandement a illustrer la grandeur et magnificence de Londres

Or d'au d'autant que ce que nous auons
a dire touchant le Seigneur Maire, sa
charge, son Election et son entree en la
noble Cité de Londres est de grande
deduction: ie diray premierement quelque chose touchant les magnifiques
Sheriefs et honorables Aldermans.

Richard. 1.

Au temps du Roy[74] Richard premier de ce

[fol. 61ᵛ]

nom, les Citoyens de Londres, desirans a-
uoir quelques vns de leur republicque,
qui eußent la charge et gouuernement
d'icelle, et n'estre plus sous la subiection

Portegreues.

des Portegreues que le Roy Williame le
Conquereur auoit establis: poursuivent si
bien enuers le Roy qu'ils obtindrent que
d'orenauant la Cité de Londres seroit gou-
uernee par deux Baillifs: ce fut en l'an, 1190.

deux Baillifs.

Et cete faßon dura iusqu'au temps du Roy

le Roy Jean ordonna
le Maire et les
Sheriefes.

Jean, en l'an 1208, que la dite Cite obtint
qu'elle pourroit ellire annuellement vn
Maire et deux Sheriefs pour le gouuernement de leur republique, et que les deux
Baillifs seroyent supprimez.

[fol. 62]

Or quant au Seigneur Maire, nous en parlerons cj apres, nous licenciant (pour les causes
susdites) de rompre l'ordre en cet endroit.

74. Roy *inserted above line.*

deux Sherifs
ordinairement.

Les Sheriefs sont ordinairement deux et
sont les seconds en dignité apres le Seigneur
Maire en la Cité de Londres et appartenances
d'icelle. Leur ellection se fait par le Seigneur
Maire, et est bien vray semblable que ce n'est
~~pas~~ sans l'auis de ses freres les honorables Aldermans.

sont elleuz par le
Seigneur Maire.

Ils sont annuels.

Ils sont elleus annuellement, et entrent en
charge enuiron la fin du mois de Septem-
bre. Celluj qui est elleu, le Seigneur
Maire le luy signifie en prenant vne cou-
pe d'argent et buuant a luy durant le
disner du iour de l'ellection, le nommant

ceremonie. en
l'ellection.

[fol. 62ᵛ]

l'office des Sheriefs.

Sheriefe. Leur charge est (entre autre)
de faire mettre a execution les Sentences
criminelles contre les traistres, rebelles, her-
retiques, murtriers, larrons et autres ~~mal~~
malfaiteurs dignes de mort (et de quelque
condition qu'ils soyent) ou autre punition
corporelle: tellement qu'en cet endroit ils
representent non seulement tout le corps
de la Cité, mais außi tout le corps du Conseil royal.   Durant le temps de leur
administration et charge, ils tienent
maison ouuerte, en laquelle sont receus
toutes gens honnestes, et d'autorité: si
que la despense qu'ils font durant leur
administration, ne monte pas moins de

dignité des sheriefs

leur liberalité

[fol. 63]

somme notable.

sept ou 8000, escus, qui est vne somme bien
notable: mais außi peuuent ils bien porter
telle charge, a cause du revenu de la Shriuauté tant de Londres que de Middlesex qu'ils ont
en fief ferme pour 300ˡˡ. starling chacun
an, et cela leur fut octroyé par le Roy Henrj, 3, et auß d'autres auantages qu'ils ont:
et außi que nul n'y est elleu quj n'ait bien
dequoy pour porter les frais qu'il y faut
faire.

les Shrifes ont la
Shriuauté de Londet
de Middlesex en
fiefferme pour 300ˡˡ
par an.

Aldermans adionts au
Maire.

Les Aldermans ont esté adioints au Seigneur
Maire pour luy aider de Conseil en sa charge qui est merueilleusement grande come
il sera dit cj apres: car comme le Seigneur.

Le Maire a tous les
affaires de la Cité sur
soy.

Maire a la charge de tous les affaires de
la Cité sur soy, a laquelle il luy seroit impos-

[fol. 63ᵛ]

sible de fournir. On lui a adioints les Aldermans comme coadiuteurs: lesquels ont

les Aldermans ont chacun le quartier pour y prendre garde.

vn chacun son quartier en la Cité pour
y prendre garde, afin qu'il n'y auienne
quelque desordre.

Chacun Alderman a vn Debitis, ou Lieutenant, le Debitis vn Conestable, et le

officiers de l'Alderman.

conestable vn Bedel, qui sont tous officiers de l'Alderman. Brief, il y a
vn si bon ordre qu'on peut dire vra-

Londres Cité de pais.

yement que Londres est vne Cité de
paix: car un chacun peut aller franche-

Grande benediction de Dieu.

ment, seurement et a quelque heure que ce
soit par toutes les rues de la ville pour ses
affaires, et peut porter (comme on dit) l'or

[fol. 64]

grande seurté.
louange du Senat de Londres.

a la main sans creinte qu'aucun lui face des-
plaisir: et cela procede de la bonne pollice
qui y est maintenue. Mais n'est ce pas vne

grande benediction de Dieu.

grande benediction de Dieu, de voir ~~de voir~~ vne si grande seureté dedans une si
grande Cité et si peuplée la ou en plusieurs
autres regions on ne feroit pas trois pas (par
maniere de dire) hors du logis, sans estre
volé, brigandé et souvent murtrj?   Or
nous parlerons de ceci plus a plain quand
nous serons sur les bonnes Loix e pollices
de cete fameuse Cité.   Poursuiuons.

distinction entre les Aldermans et le peuple.

Les Aldermans sont distinguez d'auec le
reste du peuple, par leurs grandes robes d'es-
carlate[75] rouge ou violette les iours de feste:

[fol. 64ᵛ]

la Cornette.

et les iours ouriers[76] par une Cornette de velour
noir large de 4, grans doigs: ou par vne

la longue Chaine d'or.

grande et longue chaine d'or qu'ils portent au col; chose fort louable, et quj les
rend tres venerables enuers tous: tellement
qu'on est en doute si la grauité, authori-

---

75. *above line, replacing* ~~calte te~~.
76. ouuriers *presumably intended.*

les Ephores de
Sparte. et Senateurs
Rommains.

Sainte et modeste
grauité.

té et representa*tion*[77] des Ephores de Sparte
ou des Senateurs Rommains anciene-
ment estoit plus recommandable que
celle de ceux cj. Car c'est vne grauité
qui n'est point superbe, ains benigne,
affable et en laquelle on voit certaines
traßes de la Maiesté de Dieu, quj fait
qu'ils sont d'autant[78] plus aimez et reuerez
des gens de bien, et creins et redoutez des
meschans et in domptables.

[fol. 65]

25 du Conseil
ordinaire.

L'institution premiere
des Alderma*n*s

Quant au nombre, ils sont 25, en tout
compris le Seigneur Maire.
Ils furent premierement instituez du
temps du Roy Henry, 3, en l'an 1240.
Ils estoyent 35, du commencement, et
estoyent changez annuellement, mais
quelque temps apres ils furent reduis
au nombre et ordre qu'on voit auiour-
d'hui.

Chap. 11.

De l'Ellection du Seigneur Maire. Du ser-
ment qu'il preste a sa Mai*esté*. De son entree
en la Cité de Londres, et autres triomphes
et ceremonies.

Combien que l'ordre requeroit bien

[fol. 65ᵛ]

qu'on fit mention en premier lieu du Seigneur Maire et des choses qui apartienent a
l'entree de sa charge. Toutesfois il m'a semblé bon, et plus propre (sans vouloir dimin-
uer aucune des choses qui appartiene*n*t
a son honneur et louange) de le reseruer
iusqu'a present pour les raisons dites ci
deßus.

l'ellection du Seigne*ur*
Maire et des Sheriff'

Or son ellection et celle des Shriff' se
fait a Guilde hall environ le iour de

77. *MS appears to read* representa*m*on.
78. *MS has* d'antant.

Saint Mathieu selon l'ordonnance
du Roy Jean.   Le Seigneur Maire
qui pour lors est et ses freres les honorables Aldermans font l'election en cete
sorte.   Ils choisißent celluy qui vient
en rang apres celluy de l'an present: a-

[fol. 66]

yans, toutesfois plusieurs regards. Premi-

Qualitez d'un Maire de Londres.

erement, s'il a le sauoir, iugement, prudence,
amour a la patrie et republicque, faculté en
biens et autres telles choses.   Secondement

cecj est le principal point.

s'il est de bonne et sainte Religion; car cela
leur est (surtout) commandé et recomman-
dé par sa Ma^té et son Conseil: car, deffail-
lant en quelqu'une de ces choses celluy qui
autrement seroit en rang, on y en elliroit
vn autre.   Parquoy, quiconque void[79] vn
Seigneur Maire de Londres, il peut har-
diment dire qu'il est digne d'un tel honneur:
car autrement il n'eut esté estably a cet es-

nul Maire sans estre Alderman.

tat.   On n'eslit aucun pour estre Maire
s'il n'est premierement Alderman: et

[fol. 66^v]

nul n'est choisi pour estre Alderman s'il n'est
de l'une des 12 Halles principales.   Or combien
qu'il y ait grand nombre de Halles en Londres
(selon qu'il y a plusieurs sortes d'Estas et vocations) toutesfois il y en a 12 principales, as-

12. Halles principales.

sauoir des Merciers, des Drappiers, Des Aberdashers, des Poißonniers, des Großiers, des
Vinetiers, des Épißiers, de Peletiers, des Fer-
ratiers, des Tailleurs, des Salletiers, des Ouriers de draps.   Sur toutes lesquelles (et sur

le Maire est Superintendant sur toutes les Halles.

toutes autres außj) dedans la iuridication de
Londres) le Seigneur Maire est Superintendant: combienque outre ce elles ont chacune

Gouverneurs et Maistres des Halles.

ses Gouuerneurs et Maistres d'icelles lesquels surueillent sur les ouurages de leurs

[fol 67]

occupations: tellement que si quelqu'un[80] de

bonne pollice

ceux qui sont desdites Halles ne fait son

---

79. *presumably for* voit.
80. l *inserted above line.*

deuoir en son art, ou s'il traite indeüement
ses seruiteurs et apprentis: ou si lesdits seruiteurs et apprentis ne font leur deuoir enuers leurs maistres, ils sont mandez deuant
le Gouuerneur et Maistres de leur Halle
quj les rengent a leur deuoir: les corrigeans
et chastians selon raison.

chose notable.

Il y a vn excellent et louable ordre en ces Halles;
car si quelquun, par quelque desastre, est deue-
nu poure, la Halle de laquelle il est, luy baille
maison et dequoy viure: et finalement luy
fait vne bonne somme d'argent pour se remettre sus.

[fol. 67ᵛ]

Or d'autant que ces Halles et les membres
d'icelles sont espars ça et la par tous les endroits de la Cité, et qu'un chacun d'iceux

vnion mere de paix
et concorde.

a serment d'entretenir paix et vnion en
icelle: de la vient la[81] tranquilite et seurté de laquelle nous auons parlé cj deßus.
Il faut bien dire que la cause principalle
est la grace de Dieu: mais elle se sert außj
de la dignité du Maire: qui est (a parler

Le Senat (dont le
Maire est le premier
membre) est source
des bonnes Loix.

humainement) comme la source de toutes
les bonnes Loix quj sont en Londres comme est dit ci deßus.

L'ellection du Maire et des Sheriffs se

Pourquoy se fait
l'ellection

fait quelque temps auant qu'ils soyent
mis en pleine poßeßion de leurs digni-

[fol. 68]

longtemps auant
leur entrée

tez, a fin qu'ils ayent le loisir de preparer ce qui
est neceßaire d'estre fait auant leur entrée
publique en la dite Cité: come d'embellir et
dreßer leurs maisons (selon qu'ils ont de
bonne et louanble[82] coustume) tant par pein-
tures, menuiseries que autres choses a celle
fin de[83] receuoir plus honorablement les hommes de
marque et authorité quj les viendront visiter, soit au repas ou autrement: singulierement a agrandir et parer l'entrée de leurs

---

81. la *replaces* ~~vne~~.
82. *sic.*
83. fin de *inserted to left of line.*

maisons au poßible, et mettre au deuant
de la premiere porte de chacun costé
(comme pour signe) deux gros piliers de
bois, entaillez de quelque bel ouurage tout
autour, et peints a l'auenant: combienque

[fol. 68ᵛ]

comme la dignité de Sheriefe est inferieure
a celle du Seigneur Maire, außi sont les

Piliers diuers.
pilliers des vns et des autres.

L'entree ~~du~~ du
Or pour venir a l'entree magnifique
Seigneur Maire en la
du Seigneur Maire en la Cité de Londres:
cité de Londres , le
Quand ce vient au l'endemain du iour
lendemain de S.ᵗ
Saint Symon et Jude; on voit de bon ma-
Simon et Jude.
tin par toute la Cité de grandes prepara-

les Halles.
tions.   Toutes les Hales, Compagnies et Estas
d'icelle s'aßemblent en tres honorable arroy
ayant chacun le Chapperon et liuree de sa
Conuoy tres
halle sur la longue robe de fin noir bandee
honorable.
de velour, ~~tout~~ et fourree de fines Martres,
auec vne representation merueilleuse. Et
apres avoir salué le Seigneur Maire elleu,

[fol. 69]

et prié Dieu qu'il le face prosperer, marchent
le conuoy vers la
deuant en fort bel ordre vers la Riuiere Ta-
Tames. les Barques et
mes, la ou chacune desdites Compagnies
Bateaux.
trouue les Barques et Bateaux tous prests
et magnifiquement attifez auquels entrez
le Seigneur Maire suit, accompaigné de
ses freres les magnifiques et honorables
Shriefs et Aldermans auec vn ordre
et magnificence incroiable, lesquels entrent en vne riche Barque qui leur est appre-
stee, pour le conduire a Westminster.
Or quj verroit la braueté des Barques
grande
et Bateaux de ce conuoy, leur ordre, le
magnificence.
nombre de gens, et le grand triomphe qui
y est il seroit estonné.

[fol. 69ᵛ]

Cette coustume de mener le Seigneur Maire par eau, fut introduite du temps du
commencement de
Roy Henry, 6ᵉ, en l'an 1453: car au para-
mener le Maire par
uant on y alloit a cheual, le long de la rue
eau.
de flett et Temple barre. En ce bel ordre
Henry, 6.
(donc) il est conduit a Westminster, deuant

il preste le serment
de fidelité a sa Ma^{té}.

sa Ma^{té}. ou deuant ceux quj sont ordonnez
en son nom pour receuoir de luy le serment
de fidelité. Cela fait, et les ceremonies
a ce requises accomplies, il s'en retourne
par eau, auec[84] beaucoup plus grand triomphe qu'au parauant: car les Princes et
Seigneurs du priué Conseil de sa Ma^{té}.

les Princes et
Seigneurs du Conseil
priué l'accompagnent.

luj font cet honneur de l'accompaigner
a son retour tout[85] du long.

[fol. 70]

48, trompettes.

Or quand il prend au retour de Westminster, la se trouuent, 48, trompettes
qui se diuisent en trois bandes, aßauoir, 16 en chacune bande, auec nombre

Tabours. Piffres.
Enseignes. Estandars.
Guidons.

de tabours e piffres, enseignes déployees,
estendars, guidons et plusieurs autres
beaux spectacles.

Theatre.

On a accoustumé de faire vn Theatre por-
tatif fort magnifique, tout couuert de
fueille d'or ou d'argent, en forme de mon-

le Pageant.

taigne, lequel on appelle communement 𝕻𝖆𝖌𝖊𝖆𝖓𝖙
ou mistere: au deßus duquel é par tout le
front, sont plusieurs filles tres richement
ornees, representans plusiers vertus, comme
Justice, verité, Charité, Prudence et les sem-

bestes sauuages.

blables.   On porte außj la forme de plusieurs

[fol. 70ᵛ]

bestes spectacles.

bestes sauuages et estranges, come Ellephans, vnicor-
nes, Leopards, Griffons, Chameaux, Seraines,
et les semblables, lesquelles il fait fort beau voir.

l'Artillerie.

Et cependant l'artillerie ioue son rolle, en sorte
que c'est chose estrange et épouuantable a
ouir. Mesme quelque fois on fait vne trai-

trainee de poudre.

nee de poudre a canon en rond au Cemitiere
de S^t. Paul, et sur icelle on met de six en six
piez loin vne große boette d'Artillerie, char-
gee et bien estopee, tellement que i'en ay

72, boetes d'artillerie.

quelque fois compte iusqu'a 72, pieces.
Or quand le Seigneur Maire approche
de ce lieu, on met le feu a ces flutes par le
moyen de la trainee, lesquelles chantent

84. c *inserted in space between words.*
85. *inserted above line.*

Musique infernale.	vne telle chanson, qu'il semble que ce grand temple de S^r. Paul doit choir par terre. Et

[fol. 71]

chose épouuantable.	n'y a maison es enuirons bien loin qui ne tremble bien fort.
la rue de Chepside.	Sortant de ce Cemitiere il entre en la rue de Chepside, en laquelle se trouue si grande affluance de peuple, que combien qu'elle soit
grande preße.	large de 25, pas pour le moins, on y est si preßé que plusieurs y defaillent: et y auroit grande confusion, mais il y a bon nombre d'hommes deputez pour faire large.
	Apres que toutes les Halles et Compagnies sont paßées (entre lesquelles il fait beau voir
la Halle des Sergeans.	celle des Sergeans, car outre la grand robe longue, chacun d'eux porte sa maße d'argent a la main) les Princes et Seigneurs du Conseil suiuent, puis le Pageaunt et autres misteres et triomphes: cinquante ou soixante

[fol. 71ᵛ]

soixante Bourgeois.	Bourgeois honorables, auec robes longues neuues bordees par tout d'une bande de velour, large de deux doigs, les vnes ayant les pans de deuant doubles de velour, autres de satin et autres de tafetas, comme il plait au Seigneur Maire les donner, car c'est sa liuree.
Instrumens de Musique le Port Espee.	Apres cela marchent haubois, violons, et autres Instrumens de Musique fort melodieux. Puis marche le porte Espée, habillé pompeusement, tant en habits, chaines d'or anneaux d'or qu'autres ioyaux, auec⁸⁶ son Mortier solennel sur la teste: portant l'Espée de bout en main, de laquelle le⁸⁷ fourreau est de velour blanc semé de perles fines et riches.
le S^r. Maire.	Apres luy vient le Seigneur Maire en tres

[fol. 72]

le grand Ordre du Sieg^r. Maire.	magnifique arroy, ayant son gran Ordre et tres-riche Collier autour du col, vestu d'une grande et magnifique robe d'Escarla-

86. c *inserted at end of word.*
87. *inserted above line.*

Pompe et grande
magnificence.

Ordre.

te rouge, auec le Manteau d'estat deßus,
fourré de fins Menus vair, monté sur vne
belle haquenée, en harnachee pompeuseme*n*t.
Bref, ce n'est que velour tout couuert de
boutons et fers dorez. Le Maire de l'annee precedente est a costé de luy.
Apres eux sont les Sheriefs et Aldermans
suiuans de deux en deux vestus de mesme
parure que le Seigneur Maire: excepté
que*n* lieu de Collier et Ordre, ils portent
vne grande chaine d'or, laquelle pend
en double longuement par derriere et par
deuant, richement montez außj.

[fol. 72ᵛ]

Or ce train et triomphe dure ~~dure~~ depuis les
huit heures de matin iusqu'a vne heure a-
pres midi: lors il entre en la Maison de ville
nommee Guilde hall auec tout son train,
et la est appresté vn tres excellent festin et
du tout magnifique: auquel mesme, les Princes et Seigneurs du Conseil royal aßistent, tellement qu'on estime que cette iournée là cous-
te au dit Seigne*ur* Maire, 3000, escus pour
le moins.   Or pour le dire a vn mot, c'est
vne des plus magnifiques entrées qu'on face a qui que ce soit: exceté touiours celles des
Empereurs et Rois. Außi estre Maire de
Londres est plus grande dignité en Angleterre qu'estre duc de Venize a Venise.
A trois heures apres midi de la dite iour-

[fol. 73]

née, le dit Seigneur Maire part auec mesme triomphe qu'au parauant, excepté que les Princes
et Seigneurs du Conseil royal n'y sont pas.   Et
ainsi paßant le long de la rue de Chepside, est
conduit au grand Temple de Sᵗ. Paul pour ouir
le service Diuin.   Le long de cete rue se
trouuent plus de 30, ou 40000, personnes
auec vne merueilleuse foule, curieux d'ad-
mirer cete grande magnificence.
Apres le seruice le triomphe est encore plus
grand qu'au parauant, d'autant qu'a cause
du temps quj est obscur (p*our* estre l'heure tarde)
on voit la deux ou 300, torches allumees.

la maison de ville.

despence p*our*
cette iournee.

Estre Maire a
Lon*dres* est pl*us*
qu'un Duc de Venize.

40000, personnes.

triomphe plus grand
qu'au paravant.

300, torches.

heure de nuit paisible. Et d'autant[88] que l'heure de nuit est plus coye
que de iour, la melodie des Instrumens
de musique est mieux distinguee et ouye.

[fol. 73ᵛ]

Pour conclusion il n'y a rien en cete iournee qui
ne rie par maniere de dire. C'est a dire que le peuple
apres cet excellent spectacle, se retire si ioyeux
et content que rien plus.

Or le iour de Toußains, qui est trois ou quatre iours apres, on ellit quelque excellent Docteur pour prescher au Cemitiere de Sᵗ. Paul;
la est conduit le Seigneur Maire par ses freres
les Shrief' et Aldermans, auec tous les Estas et
Halles de la Cité, en mesme equipage que
le iour de son entrée. Or ie serois trop long
si ie voulois racompter par le menu toutes
les choses quj apartienent a cete entree: toutes fois ie diray cecj pour la fin, c'est qu'il ne
se faut pas esbahir si on vse de telle magnificence a l'Entrée d'un Maire de Londres: car

[fol. 74]

estre Maire est le plus
honorable estat
d'Angleterre.

c'est un des plus excellens estas (dedans la
iuridiction d'icelle) qui soit en tout le
Royaume d'Angleterre apres la dignité
Royalle. Et de fait, les priuilleges de la

Priuilleges de Maire.

Cité portent cela, que les Rois veulent
que les Maires d'icelle, durant leur charge, ayent la premiere place, et ne cedent
a homme qui soit, la personne de leurs
Maiestez seule exceptee.

premiere institution
du Maire du temps
du Roy Jean.

La premiere institution de la Mairie
de Londres, fut du temps du Roy Jean
en l'an 1209, car au parauant, la Cité
estoit sous deux Baillifs come a esté dit.

[fol. 74ᵛ]

Chap. 12.

Des Loix et Pollices de la Cité de Londres

Maintenant que par la grace de Dieu, nous
auons descrit la Cité fleurie et ornée de ses

88. ant *inserted above line.*

singularitez et precieuses antiquitez: en
semble la magnificence du Seigneur Maire et de ses freres les magnifiques Shriff'
et honorables Aldermans, le mieux qu'il
nous a esté poßible: il nous faut dire
quelque chose touchant les Loix, Polices.
Coustumes, Privilleges et libertez, oc-
troyées a icelle par les Rois tant anciens
que modernes.
Nous auons dit des le commencement
que Brutus fut le premier fondateur
[fol. 75]
de[89] Londres, et l'appella Troye nouuelle.   Or
comme vn Tonneau Tenir ne peut le vin
quj est dedans ains se respand s'il n'a

une Cité sans lois ne
peut subsister.

des Cercles: außi vne Cité ne peut subsister ne prosperer si elle n'a des Loix
pour retenir en subiection l'insolence des
fols, et pour maintenir (et d'autant plus
faire reluire) la sageße des bons et prudens.
Les Chroniques, außi, nous tesmoignent que

Brutus porta les loix
Troyennes a Londres.

Brutus, apres auoir imposé nom a sa Cité,
y ordonna les Loix Troyennes.   Or comme
Troye estoit non seulement le chef de tout-

la prosperité de Troye
luy engendra beaucop
d'envies.

te Frigie, mais außi la plus florißante qu'
on sçeut pour lors: tellement qu'a cete cause elle estoit enuiée iusques au bout, qui fut
[fol. 75ᵛ]
en partie la cause de ~~sa de~~ sa destruction: außi
ne faut il pas douter qu'elle n'eut de tres excellentes Loix, lesquelles Brutus (qui estoit Tro-
yan) transporta a sa[90] nouvelle Troye qui est auiour-
d'huy la magnifique et florißante cité de Lon-

Julius Cæsar porta
les Loix Romaines
a Londres.

res.   Ces Loix demeurerent en estre et en
vsage iusques a Jules Cæsar qui les altera
par les Loix Romaines, lesquelles il y intro-
duisit: et celles-cj continuerent iusques

Sᵗ. Edward le
Confeßeur fit les
Loix communes,
qu'on appell auiour
d'huy partout, The
Common Lawes.

au Roy Sᵗ. Edward le Confeßeur en l'an
1060, lequel repurgea beaucoup de corruptions que le temps y auoit apportées: et d'i-
celles en tira d'autres qu'il appella les Loix

89. *Added in margin.*
90. a sa *inserted above line.*

communes qui estoyent beaucoup plus profi-
tables pour les Communautez, a cause de dequoy

[fol. 75 bis]

il leur bailla ce nom qu'elles ont encore auiour-
d'huj.   Le Roy Guillaume le Conquereur
vint apres, qui n y voulut rien changer, sinon qu'il voulut qu'elles fußent reduites en
tel langage francois qu'on les voit encore auiour-
d'huy qui est si barbare et corrompu que le
propre francois n'y entend comme rien: et
seroit bien a desirer (pour beaucoup de bien
qu'il en reuiendroit a la republique) qu'on les
remit en bonne forme de langage francois,
ce qui me semble ne seroit pas trop mal-aisé
a faire, mais i'en laiße le Jugement a plus
clair-voyant que moy, et retourne a mon propos.
  Ces Loix, selon que les Rois qui vienent
et sont venus apres ont cognu estre profita-

[fol. 75 bisᵛ]

ble, ont esté enrichies et augmentees iusques a venir a l'excellence en laquelle on
les voit a present.
Or mon intention n'est pas de traiter
icj des Loix communes a tout le Royaume, mais seulement des Loix politiques
concernant seulement la fameuse Cité
de Londres et ses dependances. Sous
lesquelles Loix, tant les Citoyens qu'autres
habitans d'icelle Cité, volontairement se
submettent, et saintement les gardent.
tellement que quand on dit de quelque chose, cela est contre les Loix de la Cité, chacun
tremble et est en effray. Et cela denotte de
tant plus la bonne pollice et administration

[fol. 76]

de Justice qui y est maintenue par le noble Senat d'icelle. Or ces Loix sont en tel nombre
que si i'auois entrepris de les coucher icj par le
menu, il faudroit un plus gros volume que
mon deßein n'est de mettre en avant pour le
present. Toutes fois i'en reciteray quelques
vnes par lesquelles on pourra iuger et des autres.

Guillaume le
Conquereur mit les
Loix communes en
francois.

plusieurs profits
viendroyent de
remettre les loix en
bon langage, repurgé
de toute barbarie.

l'intention de
l'Autheur.

cela vient de la
creinte qu'on a
d'offencer.

bonne Justice de
Londres.

1

Loy contre les mutins et traistres.

Il y a Loy en Londres contre ceux qui diront ou machineront quelque chose sinisitre, non seulement contre la Maiesté du Prince, mais außj contre le bien public de la Cité, d'estre punis selon leur merite: et außi contre les sa-chans et non reuellans, tout de mesmes.

Punition.

2

[fol. 76ᵛ]

Infracteurs de paix.

Il y a Loy contre les infracteurs de paix, singu-lierement es lieux ou se fait le seruice Diuin, come sont les Temples et lieux semblables: c'est a dire, si aucun de quelque estat et condition qu'il soit, a tiré son glaiue pour offencer quel-qu'autre en ces lieux la, il faut qu'il perde le poing.

punition.

3

Adulteres et paillars. punition.

Item contre les Adulteres et Paillars, d'estre menez a Bridwell pour la estre corrigez et refroidis de leurs folles chaleurs.

4

vagabons et faineans.

Item contre les faineans et vaccabons, et cete

[fol. 77]

cj et digne, d'estre practiquée par tout le monde, veu que faineantise et vaccabon-derie ameine tant de Jeunes gens a mau-uaise fin. La loy est telle: si les gardes de quelque quartier rencontrent quelque vaccabond ou faineant, s'il est de la cité et dit qu'il n'a point de besoigne, on trou-ue moyen de luy en faire auoir: que s'ils voyent quil ne veut[91] trauailler[92] ne rien faire, on le met par force a l'hostel nommé Bridwell: la on le contraint de trauail-ler pour gaigner sa vie, et bien souuent le baston trotte sur ses épaules s'il ne veut faire son devoir. S'il est de ~~pais~~ deßus le pais, on l'enuoye en son lieu

punition.

ceux qui ne sont de la ville.

91. t added above line.
92. r added above line.

	[fol. 77^v]
j, punition	et luy baille on argent pour s'y conduire
	2me s'il est trouué apres cela vagant et
	vaccabondant en la Juridiction de Lon-
2, punition	dres, on luy perse l'oreille auec un fer
	chaud; et bannj. Si apres on l'y retro-
3, punition	ue, il est[93] pendu et estranglé.

5

quaymans.	Item contre les quaymans et bellistres:
	s'ils sont de la Cité, les gardes les menent
	a leur quartier ou leur omosne est ordon-
	née et leur commandent de se tenir la
	et n'aller plus par les portes: et s'ils y
punition.	sont plus trouuez on les meine a Bri-
	dwell.

6

	[fol. 78]
Artisans. Gens de	Item contre tous artisans et gens de mestier
mestier.	s'ils ne font loy aux[94] leurs ouurages, ou s'ils sont
	delinquans en quelque chose appartenant
	a leurs occupations, d'estres chastiez et
punition.	corrigez par les Gouuerneurs et Maistres
	de leurs Halles.

7

rauißeurs.	Item contre ceux qui outre le gré de quelqu'un
	prenent ou rauißent aucune chose qu'il ait,
	soit argent, marchandise ou autre chose d'es-
punition.	tre punis comme larrons.

8

victuailles.	Item sur toutes victuailles et prouisions ve-
	nans d'outre mer, de ne les vendre sinon a
	la taxe du Seigneur Maire, qui y establist
	[fol. 78^v]
	vn homme expres pour en faire la distri-
	bution.
	Or ce seroit bien follement entrepris a
	moy si ie voulois descrire tout ce qui
Londres la noble.	appartient au reglement de Londres la

93. above line.
94. above line.

noble.   Toutesfois ses pollices sont si bien
ordonnees qu'il n'est poßible de mieux.
Et ie dy encore cela, que Londres peut

Pollices.
a bon droit, estre dite[95] la Cité de paix, ou pacifique:
Car, de Jour les gardes sont en tous quar-
tiers, et les Aldermans außi, pour em-
pescher qu'il ne soit fait tort a aucun,
et pour faire droit a vn chacun. De nuit
le guet est aßis par tout apres neuf heures,
auquel temps chacun se retire au son d'-

[fol. 79]

une große cloche qu'on appelle communement

Couure feu.
𝕮𝖔𝖚𝖚𝖗𝖊𝖋𝖊𝖚: et cela est de l'ordonnance
du Roy Guillaume le Conquereur.
Item (et qui est digne de grand louange) Il y a ordonnance, que des le premier iour de Nouembre iusqu'au premier

Williame le Conquerour.
iour de feurier, il y aura vne lanterne pen-
due deuant chacune maison qui est sur
rue, auec une chandelle allumee, qui soit
pour durer l'espace de, 3, heures: ce qui est
si estroitement gardé, que mesmement

Le Sʳ Maire fait bien obseruer cete ordonnance.
le Seigneur Maire prend bien souuent
la peine d'aller la nuit par les rues pour
notter et chastier les defaillans.   Cete
pollice est si vtile, qu'en tous les endroits

[fol. 79ᵛ]

de la cite on peut voir si clair qu'en plein iour
depuis les six heures de soir iusques a neuf,
quelque obscur que soit le temps,
Quand quelqu'un est en l'article de la mort

bonne et sainte ordonnance.
on clochette vne Campane sans ceßer en la
paroiße du malade, par l'espace de trois
quarts d'heure, afin que tous[96] qui l'oyent recomman-
dent a Dieu le poure pacient. S'il trespas-
se on le signifie en sonnant la cloche a
branle, autrement non. Cete bonne ordonnance fut faite du temps du bon

le bon Roy Edward, 6.
Sir Thomas Gresham.
Roy Edward, 6ᵉ, en l'an 1547: estant
Maire pour lors Sir Thomas Gresham.
Si celluy qui est trespaßé est de quelque

95. estre dite *above line.*
96. que tous *or possibly* que ceux *above line.*

Halle, tous ceux de la parroiße qui sont

[fol. 80]

honnorable conuoy. de la dite Halle, le vont accompagner pour
le mettre en terre fort honorablement, ayant
leur Chaperons sur lespaule, my partj de
noir et rouge. Auquel enterrement est

sermon funebre. fait vn excellent sermon par quelque docte
Prescheur, touchant les miseres de ce monde,
et comment le peché en est cause: l'esperan-

doctrine. ce que le repentant doit avoir au merite de
la mort de Jesus Christ. Finalement il le
clost par l'esperance de la Resurrection
derniere, et exortation a viure saintement.

oeuure charitable.   Il y a vn tel ordre en ces Halles que si quelqu'un des confraires d'une d'icelles deuient
poure par quelque inconvenient: sa Hal-

cecj est bien notable. le luy baille maison franche, et luj ordonne

[fol. 80ᵛ]

quelque bonne pension, et finalement luy
fait quelque bonne somme d'argent pour
luy aider a remettre sus. Et s'il meurt

oeuure en cete poureté, cete subvention est
recommandable. continuée a ses enfans, qui est vn ordre merueilleusement louable.

la Halle des La Halle des Haberdashers est tenue de
Haberdashers. donner a disner a, 10, poures de la Compagnie, ou autres de trois en trois mois:
et pour ce faire bailler a chacun d'iceux
un pain d'un denier, vne⁹⁷ potelle d'Ale, vne
piece d'argent vallant 4, deniers, monno-
ye d'angletere et une piece de beuf de
la valeur d'un gros en vn plat auec le

Thomas Huntlow. potage. Feu de bonne memoire Thomas

[fol. 81]

Huntlow laißa a la dite Halle⁹⁸ plusieurs heritages
pour cet effect.

Sir Jean Stodey. Sir Jean Stodey, estant Maire pour lors, laißa
la Hale des en pur don a la Halle des vinetiers ce qu'on
Haberdashers. appelle le Quadrent auquel lieu est maintenant la dite Halle, et autres tenemens a l'entour.
entre autres y a 13, maisons franches sans payer.

97. *above line.*
98. lle *above line.*

J'ay fait mention en cet endroit de ces deux
derniers Articles, non que ce soit son propre lieu,
mais pour ce que i'estois sur le propos des Halles.
Maintenant ie reuien aux polices de Londres;
puis ie diray quelque chose de ses Priuilleges et Libertez.

nulles grandes
querelles a Londres.

On ne voit point en Londres beaucoup de querelles desquelles sourdent grans scandales:

[fol. 81ᵛ]

car il y a telle pollice entre eux qu'ils tiennent
des bastons de deffence tous prests: et n'y a
guieres de Boutiques ou il n'y ait halle-
barde, bill, espieu, ou autres tels bastons,
auec lesquels ils sortent a la rue quand

querelles.

quelque batterie s'y commence, et ainsi
les separent.

oppreßeurs.

Si quelqu'un fait publiquement quelque
tort a vn autre, tout les circonstans prenent le partj de l'oppreßé, et taschent, tant
qu'ils peuuent a luy fen faire droit.

Si quelque sergent pourchaße quelcun
pour le prendre, lequel se vueille sauuer en

stope, stope.

fuyant, si le sergent crie **stope, stope**, c'est a dire
arrestez: touts sortent incontinent et l'arres-

[fol. 82]

tent: ainsi le malfaiteur ne peut eschaper.

Arrester
quelqu'un.

Si quelque sergent a charge d'emprisonner
quelqu'un, il ne fera que le toucher de sa mas-
se d'argent, lors faut que l'autre le suiue, et
s'il veut fuir, il crie **stope** etc.

Larrons

Les larrons sont poursuiuis a outrance: tellement que celluy qui est apprehendé ayant
desrobé quelque somme d'argent, bien qu'elle
ne soit pas de grand importance, il sera pendu.
Les criminels sont iugez a toutes les Seßions,
qui sont tous les mois vne fois; et sera telle

on pend en vn iour
25 ou 30 larrons.

fois qu'en vn iour on en pendra 25, ou 30,
et combien que la Loy soit ainsi rigoureuse

Loix seueres contre
les larrons en
Angleterre.

contre le larcin, neaumoins il se trouue beaucoup de poures malheureux qui n'ont ny la

[fol. 82ᵛ]

creinte de Dieu ny la Loy a seuerite d'icelle en
l'entendement, ains continuent ce mauais train

Justice diligente.

iusqu'a ce qu'ils sont apprehendez par la di-

	ligence de la Justice.
sang en batterie.	Si deux hommes s'entrebattent et y a sang il y a amende de 10, ou 12, gos.[99]
feu a la cheminée.	Si le feu[100] se prent a la cheminee d'une maison, il y a amende de[101]
Sermon.	Il y a presche general tout les dimenches au cemitiere de S^t. Paul, auquel aßiste ordinairement le Seigneur Maire, les Sherif' et Aldermans, et grande multitude de peuple.
4, iours de marché la semaine.	Il y a iour de marché, 4, fois la semaine, assauoir le lundj, mercredy, vendredj, et Samedj.

[fol. 83]

	Il y a des Tombereaux ordonnez pour tou-
les ordures.	tes le rues de la Cité: lesquels trois fois la semaine nettoyent et emportent les ordures
Londres Cité fort nette.	de la ville: tellement que par ce moyen elle demeure fort nette.
argent faux cloué.	Si quelqu'un porte quelque piece d'argent faulse, il est permis a vn chacun de la clouer au premier pillier qu'il trouue.
arrouser les rues en Esté.	Il y a commandement en Esté et temps des chaleurs, a vn chacun de ietter force eau en la rue a l'endroit de sa maison, pour euiter la corruption que peut engendrer la chaleur; et cella est d'autant plus aisé qu'en tous les
force eau a Londres.	endroits de la Cité il y a fontaine, pompe ou puits rendans force eau.

[fol. 83^v]

d'ou sont prins les Juges d'Angleterre.	Il y a vne certaine pollice en l'election des Juges laquelle ayant quelques ceremonies qui sentent leur antiquité, i'en diray ce que i'en sçay. Il ya 12, Colleges de loix
12, Colleges.	a Londres desquels il y en a, 4, princi-
4, principaux	paux desquels i'ay parlé cj deßus: les, 8,
8, moindres.	autres sont moindres, et tous ~~en~~ sont
Innes of Courte or of Chancery.	appellez, Hostels de Cour ou de Chancellerie. L'ordre est tel: quand les ieunes Escolliers des, 8, moindres Colleges, sont

99. *Presumably for* gros.
100. u *above line.*
101. bank space follows.

capables de tenir les communes disputes
qu'ils appellent 𝔐otes qui vient de *motus*
aut motio, pource quils meuvent des ques-

Inner Barresters.

tions: lors sont ils appellez, Disputeurs
dedans la Barre, ou plaideurs: et cete

[fol. 84]

dispute[102] faite, ceux qui auront bien soustenu
sont tirez de ces Colleges moindres, et mis es

1 Degré.

4 principaux, et commencent a prendre
degré de loy en l'hostel de Court et non ailleurs. Le premier degré est appellé **outer barre-**
ster, c'est a dire, Plaideurs hors de Barre. Apres

2 Degré.

cela, ils ont le degré de Lecteurs en Chancelerie,
c'est a dire Presidens sur les apprentis; et de la ils

3. Degré.

viennent a estre Lecteur es Hostels de Court, et par-
uienent la par degré d'ancienneté s'ils ne sont
empeschez par faute de sauoir et science. De

4, et dernier degré.

la ils vienent a vn degré qu'ils appellent, Sergeans de la coefe: et ce dernier degré se prend
aue beaucoup de Ceremonies et de despence,
car ~~de ce~~ de ce degré sont prins tous les Juges

[fol. 84ᵛ]

d'Angleterre.   Or auiendra que apres, 5, 7,
ou 8 ans qu'on donnera a entendre a sa
Maiesté qu'il y a faute de Sergeans a la coife

Sergeans a la coife.

pour en prendre des Juges: lors elle comman-
dera que six soient elleuz des Lecteurs de
la maison de Court. Lors a vn certain iour
ces Elleuz, aiant prié leurs parens et amis,
seront presentez a sa Maiesté, laquelle les
conferme. Adonc sont ils vestus de robes
longues, mi parties de couleur tanné vio-
lant et noire, et leur met on a chacun

le Beguin.

vn beguin de fine toile a la teste. Lors ils
donnent beucoup d'anneaux d'or, premierement a sa Ma.ᵗᵉ puis a plusieurs autres.
Puis vont disner, ou se fait vn somptueux

[fol. 85]

festin, auquel se trouuent le Seigneur
Maire, les Sheriefs et Aldermans ses freres. Apres disner ils sont conduis au

102. *Supplied from foot of previous folio.*

grand Temple de Saint Paul pour rendre
graces a Dieu, auec leurs robes my parties
et le beguin sur la teste; et doivent porter cet habit tout vn an durant.   Or
quand il faut quelque Juge en vne
place on le prend de la. Et en cet endroit
ie me contenteray de ce que i'ay dit des Pollices de Londres.

Chap. 13.

Des Priuilleges et libertez de la Cité
de Londres.

privilleges et libertez.

Les Privilleges et libertez de la noble
[fol 85ᵛ]
et triomphante Cité de Londres sont si
grans et en grand nombre, que ie ne veux
pas entreprendre de les reciter par le menu,
mais seulement quelques vns, a fin que
par iceux on vienne a la contemplation
du reste.   Ces Priuilleges luy ont esté

leurs priuilleges sont
escris en langue
Saxonique et en
mesme caracteres.

octroyez de toute ancienneté par ses premiers Rois; et confirmez par les subse-
quens et grandement augmentez: et
singulierement par Sᵗ Edward Confeßeur.
Guillaume le Conquereur leur auoit
ostez leurs Priuilleges: mais a la grand

Cet Evesque est
enseuelly en la nef du
Temple Sᵗ. Paul.

poursuite et solicitation d'un bon Eues-
ue[103] (come est dit cj deßus) ils luy furent
restituez et grandement augmentez
[fol. 86]
außi la Cité ne fut par ingrate de bene-
fice enuers le dit Evesque: car elle luy fit
dreßeßer,[104] apres son trespas vne for[105] belle tom-

en la page, 61,
de ce liure.[106]

be de marbre come on voit cj deßus en parlant
du Temple de Sᵗ. Paul.
Ces libertez furent confirmees par le

103. Euesque *intended*.
104. *For* dreßer.
105. fort *probably intended*.
106. *i.e. fol. 38, p. 222.*

Le Roy Jean les confirme et augmente.

Roy Jean 1227. et outre plus octroya
la Cité de Londres qu'elle auroit desor-
mais vn commun Seel; aux Sherifes de
auoir vn chacun d'eux clercs.

le Roy Henrj, 3, de mesme.

Elles furent außi confirmees par Henrj
3; et outre plus leur octroya de nouueau
la Conté de Midlesex.

trafique franche.

Les Bourgeois de Londres ont ce priuil-
lege de marchander et trafiquer par tout
[fol. 86ᵛ]
le Royaume d'Angleterre: et les autres ne peuuent trafiquer a Londres sans auoir la liberté de
la ville.

tous Anglois aiment le ieu de l'Arc.

Comme tous Anglois naturellement aiment et s'addonnent a tirer de l'Arc; spe-
ciallement ceux de Londres; a cause dequoy
ils ont obtenu des rois, plus*ieu*rs places vui-
des et de pasturages a l'entour de la Cité
esquelles ils s'exercent les festes.   Vray

com*mune*s entour londres.

est que les communes des villages des enuirons leur en ont autres fois fait fache-
rie et se sont mis en effet, mais ils en ont
esté chastiez.   Ce bon exercisse les

3000, tireurs.

incite souuent a faire des pris: Tellement
que i'ay autrefois compté 3000, tireurs,
[fol. 87]

3000, Archers en un pris.

tous d'une partie et prix: et au beau temps
ils font parroiße contre parroiße, en quoy
ils s'exercent si bien que c'est vne grande force pour¹⁰⁷ la Cité.

francs de peage. par tout Angleterre.

Les Citoyens de Londres peuuent mener
et ramener leurs marchandises par toute
Angleterre sans payer aucun Peage. Cela
leut fut octroyé par le Roy Henrj, 3, en

franche Garenne au tour de Londres.

l'an 1226. Il leur octroya außj puißance
de chaßer, certain circuit a l'entour de la
Cité et de ses appartenances. Et de fait, a
fin d'entretenir la poßeßion, le Seigneur
Maire, vne fois l'an, et accompagné de ses
freres les Sherifs et Aldermans, et de plus-

107. r *above line.*

la chaße du Maire.

ieurs autres Citoyens, vont faire la chasse[108]

[fol. 87ᵛ]
Pour plus grande Illustration de Singularitez de Londres, il faudroit que ie miße
en auant, singulierement les bonnes mœurs,
l'honesteté, (et surtout) la Charité des nobles
citoyens de Londres. Et particuliere-
ment la Pieté de plusieurs, lesquels ont
si bien profité en l'escole de Jesus Christ,
que quand il viendra iuger les vifs et les
morts, plusieurs viendront[109] voire et[110] grand nombre,
de poures bannis pour la querelle de Jesus
Christ, aportans et luy presentant le biens qu'ils ont receuz d'eux en leur grande
neceßité: et lors ils orront la voix du Seigneur
qui leur dira: J'ay esté estranger, et vous m'
auez receu, iouißez de la vie eternelle.

[fol. 88]
Voila la somme de ce que i'ay peu auoir cognoißance des beautez, bontez et perfections
de cete tant[111] florißante, et triomphante Cité

Priere de l'Autheur.

de Londres. Le Seigneur, Eternel, et Tout puis-
sant Dieu la maintiene et face prosperer de
plus en plus. Maintiene außj et rempliße de
ses graces le noble Magistrat et Senat d'icelle,
vueille finallement prendre sous sa protection tous les bons et vertueux Citoyens et
habitans d'icelle iusqu'a la fin. Amen

Fin.

[fol. 88ᵛ is set out with lead-ruled lines and red lines for margins,
but contains no text]

108. *Despite the abrupt transition to the conclusion, there is no
indication that anything has been omitted since* se *was
intended simply to complete the word* chasse *and was not
repeated at the top of the verso, as would have been the
scribe's normal practice. The aim appears to have been to
begin the conclusion on the next blank side. This is also
indicated by the original pagination, in which fol. 87 was
numbered, probably in the hand of the orginal scribe, as 161,
and fol. 87ᵛ as 162.*
109. *inserted above line.*
110. et *seems to an error for* en.
111. t *inserted above line.*

SOURCES AND WORKS CITED IN NOTES

Manuscripts

Bethlem Royal Hospital
Bridewell Court Book, vol iii

British Library
Additional Manuscripts
Cottonian Manuscripts
Harleian Manuscripts
Lansdowne Manuscripts

Folger Shakespeare Library
V.a.316
Journal of Georg van Schwarzstat

Lambeth Palace Library
C.M. VIII
Papers relating to the Great Tithe cause

London Metropolitan Archives
CLC/199/TC/024/MS09680
St Katharine's by the Tower, constables'
accounts
CLC/199/TF/024/MS09774
St Katharine's by the Tower, plan 1687
CLC/210/B/001/MS12806/002
Christ's Hospital, governors' minutes
CLC/210/C/001/MS12819/002
Christ's Hospital, accounts
CLC/210/G/A/004/MS12805
Christ's Hospital, plan book
CLC/210/G/BCA/034/MS13008
Christ's Hospital, papers relating to
Castel estate
CLC/210/G/BCA/039/MS13013
Christ's Hospital, papers relating to
Castel estate
CLC/210/G/BCA/040/MS13014
Christ's Hospital, papers relating to
Castel estate

CLC/262/MS024643
Description of London by William Smith
CLC/313/B/001/MS25504
St Paul's Cathedral archive, Liber L
CLC/W/HF/001/MS04069/001
Cornhill wardmote inquest book
COL/AD/01/013
Letter Book N
COL/CA/01/01/012-050
Repertories of the court of aldermen
COL/CC/01/01/005-021
Journals of the court of common council
COL/RMD/PA/01/001
Remembrancia, volume 1

Mercers' Company
Register of Writings, vol. ii

Public Record Office
PROB 11
Prerogative Court of Canterbury, wills
SP12
State Papers Domestic, Elizabeth I

Suffolk Records Office
E2/29/1.1
Thomas Cullum, account book

University of Ghent Library
MS 2466
Lucas de Heere album of paintings;
see de Heere c.1574b

Westminster Diocesan Archive
MS A.7
Newsletters

Printed Works, Theses and Short References

Acts of Court. 1936. *Acts of Court of the Mercers' Company, 1453-1574* (Cambridge)

Adams, S. (ed.). 1996. *Household Accounts and Disbursement Books of Robert Dudley Earl of Leicester*, Camden fifth series vol. 6 (Cambridge)

Adams, S., Archer, I. W., Bernard, G. (eds). 2003. 'A "Journall" of matters of state', in Archer, I. W. et al (ed.): 52-122

Adams, S. and Greengrass, M. (eds). 2003. 'Memoires et procedures de ma negociacion en Angleterre (8 October 1582-8 October 1583) by Jean Malliet, councilor of Geneva', in Archer et al. (eds) 2003: 137-96

Allen, M. 2012. *Mints and Money in Medieval England* (Cambridge).

Amyot, J. (trans.). 1554. *Sept livres des Histoire de Diodore Sicilien, nouvellement traduyt de Gre en Françoys* (Paris)

Amyot, J. (trans.). 1558. *Les Vies des Hommes illustres Grecs et Romains, comparees l'une avec l'autre ... translatees de Grec en François* (Paris)

Andrews, J., Briggs, A., Porter, R., Tucker, P., Waddington, K. 1997. *The History of Bethlem* (London and New York)

Arber, E. (ed.) 1875-94. *Transcript of the Registers of the Stationers' Company, 1554-1640*, 5 vols (London)

Archer, I. W. 1991. *The Pursuit of Stability: Social Relations in Elizabethan London* (Cambridge)

Archer, I. W. 1995. 'The nostalgia of John Stow' in D. Smith, R. Strier, and D. Bevington (eds), *The theatrical city. Culture, theatre, and politics in London, 1576-1649* (Cambridge): 17-34

Archer, I. W. 2001a. 'The burden of taxation on sixteenth-century London', *Historical Journal*, 44.3: 599-627

Archer, I. W. 2001b. 'Government in early modern London: the challenge of the suburbs', in P. Clark and R. Gillespie (eds), *Two Capitals. London and Dublin, 1500-1800* (Oxford): 13-47

Archer, I. W. 2002. 'The livery companies and charity in the sixteenth and seventeenth centuries', in I. Gadd and P. Wallis (eds), *Guilds, Society and Economy in London, 1450-1800* (London): 15-28

Archer, I. W. 2004a. 'John Stow, citizen and historian', in Ian Gadd and Alexandra Gillsepie (eds), *John Stow (1525-1604) and the making of the English past: studies in early modern culture and the history of the book* (London): 13-26

Archer, I. W. 2004b. 'Lambe, William (d. 1580)', *ODNB*

Archer, I. W. 2005. 'Discourses of history in Elizabethan and early Stuart London', *Huntington Library Quarterly*, 68:1 and 2: 205-26

Archer, I. W. 2007. 'The charity of London widows in the later sixteenth and early seventeenth centuries', in N. Jones and D. Woolf (eds), *Local identities in late medieval and early modern England* (Basingstoke): 178-206

Archer, I. W. 2008. 'Ramsey, Mary, Lady Ramsey (d. 1601)', *ODNB* (online only)

Archer, I. W. 2009. 'The city of London and the theatre' in R. Dutton (ed.), *The Oxford Handbook of Early Modern Theatre* (Oxford): 396-412

Archer, I. W. 2012. 'The city of London and river pageantry, 1400-1856', in S. Doran (ed.), *Royal River. Power, pageantry and the Thames* (London): 80-5

Archer, I. W., Barron, C. M., Harding, V. (eds) 1988. *Hugh Alley's Caveat: the Markets of London in 1598, Folger Ms V. a. 318*, LTS 137 (London)

Archer, I. W. et al (eds). 2003. *Religion, Politics, and Society in Sixteenth-Century England*, Camden Society fifth series 22 (London)

Archer, I. W. and Price, F. D. (eds). 2011. *English Historical Documents*, Va, *1558-1603* (London)

Ashbee, J. 2008. 'The structure and function of the White Tower, 1150-1485', in Impey 2008: 140-59

Ashe, L. 2013. 'Holinshed and mythical history', in P. Kewes, I. W. Archer, and F. Heal (eds), *The Oxford handbook of Holinshed's Chronicles* (Oxford): 153-69

Ashton, R. 1979. *The City and the Court 1603-1643* (Cambridge)

Bacon, Francis. 1996. *Collected Works*, 12 vols, 1878, repr. 1996 (London)

B & H Map. 1572. The map of London in vol. 1 of G. Braun and F. Hogenberg, *Civitates Orbis Terrarum*, 6 vols (Antwerp, Cologne, 1572-1617). See Fig. 1

Baker, J. H. 1984. *The Order of Serjeants at Law: a chronicle of creations, with related texts and a historical introduction* (London)

Baker, J. H. (ed.). 2001. *Readers and Readings in the Inns of Court and Chancery*, Selden Society supplementary series, 13 (London)

Baker, J. H. 2002. *An Introduction to English Legal History* (London)

Baker, J. H. 2004. Baker, 'Bendlowes, William (1516-1584)', *ODNB*

Barker, F. and Jackson, P. 2008. *The Pleasures of London*, LTS 167

Barlow, F. 1986. Barlow, *Thomas Becket* (London)

Barron, C. M. 1970. 'The government of London and its relations with the Crown, 1400-1450', University of London PhD. Thesis

Barron, C. M. 1974. *The Medieval Guildhall of London* (London)

Barron, C. M. 2004a. *London in the Later Middle Ages: Government and People 1200-1500* (Oxford)

Barron, C. M. 2004b. 'Eyre, Simon (*c*.1395-1458)', *ODNB*

Barron, C. M., Coleman, C. and Gobbi, C. 1983. 'The London journal of Alessandro Magno, 1562', *The London Journal* 9: 136-52

Barron, C. M. and Davis, M. (ed.). 2007. *The Religious Houses of London and Middlesex* (London)

Bateson, M. 1902. 'A London municipal collection of the reign of John', *English Historical Review* 17: 480-511, 7-30

Beaven, A. B. (1908-13). *The Aldermen of the City of London, Temp. Henry III-1912*, 2 vols (London)

Beilin, E. V. 2004. 'Martin, Dorcas, Lady Martin (1536/7-1599)', *ODNB* (2004)

Benbow, R. M. 1993. 'Notes to Index of London Citizens involved in City Government, 1558-1603', typescript, 2 vols (in library of the Institute of Historical Research, University of London, at shelfmark BL.518/Ben)

Bentley, R. (trans.) and Walpole, H. (ed.). 1757. *A journey into England. By Paul Hentzner. MD MDXCVIII* (Twickenham)

Bergeron, D. W. 1971. *English civic pageantry, 1558-1642* (London)

Berossos. 1552. *Berosi,... Antiquitatum... libri quinque, cum commentariis Joannis Annii Viterbensis* (Antwerp); see also Nanni 1498

Berry, H. (ed.). 1979. *The first Public Playhouse: the Theatre in Shoreditch 1576-98* (Montreal)

Berry, H. 2000. 'The view of London from the north and the playhouses in Holywell', *Shakespeare Survey* 53: 196-212

Bersuire, P. (trans.). 1515. *Le Premier volume des Grans décades de "Titus Livius", translatées de latin en françois, nouvellement corrigées et amendées. Et ensuyvant les faictz dudit "Titus Livius", aucunes additions de plusieurs grans historiographes si comme Orose, Saluste, Suétone et Lucain*, 3 vols (Paris)

Bibliographie Universelle. Bibliographie Universelle (Michaud), Nouvelle édition, 45 vols (Paris, 1854-65)

Bicknell, S. 1996. *The History of the English Organ* (Cambridge)

Bignami Odier, J. 1962. 'Les fonds de la reine à la Bibliothèque Vaticane', in *Collectanea Vaticana in Honorem Anselmi M. Card. Albareda a Bibliotheca Apostolica edita*, Studi e Testi 219-20 (Città del Vaticano), vol. 1: 159-89

Bindoff, S. T. (ed.). 1982. *The History of Parliament: the House of Commons 1509-1558*, 3 vols (London)

Binski, P. 1995. *Westminster Abbey and the Plantagenets; Kingship and the Representation of Power, 1200-1400* (New Haven and London)

Biondo Flavio. 2005-10. *Biondo Flavio's Italia Illustrata: text, translation, and commentary*, ed. C. J. Castner, 2 vols (Binghampton, N.Y.)

Birch, W. de Gray. 1887. *The Historical Charters and Constitutional Documents of the City of London* (London)

Bishop, J. 2011. '*Utopia* and civic politics in mid sixteenth-century London', *Historical Journal* 54.5: 933-953

Blackmore, H. L. 1976. *The Armouries of the Tower of London. 1. Ordnance* (London, 1976)

Blanchard, I. 2004a. 'Gresham, Sir Thomas (*c*.1518-1579)', *ODNB*

Blanchard, I. 2004b 'Gresham, Sir Richard, including Sir John Gresham, c.1485-1549', ODNB

Blanchard, I. 2004c. 'Vaughan, Stephen (d. 1549)', ODNB

Blatcher, M. 1978. *The Court of King's Bench 1450-1550:a Study in Self-Help* (London)

de Blignières, A. 1851. *Essai sur Amyot et les traducterus français au XVIᵉ siècle* (Paris)

Blok, F. F. 2000. *Isaac Vossius and his Circle: his life until his farewell to Queen Christina of Sweden 1618-1655* (Groningen)

Boersma, O., and Jelsma, A. J. (eds). 1997. *Unity in multiformity. The minutes of the coetus of London, 1575 and the consistory minutes of the Italian church of London, 1576-1591*, Huguenot Society 59 (London)

Bonnardot, A. 1880. *Gilles Corrozet et Germain Brices. Études bibliographiques sur ces deux historiens de Paris* (Paris)

Bowler, H. (ed.). 1934. *London Sessions Records 1605-1685*, Catholic Records Society 34

Bowsher, D. et al. 2007. *The London Guildhall. An archaeological history of a neighbourhood from early medieval to modern times*, 2 vols, MOLAS Monograph 36, (London)

Bowsher, J. 2012. *Shakespeare's London Theatreland. Archaeology, History and Drama* (London)

Braines, W. W. 1917. 'The site of the Theatre, Shoreditch', *London Topographical Record* 11: 1-27

Braines, W. W. 1924. *The site of the Globe Playhouse, Southwark* (London)

Brigden, S. 1988. *London and the Reformation* (Oxford)

Brooke, C.N. L. and Keir, G. 1975. *London 800–1216: the shaping of a city* (London)

A breefe discourse declaring and approving the necessarie maintenance of the laudable customes of London (1584)

Brooks, C. W. 1986. *Pettyfoggers and Vipers of the Commonwealth: the 'lower branch' of the Legal Profession in Early Modern England* (Cambridge)

Burch, M., Treveil, P., and Keene, D. 2011. *The development of early medieval and later Poultry and Cheapside. Excavations at 1 Poultry and vicinity, City of London*, MOLA Monograph 38 (London)

Calabi, D. and Keene, D. 2007. 'Exchanges and cultural transfer in European cities, c.1500-1700', in D. Calabi and S. T. Christensen (eds), *Cities and Cultural Exchange in Europe, 1400-1700*, (Cambridge): 286-314

Cal LBG. Calendar of Letter-Books of the City of London ... Letter-Book G., ed. R. R. Sharpe (London, 1895)

Cal LBH. Calendar of Letter-Books of the City of London ... Letter-Book H, ed. R. R. Sharpe (London, 1907)

Cal LBK. Calendar of Letter-Books of the City of London ... Letter-Book K., ed. R. R. Sharpe (London, 1911)

Callmer, C. ed. 1971. *Catalogus codicum manu scriptorum Bibliothecae Regiae Holmiensis C. Annum MDCL conductu et auspicio Isaac Vossii conscriptus* (Stockholm)

Carlin, M. 1996. *Medieval Southwark* (London and Rio Grande)

Carpenter, E. F. 1966. *A House of Kings: the History of Westminster Abbey* (London)

Carter, P. R. N. 2004. 'Mason, Sir John (c.1503-1566)', ODNB

Cavert, W. 2011. 'Producing Pollution. Coal, Smoke and Society in London, 1550-1750', Northwestern University Ph.D. thesis

Cerasano, S. P. 1991. 'The Master of the Bears in Art and Enterprise', *Medieval and Renaissance Drama in England* 5: 195-209

Challis, C. 1992. *A New History of the Royal Mint* (Cambridge)

C. E. Challis, C. E. 2004. 'Martin, Sir Richard (1533/4–1617)', ODNB

Chambers, E. K. 1924. *The Elizabethan Stage* 4 vols (London)

Chaney, E.P. de G. 1981. '"Philanthropy in Italy": English observations on Italian hospitals', in T. Riis (ed.), *Aspects of Poverty in Early Modern Europe* (Florence): 183-217

Chiesa, P, ed. and trans. 1997. Bonvesin da la Riva, *De Magnalibus Mediolani. Meraviglie di Milan* (Milan)

Chotzen, Th. M. and Draak, A. M. E. (eds). 1937. *Beschriving der Britische eilanden door Lucas de Heere* (Antwerp)

Churchyard, Thomas. 1579. *The miserie of Flanders, the calamitie of France, misfortune of Portugale, unquietness of Ireland, troubles of Scotland, and the blessed state of England* (London)

Coates, R.1998. 'A new explanation of the name of London', *Transactions of the Philological Society* 96.2: 203-29

Collinson, P. 1983. 'The Elizabethan puritans and the foreign reformed churches in London', in his *Godly People: Essays on English Protestantism and Puritanism* (London): 245-72

Collinson, P. 2001. 'John Stow and nostalgic antiquarianism', in J. Merritt (ed.), *Imagining early modern London: perceptions and portrayals of the city from Stow to Strype, 1698-1720* (Cambridge): 27-51

Copperplate Map. See Figs 3-5. Three surviving plates out of at least fifteen of a map of London surveyed between 1553 and 1559, probably towards the latter part of that period, see. A. Saunders and J. Schofield (eds), *Tudor London: a map and a view*, LTS 159 (2001). For later versions of it, see B & H Map, Woodcut Map

Corrozet, G. 1532. *La Fleur des antiquitez, singularitez et excellences de la plus que noble et triomphante ville et cité de Paris , capitale du royaulme de France avec la généalogie du roy Françoys premier de ce nom* (Paris). The enlarged second impression of 1532 was reprinted by 'Le Bibliophile Jacob' (Paul Lacroix) in 1874 (Paris)

Corrozet, G. 1533. *La Fleur des antiquitez, singularitez et excellences de la noble et triomphante ville et cité de Paris, capitale du royaulme de France, adjoustées oultre la première impression plusieurs singularitez estans en ladicte ville, avec la généalogie du roy Françoys premier* (Paris)

Corrozet, G. 1539. *La fleur des Antiquitez, singularitez & excellences de la noble & triomphante ville, & cité, de Paris, Capitalle du royaulme de France. Auec la genealogie du roy Francoys premier de ce nom. De nouueau ont este adioustees plusieurs belles singularitez* (Paris)

Corrozet, G. 1550. *Les Antiquitez, histoires et singularitez de Paris, ville capitale du Royaume de France* (Paris)

Corrozet, G. 1561. *Les Antiquitez, chroniques et singularitez de Paris, ville capitale du royaume de France, avec les fondations et bastimens des lieux : les sépulchres et épitaphes des princes, princesses et autres personnes illustres : corrigées et augmentées pour la seconde édition par G.Corrozet Parisien* (Paris)

Corrozet, G. 1571. *Les Antiquitez, chroniques et singularitez de Paris, ville capitale du royaume de France ... recueillies par feu Gilles Corrozet,*

Augmentées de nouveau de plusieurs choses mémorables (Paris)

Corrozet, G. 1577. *Les Antiquitez, histoires, croniques et singularitez de la grande & excellente cité de Paris ... Avec les fondations & bastimens des lieux: Les sepulchres & Epitaphes des princes, princesses & autres personnes illustres. Auteur en partie, Gilles Corrozet ... mais beaucoup plus augmentees, par N. B. Parisien*

Cotgrave, R. 1673. *A French and English Dictionary composed by Mr. Randle Cotgrave* (London)

CPR 1441-1446. *Calendar of Patent Rolls. Henry VI*, vol 4 (London, 1908)

CPR Edw. VI. *Calendar of Patent Rolls. Edward VI*, 6 vols (London, 1924-9)

CPR Philip & Mary. *Calendar of Patent Rolls, Philip and Mary*, 4 vols (London, 1937-9)

Crawford, A. 1971. *History of the Vintners' Company* (London)

Cressy, D. 2000. 'The downfall of Cheapside Cross', in D. Cressy, *Travesties and Transgressions in Tudor and Stuart England* (Oxford): 234-50

Crowley, R. 1575. *A sermon made in the chappel at the Gylde Halle in London, the. xxix. day of September, 1574 before the Lord Maior and the whole state of the citie, then assembled for the chusing of their Maior that shuld then succede in the gouernme[n]t of the same citie* (London)

Cruden, R. P. 1843. *The History of the Town of Gravesend in the county of Kent and of the Port of London* (London)

CSP Foreign, Edw. VI. *Calendar of State Papers, Foreign. Edward VI* (London, 1861)

CSP Foreign, Elizabeth. *Calendar of State Papers Foreign. Elizabeth*, 23 vols (London, 1863-1950)

CSP Foreign, Mary. *Calendar of State Papers, Foreign. Mary* (London, 1861)

CSP Simancas. *Calendar of Letters and State Papers relating to English Affairs preserved principally in the Archives of Simancas*, 4 vols (London, 1892-9)

CSP Spain. *Calendar of Letters, Despatches and State Papers relating to the negotiations between England and Spain preserved in the Archives at Simancas and elsewhere*, 13 vols (London, 1862-1954)

CSP Venetian. *Calendar of State Papers and Manuscripts relating to English Affairs, existing in the Archives of Venice and other Libraries of Northern Italy*, 38 vols (London, 1864-1947)

Cyuile and vncyuile life a discourse very profitable, pleasant, and fit to bee read of all nobilitie and gentlemen : where, in forme of a dialoge is disputed, what order of lyfe best beseemeth a gentleman in all ages and times ... (1579, London)

Dart, J. 1723. *Westmonasterium: or the History and Antiquities of St Peter's Westminster* (London)

de Beer, E. S. 1941. 'The early history of London street lighting', *History* 25.100: 311-24

Deloney, T. 1639. *The Gentle Craft. The second part* (London)

Dérens, J. 1980. 'Commentaire', in *Le plan de Paris par Truschet et Hoyau 1550, dit plan de Bâle : Bibliothèque Publique de L'Université de Bâle, AA 124* (Zürich)

Devereux, E. J. 2000. 'Empty tuns and unfruitful grafts: Richard Grafton's historical publications', *Sixteenth Century Journal* 21: 33-56

Dietz, B. ed. 1972. *The Port and Trade of early Elizabethan London Documents*, LRS 8

Dillon, J. 2008. 'Clerkenwell and Smithfield as a neglected home of London theater', *Huntington Library Quarterly* 71.1: 115-35

Dobb, C. 1964. 'London's prisons', *Shakespeare Survey* 17: 87-100

Dobson, M. 2008. *The Army of the Roman Republic: the second century, Polybius and the camps at Numantia, Spain* (Oxford)

Dodgson, J. M. 1996. 'A linguistic analysis of the place-names of the Burghal Hidage' in D. Hill and A. R. Rumble (eds), *The defence of Wessex: the Burghal Hidage and Anglo-Saxon fortifications* (Manchester): 98-122

Dollinger, P. 1964. *La Hanse (XIIᵉ-XVIIIᵉ siècles)* (Paris)

Doran, S. 1996. *Monarchy and Matrimony: the courtships of Elizabeth I* (London)

Douce, F. (ed). 1811. *The Customs of London otherwise called Arnold's Chronicle* (London)

Dugdale, W. 1658. *The History of St Paul's Cathedral in London from its foundation untill these times* (London)

Edelen, G. (ed.). 1968. *William Harrison, The Description of England* (Ithaca)

Egan, G. 2009. 'Theatre in Shoreditch', in R. Dutton (ed.), *Oxford Handbook to Early Modern Theatre* (Oxford): 169-77

Eichberger, D. 2003. 'A noble residence for a female regent: Margaret of Austria and the 'Court of Savoy in Mechlen', in H. Hills (ed.), *Architecture and the politics of Gender in Early Modern Europe* (Aldershot): 25-46

Ekwall, E. 1965. *Street-names of the City of London* (Oxford)

Fabyan, R. 1811. *The new chronicles of England and France : in two parts, reprinted from Pinsent's edition of 1516 collated with later editions*, with preface and index by Henry Ellis (London)

Fagel, R. 2005. 'Immigrant roots: the geographical origins of newcomers from the Low Countries in Tudor England', in Nigel Goose and Lien Bich Luu (eds), *Immigrants in Tudor and early Stuart England* (Brighton): 41-56

Fairholt, F. W. 1866. 'On an inventory of the goods of Sir Thomas Ramsey, lord mayor of London in 1577', *Archaeologia* 40: 311-42

Favier, J. 1970. *Les Contribuables Parisiens à la fin de la Guerre de Cent Ans* (Paris)

Felici, L. 2009. 'Theodor Zwinger's *Methodus Apodemica*: an observatory of the city as political space in the late sixteenth century', *Cromohs* 14: 1-18. <URL: http://www.cromohs. unifi.it/14_2009/felici_zwinger.html >

Ferguson, A. B. 1993. *Utter Antiquity: perceptions of Prehistory in Renaissance England* (Duke, NC)

Ferguson, M. G. 2004. 'Grafton, Richard, c.1511-1572', *ODNB*

Ffoulkes, C. J. 1916. *The Armouries of the Tower of London*, 2 vols. (London)

Field, John. 1583. *A Godly Exhortation by Occasion of this Late Judgement of God Showed at Paris Garden* (London)

FitzStephen, William. 'Description of London' (written 1173-4): see Robertson (1877)

Foster, F. F. 1977. *The Politics of Stability: a Portrait of the Rulers in Elizabethan London* (London)

Freeman, A. 1973. 'Marlowe, Kyd and the Dutch Church Libel', *English Literary Renaissance*, 3: 44-52

Gairdner, J. (ed.).1880. *Three fifteenth-century chronicles with historical memoranda* Camden Society, new series, 28 (London)

Galloway, J., Keene, D. and Murphy, M. 1996. 'Fuelling the city. Production and distribution of firewood and fuel in London's region, 1290-

1400', *Economic History Review*, 49: 447-72

Garzoni, T. 1585 *La piazza universale di tutte le professioni del mondo. Di Tommaso Garzoni da Bagnocauallo. Con l'aggiunta di alcune bellissime annotazioni à discorso per discorso* (Venice)

Gascoigne, George. 1576. *The spoyle of Antwerpe. Faithfully reported by a true Englishman who was present at the same* (London)

Geoffrey of Monmouth. *The History of the Kings of Britain*, completed about 1136. Cited here by book and chapter numbers, as in the widely available translation by L. Thorpe (Harmondsworth, 1966). For a good Latin text with English translation, see Reeve, M. D. (ed.) and Wright, N. (trans). 2007. *The History of the Kings of Britain: an edition and translation of De Gestis Britonum (Historia regum Britanniae) / Geoffrey of Monmouth* (Woodbridge), which adopts a new division into sections

Geoffrey of Monmouth. 1508. *Britanie utriusque regum et principum origo et gesta insignia ab Galfrido Monumentensi ex antiquissis Britannici sermonis monumentis in latinum sermonem traducta*, ed. I. Cavellatus (Paris) [also a Paris edition of 1517]

Géraud, H. (ed.). 1837. *Paris sous Phillippe-le-Bel. D'après les documents originaux et notamment d'après un manuscrit contenant 'Le Rôle de Taille' imposée sur les habitants de Paris en 1292* (Paris)

Giovio, Paolo. 1548. *Descriptio Britanniae, Scotiae, Hyberniae, et Orchadum, ex libro Pauli Iouii, Episcopi Nucer: de imperiis, et gentibus cogniti orbis cum eius operis prohemio* (Venice)

Glover, E. 1971. *Vintners' Hall* (London)

Goldring, Elizabeth, Eales, Faith, Clarke, Elizabeth, and Archer, Jayne Elisabeth (eds). 2014. *John Nichols's The Progresses and Public Processions of Elizabeth I: A new edition of primary sources*, 5 vols (Oxford)

Goose, Nigel. 2005. 'Xenophobia in Elizabethan and early Stuart London: an epithet too far?', in Nigel Goose and Lien Luu (eds), *Immigrants in Tudor and early Stuart England* (Brighton): 110-35

Grafton, R. *Abridgement*. 1562 etc. *An Abridgement of the Chronicles of England gathered by Richard Grafton, citizen of London* (London: 1562, 1563, 1564, 1570 and 1572). These are the editions that appeared before Grenade completed his work in 1578

Grafton, R. *Chronicle*. 1569. *A chronicle at large and meere history of the affayres of England and the kinges of the same; deduced from the Creation of the worlde, vnto the first habitation of thys island: and so by continuance vnto the first yere of the reigne of our most deere and souereigne Lady Queene Elizabeth* (London)

Greenway, D. ed. 1996. Henry, Archdeacon of Huntingdon, *Historia Anglorum The History of the English People*, ed. and trans D. Greenway (Oxford)

Grenade, L. de. 1572. *Traité de l'Oraison et de la Meditation*, 2 vols (Paris)

Grenade, L. de. 1578. *Tutte l'opere del R. P. F. Luigi di Granata... tradotte di spagnuolo in italiano da diversi autori, et adornate di postille, che monstran le sententie più notabili, e l'autorità della Scrittura* (Venice)

Grenade, L. de. 1579. *La Guide des Pecheurs*, rev. edn. (Paris)

Griffiths, P. 2000. 'Politics made visible: order, residence and uniformity in Cheapside', in P. Griffiths and M.Jenner (eds), *Londinopolis. Essays in the Cultural and Social History of Early Modern London* (Manchester): 176-96

Griffiths, P. 2003. 'Contesting London Bridewell, 1576-1580', *Journal of British Studies* 42.3: 283-315

Griffiths, P. 2008. *Lost Londons: change, crime, and control in the capital city, 1550-1660* (Cambridge)

Gunn, S. J. 2010. 'Archery practice in early Tudor England', *Past and Present* 209.1: 53-81

Hakluyt, R. 1903-5. *The principal navigations, voyages, traffiques & discoveries of the English nation ...*, 12 vols, Hakluyt Society (Glasgow)

Hamilton, W. D. (ed.). 1875-7. *A chronicle of England during the reigns of the Tudors* [Wriothesley's Chronicle], 2 vols, Camden Society, new series, 11 and 20 (London)

Hammel-Kiesow, R. 2000. *Die Hanse* (Munich)

Hardyng, J. 1543/4. *The Chronicle of John Hardyng* [with continuation from reign of Edward IV to present, by R. Grafton] (London; facsimile reprint Amsterdam, 1976)

Harkness, D. 2001. 'Maps, spiders, and tulips: The Cole-Ortelius-L'Obel family and the practice of science in early modern London', in R. Vigne and C. Littleton (eds), *From strangers to citizens. The integration of immigrant communities in Britain, Ireland, and colonial America, 1550-1750*: 184-96 (Brighton, Huguenot Society)

Hartley, T. E. (ed.). 1981-95. *Proceedings in the Parliaments of Elizabeth I*, 3 vols (Leicester)

Harvey, P. 1980. *The History of Topographical Maps. Symbols, Pictures and Survey* (London)

Harvey, P. D. A. 1987. 'Local and Regional Cartography in Medieval Europe', in J. B. Harley and D. Woodward (eds), *The History of Cartography*, vol. 1, *Cartography in Prehistoric, Ancient and Medieval Europe and the Mediterranean* (Chicago and London): 464-501

de Heere, Lucas. c.1574a. Théâtre de tous les peuples et nations de la terre avec leurs habits et ornemens divers, tant anciens que modernes, diligemment depeints au naturel par Luc Dheere peintre et sculpteur Gantois, BHSL-HS-2466 (University Library Ghent, MS 2466)

de Heere, Lucas. c.1574b. 'Corte Beschryuinghe van Engheland, Scotland ende Irland'. BL, Additional MS 28330 (includes a number of illustrations presumably once part of the album de Heere c.1574a). For the edition of this text, see Chotzen and Draak 1937

Herrup, C. B. 1987. *The Common Peace: Participation and the criminal law in seventeenth-century England* (Cambridge)

Hill, T. 2010. *Pageantry and Power: a Cultural History of the Early Modern Lord Mayor's Show, 1585-1639* (Manchester)

Hilts, C. 2012. 'Raising the Curtain: Excavating Shakespeare's Lost Playhouse', *Current Archaeology*, 229: 10-13

HMC Hatfield. *Calendar of the manuscripts of ... the Marquis of Salisbury ... at Hatfield House* (Historical Manuscripts Commission, London, 1883 onwards)

Hodges, E. 2008. *Urban Poetics and the French Renaissance* (Aldershot)

Holinshed, R. 1587. *Chronicles of England, Scotland and Ireland* (London) [also 1577 edition]. An online edition of the text of both editions is available at cems.ox.ac.uk/holinshed, albeit one retaining the misleading volume divisions introduced by Early English Books Online. Our references follow the sixteenth-century volume divisions, not those of later editors

Hone, W. 1823. *Ancient Mysteries described: especially the English Miracle Plays* (London)

Hornblower, S. and Spawforth, A., eds. 2003. *Oxford Classical Dictionary*, 3rd ed. revised (Oxford)

House, A. P. 2006. 'The City of London and the problem of the liberties, c.1540 - c.1640', University of Oxford D.Phil. thesis

Howell, J. 1650. *Epistolæ Ho-elianæ familiar letters domestic and forren divided into sundry sections, partly historicall, politicall, philosophicall, vpon emergent occasions* (London)

Hughes, P. L. and Larkin, Larkin, J. F. (eds). 1964-9. *Tudor Royal Proclamations* 3 vols (London)

Huguet, E. (1925). *Dictionnaire de la Langue Française du Seizième Siècle*, vol. 1 (Paris)

Humpherus, H. 1874-86. *History of the origins and progress of the Company of Watermen and Lightermen of the river Thames, with numerous historical notes: 1514-1859*, 3 vols (London)

Hyde, J. K. 1966. 'Medieval descriptions of cities', *Bulletin of the John Rylands Library*, 48:308-40

Impey, E. (ed.). 2008. *The White Tower* (New Haven and London)

Ingram, Martin. 2002. 'Regulating sex in pre-Reformation London', in G. W. Bernard and S. J. Gunn (eds), *Authority and Consent in Tudor England: Essays presented to C.S.L. Davies* (Aldershot): 79-95

Ingram, W. 1992. *The Business of Playing: the beginnings of the adult professional theatre in Elizabethan London* (Ithaca)

James, C. 1810. *New and Enlarged Military Dictionary, in French and English; in which are explained the principal terms ... of all the sciences that are ... necessary for an Officer and Engineer ...*, 2 vols, Third Edition (London)

Jamison, C. 1952. *The History of the Royal Hospital of St Katharine by the Tower* (Oxford)

Jansson, M. and Rogozhul, N. (eds.). 1994. *England and the north. The Russian embassy of 1613-14* (Philadelphia)

Jeaffreson, W. C. (ed.). 1886-92. *Middlesex County Records*, 4 vols (London)

Jenner, M. 1992. 'Early modern conceptions of cleanliness and dirt as reflected in the environmental regulation of the city of London, c.1530 - c.1700', University of Oxford D.Phil. thesis

Jewitt, L., and Hope, W. H. St John. 1895. *The Corporation Plate and Insignia of Office of the Cities and Towns of England and Wales* (London), includes 'large additions' from Hope

Johnson, A. H. 1914-22. *History of the Worshipful Company of Drapers of London*, 4 vols (London)

Johnson, D. J. 1969. *Southwark and the City* (London)

Kathman, D. 2004. 'Smith, William (*c.*1550-1618)', *ODNB*

Keay, A. (ed.). 2001. *The Elizabethan Tower of London: the Haiward and Gascoyne plan of 1597*, LTS 158

Keay, A. and Harris, R. B. 2008. A. Keay and R. B. Harris, 'The White Tower, 1485-1642' in Impey 2008: 161-77

Keene, D. 1989. 'New discoveries at the Hanseatic Steelyard in London', *Hansische Geschichtsblätter* 107: 15-25

Keene, D. 1985. *Cheapside Before the Great Fire* (London)

Keene, D. 1997. 'The setting of the Royal Exchange: continuity and change in the financial district of the City of London, c.1300-1871', in A. Saunders (ed.), *The Royal Exchange*, LTS 152: 253-71

Keene, D. 1999. 'Wardrobes in the City: houses of consumption, finance and power', in M. Prestwich, R. Britnell, and R. Frame (eds.), *Thirteenth-Century England VII* (Woodbridge): 61-79

Keene, D. 2001. 'Issues of water in medieval London, to *c.*1300', *Urban History* 28: 161-81

Keene, D. 2004. D. Keene, 'Henry fitz Ailwin (d. 1212), *ODNB*

Keene, D. 2008a. 'Tall Buildings in Medieval London: Precipitation, Aspiration and Thrills', *The London Journal*, 33.3: 201–215

Keene, D. 2008b. 'Text, visualisation and politics: London, 1150-1250', *Transactions of the Royal Historical Society*, 6th series, 18: 69-99

Keene, D. 2011. 'Crisis management in London's food supply', in B. Dodds and C. D. Liddy (eds), *Commercial Activity, Markets and Entrepreneurs in the Middle Ages: Essays in Honour of Richard Britnell* (Woodbridge): 45-62

Keene, D., and Harding, V. (1987), *Historical Gazetteer of London before the Great Fire, I, Cheapside* (microfiche, Cambridge)

Keene, D., Burns, A., and Saint, A. (eds.) 2004. *St Paul's; the Cathedral Church of London, 604-2004* (New Haven and London)

Kendrick, T. D. 1950. *British Antiquity* (London)

Kingdon, J. A. 1901. *Richard Grafton, Citizen and Grocer of London* (London)

Kingsford, C. L. 1916-20. 'Historical Notes on Mediaeval London Houses', *London Topographical Record*, 10: 44-144; 11: 28-81; 12: 1-66

Kingsford, C. L. 1920. 'Paris Garden and the Bear-baiting', *Archaeologia* 70: 155-78

Kirk [R. E. G] and Kirk [E. F.] (eds.) 1900-1908. *Returns of Aliens dwelling in the city and suburbs of London from the reign of Henry VIII to that of James I,* Huguenot Society of London vol. 10, 4 parts (Aberdeen)

Kitching, C. (ed.) 1980. *London and Middlesex Chantry Certificates, 1548*, LRS 16

Knights, M. 2011. 'Commonwealth: the social, cultural, and conceptual contexts of an early modern keyword', *Historical Journal*, 54:3: 659-87

Krem, J. 1994. *Jean Lemaire des Belges's Les Illustrations de Gaule et singularitez de Troye. The Trojan Legend in the Late Middle Ages and Early Renaissance* (New York)

K W. The History of the King's Works, vols 1-4 (Middle Ages to 1660), general ed. H. M. Colvin (London, 1963-82)

Lake, P. 2001. 'From Troynouvant to Heliogabulus' Rome and back: "order" and its others in the London of John Stow', in J. Merritt (ed.), *Imagining early modern London: perceptions and portrayals of the city from Stow to Strype, 1698-1720*: 217-49 (Cambridge)

Lancashire, Anne. 2002. *London Civic Theatre. City Drama and Pageantry from Roman Times to 1558* (Cambridge)

Lang, R. G. (ed.). 1993. *Tudor Subsidy Rolls. Two Tudor Subsidy Rolls for the City of London: 1541 and 1582*, LRS 29

L & P Hen. VIII. Letters and Papers, Foreign and Domestic, Henry VIII, 21 vols, plus 2 vols of Addenda (London, 1920-32)

Langdon, J. 2007. 'The efficiency of water transport in medieval England', in J. Blair (ed.), *Waterways andCcanal-building in Medieval England,* (Oxford): 110-32.

Lappenberg, J. M. 1851. *Urkundliche Geschichte des Hansischen Stahlhofes zu London*, 2 parts (Hamburg)

Leland, J. 1543. *Genethlicon illustrissimi Edwardi principis Cambriae* (London), unpaginated

Le Roux de Lincy, A. J. V. and Tisserand, L. M. (eds). 1867. *Paris et ses Historiens aux XIVe et XVe siècles* (Paris)

Les Manuscrits. 1964. *Les Manuscrits de la reine de Suède au Vatican, réédition du catalogue de Montfaucon et cotes actuelle,* (Città del Vaticano) *Studi e Testi* 238

Les rues et eglises. 1500. *Les rues et eglises de Paris auec la despense qui se fait par chascun jour* (Paris). Copy dated approximately to 1500 in BL, at C. 32.c.13. Reprinted from a different edition of about that date (Paris, 1867)

Levy, F. L. 1967. *Tudor Historical Thought* (San Marino, CA)

Liaroutzos, C. (1998). *Le pays et la mémoire. Pratiques et représentations de l'espace français chez Gilles Corrozet et Charles Estienne* (Paris)

Lily, G. 1548a. *Chronicon sive Brevis enumeratio regum et principum, in quos uariante fortuna, Britanniae imperium diversis temporibus translatum est.* In Giovio, Paolo (1548)

Lily, G. 1548b, *Virorum aliquot in Britannia qui nostro seculo eruditione & doctrina clari, memoralesque fuerunt elogia,* in Giovio, Paolo (1548).

Littleton, C. G. D. 1996. 'Geneva on Threadneedle Street: the French church of London and its congregation, 1560-1625' University of Michigan Ph.D. thesis

Littré. 2005. *Le nouveau Littré,* ed. C. Blum (Paris)

Lloyd, T. H. 1991. *England and the German Hanse, 1157-1611. A study of their trade and commercial diplomacy* (Cambridge)

Lobel, M. D. (ed.). 1989. *The City of London from Prehistoric Times to c.1520,* The British Atlas of Historic Towns, vol. 3 (Oxford)

Luard, H. R. (ed.) 1865. *Annales Monasterii de Waverleia,* in *Annales Monastici* ii. 127-411 (London), 127-411

Luard, H. R. (ed.) 1866. *Annales Monasterii de Bermundeseia,* in *Annales Monastici* iii. 421-87 (London)

Luard, H. R. ed. 1872-3. *Chronica Major Matthaei Parisiensis, Monachi Sancti Albani, Chronica Majora,* 7 vols (London, 1872-83)

Lucidus, J. 1546. *Ioannis Lucidi Samothei viri clarissimi opusculum de eme[dationibus temporum ab orbe condito ad hanc vsque nostram aetatem: ixta veram ac rectam chronographiam ex antiquis ac probatissimis authoribus excerptum; in hoc volumini habentur haec, diligntissime recognita &emendata* (Venice)

Luu, Lien Bich. 2005a. *Immigrants and the Industries of London, 1500-1700* (Aldershot)

Luu, Lien Bich. 2005b. 'Natural born versus stranger born subjects: aliens and their status in Elizabethan London', in N. Goose and L. Luu (eds), *Immigrants in Tudor and early Stuart England:* 57-75 (Brighton)

MacCulloch, D. A. 1999. *Tudor Church militant: Edward VI and the Protestant Reformation* (London)

Machyn. 1848. *The Diary of Henry Machyn: Citizen and Merchant-Taylor of London, from A.D. 1550 to A.D. 1563,* ed. J. G. Nichols (London, Camden Society, old series 42)

MacClure, M. 1958. *The Paul's Cross Sermons, 1544-1642* (Toronto)

McConville, S. 1981. *A History of English Prison Administration,* vol 1. *1750-1877* (London)

McDermott, J. 2001. *Martin Frobisher: Elizabethan privateer* (London)

McGrath, P. and J. Rowe, J. 1991. 'Imprisonment of catholics for religion under Elizabeth I', *Recusant History,* 20.4: 415-35

Mackinder, A. et al. 2013, *The Hope Playhouse, Animal Baiting and Later Industrial Activity at Bear Gardens on Bankside. Excavations at Riverside House and New Globe Walk, Southwark, 1999-2000,* MOLA Archaeology Studies 25 (London)

Manley, L. 1995a. *Literature and Culture in Early Modern London* (Cambridge)

Manley, L. 1995b. 'Of sites and rites', in D. Smith, R. Strier and D. Bevington (eds), *The theatrical city. Culture, theatre, and politics in London, 1576-1649* (Cambridge): 35-54

Marot, Cl. 1556. *Trois premiers livres de la Métamorphose d'Ovide traduictz en vers françois, le premier et second par Cl. Marot, le tiers par B. Aneau* (Lyon)

Marshall, P. 2002. *Beliefs and the Dead in Reformation England* (Oxford)

Mason, E. (ed.). 1988, *Westminster Abbey Charters, 1066-c.1214.* LRS 25

Masters, B. R. 1974., *The Public Markets of the City of London surveyed by William Leybourn in 1677,* LTS 117 (London)

Masters, B. 1984. *Chamber Accounts of the Sixteenth Century*, LRS 20

Mateer, D. 2006. 'New light on the early history of the Theater in Shoreditch', *English Literary Renaissance* 36: 335-75

Merritt, J. F. 2001. 'The cradle of Laudianism: Westminster Abbey, 1558-1630', *Journal of Ecclesiastical History* 52: 623-46

de Meyier, K. A. 1947. *Paul en Alexandre Petau en geschiedenis van hun hanschriften, voornamelijk op grond van Petau-handschriften in de Universiteitsbibliotheek te Leiden* (Leiden)

Michel, F. 1840. *Histoire des ducs de Normandie et des rois d'Angleterre: publiées entiers pour la première fois, d'après deux manuscrits de la Bibliothèque du Roi* (Paris)

Minson, S. 2013. 'Political culture and urban space in early Tudor London', University of Oxford D.Phil. thesis

de Monfaucon, B. 1739. *Bibliotheca bibliothecarum manuscriptorum nova*, 2 vols (Paris)

Moore, N. 1918. *The History of St Bartholomew's Hospital*, 2 vols (London)

Morrissey, M. 2011. *Politics and the Paul's Cross sermons 1558-1642* (Oxford)

Murray, A. 1978. *Reason and Society in the Middle Ages* (Oxford, reprinted 1991)

Nanni, J. 1498. *Commentaria fratris Joannis Annii Viterbiensis super opera diversorum auctorum de antiquitatibus loquentium* (Rome). See also Berossos 1552

Nearing, Homer. 1948. 'Julius Caesar and the Tower of London', *Modern Language Notes* 63: 228-43.

Nichols, J. G. 1831. *London Pageants* (London)

Nichols, J. G. (ed.). 1850. *Chronicle of Jane and Mary. The chronicle of Queen Jane, and of two years of Queen Mary and especially of the rebellion of Sir Thomas Wyat, written by a resident in the Tower of London*, Camden Society, old series, 48

Nichols, J. G. 1859. *The Fishmongers' Pageant on Lord Mayor's Day, 1616. Chrysanaleia, or the Golden Fishing, devised by Anthony Munday, ... Represented in twelve plates by Henry Shaw, ... from contemporary drawings in the possession of the Worshipful Company of Fishmongers. Accompanied with an historical introduction, and an appendix of various illustrative documents* (London)

Norton, G. 1869. *Commentaries on the History, Constitution, and Chartered Franchises of the City of London* (third edition, London)

Norton, Thomas. 1574-5. 'Instructions to the lord mayor of London, 1574-5', in J.P. Collier (ed.), *Illustrations of Old English Literature*, 3 vols (London, 1866): iii, item 8

Number. 1582/3. *The number of all those that hath dyed in the citie of London and the liberties of the same from 28 of December 1581 unto 27 December 1582, with the christenings* (London, n.d.)

Nutton, V. 2004. 'Linacre, Thomas (c.1460 - 1524) ', *ODNB*

O'Brien, B. 1999. *God's Peace and the King's Peace. The Laws of Edward the Confessor* (Philadelphia)

O'Neilly, J. G. and L.E. Tanner, L. E. 1966. 'The shrine of St Edward the Confessor', *Archaeologia* 100: 129-54

Orders. 1582. *Orders appointed to bee executed in the citie of London, for setting roges and idle persons to work* (London)

Ordre. 1568. *The Ordre of my Lorde Mayor, the aldermen and the shiriffes, for their metinges and wearynge of theyr apparel throughout the yeare* (1568)

Orlin, L. C. 2008. 'The Character of Sir Martin Barnham, Knight, by his son Sir Francis Barnham', in James Dutcher and Anne Lake Prescott (eds), *Renaissance Historicisms. Essays in Honor of Arthur F. Kinney*, (Newark, N.J.,): 259-90

Parnell, G. 1993. *The Tower of London* (London)

Patten, W. 1548. *The expedicion into Scotla[n]de of the most woorthely fortunate Prince Edward, Duke of Soomerset* (reprint, Amsterdam, New York, 1972)

Patterson, A. ed. 1998. *The Trial of Nicholas Throckmorton*, (Toronto)

Pauls, P. and Boswell, J. C. 1989. *Register of Sermons Preached at Paul's Cross, 1534-1642*, enlarged edition of appendix to Maclure 1958 (Ottawa)

Pearl, Valerie. 1961. *London and the Outbreak of the Puritan revolution: City Government and National politics, 1625-1643* (Oxford)

Pettegree, A. 1986. *Foreign Protestant Communities in Sixteenth-Century London* (Oxford)

Pinto, J. A. 1976. 'Origins and Development of the Ichnographic City Plan', *Journal of the Society of Architectural Historians*, 35:1: 35-50

Porder, R. 1570. *A sermon of Gods fearefull threatenings for idolatry preached in Paules churche the xvi daye of Maye 1570* (London)

Potter, D. 1993-4. 'Les allemands et les armées françaises au XVIe siècle. Jean-Phillipe Rhingrave, chef des lansquenets: étude, suivi de sa correspondence een France, 1548-1566', in two parts *Francia* 20/2: 1-20 (pt 1); 21/2: 1-61 (pt 2).

Prest, W. 1972. *The inns of court under Elizabeth I and the early Stuarts, 1590-1640* (London)

Price, J. E. 1886. *A Descriptive Account of the Guildhall of the City of London* (London)

Pugh, R. B. 1968. *Imprisonment in Medieval England* (Cambridge)

Ramsay, G. D. 1975. *The City of London in international politics at the accession of Elizabeth Tudor* (Manchester)

Raven, J. 2007. *The Business of Books* (New Haven and London)

Rawcliffe, C. 2013. *Urban bodies. Communal health in late medieval English towns and cities* (Woodbridge)

Reddaway, T. F. 1963. 'Goldsmith's Row in Cheapside, 1558-1645', *Guildhall Miscellany* 2 no. 3 (Oct., 1963): 181-206

Register of St Dunstan. The register of St. Dunstan in the East, London, vol. 1, *1553-1644*, ed. A. W. Hughes Clarke (Harleian Soc. 1939).

Reiester booke. The reiester booke of Saynte De'nis, Backchurch parishe (city of London) for maryages, christenyges, and buryalles, begynnynge in the yeare of Our Lord God 1538, ed. J. L. Chester (Harleian Soc. v, 1878)

Rexroth, F. 2007. *Deviance and Power in Late Medieval London* (Cambridge)

Riley, H. T. (ed.). 1859. *Liber Albus, compiled A. D. 1419*, vol. 1 of *Munimenta Gildhallæ Londoniensis*, 3 vols (London, 1859-62)

Riley, H. T. ed. 1860. *Liber Custumarum, compiled in the early part of the fourteenth century*, vol. II, in two parts, of *Munimenta Gildhallæ Londoniensis*, 3 vols (London, 1859-62)

Robertson, J. C. (ed.). 1875. 'Vita Sancti Thomæ Cantuariensis Archiepiscopi et Martyris, auctore Willelmo filio Sephani' in *Materials for the History of Thomas Becket, Archbishop of Canterbury*, 7

vols (1875-83), vol iii. FitzStephen's description of London is on pp. 1-13.

Robertson, J. C. 1996. 'Reckoning with London: interpreting the bills of mortality before John Graunt', *Urban History*, 23: 325-50

Roskell, J. S., Clark, L., Rawcliffe, C., eds. 1993. *The History of Parliament: the House of Commons 1386-1421*.

Rye, W. B. 1865. *England as seen by foreigners in the days of Elizabeth and James I* (1865)

Salel, H. (trans.). 1545. *Les dix premiers livres de l'Iliade d'Homère prince des poetes: Traduictz en vers Francois, par M. Hugues Salel* (Paris)

Salel, H. (trans.) 1570. *Les Iliades d'Homère... traduict de grec en vers françoys par M. Hugues Salel,... L'augmentation outre les précédentes impressions ; l'Umbre dudict Salel par Olivier de Magny, avec le premier et second de l'Odissée d'Homère, par Jaques Peletier,... Autres poésies par P. de Ronsard... et par autres poètes de ce temps, à l'imitation dudit Homèreen françois* (Paris)

Saliat. P. (trans.). 1556. *Les Neuf livres des histoires de Hérodote, Traduit de grec en françois par Pierre Saliat* (Paris)

Samuel, M. 1989. 'The fifteenth-century garner at Leadenhall, London', *The Antiquaries Journal* 69: 118-53

Sandford, F. 1677. *A genealogical history of the kings and queens of England, and monarchs of Great Britain, from the conquest, anno. 1066 to the year 1677* (London)

Saunders, A. 1997. *The Royal Exchange*, LTS 152

Saunders, J. 1997. 'English cathedral choirs and choirmen 1558 to the civil war: an occupational study', University of Cambridge Ph.D. thesis

Sayle, R. T. D. (ed.) 1931. *Lord Mayors' Pageants of the Merchant Tailors' Company* (London)

Scattergood, J. 1996. 'Misrepresenting the city: genre, intertextuality and William fitz Stephen's *Description of London (c.1173)*', in *London and Europe in the later Middle Ages*, ed. J. Boffey and P. King (London), 1-34

Schlueter, J. 2011. *The Album Amicorum and the London of Shakespeare's Time* (London)

Schofield, J. (ed.). 1987. *The London surveys of Ralph Treswell*, LTS 135

Scouloudi, Irene. 1985. *Returns of strangers in the metropolis, 1593, 1627, 1635, 1639*, Huguenot Society publications, 57

Sellberg, E. 2014. 'Petrus Ramus', in *The Stanford Encyclopedia of Philosophy*, ed. E. N. Zalta (Spring 2014 Edition), forthcoming URL <http://plato.stanford.edu/archives/spr2014/entries/ramus/>.

Selwood, Jacob. 2010. *Diversity and Difference in early modern London* (Aldershot)

Serpetro, N. 1653. *Il Mercato delle Maraviglie della Natura overo Istoria Naturale* (Venice). The Dedication of this work uses the term *fondaco* rather than *mercato*

Shapiro, B. 2000. *A culture of fact. England 1550-1720* (Ithaca)

Sharpe, R. R. (ed.). 1889-90. *Calendar of Wills proved and enrolled in the Court of Husting, London, A. D. 1258-A.D. 1688*, 2 vols (London)

Sherlock, Peter. 2005. 'Henry VII's miraculum orbis: royal commemoration at Westminster Abbey 1500-1700', in F.W. Kent and Charles Zika (eds), *Rituals, images and words; varieties of cultural expression in late medieval and early modern Europe* (Turnhout): 177-99.

Shoemaker, R. 2004. *The London Mob. Violence and Disorder in Eighteenth-Century England* (London)

Simpson, Alan. 1961. *The Wealth of the Gentry* (1961)

Skelton, R. A. 1966. 'Introduction' in *Braun and Hogenberg Civitates Orbis Terrarum, 1572-1618*, facsimile reproduction, 3 vols (Cleveland and New York): vol. 1, vii-xxi

Skelton, R. A. 1970. *County Atlases of the British Isles, 1579-1850*

Skenazi, C. 2003. Skenazi, *Le poète architecte en France: construction d'une imaginaire monarchique* (Paris)

Slack, Paul. 1980. 'Social Policy and the Constraints of Government', in. J. Loach and R. Tittler (eds), *The mid-Tudor polity, c.1540-1560* (London): 94-115

Slack, Paul. 1985. *The Impact of Plague in Tudor and Stuart England* (London)

Slack, Paul. 2000. 'Perceptions of the metropolis in seventeenth-century England', in P. Burke, B, Harrison, and P. Slack (eds), *Civil Histories: Essays presented to Sir Keith Thomas* (Oxford): 161-80.

Smuts, R. Malcolm (ed.). 2007. 'The Whole Royal and Magnificent Entertainment, ed. R. Malcolm Smuts', in *Thomas Middleton. The Collected Works*, eds Gary Taylor and John Lavagnino, 2 vols (Oxford), 1. 219-79.

Sneyd, C. A. ed. and trans. 1847. *A Relation or rather a true account of the Island of England ... about the year 1500* Camden Society, old series 37 (London)

Soar, H. D. 1988. 'Prince Arthur's knights: some notes on a sixteenth-century Society of Archers', *Journal of the Society of Archer Antiquaries* 31: 31-9

Spufford, P. 1986. *Handbook of Medieval Exchange* (London)

Stapleton, T. (ed.). 1846. *De Antiquis Legibus Liber. Cronica maiorum et vicecomitum Londondoniarum*, Camden Society, old series (London)

Statutes. Statutes of the Realm, ed. A. Luders et al., 11 vols (1810-28)

Stein, P. 1999. *Roman Law in European History* (Cambridge)

Stevenson, L. C. 1984. *Praise and Paradox: Merchants and Craftsmen in Elizabethan Popular Literature* (Cambridge)

Stone, L. 1965. *The Crisis of the Aristocracy 1558-1642* (Oxford)

Stow, *Summarie* 1565, etc. J. Stow, *A Summarie of Englyshe Chronicles* (London, 1565, 1566a, 1566b, 1567, 1570, 1573, 1575). These are all the editions that appeared before Grenade completed his text in 1578. There are minor variations in the spelling and wording of the titles and Stow is not always clearly identified as the author. The 1566a edition is in a larger format than 1566b.

Stow, *Survey*. John Stow, *A Survey of London, reprinted from the text of 1603*, introduction and notes by C. L. Kingsford (Oxford, 1908; corrected impression, 1971)

Stubbs, W. (ed.). 1882. *Annales Londonienses and Annales Paulini* in *Chronicles, Edward I and Edward II* vol 2 (London)

Survey of London. 50 vols 1900 to date (London)

Sutton, A. F. 2005. *The Mercery of London: Trade, Goods and People, 1130-1578* (Aldershot)

Tatton-Brown, T. W. T. and Mortimer, R. (eds) 2003. *Westminster Abbey: the Lady Chapel of Henry VII* (Woodbridge).

Tawney, R. H. and Power, E. (eds) 1924. *Tudor Economic Documents*, 3 vols (London)

Te Brake, W. H. 1975. 'Air pollution and fuel crisis in Pre-Industrial London, 1250-1650', *Technology and Culture*, 16 (1975): 337-59

The History of the Sheriffdom of the City of London. 1723 (London)

Thirsk, J. 1978. *Economic policy and projects: the development of a consumer society in early modern England* (Oxford)

Thoison, E. 1886, 1887, 1888. 'Saint Mathurin: légende – reliques, pèlerinages – iconographie', distributed in parts through vols 4-6 of *Annales de la Société historique et archéologique du Gâtinais* (1882-8)

Thoison, E. 1888a. *Les séjours des Rois de France dans le Gâtinais (481-1789), Documents publiés par la Société historique et archéologique du Gâtinais* (Paris and Orléans 1888), vol. 2

Thomas, A. H. and Thornley, I. D. (eds), 1938. *The Great Chronicle of London* (London)

Thomas, C., Sloane, B., Phillpotts, C. 1997. *Excavations at the Priory and Hospital of St Mary Spital, London* (London)

Thorne, S. and Baker, J. H. (eds). 1990. *Readings and Moots at the Inns of Court in the fifteenth century*, vol 2, Selden Society 105 (London)

Tittler, R. 2004. 'Bacon, Sir Nicholas (1510-1579)', *ODNB*

Trapp, J. B. 2004. 'Colet, John (1467-1519)', *ODNB*

Trim, D. J. B. 2004. 'Chester, Edward (d. 1577)', *ODNB*

Tucker, P. 2007. *Law Courts and Lawyers in the City of London, 1300-1550* (Cambridge)

Tudor-Craig, P. (ed.). 2004. *'Old St Paul's'. The Society of Antiquaries' Diptych, 1616*, LTS 163

VCH Essex. A History of the County of Essex (*The Victoria History of the Counties of England*) 11 vols to date (London, 1903-2012)

VCH Hertford. A History of the County of Hertford (*The Victoria History of the Counties of England*), 4 vols (London, 1908-14)

VCH Somerset. A History of the County of Somerset (*The Victoria History of the Counties of England*) 10 vols (London, 1906-2010)

von Bülow, G. (ed.). 1892. 'Diary of the journey of Philip Julius, duke of Stettin-Pomerania through England in the year 1602', *Transactions of the Royal Historical Society*, new series 6: 1-67

von Bülow, G. (ed.), 'Journey through England and Scotland made by Lupold von Wedel in the years 1584 and 1585', *Transactions of the Royal Historical Society*, second series, 9 (1895), 223-70

Ward, J. P. 1997. *Metropolitan Communities: Trade guilds, Identity and Change in Early Modern London* (Stanford)

Warkentin, G. (ed.). 2004. *The queen's majesty's passage and related documents* (Toronto, 2004)

Warning to London. 1577. *A warning to London by the fall of Antwerp to the tune if Row wel ye mariners* (London)

Watson, A. G. 1969. *The Manuscripts of Henry Savile of Banke* (London)

Weever, J. 1631. *Ancient funerall monuments within the united Monarchie of Great Britaine and Ireland, and the lands adjacent, with the dissolved Monasteries therein contained* (London)

Werbrugghe, G. P. and Wickersham, J. M. (introd. and trans). 1996. *Berossos and Manetho* (Ann Arbor)

Werner, H. 1999. 'A German eye-witness to Troia Nova Triumphans: is Dekker's text a reliable description of the event?', *Notes and Queries* 46: 251-4

Wheatley, A. 2008. 'The White Tower in Medieval Myth and Legend', in Impey 2008: 277-88

Wheatley, Chloe. 2002. 'The pocket books of early modern England', in H.S. Turner (ed.), *The culture of capital: property, cities, and knowledge in early modern England*: 183-202 (London)

White, Thomas. 1578a. *A sermon preached at Pawles Crosse on Sunday the ninth of Decemberthirde of November 1576 in the time of plague* (London)

White, Thomas. 1578b. *A sermon preached at Pawles Crosse on Sunday the thirde of November 1577 in the time of plague* (London)

Wickham, G., Berry, H. and W. Ingram, W. (eds), *English Professional Theatre, 1530-1660* (Cambridge, 2000)

Wilkinson, R. 1825. *Londina Illustrata* (London)

Willan, T. S. 1956. *The Early History of the Russia Company, 1553-1603* (Manchester)

Williams, C. (ed.). 1937. *Thomas Platter's travels in England, 1599* (London)

Willis, J. 2010. *Church music and Protestantism in post-Reformation England : discourses, sites and identities* (Farnham)

Wilmart, A. (ed.). 1937-45. *Codices Reginenses Latini*, 2 vols (Bibliotheca Vaticana) [covers only BAV Reg. Lat. 1-500]

Wilson, F. P. 1930. *The Plague in Shakespeare's London* (Oxford)

Withington, R. 1918-20. *English Pageantry, an Historical Outline*, 2 vols (Cambridge, Mass.)

Woodcut Map. A woodcut version, produced between 1561 and 1570, of the Copperplate Map (q.v.); formerly mistakenly attributed to Ralph Agas. Reproduced in A. Prockter, R. Taylor and J. Fisher, *The A to Z of Elizabethan London*, LTS 122 (1979)

Woolf, D. R. 2000. *Reading History in Early Modern England* (Cambridge)

Woolf, D. R. 2003. *The Social Circulation of the Past: English Historical Culture, 1500-1730culture in England, 1500-1730* (Oxford)

Woolf, D. R. 2005. 'From hystoryes to the historical: five transitions in thinking about the past, 1500-1700', *Huntington Library Quarterly*, 68:1 and 2: 33-70

Wright, T. (ed.). 1838. *Queen Elizabeth and her times*, 2 vols (London)

Wunderli, R. 1990. 'The evasion of the office of alderman in London, 1523-1672', *The London Journal* 15: 3-18

Wyngaerde. *The Panorama of London circa 1544 by Anthonis van den Wyngaerde*, ed. H. Colvin and S. Foister, LTS 151 (London, 1996)

Zwinger, T. 1577. *Methodus Apodemica in eorum gratiam qvi cum fructu quocunque tandem uitæ genere peregrinari cupiunt* (Basel)

INDEX

Unless stated to the contrary, all entries relate to London and people associated with it. The French text is not indexed, but names and subjects there can be identified from the English translation.